D1756893

Between 1651 and 1740 hundreds of fables, fable collections, and biographies of the ancient Greek slave Aesop were published in England. In *The English Fable*, Jayne Elizabeth Lewis describes the national obsession with Aesop's fables during this period as both a figural response to sociopolitical crisis, and an antidote to emerging anxieties about authorship. Lewis traces the role that fable collections, Augustan fable theory, and debates about the figure of Aesop played in the formation of a modern, literate, and self-consciously English culture, and shows how three Augustan writers – John Dryden, Anne Finch, and John Gay – experimented with the seemingly marginal symbolic form of fable to gain access to new centers of English culture. Often interpreted as a discourse of the dispossessed, the fable offered Augustan writers a unique form of cultural authority.

CAMBRIDGE STUDIES IN EIGHTEENTH-CENTURY
ENGLISH LITERATURE AND THOUGHT 28

The English Fable

CAMBRIDGE STUDIES IN EIGHTEENTH-CENTURY
ENGLISH LITERATURE AND THOUGHT

General Editors Professor Howard Erskine-Hill; Litt. D., FBA, *Pembroke College, Cambridge*, and Professor John Richetti, *University of Pennsylvania*

Editorial Board Morris Brownell, *University of Nevada*
Leopold Damrosch, *Harvard University*
J. Paul Hunter, *University of Chicago*
Isobel Grundy, *University of Alberta*
Lawrence Lipking, *Northwestern University*
Harold Love, *Monash University*
Claude Rawson, *Yale University*
Pat Rogers, *University of South Florida*
James Sambrook, *University of Southampton*

Some recent titles

Writing and the Rise of Finance: Capital Satires of the Early Eighteenth Century
by Colin Nicholson

Locke, Literary Criticism, and Philosophy by William Walker

Poetry and Jacobite Politics in Eighteenth-Century Britain and Ireland
by Murray G. H. Pittock

The Story of the Voyage in Eighteenth-Century England
by Philip Edwards

Edmond Malone: A Literary Biography by Peter Martin
Swift's Parody by Robert Phiddian

Rural Life in Eighteenth-Century English Poetry
by John Goodridge

The English Fable: Aesop and Literary Culture, 1651–1740
by Jayne Elizabeth Lewis

A complete list of books in this series is given at the end of the volume.

The English Fable

Aesop and Literary Culture, 1651–1740

JAYNE ELIZABETH LEWIS

University of California, Los Angeles

CAMBRIDGE UNIVERSITY PRESS
Cambridge, New York, Melbourne, Madrid, Cape Town, Singapore, São Paulo

Cambridge University Press
The Edinburgh Building, Cambridge CB2 2RU, UK

Published in the United States of America by Cambridge University Press, New York

www.cambridge.org
Information on this title: www.cambridge.org/9780521481113

© Cambridge University Press 1996

This publication is in copyright. Subject to statutory exception
and to the provisions of relevant collective licensing agreements,
no reproduction of any part may take place without
the written permission of Cambridge University Press.

First published 1996
Hardback version transferred to digital printing 2006
Digitally printed first paperback version 2006

A catalogue record for this publication is available from the British Library

Library of Congress Cataloguing in Publication data
Lewis, Jayne Elizabeth
The English fable: Aesop and literary culture, 1651–1740 / Jayne Elizabeth Lewis.
p.   cm. – (Cambridge studies in eighteenth-century English literature and thought: 28)
Includes bibliographical references and index.
ISBN 0 521 48111 2 (hardback)
1. English literature – 18th century – History and criticism.
2. Fables, English – History and criticism.
3. English literature – Early modern, 1500–1700 – History and criticism.
4. Aesop – Influence.   5. Dryden, John, 1631–1700. Fables.
6. Gay, John, 1685–1732. Fables.
7. Winchilsea, Anne Kingsmill Finch, Countess of, 1661–1720 – Criticism and interpretation.
8. Politics and literature – Great Britain – History – 17th century.
9. Politics and literature – Great Britain – History – 18th century.
10. English literature – Greek influences.
11. Aesop's fables – Parodies, imitations, etc.
12. Animals in literature.   I. Title.   III. Series.
PR448.F34L49   1996
820.9′005 – dc20   95–8403   CIP

ISBN-13 978-0-521-48111-3 hardback
ISBN-10 0-521-48111-2 hardback

ISBN-13 978-0-521-02531-7 paperback
ISBN-10 0-521-02531-1 paperback

Contents

List of illustrations   *page* viii
Acknowledgments   ix

Introduction   The English fable   1

1   Aesopian examples: the English fable collection and its authors,   14
     1651–1740

2   "The first pieces of wit": Augustan fable theory and the birth of   48
     the book

3   Common and uncommon characters: the lives of Aesop   71

4   Brutal transactions, "mysterious writ": Aesop's fables and   99
     Dryden's later poetry

5   In her "transparent Laberynth": obstructions of poetic justice in   128
     Anne Finch's fables

6   Risking contradiction: John Gay's *Fables* and the matter of   156
     reading

7   The moral   185

Notes   190
Bibliography   223
Index   230

Illustrations

1   Frontispiece to John Ogilby, *Fables of Æsop, Paraphras'd in Verse*,   *page* 16
    London, 1651. By kind permission of Henry E. Huntington
    Library.

2   Plate from John Locke, *Æsop's Fables*, London, 1703. By kind   42
    permission of William Andrews Clark Memorial Library, UCLA.

3   Frontispiece to Francis Barlow, *Æsop's Fables, with his Life*, London, 74
    1687. By kind permission of Henry E. Huntington Library.

4   Frontispiece to Roger L'Estrange, *Fables of Æsop and Other Eminent*   75
    Mythologists, London, 1692. By kind permission of William Andrews
    Clark Memorial Library, UCLA.

5   Frontispiece to Samuel Croxall, *Fables of Æsop and Others*, London,   76
    1722. By kind permission of William Andrews Clark Memorial
    Library, UCLA.

6   Plate from Francis Barlow, *Æsop's Fables, with his Life*, London,   81
    1687. By kind permission of Henry E. Huntington Library.

7   Plate from Francis Barlow, *Æsop's Fables, with his Life*, London,   87
    1687. By kind permission of Henry E. Huntington Library.

8   John Wootten, plate from John Gay, *Fables*, London, 1727. By   170
    kind permission of William Andrews Clark Memorial Library,
    UCLA.

9   Gerard Scotin, plate from *Fables of the Late Mr. Gay*, London, 1738.   175
    By kind permission of William Andrews Clark Memorial Library,
    UCLA.

Acknowledgments

Aesop's fable of the jay in peacock's feathers provides an apt image for what it has often felt like not only to put Aesop in scholarly dress but indeed to write an academic book at all. In the fable, a slightly mangy and very unremarkable bird decides to dress like her infinitely more elegant cousins, the peacocks; she boldly sashays into public, clad in their splendid feathers. The jay's avian superiors see instantly through her disguise. They pluck her borrowed finery apart, exposing her true colors and thereby confirming their own inimitable virtue and authenticity. My deepest thanks, therefore, are due to the true peacocks who, rather than strip the author of her plumes, decided instead to recognize her as one of their own.

Among the very rarest of these *aves in terra* is Margaret Anne Doody, without the example of whose exuberance, imagination, and sheer brilliance this project would have been unthinkable. I am also extremely grateful to the many sensible words of Richard Kroll, whose unfailing rigor, patience, guidance, and good faith were with me through thick and thin. Others read parts of the manuscript, generously shared their ideas about it, and offered relief to the sinking spirit: Carol Barash, Anne Becher, Toni Bowers, Helen Deutsch, Julia Douthwaite, Dianne Dugaw, H. A. Kelly, Deidre Lynch, Maryclaire Moroney, Sheila Newbury, Max Novak, Alan Roper, Debora Shuger, Hilary Schor, Victoria Silver, Susan Staves, James Turner, and Rob Watson. Florian Stuber is owed special thanks for sharing an Aesopian obsession at least equal to my own. Very early versions of this book profited immeasurably from the society of John Archer, Madeleine Brainerd, Hunter Cadzow, Aileen Douglas, Siobhán Kilfeather, and Yopie Prins, and from the generous attention of Earl Miner and Froma Zeitlin. My readers and editors at Cambridge University Press have contributed far more than words can say. So, in a different way, has Blake Allmendinger; Claire McEachern offered unfailing encouragement and support. Nancy Glazener demonstrated heroic devotion to this manuscript at every stage and in every possible incarnation; no stories could have been told and no morals could have been found, here or elsewhere, without her.

Hilary Kaplan and Patricia Juliana Smith provided valuable research assistance, and Margery Kingsley true intellectual sustenance. Josie Dixon has been an exemplary editor. The very efficient staffs of the William Andrews Clark, Henry E. Huntington, Firestone, Widener, Bodleian, and British Libraries made research much less taxing than it might have been. Generous fellowships from the American Council of Learned Societies, the National Endowment for the Humanities, and the University of California President's Fund gave me time to write. A portion of Chapter 2 appeared in *The Eighteenth Century: Theory and Interpretation* (32 (1991), pp. 99–118.

To Eldon and Stella Lewis – a father without parallel and a mother beyond compare – this book is dedicated.

Introduction

The English fable

> In Fable, all Things hold discourse;
> Then Words, no doubt, must talk, of course.
>
> "Ay and No: A Fable" (1726)

During the turbulent decades that divided the English Civil Wars from the entrenchment of Georgian culture in the middle of the eighteenth century, a torrent of animal fables flooded England. Bred by native presses and imported from abroad, fables found their way into every pocket of contest and change. They proliferated in Whig pamphlets and in Tory periodicals, in the ideal syllabi of education reformers and in grammar school textbooks steeped in humanist tradition. Countless popular collections gathered up the apologues attributed to the ancient slave Aesop, then farmed them out to the pages of high neoclassical poetry. The libertine heroes of Restoration comedy tendered fables as tokens of wit; the distressed heroines of sentimental fiction turned them into emblems of domestic horror. Late Stuart censors and Whig clergymen, satirists and scholars, dancing masters and deans, Grub Street hacks and men of eminently polite letters all found room for short, moralized speaking animal narratives in their own writing: 1697 even brought Aesop from Paris to the London stage.[1] So when in 1711 Joseph Addison's Mr. Spectator observed that fables have "been still highly valued, not only in times of the greatest Simplicity, but among the most polite Ages of Mankind," he simply transposed onto history their remarkable stability within the competing currencies of contemporary English culture.[2]

This book aims to account for that stability. It asks what about fables encouraged their survival, indeed their proliferation, in a contentious and transitional age. It asks what about that age, impatient with so many long-standing genres, disposed it so kindly toward Aesop's fables – the most ancient and, in their unvarying division between story and moral, the most rigid of symbolic forms. Such questions seem obvious ones to raise. But while Augustan literary critics always kept an eye on Aesop – even regarding his fables as prototypes of the "Epick Poem," and of every "legitimate Dramatick Poem, either of the Comick or the Tragick kind" – the fate of fable criticism since has been a sorry one.[3] Strangely subterranean and fragmented, Aesopian scholarship has survived mainly in unpublished doctoral disserta-

1

tions and relatively brief critical essays.[4] At its most public, it has been swallowed up in sweeping overviews that either lump late seventeenth- and early eighteenth-century English fables with their continental counterparts or span millennia of Aesopian practice.[5] Occasionally, the English fable collection wins honorable mention as a source for canonical writers like John Dryden,[6] and a giant step toward rescuing it from obscurity is taken by Annabel Patterson's recent *Fables of Power*, which devotes more than a chapter to Aesop's involvement in Restoration and early eighteenth-century political history.[7] But on the whole, it has been remarkably easy to overlook fables as a significant presence in Augustan literature; critical interest instead has centered on innovations within established genres (pastoral, satire, epic) or on the emergence of allegedly new ones (the periodical essay, the novel).[8] Little altered from their original form, Aesop's fables could, and did, appear in all of these changing verbal contexts: as Patterson suggests, sometimes they are better understood as a "function" than as a genre.[9] But the English fable also has a life of its own, and it is one whose whole story has yet to be told.

My version of the story begins in 1651, the year of John Ogilby's *Fables of Æsop, Paraphras'd in Verse and Adorn'd with Sculptures*. It ends in 1740, the year that several fables decamped from Samuel Richardson's *Æsop's Fables* (1739) to take up residence in his first novel, *Pamela*. Throughout the intervening decades hundreds of imaginary animals quarrelled, inveigled, pontificated, and schemed in prose and verse, in English, French, and Latin, alongside supporting illustrations and unadorned. Not surprisingly, the years that divide Ogilby from Richardson were also dominated by the vigorous and incessant renegotiation of the terms of English social and political life – an invariably conflictual process whose improbable end, as historians like J.H. Plumb and W.A. Speck have shown, was the formation of modern England as a stable socio-linguistic entity.[10] As if to advertise fables" fitness for such a cultural battlefield, the two most popular of the many fable collections to materialize between 1651 and 1740 were Roger L'Estrange's Stuart-sympathizing *Fables of Æsop and Other Eminent Mythologists* (1692 and 1699) and Samuel Croxall's virulently Hanoverian *Fables of Æsop and Others* (1722). Likewise, the period's most trenchant articulation of the predations and paradoxes that secure a prosperous English modernity took the form of a fable – Bernard Mandeville's ever-expanding and endlessly reprinted *Fable of the Bees*.[11] I start with Ogilby because his half-tendentious, half-conciliatory collection, in its fifth edition by 1670, pushed Aesop's fables onto the track that they would follow for the next ninety years. I stop with Richardson because his self-conscious revision of the English fable collection set out to summarize the sociopolitical contests that had been waged between its covers.

In many ways, the story I want to tell follows from Patterson's, whose title, *Fables of Power*, reflects her argument that fables, in this period as in others, are a form of covert political criticism – one that may be traced back to ancient Greece, where Aesop himself was a slave obliged to cloak trenchant philosophical and political analysis in self-protective riddles. At the same time, the better to track Aesop through late Stuart and Williamite England, Patterson identifies more specific continuities with diverse Tudor and early Stuart fabulists. She thereby demonstrates the history of commonality that, at least in England, made fables available to virtually anyone anywhere in the political spectrum. In Patterson's analysis, those at the extremes of the spectrum seem to have resorted to fables more often than those at the center – as we might expect if fables did indeed originate as slave discourse. My own argument, however, emphasizes fables" aptitude for reactive mediation between opposing sides – an aptitude which the Augustans recognized and whose resulting irony they found hugely amusing. As obvious as it is covert, a fable hotly pursues a single, highly interested perspective at the same time that it invites appropriation by competing interests. Coupled with a perverse confidence in its own cultural usefulness, I suggest, it is its desire to dramatize such paradoxes – and the resulting convulsion of authority – in the empirically available space of the printed page that most consistently distinguishes the late seventeenth- and early eighteenth-century English fable from its Aesopian ancestors and descendants.

In speaking of "the English fable," I risk flattening an amazingly diverse assortment of literary exercises undertaken in Aesop's name. So throughout this book, it will often be most fitting to speak of "fables" rather than of "the fable." Nonetheless, the idea of an *English* fable is always implicit, as it was for many Augustan fabulists. Twenty years ago, Mary Pritchard pointed out that the first major fabulist after the English Civil Wars, John Ogilby, was determined to make his long verse fables be about England – both about the Commonwealth that the disappointed Royalist saw around him and about the monarchy that he thought should be restored. Without presuming that all English fabulists after Ogilby (who was after all a Scot by birth) were up to the same thing, we can say that many of them did shoulder an explicitly and increasingly English task. Ubiquitous topical references to national and party politics are only the most obvious ways in which the fable was made "English": Aesop's fables were also used to teach English to English schoolchildren, and to wrestle other languages into line with English grammatical patterns. And many fabulists, posing as translators, self-consciously appropriated French fables by Jean de la Fontaine and Antoine Houdart de la Motte, among others; often this was to make an English fable more contentious, tentative and irregular than its "original." English fabulists were never as systematic as their French counterparts, and on the surface, their differences both from each other and from the neoclassical model that a few of them emulated belie a coherent cultural enterprise. But in fact, just as a fiction of opposition became legible as a sign of British liberty, thus a point of national pride, so diversity within the fable collection claimed that collection's contents for an emerging England.

Such claims were staked not only in individual fables and fable collections but also in a burgeoning commentary *about* fables – what they are, where they come from, what they ought to do. If Augustan writers were much exercised over the question of what makes a good fable, it was not least because, following the tropological crises of the Civil Wars that I describe more fully below, they were already notoriously worried about how figurative language itself should (or could) be used.[12] Few fabulists sent their collections into the marketplace without a lengthy prefatory statement of intent. My first two chapters lean heavily upon such prefaces, for these convey a new and significant determination to see fables in formal as well as functional terms – or, more accurately, to see Aesopian form as itself a culturally formative function. While Patterson's stimulating discussion of them is comprehensive, Chapter 3 treats the biographies of Aesop that also accompanied all the best fable collections as allegories of that function, and therefore as one opportunity that assorted fabulists took to venture their surprisingly convergent opinions as to how figurative language should work to make a coherent modern England.

To English writers after the Civil Wars, "modernity" often implied the presence of print culture. Practically speaking, the print explosion in the middle of the seventeenth century made the Aesop craze possible; historically speaking, it made possible modern English culture itself.[13] Fabulists from Ogilby to Richardson therefore naturally belabored their own fables" inescapably typographic dimensions. Prefaces to fable collections major and minor often stressed the physical features of the texts at hand. Fables themselves were wont to pun on their own typography: "Upon a magpye always look asquint," warned one Aesop of the 1670s, playing with the Latin word for crow. "Pica's a letter and puts things in print." Similarly, Francis Barlow's frontispiece to the popular and enduring *Æsop's Fables, with his Life* (1666, 1687) invited its readers to "See here how natures Book unclasped lies,/Whose pages Aesop reads with pearcing eyes." In my argument, then, Aesopian self-consciousness reflects not only contemporary thinking about figurative language but also an obsessive perception that figurative language is inseparable from the material forms (the very printed pages) that convey it. In turn, the relative, if superficial, egalitarianism of an increasingly book-based society demanded new constructions of political marginalization and opposition – the very situations that, as Patterson and others have shown, motivate Aesopian representation.

Hence this study ends with three poets – John Dryden, Anne Finch, and John Gay – who used Aesopian method to comment on contemporary politics of representation. As my early chapters suggest, those politics were permanently altered by the necessity of grounding and maintaining literary authority within the culturally constructive province of the page. Dryden, Finch, and Gay were all excluded from political culture, variously by virtue of Stuart loyalty (Dryden and Finch), religious faith (Dryden), gender (Finch), and party sympathy (Finch and Gay). Fables, however, allowed each of these writers to continue to participate in literary culture. And, as fabulists, all managed to pose the very questions about cultural authority that their political predicaments threatened to silence. These questions were legible because of the features (examined in my first three chapters) that con-temporary fabulists, fable theorists, and biographers of Aesop had built into Aesopian style. By the time that Dryden, Finch, and Gay went Aesopian, that is, English readers were already trained (sometimes literally, by schools that used fables to teach reading) to interpret the self-reflexive performance of written signs as itself a most enlightening type of political commentary, and to judge sensible figures that proved capable of reactive mediation the most worthy bearers of cultural authority.

What did the Augustans consider a good fable? One that could "carry a double meaning," Charles Montagu and Matthew Prior maintained, but also one "conformable to [...] Nature."[14] One unsullied by "Frothy *Jests*, and jingling *Witticism*," declared Roger L'Estrange, but also one with an appended "Reflexion" that could expose its many layers of meaning.[15] "'Tis a feign'd or disguis'd Discourse," decided Richard Blackmore, even as his contemporaries held that "a whole Fable ought to be related in [...] common and general Circumstances."[16] A fable that earned its keep, apparently, had somehow to be at once plain and devious; it was honor-bound to teeter along the ledge separating the language of "common" things from a more intricate, less innocent, "Discourse."

While to the post-romantic ear such requirements can sound incompatible, England's peculiar linguistic climate after the Civil Wars easily sustained both of them. As Gerard Reedy has shown, extreme skepticism about the integrity of figurative language was one of the most important legacies of the Civil Wars of the 1640s. As Reedy explains, both the demythologizing Puritans and the Cavaliers in retaliation twisted and politicized most existing symbolic modes. A casualty of the wars was therefore the notion of plausible conjunction between "phenomenal" signs and "noumenal" meanings. One response to this figural crisis, epitomized in the linguistic endeavours of the Royal Society, was to attempt to build a reliable bridge, in Abraham Cowley's formulation, "from Words, which are but Pictures of the Thought,/ To Things, the Minds right Object."[17] Thomas Sprat's call for a verbal system made up of "larger, fairer and more moving Images" that could "represent *Truth*, cloth'd with Bodies, and [...] bring Knowledge back again to our very Senses, whence it was first derived" became the credo of modern scientific discourse.[18] Crusades for a universal character that would "immediately represent Things, and the Sources of Words,"[19] sense-based pedagogical reforms, and inquiries into the material and political origins of writing all labored to revise linguistic signs so that they might reclaim the cultural authority they had lost.[20] Meanwhile, throughout the later seventeenth century, works by the French theriophilists who had mobilized in reaction to Cartesian automatism were translated into English. Arguing that animals can reason and develop language, the theriophilists implicitly located the foundations of all human habits of representation in the sensible particulars that make up even animal cognition.[21] The same convincing particles resurface in Lockean epistemology as the grounds both of knowledge and of the words we use to convey it.

Not everyone, of course, reveled in the discrete sensible elements of human language, or even necessarily believed in them. Murray Cohen, for example, suggests that by the early eighteenth century, language philosophy itself had lost its "revolutionary fervor": an interest in "syntactical structures" and "logical universals" began to replace referential "correspondence theor[ies]" of the sign, just as poetic tastes wandered from the "discrete image-units" typical of Dryden and Cowley to the "excursion and verse paragraphs" we find in, say Pope.[22] At the same time, writers like Jonathan Swift were quick to snicker at contemporary quests for a language isomorphic with the phenomenal world.[23] Taken straight or held at a distance, a corporeal, even corpuscular, linguistic sensibility went hand in hand with a practical skepticism about how these elements might be combined to form authoritative meanings. This is why the Latin poet Lucretius's account of language's origins in the material world of jarring atoms and animal instincts was so often translated and remarked (albeit ambivalently) throughout the later seventeenth century.[24] As Richard Kroll has shown, because the rhetorical operations of Lucretius's own writing tended to exemplify proposed continuities between the natural world of colliding "Seeds" and the human world of differing signs, De rerum natura became the foundation of a new literary protocol, one bound to acknowledge the phenomenal nature of all writing. A similar protocol governed emerging literary forms that required reading to proceed naturalistically, by way of probabilistic inference from one discrete, graphic sign to another.[25] Highly legislated structures like emblem and allegory thus gave way to the composite and historically responsive literary models epitomized in Dryden's political poetry and in the pointedly ornamented actions of Restoration drama.[26] Even lofty genres like the epic began to be seen in atomistic and material terms, and, following the iconoclasms of the pugnacious classicist Richard Bentley, in terms also of their erratic passage through history: Henry Felton's Dissertation on Reading the Classics (1709) mocked the very popular theory that the Iliad and the Odyssey were merely "loose, independent Pieces tacked together" and that these poems had "rise[n] in beautiful Order out of millions of Letters eternally shaken together."[27] Thomas Blackwell's *Enquiry into the Life and Writings of Homer* (1730) was less interested in admiring Homer's formal integrity than in analyzing the "Concourse of natural Causes [that] conspired to produce and cultivate his mighty Genius."[28]

Crucially, the emergence of probabilist and materialist linguistic values accompanied a growing preoccupation with textual representation – with the history of writing, with the evils of print culture, with the phenomenology of reading. While obviously print culture did not emerge *ex nihilo* after the English Civil Wars, it did flourish in England after 1650. And its efflorescence is wonderfully coherent with the contemporary supposition that language can be culturally constructive only as long as it is closely monitored, leashed to its roots in the sensible world. After all, pages – particularly the printed ones that can be bought and sold – manifestly turn words into material, fungible things. They allow readers to examine how meanings are constructed, and they seem to admit, indiscriminately, the arguments of opposing sides. Small wonder, then, that throughout our period more and more cultural authority should have come to lodge in books, or that the printed page should have shaped symbolic forms like drama and the visual arts.[29]

The shift to skeptical, sensible, and text-centered linguistic practices after the English Civil Wars inevitably provoked a search for new metaphors, for more empirical and evidentiary figures of speech. Accountable to the discrete, sensible, and presumably universal grounds of human experience, these new tropes would need to be accountable, as well, to the page on which they appeared. At the same time, a stubborn suspicion of language demanded that verbal *forms* confess their own artifice. Evidently a good fable fit this new, if paradoxical, cultural bill. Aesopian collections never pretended to contain anything other than "loose, independent Pieces" and thus fables themselves seemed to possess a grubby integrity that other genres lacked. Together with their use of animal actors and their simple grammatical structure, fables' appeal to readers of all stages and walks of life made them the figures of choice in a culture officially hostile to figuration. Typically, the title of one popular collection of 1720 boasted contents suitable "for all Degrees of Men, and Circumstances of Life."

At the same time, though, fabulists and theorists of fable found ways to expose such boasts as empty ones, to demonstrate the artifice and interestedness of even the most modest symbolic structures. Fables finally harbor little reverence toward their own pretense that signs naturally point to a single meaning, that there can be pure bonds between words and things, that such bonds would be particularly equitable or reassuring if they did exist. Material signs ultimately commanded unanimous consent only when the way they became meaningful was made evident as well. More than their superficial invocation of the sensible world, it is fables' demonstration of their own contingency – of the ways meaning is made – that, in Augustan eyes, invested them with something akin to natural authority. Indeed, fables' thematic preoccupation with the phenomenal world may be seen as a trope for the concrete acts of meaning-making that they perform structurally. More than their actual invocation of sensible things, it was this complex materiality that made fables antidotes to a figural crisis that was also a political and cultural one.

For example, the average fable went like this:

> The Crow with laden beak to tree retires,
> The Fox to gette her prey her forme admires,
> While she to show her gratitude not small,
> Offering to give her thanks, her prize lets fall.
>
> Morall
>
> Shun faithless flatters, Harlots, jilting tars,
> They are fooles hopes and youths deceitefull snares.[30]

In such fables, as any child will know, "Things hold discourse."[31] Foxes and crows, lambs and wolves, oxen and toads, haystacks and nettles, tulips and hens all exchange words. Words themselves thus prove their continuity with things: they acquire a reassuring solidity, one only confirmed when fables are "illustrated with proper Pictures." Thus when a hungry fox spies a crow with a piece of cheese in her beak and flatters her into opening her mouth to sing for him, it is not a word but a thing – the cheese – that tumbles out, to land between the fox's waiting jaws. Such transactions may not be equally agreeable to both individuals involved, but they do verify a symbolic economy in which objects are demonstrably equivalent to verbal signs, and *vice versa*. And all of the elements of a fable, its animal characters included, work to confirm this equivalence.

On the other hand, Aesopian conversations themselves are seldom amicable. They usually end with one party's murder or discomfiture by the other: indeed, a fable is the only literary form in which the principal characters regularly devour one another. Aesopian debates thus visibly ground language not only in the material world to which its elements correspond, one-to-one, but also in the realm of frequently brutal power relations. And thereby fables weld together the material, the political, and the symbolic. However turbulent or unreliable any one of these registers might seem to be in and of itself, the enduring point of a fable is that none can be isolated from the others. Fables themselves are thus not only referential verbal forms; they are also performative, actively bringing different modes of reference to bear upon one another. And because they do so consistently and predictably, they initiated generations of English readers into a common understanding of symbolic practice. This shared symbology in turn may be seen as the foundation of the other figural structures that began to alter or appear during the Augustan period.

Likewise, fables' visceral plots always generate explicit morals – interpretations that turn the preceding stories into convincing figures for home truths: "Do not trust any body"; "it is a sentence of law, we may keep off force by force"; "it is better to live with like"; "thou shalt have equal dealings with thy equals."[32] Thematically such morals advise how to negotiate a ravenous and capricious world. Structurally, though, the very presence of a moral signals each fable's membership within a stable set of symbolic conventions, one in which concrete examples instill socially relevant precepts. It makes double sense, then, that fables should have thrived during a period of self-conscious and often strife-ridden cultural construction. As they close gaps between tangible matter and culturally constitutive signs, they promise to resolve seemingly irreconcilable differences within a single set of assumptions about signification.

Since fables guide symbolic action back to its manifest origins in the physical world, they naturally require a reader to attend to their own material ground, that is, to the page that harbors them. And indeed English fabulists from Ogilby to Richardson proved almost preternaturally conscious of fables' graphic and typographic dimensions. For such writers, exploring the figural potential of the printed page went hand in hand with using speaking animals to align language with the sensible world, to press political arguments or to inculcate codes of social and cognitive behavior. Often visibly driven by a combative sociopolitical context, and by a determination to confer on words the status of objects, this textual self-consciousness perfectly suited Aesop's fables to the cultural climate of Augustan England. Their explicit textuality meant that fables very concretely satisfied a contemporary hunger to know the sensible origins of culturally constitutive signs. It is what helped them truly quench a post-Civil War thirst for a symbolic form that could accommodate competing sociopolitical positions. In Augustan culture the status of the book ultimately conditioned that of the fable, which at its simplest taught children how to read English, and thus how to inhabit, and eventually reproduce, a text-centered culture. At their most complex, fables challenged the foundations of literary authority, boldly dramatizing its extreme contingency. But instead of undermining a literate model of cultural authority, such dramatizations only verified its appropriateness to a nation whose political identity was already visibly constituted – visibly defined by and through negotiation.[33]

Classicists like Jack Winkler and Gregory Nagy have shown how, from their origins in earliest antiquity forward, fables have always grounded symbolic structures in the world of tangible things.[34] Romantic and post-romantic philosophers as diverse as Georg Hegel and Roland Barthes have identified fables with the beginnings of myth,[35] while literary scholars like Patterson and H.P. Blackham have explored their ability to encode subterranean narratives that speak to and for politically disadvantaged groups.[36] And no observer has ignored fables' primacy both in western habits of representation and in the symbolic experience of individuals, who typically encounter them in early childhood.[37] Between 1651 and 1740 English fabulists brought all of these native traits to bear upon an investigation of the signifying potential of books, which they increasingly perceived as the arbiters of potentially catastrophic sociopolitical differences. Even when Addison recalled Plato's famous story about how Socrates told a fable on the morning of his execution, he had the antique philosopher first imagine how "a Man of good Genius for a Fable" would "represent the Nature of Pleasure and Pain in that way of Writing."[38] To Addison and his fellow Augustans, fables were a "way of Writing" with special ties to the unwritten world. The syllogism that provides the quotation which heads this introduction, then, was practically a foregone conclusion by the time it appeared, anonymously, in 1726. If in fables all things hold discourse, then in a world where authoritative language itself increasingly takes the form of tangible and portable things ("Writing," letters), words too "must talk of course." And their conversation is necessarily an integral part of any meaning put forward on the surface of the page. Aesop's fables continually enact this recognition. Their official employment in English schools only literalizes their primary function. Simply put, that function was to inculcate a text-based set of assumptions and cognitive strategies which, if shared, could actively create a coherent modern community of readers. In my view, their common stock in the formation of this community frames, and thereby forces us to reconsider, the political critiques and apparent subversions so openly at play in English fables written between 1651 and 1740.

A word, finally, about the boundaries of this book. First, in the late seventeenth and early eighteenth centuries, the term "fable" was polyvalent. It could signify a lie, any "feign'd or devis'd discourse," a plot, a hieroglyph, a parable, a myth.[39] Here, I treat mainly short, moralized speaking animal narratives, many of which were conspicuously attributed to Aesop. Though often hailed as "the First who purposely made use of this Mode of Writing," Aesop was not the only figure that English writers identified with fables.[40] The Brahmin philosopher Pilpay (a.k.a. Bidpai and Doni) had several volumes of "instructive and entertaining" fables to his credit by the mid-eighteenth century.[41] Persian tales, particularly those of Scheherazade, remained popular throughout the century,[42] and in 1711, Mr. Spectator announced that the French fabulist Jean de la Fontaine had "come more into Vogue than any other Writer of our Time."[43] Above all, the Latin poet Phaedrus, whom La Fontaine himself mentioned admiringly in his own fables, achieved considerable eminence among the Augustans. Matthew Prior and William Somerfield translated some of his fables. Philip Ayres and Roger L'Estrange included him in their fable collections; translations of his fables were published in 1646, 1651, and 1710, and in Christopher Smart's acclaimed edition of 1760. Richard Bentley's *Phaedri Fabulae Aesopiae* appeared in 1726. But just as the freed Roman slave defined himself in terms of Aesop – boasting for example that he had "polish[ed]" his more antique Greek "source" – so was it Aesop who dominated English discussions of fable and fable collections. When in 1703 one fabulist noted that "all Fables have since [Aesop's time] come under the Shelter of his Name, as an Acknowledgment of his peculiar Excellency, and Talent in that Sort of Performance,"[44] he was merely confirming that "Aesop," not "Phaedrus" or "Pilpay," had become shorthand for a specific discursive method, or symbolic "Performance."

Finally, and obviously, fables are unique neither to England nor to the later seventeenth and early eighteenth centuries: Aesop was presumably a contemporary of Homer, and Greek and Latin writing is studded with the fables to which France would prove as appreciative an heir as England. In Spain Velasquez painted Aesop's imaginary portrait, and in the latter half of the eighteenth century, German romantic writers like Herder and Lessing felt fables' primitive allure.[45] Above all, writers like La Fontaine, La Motte, François Fénélon, Pierre Boissat, and Jean Baudoin not only inducted the fable into the neoclassical pantheon of respected literary forms but also crafted a theory of fable that was far more systematic than its English counterpart, which it sporadically influenced. Against these parallel traditions, Augustan Aesopianism stands in interesting relief. The diversity within the English fable collection, its bulk and exuberance, its self-conscious enthusiasm for the new cultural authority of the printed page, and its equally self-conscious Englishness all set the English fable apart.

Meanwhile, in England itself, Ogilby's fable collection no more commemorates the birth of Aesop's fables than Richardson's marks their demise. Fables often appear in English and Scottish literature: Chaucer's "Nun's Priest's Tale" (1387) and Robert Henryson's *Morall Fabillis* (1485) are the best known examples, but even King Alfred is supposed to have translated some Latin apologues.[46] As early as 1486 William Caxton's printing press brought England the Aesopian collection proper, along with what was at the time Aesop's definitive biography. The Renaissance in turn produced some redactions of the collection, both in Latin schoolbooks and in the vernacular. Edmund Spenser's Aesopian *Mother Hubberds Tale* (1591) is one of the most resonant political allegories of the sixteenth century, and writers from John Lydgate to John Milton were wont to repeat what "Æsop's Chronicles averre."[47] In what would prove to be the most fertile breeding ground for the fables of our period, Civil War ballads and broadsides claimed Aesop for Parliamentarian and Royalist causes alike.[48]

Similarly, after Richardson, Robert Dodsley published the *Select Fables of Esop* (1764), with a prefatory "Essay on Fable" that abstracted some of the fable theories that had been put forward in the earlier part of the eighteenth century.[49] Thomas Bewick produced a series of naturalistically illustrated fable collections in 1779, 1784, 1814, and 1818, even appending engravings of the headstones of England's leading fabulists to one volume. Editions of Croxall's *Fables* continued to appear through the end of the eighteenth century; Edward Moore, Christopher Smart and even William Godwin all contrived fable collections of their own.[50] More revealing of new trends in fable-writing, fables designed to regulate the conduct of "the fair sex" were *en vogue* from the 1740s through the 1770s.[51] Later, didactic fictions by Maria Edgeworth and Anna Barbauld made fables the staple of children's literature that they remain to the present day.[52]

Still, *Aesop's* fables had a specific and finite meaning for readers and writers in late seventeenth- and early eighteenth-century England. Each of the chapters that follows explores some aspect of that meaning, and all suggest that Aesop's fables were intimately involved with the emergence of a self-consciously literate culture – one in which the printed page, with its unique claims to continuity with the world of sensible and portable objects, gradually absorbs and regulates sociopolitical conflict, and thereby becomes the chief bearer both of cultural authority and of authorial identity. My first three chapters consider Aesop's fables in the aggregate, as a phenomenon within English print culture between 1651 and 1740. My last three chapters explore the work of three neoclassical poets – Dryden, Finch, and Gay – who used fables to renegotiate the terms of literary authority in an increasingly book-centered culture.

In particular, Chapter 1 surveys fable collections ranging in size from L'Estrange's mammoth *Fables of Æsop and Other Eminent Mythologists* to the sixpenny pamphlets that Grub Street hacks churned out in Aesop's name around the turn of the century. Chapter 2 investigates Augustan fable theory, particularly as it sought to identify fables with the origins of writing, and thereby to protect modern texts from readerly invasion. Chapter 3 looks at Aesop's role as a cultural icon in England between 1651 and 1740. Each of these chapters analyzes a different aspect of Aesopian method – its practical application in Augustan fable collections, its theoretical profile, its allegorization in the figure of Aesop. But all maintain that that method prevailed in English writing for nearly a century because of its capacity for reactive mediation between opposing sides, and because of its perceived ability to naturalize and stabilize the printed page as an ironically centerless center of cultural authority.

In the second half of this study, Dryden, Finch, and Gay merit special attention because, of the many neoclassical poets who employed Aesopian method, these three most fully exploited its capacity to analyze literate culture from within it. Publishing at roughly generational intervals – in 1687, 1713, and 1738 – all used fables to orient themselves to an England understood as a symbolic, indeed literary, entity. Dryden's *The Hind and the Panther* was preoccupied with the figure and future of England. A refugee from the disbanded Stuart court, Finch used fables to make herself present to a new English reading public. It was as a fabulist that Gay was monumentalized as an English poetic paragon. Aesop's fables gave each of these writers a way of exposing, but also of exploiting, the new foundations of literary and cultural authority in contemporary England. So Chapter 4 places Dryden's eleventh-hour attraction to Aesop's fables in the context of his conversion to Roman Catholicism. His new position as a political outsider, I suggest, made him especially receptive to the figural possibilities that lurk in a self-consciously material text. Finch's translations of La Fontaine and the Aesopian subtext of her *Miscellany Poems* (1713) are seen to explicate the links between textual and sexual politics in early eighteenth-century England. Finally, I show how Gay's two series of fables (1727 and 1738) used Aesopian strategies to illuminate the guilty ironies that underlie modern English signifying conventions and habits of reading.

To an outsider, Aesop's fables' efflorescence between 1651 and 1740 can look either predictable or surprising. To the extent that all of Aesop's figures are grounded in the sensible world from which particular significances demonstrably emerge, it seems inevitable that fables should have been so fashionable in late seventeenth- and early eighteenth-century England. To the extent that fables are also improbable, restless, and potentially multivalent, however, they also reveal the pretensions, exclusions, and contradictions that underlie a symbolic system perhaps inordinately proud of its own clarity, concreteness, and accessibility "to all Degrees of Men and Circumstances of Life." In the largest sense, this book thus asks how fables both reveal and reproduce the signifying habits of modernity, especially insofar as these are located on the theoretically egalitarian page. The English fable between 1651 and 1740 gives us a glimpse of a culture's ambivalent foundation – which is of course one of our own.

Aesopian examples:
the English fable collection and its authors,
1651–1740

Examples are Best Precepts, and a Tale
Adorn'd with Sculpture better may prevaile
To make Men lesser Beasts than all the Store
Of tedious Volumes vext the World before.

John Ogilby, Frontispiece,
Fables of Æsop, Paraphras'd in Verse (1651)

There was a Controversie Started betwixt a *Lyon* and a *Man*, which was the Braver and Stronger Creature of the Two. Why look ye, says the Man (after a long Dispute), we'll appeal to that Statue there, and so he shew'd him the Figure of a *Man*, cut in Stone, with a *Lyon* under his Feet. Well! says the *Lyon*, if *We* had been brought up to Painting and Carving, as *You* are, where you have One *Lyon* under the Feet of a *Man*, you should have had *Twenty Men* under the Paw of a *Lyon*.

Roger L'Estrange, "A Lyon and a Man"
Fables of Æsop and Other Eminent Mythologists (1692)

On May 10, 1665, literate Londoners had the chance to participate in a curious event – a "Standing Lottery of his Own Books, Design'd and [...] Executed by the AUTHOR."[1] Pronounced by his contemporaries "one of the Prodigies of our Age,"[2] this enterprising "AUTHOR" was John Ogilby, and his lottery featured a store of folio volumes ranging from Ogilby's translations of Virgil (1649) and Homer (1660) to his elaborately engraved edition of the English Bible, to what was to become his most celebrated achievement – a verse paraphrase of Aesop's fables, extravagantly "adorn'd with Sculptures," and valued at the equally extravagant price of three pounds.

Staged only five years after the Restoration of the Stuart monarchy, in the early days of the great plague, Ogilby's lottery shared the capricious temper of the times as it enticed "Adventurers" to put 40 shillings "into the hands of Fortune."[3] Unlike earlier lotteries, whose proceeds usually went to support national interests, particularly in the colonies, Ogilby's was meant to promote his status as "AUTHOR." Evidently the venture did yield a "handsom Stock of Reputation" – so "handsom" a "Stock," in fact, that Ogilby "erected" a second lottery in 1668 and, "still covetous of Fame," a third in 1669.[4] His schemes mark a crucial intersection between the history of authorship and English sociopolitical history. Undeniably a man of "excellent inventive and prudentiall wit,"[5] Ogilby linked his image as an author to the economic investments of a new reading public. His lotteries were a means of cunning self-promotion in a tumultuous world where, as Ogilby himself advertised, Fortune's favors are but "blind[ly] dispenc[ed]," and then more often "on the wrong side, than on the right."[6]

Among Fortune's beneficiaries in 1665 was Samuel Pepys, who won a folio copy of Ogilby's *Fables of Aesop, Paraphras'd in Verse*. Pepys was already in possession of the first edition of *Fables*, published in quarto in 1651; from it he had even "read to my wife a fable or two" on a spring evening in 1663.[7] And by June of 1666 he was looking forward to yet another folio edition of Ogilby's Aesop, which he expected to be "very fine and very satyricall,"[8] and which finally materialized in 1668. In fact, by the time of Ogilby's death in 1676, *Fables* had gone into five editions; his *Aesopics* – a variation on the *Fables* allegedly produced because "people did [. . .] suspect, or would not beleeve that 'twas he was the author of the paraphrase upon Æsop"[9] – had appeared in three. Altogether, in popularity Ogilby's Aesopian excursions handily surpassed his *Aeneid* (four printings), his *Iliads* and his *Odyssey* (printed once each). And while in some circles, as Walter Scott would put it, Ogilby's "name" was to "become almost proverbial for a bad Poet," thanks to his overweening translations of the great classical epics, *Fables* was more genially acknowledged as "the chief of all" Ogilby's works. "Compos'd *propria Minerva*," Edward Phillips opined, Ogilby's Aesop "for Ingenuity & Fancy, besides the Invention of new Fables, is generally confess't to have exceeded what ever hath been done before in that kind."[10]

What exactly had Ogilby wrought? To hear high Augustans like Pope and Dryden tell it, precious little. On the contrary, Pope's slighting allusion to "Ogilby the great" in *The Dunciad* comes with a footnote that jabs at him for "sending into the world" too "many large *Volumes*," all "printed [. . .] on *special good Paper*, and in a *very good Letter*."[11] *Fables* was surely one such volume. To produce it, Ogilby had blithely raised the familiar speaking animal stories told by an antique slave into elaborate iambic couplets, "adorn[ing]" them with "Sculptures" as handsome as those that graced his epic translations. The caption beneath the facing image of an Aesop himself very far from elegance (plate 1) ambitiously declared that, since "Examples are best Precepts," the following pages easily outstripped "tedious Volumes" of the past both in their likelihood of pleasing and in their didactic efficacy. An early panegyric praised Ogilby for correcting the misguided efforts of earlier "Rimers" who had "vex'd [Aesop's] Ghost" and "stain[ed] fair Paper" with their clumsier

Examples are past Precepts; And a Tale
Adorn'd with Sculpture better may prevaile
To make Men lesser Beasts, than all the Store
Of tedious Volumes, vext the World before.

1   Frontiespiece to John Ogilby, *Fables of Æsop, Paraphras'd in Verse*, London, 1651.

efforts.[12] By 1665 Ogilby had added marginal notes that glossed the fables
with references to the likes of Ovid, Euripides, and Cicero. He had also
jettisoned Francis Cleyn's relatively modest "Sculptures" in favor of more
accomplished images by Wenceslaus Hollar and Robert Stoope.[13] If Ogilby's
achievement was to elevate Aesop's fables, he did so by making the most of
every aspect of the printed page.

Certainly, Aesop's fables themselves were nothing new. Nor even was their adaptation to the latest in print technology. When William Caxton had set up the first English press near the end of the fifteenth century, *The Book of the Subtyll Histories of Æsop* (1486) was among the first things that he printed, and in the sixteenth century William Bullokar had published a new prose collection meant to demonstrate, in type, his own eccentric orthographic schemes.[14] Ogilby's rendering of Aesop into English verse was not unprecedented either: at least two earlier collections had already turned them to poetry.[15] What *was* new about Ogilby's *Fables* was their use of the physical body of the book to establish the fame of a modern English poet, as well as to integrate the poetic present with the classical past. This poetic present was also a political present, as Pepys's expectation that Ogilby's next edition of fables would be "satyricall" suggests and as the two most thorough critical discussions of Ogilby's collection to date have shown.[16] Ogilby's *Fables* brimmed with puns and topical references that made them recognizably, distinctively English, even as they bore witness to an England, fraught with barely disguised conflict, that had not existed before the recent Civil Wars. Pepys's anticipation of a new volume equally "fine and [. . .] satyricall" implies that, for contemporary readers, the collection's up-to-the-minute Englishness was in turn bound up with its status as a visually appealing, possessible object.

With so much to recommend them, Ogilby's collections caught on in a way that their predecessors had not, sparking a craze for Aesop's fables that would last for almost 90 years. While they could seldom match Ogilby's ornate example, the droves of fable collections published in its wake took comparable advantage of new print techniques and of the appetite for textual experience that they whetted. Many incorporated detailed plates and variable typefaces. Others divided individual fables into numbered episodes, each of which exhibited some rudiment of English sentence structure. Polyglot collections like Francis Barlow's *Æsop's Fables, with his Life* (1666; 1687) dexterously juxtaposed the same story in different types corresponding to the different languages on display (English, French, and Latin). So that "the signification of the one [language] might be learnt from the other," John Locke's English–Latin fable collection of 1703 offered cognates "always printed in the same Character, to shew their correspondence."[17] When Samuel Richardson typeset his own edition of Aesop's fables in 1739, he used state-of-the-art copper plates that were guaranteed to boost sales.

English fabulists copied more than Ogilby's technological opportunism, though. They were equally eager to reproduce those aspects of his collection that distracted attention from its bookishness. For example, later collections often displayed portraits of the storyteller Aesop very like the one that presided over Ogilby's frontispiece. Thus while they now subsisted between two covers, the fables printed in a given collection frequently appeared to have started out as tales told in the natural world. What's more, like Ogilby's, the fables themselves narrated the adventures of greedy dogs and ambitious frogs, crafty foxes and ruthless wolves. Plots so visceral – and actors so very natural – confirmed the declaration, boldly posted on Ogilby's frontispiece, that "Examples are best Precepts." Obvious offspring of the printing press though they might be, Aesop's fables nonetheless purported to supply natural and concrete "Examples" that could drive home otherwise abstract or unpalatable "Precepts." Aesopian examples, apparently, could insinuate moral, grammatical, and political principles without the visible intervention of a human author, much as Ogilby's unorthodox manner of marketing his work subordinated authorial "fame" to Fortune's whimsy and to a new reading public's love of risk and acquisition.

In itself, again, this figural strategy was scarcely novel. As John Wallace has shown, many Renaissance writers had already developed a theory of exemplarity – of sensuous particulars aimed at the "seduction" of recalcitrant readers – which Ogilby only (indeed belatedly) echoes.[18] Indeed, in his *Mother Hubberds Tale* (1591) and *Shepheardes Calender* (1579), Edmund Spenser had dispatched Aesopian examples themselves. Ogilby's contention that "Examples are best Precepts" – even its realization in Aesopian practice – would thus seem to look as far back as forward.

Yet why should Aesopian exemplarity need to be original in order to be significant? More important are its sudden wide currency beginning with Ogilby, and its articulation in a cultural form – the printed fable collection – which could complicate and even animate the literary commonplace that justifies a fable collection in the first place. Ogilby's own epigraph expands the maxim that "Examples are best Precepts" in just this direction: What counts as an example is more than a simple story that appeals directly to the senses. As an example of an example, Ogilby offers "a Tale,/Adorn'd with Sculpture." Not only would such examples be unrepresentable outside a culture with a developing taste for printed matter; Ogilby further suggests that the example which "better may prevaile" is the one that, in textual space, manifests skepticism about the authenticity and innocence of examples themselves. Aesopian examples are persuasive – in the words of one of Ogilby's heirs, they allow authors to be "secure in [their] Representation" – because they make the real (and really insecure) conditions of "Representation" a visible element of their own meaning.[19] Fables' authority depends on their ability to demonstrate their own provisional status as authoritative signs.

Aesopian practice confirms this interpretation of Ogilby's maxim, as we can see in an example of our own. The fable of the lion and the man (quoted at the head of this chapter) is ubiquitous in contemporary collections; it even moonlighted in periodicals like Addison and Steele's *Spectator* and in didactic works like Elizabeth Griffith's *Letters between Henry and Frances* (1757).[20] In the story a lion points out that a visible "Figure" depicting "a *Man* [...] with a *Lyon* under his Feet," means not (as the man would have it) that one species is

"Braver and Stronger" than another but only that whoever controls the methods and materials of representation at a given moment will also determine a figure's meaning. Paradoxically, the fable employs a sensible image – a speaking lion – to show that such images are always vulnerable to appropriation and inversion.[21] Ogilby's lion is admirably clear on the concept: Inspecting the image of "a *Lion*'s head in a *Man*'s bosome laid," he maintains that this is "no sufficient Proof" of human superiority. For "could we, well as you, our Stories cut,/We might, and justly, put/Your lying Heads beneath/Our Conquering Foot."[22]

While Ogilby's axiom that "Examples are best Precepts" properly headnotes Aesopian practice after 1651, thus, actual fables just as properly undercut this axiom – as indeed does Ogilby's own addendum to it. Augustan fables not only compounded verbal abstractions with the convincing material of the sensible world. They also made it clear that literary authority – issuing ultimately in authorial reputation – takes shape only through compromise with existing power relations, and with prevailing theories and practices of representation. Its talent for compounding prudential skepticism with empirical security sets an Aesopian fable apart from other kinds of example. And their eagerness to exploit this kind of figuration in order to institute a new form of symbolic authority distinguishes the work of English fabulists from Ogilby to Samuel Richardson. The "AUTHOR[S]" of the most prominent fable collections differed widely on many a score; and as a group they proved more self-conscious than the fabulists whose less celebrated collections I consider after them. Just the same, we can trace a common commitment from the inception of the self-consciously English fable collection to the Aesopically inflected novels of the 1740s.

Prevailing tales: the major collections

More than one European country adopted fables into a native literary tradition during the late seventeenth and eighteenth centuries, and the major fable collections produced in England between 1651 and 1740 are no exception. Despite their differences from one another, they are very uniquely and deliberately English, and together they consitute a figural response, often self-consciously organized within the English language, to England's notoriously unstable political history and the crisis of signification that that history wrought.[23] Ogilby's own *Fables* "englished" the fable collection partly by incorporating political slang left over from the wars. Often posing as translators or teachers of written English, later fabulists consistently situated themselves amid the different competitions that characterized not only England's political experience between the Civil Wars and the death of Walpole but also its emerging literary marketplace and commercial culture generally.[24] In their very diversity, the fable collections reflected the demands and desires that vied in the world around them. They ranged in price from a penny to several pounds, and in size from a "Pocket Manual" to that of "a Folio more than double that Bulk."[25] Their authors could be as obscure as an anonymous Grub Street hack or as eminent as John Locke. Likewise, their illustrators could be unknowns or celebrated artists like Francis Barlow, their readers barely literate children or aged and illustrious poets. The object of a fable collection could be to teach schoolboys how to read English, French, or Latin. But it could also be to preach proper conduct to young ladies or to argue for a complex political perspective that might, in turn, be Whig or Tory, Williamite or Stuart.

It is fitting that Aesop's fables themselves tell tales of competition among individuals of radically different stripe. Set in a world where power is never balanced and self-interest decides value, their themes mirror the instability of the England in which they were put to use. After beginning with the story of the cock who digs up a precious gem, only to announce that he would have preferred a barleycorn, a typical collection went on to tell of a wolf with a craving for mutton who accuses a lamb of sullying his drinking water and then devours him. A jay strutting in peacock's feathers is plucked apart for her pretensions. A frog explodes when she tries to puff herself up to the size of an ox. A wolf hires a stork to fish the lamb bones out of his throat and, when she demands remuneration, reminds her that his sparing her head should be compensation enough. A fox trapped in a well persuades the goat stuck with him to offer his head for a step ladder; gaining freedom, the fox leaves the goat to perish, jeering over his shoulder that his ex-partner has not "half so much Brains as you have Beard."[26] Since Aesop's plots uncover craft and machination in the service of brutal desire, the morals attached to them were usually cynical and pragmatic: "A Wise Man [...] leaves Nothing to Chance more than he needs must." "In a Wallowing Qualm, a Man's Heart and Resolution fail him, for want of Fit Matter to Work upon." "Perfidious people are naturally to be suspected in reports that favour their own interest."[27]

Skeptical and combative though their themes and morals might be, however, Augustan fable collections also practiced a strikingly conciliatory figural method. Structurally they employed a "Method of recommending [...] Principles by pleasing Images."[28] Practically, fables provided primary reading material to most English grammar schools, thereby supplying a reservoir of shared figures to several otherwise divided generations of readers and writers. In other words, Augustan fable collections struck a delicate balance between a mode of representation so simple and sensible as to seem unmediated – almost non-linguistic – and the admission that all authoritative signs can be appropriated, manipulated, and inverted. A less than flattering view of the human reader prompted Ogilby's own commitment to this delicate equipoise. His famous epigraph maintains that fables' primary task is to "make Men lesser Beasts," to offer precepts "Men" can agree upon and that can forestall reversion to what we may fairly call a state of nature. Ironically, it is only by commissioning the sensible, familiar, but also belligerent elements of that state that fabulists may forestall such reversions, for only these elements are deemed genuinely and universally impressive.

It is not surprising then that Ogilby's first Aesopian quarto should have appeared in the same year as Thomas Hobbes's *Leviathan* (1651). Hobbes found the germ of cultural stability in a *rapprochement* between human signifying practice and the state of nature. He argued that "Man"'s native penchant for conflict can be averted only when "Men" craft a consensual sign system. Thus a brutal and divisive "Nature" composes itself into the "Artificial Animal" of social order. What holds this prodigious beast together are symbolic tokens which its members have agreed to exchange. Hobbes allowed these tokens to be words themselves, as long as they remain grounded in the shared sensible world, and as long as those who use them consent to do so in the same way.[29] As Ogilby's epigraph makes clear, fables (particularly when "adorn'd" with impressive "Sculptures") are perfect candidates to become such tokens. And the persuasive image of Hobbes's own Leviathan predictably bears more than a passing resemblance to the beasts in Aesop's menagerie.

But Hobbesian theory also promises that clashing appetites will continue to drive, and divert, the traffic of signs. Especially when viewed in light of its metamorphoses over the 1650s and 1660s, Ogilby's fable collection acts out this promise and the paradox that attends it. In the first edition of *Fables*, the former dancing master, theater manager, and Royalist soldier offered Cromwellian London eighty-one "Tale[s] adorn'd with Sculpture." Alluding to the recent wars, he guaranteed that any one of these "Tale[s]" could "make Men lesser Beasts." Laudatory poems by James Shirley and William Davenant praised Ogilby's "humble Moralls" for their ability both to "convince the subtile, and the Simple gaine." In Davenant's far from unshared view, Ogilby's fables "invade[d]" their reader's "will" not with "force" but rather with homely imagery to which all and sundry are naturally amenable.[30]

Despite the high aroma of conciliation emanating from *Fables*, however, Davenant sent his verses "from the Tower," and Ogilby pointedly dedicated the volume to the royalist Heneage Finch. As both Annabel Patterson and Mary Pritchard have shown, individual fables were fraught with royalist dogma. The Aesopian canon already housed simple stories about amphibian monarchies, ingenuous trees that lend woodsman wood for their axe handles, and foxes that grow so accustomed to the sight of "the Scepter'd *Lion*" that the latter loses all power to awe, hence rule. In Ogilby's hands, such narratives became intricate political allegories, some critically sympathetic to the royalist cause, others hostile to the government that had supplanted it.[31] To complete the picture, ominous images of decapitation haunt Francis Cleyn's "Sculptures." Such gestures undercut the fables' superficial pursuit of the peaceable authority of the naturalized and textualized example by conspicuously, even violently, twisting the implications of individual signs.

Just so, in 1660, the fabulist himself was to be found designing "Ænigmatical Emblems" for the triumphal arches at Charles II's coronation. He went on to become Master of the Royal Imprimerie and, at the end of the decade, Cosmographer Royal, in which capacity he devised elaborate atlases of the world's continents as well as road maps of England that instituted the statute mile. Ogilby took easily to a position of cultural authority, and his Aesop just as effortlessly traveled with him from the margins to the mainstream of seventeenth-century literary culture. The contemporary value of Ogilby's fables, in other words, was not restricted to the political critique they mounted. Rather, equally viable in two very different Englands, they offered literary figures that acknowledged the factional, and fictional, nature of all meaningful signs even as they continued to identify themselves with a natural world whose preceptive authority few wished to deny. Ogilby's fables thus confirmed the vision of efficacious symbolic order set forth in *Leviathan*. Unlike Hobbes's treatise, however, Ogilby's fables and others like them proved structurally equipped to comment on the ironic juxtaposition of two axes of signification, one combative and motivated, the other busy minting a new symbolic currency that could create cultural coherence.

For example, when Bernard Mandeville applied Hobbes's argument to a modern commercial society, he naturally did so in the form of a fable. It is even a lion who, in one of the footnotes to *The Fable of the Bees* (first complete edition, 1729), remarks that, in successful human societies, "Millions [...] well-join'd together [...] compose the strong *Leviathan*."[32] Mandeville's fable earmarks "private Vices" as the predicates of "publick Benefits," injustice and disproportionate lack as prerequisites of cultural order. Fabulists like Ogilby had already made this paradox a feature of signification itself. Ogilby's headstrong, truculent animals often comment ironically on their own absorption into a stable and transmissible symbolic system: "Here I the Emblem of fond Mortals sit,/That lose the Substance for an empty Bit," one dog mourns, after he has dropped a shoulder of mutton by snapping at its reflection. The dog's own words reveal what made him a significant object. He is thus a convincing reminder not only of the follies of unbridled desire ("an Emblem of fond Mortals") but also of the greed and guile that turn meaningless "Substance" into meaningful sign.[33]

Throughout all of Ogilby's collections, fables like "The Dog and the Shadow" meld sensible images ("Sculptures") with linguistic structures ("Tales") that document those images' progress toward the status of memorable and authoritative signs. A similar desire to demystify the act of attaching moral and political significance to phenomenal signs apparently motivated the other major collection of the Restoration period, the celebrated artist Francis Barlow's *Æsop's Fables with his Life*. While English readers identified Ogilby's Aesop with its writer, they associated Barlow's equally sumptuous and oft-reprinted volume with its illustrator.[34] For a first edition of 1666, however, Barlow commissioned the text of the fables (in English, French, and Latin) from one Thomas Philipott. Then for a new edition of 1687 he invited the "ingenious" playwright, poet, and romance writer Aphra Behn to "perform the English Poetry."[35] Behn obliged and the resulting collection flourished well into the eighteenth century.

In his dedication to the Earl of Devonshire, Barlow claimed a special symbolic status for "his" fables – "a thing," he declared, "much practis'd by the Ancient *Greeks* and the *Orientals*" who used them as "Portraitures in their Temples, design'd as Memorial Characters of Philosophic Notions to be the Subject of Adoration." In place of these antique idols, Barlow ostentatiously offers his own modern English readers a "Book, ascrib'd to Esop in a Plain and Simple Form." As the "Plain and Simple" book supplants the arcane icons of the past, it openly confesses its own political and historical contingency; equally transparent are its fictive strategies for recommending "the conduct of Life." After all, Barlow points out, " 'tis the Misfortune of Mankind, that the present Times as little dare to relate Truths, as the Future can know them." Obviously fictional and factional, Barlow's carefully fused "Ornaments of Sculptures and Poetry" further Ogilby's quest for a symbolic form that might wed a picture's immediate impact to language's power of skeptical exposition.

Each a quatrain with a moralizing couplet tacked onto it, Behn's fables deftly "perform[ed]" the Aesopian premises that Barlow's dedication had sketched. Behn feminized a number of Aesop's fables, somewhat improbably turning the "kingly Eagle" who steals a young fox into a female, along with the kid whom a wolf woos away from its mother. A female ape begs in vain for an inch of a fox's tail to "vaile" her "bum" and the fable of the dog in the manger is moralized as a story about how "aged Lovers" who court "young Beautys [...]/Keepe off those joys they want the power to give" (p. 59). Behn's verses not only bent fables with the crowbar of witty feminism she had perfected in the Restoration theater; writing in the last days of the Stuart monarchy, which she supported, Behn also included barely oblique references to the Stuart predicament. To the brief chronicle of a family of adders whom "the Porcupines deceiv'd/Of their warme Nest which cou'd not be retriev'd," for example, she appended the observation that "Crownes got by force are often times made good,/By the more rough designes of warr, and blood" (p. 81). Other fables, like that of the mouse who saves a lion from a snare by gnawing through the ropes, caution their readers not to "despise the service of a Slave" since "an Oak did once our glorious Monarch save" (p. 47). More than veiled political commentary, Behn's fables fulfilled Barlow's dedicatory promise that the "Plain and Simple Form" of the Aesopian example ought to convey the impossibility of "relat[ing] Truths." Because each fable also appeared in French and Latin versions that were unmolested by tendentious reference, Behn's "Plain and Simple" English verses all the more plainly displayed their own distortions. And since these same verses were printed as captions to Barlow's illustrations, throughout the collection visual images were virtually soldered to tendentious English words. The resulting figures effectively ironized – even parodied – the very notion of an indisputable emblem.

The revised edition of Barlow's collection appeared just before James II's abdication and the accession of William and Mary. The next fifteen years saw a fresh flurry of Aesopian activity, particularly by writers who, like Behn, sympathized with the lost Stuart cause. The simplest explanation for the rash of fable collections during the Williamite period is that fables' seemingly innocent preoccupation with animal affairs made them safe, while yet exceptionally convincing, ways to resist the prevailing political tide. While many fables were written from the ruling side, this explanation can begin to account for the most copious, notorious, and widely read fable collection of the 1690s, Roger L'Estrange's immense *Fables of Æsop and Other Eminent Mythologists* (1692 and 1699).

By his own confession, L'Estrange was already "on the wrong Side of Fourscore" when he published the first edition of his *Eminent Mythologists*.[36] A Cavalier who had prudently spent the middle of the seventeenth century abroad, he became a prolific propagandist for the Stuarts after the Restoration, publishing a blizzard of pamphlets and two newspapers that, along with his watchdog post as Surveyor of the Press and Chief Licenser, presciently earned him the Aesopian nickname "Towzer."[37] Throughout the reigns of the last Stuart kings, L'Estrange's jobs as censor and propagandist put him in exactly the spot where old (centripetal) images of sovereign right met the new (centrifugal) cultural authority of the printing press. Predictably, his Stuart and Roman Catholic sympathies ousted him from this influential position in 1688. No less enterprising than Ogilby, L'Estrange thereupon launched a remarkably successful career translating Seneca, Tacitus, and Terence, as well as select modern texts in French and Spanish. *Eminent Mythologists* belongs to this paradoxical period of political disenfranchisement and swelling belletristic prestige. Officially L'Estrange's collection is also a translation, of Aesop and a number of "Other Eminent Mythologists," ancient and modern.[38] The identities of these other mythologists merge into that of Aesop, whose portrait and biography, as in Barlow's *Fables*, are an integral part of the collection. L'Estrange's own likeness – flowing Cavalier ringlets, canine bone structure and all – appears at the beginning of the volume, so that readers so inclined could also identify the motley and gargantuan collection with a single English author.

Rendered in a pithy and colloquial prose with morals and long "Reflexions" that offered a clandestine protest against the constitutional structure of the new political order,[39] L'Estrange's versions of Aesop's fables looked and sounded quite unlike Ogilby's intricate verses, or even Behn's quipping quatrains. Nor were L'Estrange's fables illustrated, though his preface described them as "Precepts in Emblem," as "Emblem[s] and Figure[s]," even as "Images of Things."[40] However, it is this very assumption that graphic signs – the words that communicate the fable, in conjunction with the words that moralized and reflected on it – can persuade as powerfully as images do that placed *Eminent Mythologists* in line with its recent English predecessors. As was the case with earlier Aesops, L'Estrange's collection was more than Jacobite propaganda tucked under "the Vaile of *Emblem*, and *Figure*."[41] Like them, it mixes political reaction with an almost obsessive attention to the sensible and potentially mediatory properties of the printed page.

Whereas Ogilby and Barlow had dedicated their work to notable aristocrats, L'Estrange officially intended his collection to be used in English classrooms, where it might instill a proper sense of the English language. His long and lively preface scorns the "Book" of Aesop's fables as he maintained it had been "universally Read, and Taught in All our Schools" (sig. B4r). For too long, L'Estrange claimed, Aesop's fables had languished in the form of empty "Rhapsody," foaming with "Insipid *Twittle-Twattles*, Frothy *Jests*, and Jingling *Witticisms*." The English language had languished right along with them, for, rife with nonsensical word games, the old Aesops had taught children to read "as we teach *Pyes* and *Parrots*, that pronounce the Words without so much as Guessing at the Meaning of them; Or to take it Another Way, the Boys Break their Teeth upon the Shells, without ever coming near the Kernel" (sig. B2r).[42]

Although his pedagogical approach makes L'Estrange a different breed of author from Ogilby or Barlow, or Behn, he shared their conviction that modern fables could coax signs away from obscurity and excessive figurality into a more durable and trustworthy symbolic register. As his contempt for "pronounc[ing]" suggests, that register is implicitly textual. L'Estrange even maintained that fables affect their readers as sense experience does, impressing reading minds as writing might a page: "Children are but *Blank Paper*, ready Indifferently for any Impression, Good or Bad, and it is much in the Power of the first Comer, to Write Saint, or Devil upon't, which of the two he pleases" (sig. A2v). As primary reading material, fables openly wielded "the Power of the first Comer." Like Ogilby's preceptive examples and Barlow's "Ornaments of Sculptures and Poetry," L'Estrange's fables capitalize on the materiality of the text, transferring to self-revealing graphic signs more and more of the powerful immmediacy that iconic signs had once possessed. It seems unlikely that L'Estrange really expected his fables to be used in "the Schools." Instead, his speculations about how printed fables viscerally impress young readers build a trope for Aesopian authority. This trope in turn openly acknowledges the pages of the fable collection to be a proper arena of political activity. Once that activity is conceded to be a matter of making meaning, the physical body of the fable collection can be seen to participate in its moral, political, and thematic mission.

Though eighteenth-century readers complained about its raunchy and colloquial style, its Jacobite morals, even L'Estrange's fondness for the contractions and abbreviations that made it speak almost *too* current an English, *Eminent Mythologists* remained the most popular collection in the nation for the next thirty years.[43] Other Aesops came and went without attracting half the notice that it did. None was more often abridged, revised, and discussed. But in 1722 the Whig clergyman Samuel Croxall decided that the time was ripe for a new collection of Aesop's fables. He proceeded to devise one whose political sensibilities aggressively countered and ultimately deposed L'Estrange's "eminent mythologists," with new editions proliferating well into the twentieth century.

Writing in the self-congratulatory pseudo-stability of early Georgian England, Croxall touted his *Fables of Æsop and Others* as a patriotic antidote to L'Estrange's *Eminent Mythologists*. His dedicatee was the five-year-old Baron Halifax, whom Croxall depicted as an English political hero in the making, already precociously adept in the "English Tongue" and "by Birth intitled to a Share in the Administration of the Government."[44] Croxall filched L'Estrange's trope of the Aesopically influenced English reader in order to promote his own *Fables* as a book with consequences for the nation: In theory, if Halifax ingested its contents early, then later the "Country [would] feel the Benefit of these Lectures of Morality" (sig. A5r). Thus would Croxall's Aesop personally advance "the Peace and Prosperity of my Country" (sig. A6v). Superficially, this approving image of a peaceful and prosperous Britain set Croxall against the confirmed malcontent L'Estrange, whom Croxall claimed had twisted the fables so as to exaggerate "Party Animosities" and "factious Division." It was in order to endorse and replicate the "liberal" politics of Hanoverian Britain that Croxall resolved to detoxify L'Estrange's "pernicious ... Principles, coin'd and suited to promote the Growth, and serve the Ends of Popery and Arbitrary Power" (sig. B5v). His acrid preface parrots L'Estrange's diatribe against earlier collections to express contempt for the "Insufficiency of *L'Estrange*'s own Performance." In Croxall's book, this frightful "Insufficiency" went beyond objectionable political views to encompass the "insipid and flat" morals and "course and uncouth [...] Style and Diction" that, like those views, had diverted Aesop's fables from the "Purpose for which they were principally intended" (sigs. B4v–r). Insisting that this "Purpose" was to argue against political absolutism, Croxall revised L'Estrange's fables so that they would better suit the "Children of *Britain*," who are "born with free Blood in their Veins; and suck in Liberty with their very Milk" (sig. B5r).

It is not hard to catch the ironic resemblance between Croxall's conception of what a fable collection should be and that of his loathed predecessor. Like

L'Estrange, Croxall implied that the future of England's linguistic and political integrity depended on the proper transmission of Aesop's fables to a new generation of English readers. To this end, he too stressed the material ties that bind the Aesopian text to the phenomenal world that it depicts. Thus one of Croxall's most strident criticisms of L'Estrange's stupendous folio was that it was physically inadequate to the task of impressing the appropriate "Morality" on the "blank Paper" of its reader's mind. L'Estrange, Croxall charged, had "swell'd [the collection] to so voluminous a Bulk, . . . I don't see how it can suit the Hand or Pocket, of the Generality of Children" (sig. B8v). L'Estrange's "noxious Principles" were inseparable from his "Prolixity." As cumbersome textual matter, his fables embodied their author's unpalatable political designs. Nonetheless, this very materiality became the condition of Croxall's own opposition to L'Estrange. It permitted him to point the fables plausibly in new directions and thus it demonstrated not simply the reassuring substantiality of written signs but also how easily they can be stolen and deformed. For example, Croxall took L'Estrange's version of "A Lyon and a Man," literally inverted its title to "The Forrester and the Lion," and applied its moral directly to writing, noting tersely that "contending Parties are very likely to appeal the Truth to Records written by their own Side."[45]

As Richardson would observe, the "depreciating of *Lestrange's* Work seems to be the Corner-Stone of [Croxall's] own Building."[46] From an Aesopian perspective, this "depreciating" is both a natural action and a textual strategy; it is equally constructive and destructive. To show L'Estrange's unjust "Manner of drawing his Reflections," for instance, Croxall cited Old Towzer's version of the fable of a dog who describes his life of leisure to a wolf. In the fable, the wolf is nearly persuaded to join the dog on the other side of the fence – until he notices the marks that the dog's collar has worn into his fur. The wolf interprets these marks as badges of servitude and flees. In L'Estrange's view, the moral of the fable was that freedom of mind is preferable to mental bondage. Croxall disagreed, seeing such a conclusion as a debased apology for political oppression. Rather than simply shift the moral, however, Croxall turned the fable itself into a vivid example of L'Estrange's willingness to "perver[t . . .] Sense and Meaning" (sig. B6r). Croxall himself becomes the wolfish reader who easily sees through the dog L'Estrange's "long, tedious, amusing Reflection, without one Word to the Purpose." The "Reflection" is, in Croxall's eyes, a flagitious attempt to "justify Slavery":

He tells us at last *that the Freedom which Æsop is so tender of here, is to be understood as the Freedom of the Mind.* Nobody ever understood it so . . . If the Wolf was sensible how sweet the Freedom of the Mind was, and had concern for the liberty of his person, he might have ventur'd to have gone with the Dog well enough: But then he would have sav'd *L'Estrange* the spoiling of one of the best Fables of the whole Collection. However, this may serve for a Pattern of that Gentleman's Candour and Ingenuity in the Manner of drawing his Reflections. (sig. B7v)

For Croxall – as ironically for the Stuart-sympathizing fabulists of the last
century – fables embody not only morals but also "Manner[s] of drawing
[...] Reflections." They translate often contentious literary relations into a
sensible "Pattern." That pattern accommodates the new author himself, and
it in turn becomes an integral part of the story a fable tells. Indeed, it makes
possible the fable's replication across parties and generations, creating a
coherence within conflict – authorial integrity within a dispute about
authority – that neither Croxall nor L'Estrange acknowledged directly.

   In 1739, however, Samuel Richardson did acknowledge it. As Margaret
Anne Doody suggests, the London printer's interest in Aesop, resulting in his
popular *Æsop's Fables*, may betray a nascent sympathy to the Jacobite cause.[47]
Certainly, it was L'Estrange, not Croxall, whose text Richardson finally
decided to abridge and illustrate. In any event, Richardson was no mean
entrepreneur, and he quite unapologetically aimed to mold his readers'
morals. He thus naturally wanted to make the fables in this new collection as
physically impressive as possible. Just as Ogilby had found Aesop's fables the
kind of graphic "Examples" that may best "prevaile" over their readers, just
as L'Estrange deemed them the most persistent of the primary characters that
one could hope to engrave on children's brains, and just as Croxall
pronounced them as digestible as the "Milk of Liberty," so Richardson,
"sensible of the alluring Force which Cuts or Pictures, suited to the respective
Subjects, have on the Minds of Children," took care to include "in a quite
new Manner, engraved on Copper-Plates, at no small Expence, the Subject
of every Fable." Illustrations would further "excite [readers'] Curiosity, and
stimulate their Attention, [...] especially as [they] are distinctly referred both
to Page and Fable in every Representation" (p. xi).

   But if the physical properties of the page promised to forge a happy
coherence among author, reader, signifier, and signified, the fabulist still had
to account for the split political personality of the English fable collection, as
exemplified in the glaring discrepancies between Croxall's *Fables* and those
of L'Estrange. Richardson's preface scrupulously weighs the relative merits
of "the Knight" (L'Estrange) and the "Worthy Gentleman" (Croxall), and
finds that the latter "has strained the natural Import of some of the Fables
near as much one way, as Sir Roger has done the other" (p. viii). For
Richardson, however, such "strain[ing]" may be explained as a consequence
of historical accident, and he specifically defended L'Estrange by reasoning
that, "were the Time in which he wrote considered, the Civil Wars so lately
concluded in his View, and the Anarchy introduced by them, it is the less
wonder that one Extreme produced another in the opposite Party, in its
Turn" (p. vi).

   As he conceded authorial vulnerability to historical and political circumstance, Richardson *de facto* admitted those same circumstances as key features
of every figure. His own collection could yield "better-adapted and more

forcible Morals' precisely because in both preface and in practice it recognized that signs acquire meaning in a contentious and reversible world. Richardson thus had no trouble imagining Croxall and L'Estrange in reversed positions: "Had [the former] lived when Sir *Roger* did, he might have been the *Lestrange* of the one *Court*; as *Lestrange*, had he been in his place, might have taken Orders and become *Chaplain* in the other" (p. ix). The two authors could have cancelled each other out; instead, they demonstrate the same provisional model of symbolic authority.

What made the fables in the English collection contestable was also what made them durable, reproducible, and effective – their "natural Import," their tendency to reduce complex symbolic systems into discrete, concrete, historically responsive terms whose maneuvers could be monitored and whose origins could be investigated. As he strove to reconcile Croxall and L'Estrange in the "natural" space of his own text, Richardson perforce conceded that an individual figure's "natural Import" is never entirely separable from its use, and therefore that symbolic authority survives only through its conscious alienation. This is in many ways the moral of the two epistolary novels that Richardson published in the 1740s, and it is no accident that the letter writers in both *Pamela* (1740) and *Clarissa* (1747–1748) make liberal use of Aesop's fables. In the fifth edition of *Pamela*, an advertisement for Richardson's *Fables* even slyly footnoted Pamela's allusion to "the grasshopper in the fable, which I have read of in my lady's books."[48] The links between Richardson's novels (which looked toward the future of English fiction) and his fables (which mark the end of the Aesopian period as I have described it) are not only literal ones. First, Richardson's work has never been known for its tropological richness. On the contrary, he disavowed all sympathy with his most metaphorically accomplished character, Lovelace, whose narcissistic but self-immolating enthusiasm for convoluted imagery brands him a libertine. Aesop's fables, on the other hand, supply Richardson's correspondents with images so natural, so shareable, and so carefully and conspicuously invested with meaning that they seem to avoid the predatory centerlessness of Lovelacean figuration.

Furthermore, in both *Pamela* and *Clarissa* the most meaningful signs are the words that make up individual letters – minute textual particulars burdened with the task of representing their authors to a world of jealous and acquisitive readers. Both of Richardson's besieged heroines are anxious because they recognize that these graphic signs are continuous with their own bodies and minds – with "Virtue" in Pamela's case, and with moral and spiritual integrity in Clarissa's. For the same reason, both heroines understand, and experience, interpretation (readers' assignment of morals and meanings) as violence. As Terry Castle and other feminist readers of Richardson have shown, this is what makes the symbolic texture of *Clarissa* in particular so very agonized and agonizing.[49] English fabulists from Ogilby forward, though, had sculpted Aesop's fables into concrete textual figures that demonstrated these very trepidations and thereby stood a chance of weathering them.[50] In Richardson's novels, these same fables thus naturally supply a symbolic currency common even to characters as antagonistic as Lovelace and Clarissa. More important, they work almost as forcibly as sensible impressions to control and limit a letter writer's meaning, without denying the fragility of all claims to symbolic mastery.

Pamela offers an especially clear case in point. Because Richardson's laboring-class heroine cribs her fables from her dead mistress's library, Aesop demonstrably mediates between the aristocratic Lady B – and her nominal servant Pamela. And as Pamela claims to have consulted "a *book* of Fables" (p. 109) – not, for instance, the gossip of other household menials – fables' textual status supersedes even their conventional appeal to the natural world. Early in her one-sided correspondence with her parents, Pamela uses Aesop to figure her own deracinating upbringing by Lady B, an upbringing that, she claims, has made her "like the grasshopper in the fable." Pamela goes on to reproduce, *verbatim*, the tale of "a hungry grass-hopper (*as suppose it was poor me*)" who, "having sung out the whole season" of summer, come wintertime "beg[s] charity" of a colony of industrious ants (Pamela's reader-parents), only to be told to "dance in winter to the tunes you sung in summer" (p. 108).

Pamela applies the fable directly to herself: "So I shall make a fine figure with my singing and dancing, when I come home to you" (p. 108). The fable participates in Aesopian tradition not just because the author so ostentatiously adopts it as her own ("suppose [the grasshopper] was poor me") but also because in so doing she uses a piece of text, lifted from a different book, to foreground the process through which meaningful figures themselves are constructed. This in turn lets Pamela rearrange a conventional relationship between the figural and the literal. Pamela is literally as like Aesop's grasshopper as she can be, for she was taught exactly the arts – "singing and dancing" – that he perfected. But she uses the image of the grasshopper to project a personal future in which, returning to her parents' humble household, she wryly expects to "make a fine figure" as useless as the one the grasshopper cuts at the end of the story. The Aesopian example regulates a delicate exchange between the literal and the figural. It witnesses the transformation of the one into the other. This is why Pamela intuitively uses it to guide her parents' reading of her: It gives her authority over the self-portrait her letters compulsively paint. Significantly, in the long run Pamela manages to keep the most undesirable of future selves – the "figure" of the feckless servant girl ignominiously returned to her roots – from materializing. Seen from this perspective, Aesop's fable manages the ratio between the material and symbolic aspects of the author's own character.

In *Clarissa*, the stakes are higher, and Aesop's fables are accordingly much in evidence, in Lovelace's letters as well as in Clarissa's. Whereas Lovelace applies most of his fables to others, Clarissa shares Pamela's inclination to shield herself (or at least her social image) with Aesopian imagery.[51] For instance, when Lovelace pretends to propose to dress her in his sister's clothes and take her to meet his family, Clarissa declines by comparing herself to "the jay in the fable" (p. 456) who masqueraded in peacock feathers only to be stripped of her borrowed finery by its rightful owners. Like Pamela, Clarissa uses the Aesopian figure to control the figural destiny of her own body in the social and symbolic space where her letters too acquire their meanings.

Aside from Clarissa's body, those letters are the most imperiled and material signs in Richardson's novel. It is thus appropriate that Clarissa's most memorable fable appears in the "odd letter," written after Lovelace rapes her, that she "throw[s . . .] in fragments under the table" (p. 889). The "fragments" offer their own graphic testimony to the state of their author's mind and body; the scribbled fable condenses this terrible equation of mind, body, and letter into a single figure. In the story, "a lady [who] took a great fancy to a young lion, or a bear, I forget which – but a bear, or a tiger" is "tor[n . . .] in pieces" when the animal "resume[s] its nature" and seeks to "satisfy its hungry maw" (p. 891). Clarissa moralizes this chilling tale by asking "who was most to blame, [. . .t]he brute, or the lady?" She concludes that it was "the lady, surely. – For what *she* did, was *out* of nature, *out* of character at least: what *it* did, was *in* its own nature" (p. 891). Although Clarissa casts herself as the lady in the fable in order to maintain a sense of agency – and supplies a moral for the same reason – the fable itself serves less to protect its teller's physical body than to confirm the yoked fragmentations of body, letter, and meaning in a way that later will protect her symbolic body – her reputation.

Clarissa's fable of the lady broken to bits by the beast she befriended has itself begun to break down: Was "the brute" a lion or a tiger or a bear? Was the lady's "great fancy" for the creature as unnatural as she wishes to believe? Because it refuses to answer these questions, yet remains an impressive image, the fable takes us to the apocalyptic edge of the history of Aesopian figuration in England, at least as it had been theorized and practiced in the major fable collections from Ogilby to Richardson. As Ogilby's exemplifications of Hobbesian sign theory had made apparent, fables themselves reveal brutal nature masquerading in social and even typographical character. Via his epistolary heroines – the authors in his own texts – Richardson smuggled fables' power of revelation out of the fable collection and into the English novel. But unlike the other fabulists we have seen, including Richardson himself, his female fabulists are utterly powerless. In their hands, the talent for reactive mediation that had given the Aesopian example its cultural cachet was finally swallowed up by its capacity to demonstrate the violence that makes things mean.

Significant miniatures: the minor collections

The fabulists we have met so far were only the most eminent Aesopians of their day. Along with their high visibility as "AUTHOR[S]" and the extraordinary longevity of their work, their self-consciousness as the sculptors of a new form of symbolic authority sets them apart from the droves of other fabulists whose collections inundated both the popular press and English classrooms between 1651 and 1740. Like their more illustrious counterparts, however, the "minor" collections made it clear that "things" do not "hold discourse" without some authorial hugger-mugger behind the scenes. At the same time, in order to impress their readers, these same collections relied on fables' well-publicized close kinship with natural signs to impress their readers. Particularly since many of them were designed for schools or for quick and easy consumption, the relatively obscure Aesops to which we now turn trained English readers to tolerate the resulting paradox, even to expect it. Both in their manner of ordering and moralizing their fables, and in their prefatory catalogues of fables' distinguishing traits, they thus paved the way for the more self-reflexive and complex collections we have been examining.

Among their distinguishing features, one of the most conspicuous was fables' urgent address to the eye. Despite their alleged origins in oral culture, fables were identified with "pleasing Images," not sounds. Edmund Arwaker's collection of 1708 described them in typically pictorial terms:

A Man that would describe another Man's Person to me, must need a great many Words, & yet after all perhaps give me but a very imperfect Idea of him; but he that shows me his Picture well-painted, though it be in Miniature, does all this much better at one View and in a Moment. It is the same thing in Writing: a Man may drag up the Artillery of twenty Heavy Ornaments to attack a Vice, one of which may strike by the Way, the rest be either not understood, or not remembered. But a Fable shall describe the sordidness of this Vice at once, and convince us pleasantly and quickly.[52]

The preface to Robert Samber's popular 1721 translation of Antoine Houdart de la Motte's *Fables nouvelles* (1719) also described the fabulist as a writer who "by Discourse paints to the Ears."[53] In 1689 Philip Ayres found that writing fables is "like the Placing of Pictures before [readers'] Eyes, whereby more firm and lasting Impressions of Virtue may be fix'd in them, than by plain parallel Rules and Maxims." John Jackson compared a "Fable" to "a Picture or Image of Truth," and characterized every fable in his collection as a "painted Scene."[54]

Ut pictura poesis is of course one of the oldest literary principles in the book, and it is not surprising to find so many fabulists staking claims to it. As they became more and more like images, fables were expected to make ever "more firm and lasting Impressions" on their readers. But, as La Motte hints, they were never expected absolutely to abandon the verbal register that lent them a skeptical reflexivity. Indeed, many of the collections whose prefaces treat fables as images actually lack illustrations. Instead their visible activity takes place typographically, in the form of demonstratively yoked typefaces.

Another reason that editors of fable collections likened their contents to "miniature" pictures was because they reckoned diminutive size a virtue: English fabulists readily adopted La Fontaine's maxim that "Brevity is the Soul of Fable." Addison described fables as "Pieces." Richardson and Croxall deliberately scaled their collections down to "such a *Size*, as should be fit for the *Hands* and *Pockets* for which it was principally designed."[55] Meanwhile, an extremely anglicized La Motte grumbled that fables' "laconick Original," Aesop could even be "too concise, and I have often wonder'd at it, for he was a Greek, and they are great Talkers in that Country, as witness our divine Homer." *Æsop Naturaliz'd* (1711) noted flat out that "One reason why Stories and Fables seem most suitably contrived to Inform the Understanding is ... because they are unusually short; and the shortest way to Instruction is the Best; they only aim to teach us one Point at a Time, and are Quick in doing it."[56]

Like their affinity with images, fables' brevity claimed them for a symbology which assumes that the perceptible world is itself organized in particles, and that therefore the most penetrating signs will also be the most irreducible and concrete. As they had been in the sixteenth century, fables were tirelessly likened to compact, palatable substances that, in L'Estrange's words, "go kindly down." They were touted as "Chymical drops," as nuts, as "Chinks" and "Crannies" of light, as "Gilt and Sweeten'd ... Pills and Potions," as honey-rimmed cups. Traditionally such analogies suggested sweet deception, and could be applied, as in Sidney's *Defence of Poetry* (1595), to figurative language generally. Augustan fabulists used these metaphors more precisely to stress fables' likeness to particular small things. Their lilliputian size physically "adapted [fables] to the Palate and Capacity" of those who took them in.

But fables' compactness equipped them for cultural action as well as for natural impact: it made them easy to transport from text to text, and indeed from language to language. And it aligned them with a symbolic system in which items acquire authority, significance, and value according to their capacity for transportation and exchange.[57] The fact that fables were most often preserved in collections not only invokes a cultural system that identifies knowledge with accumulation. It also displays the instability of resulting systems of meaning, insofar as these consist of many discrete restless particles. Augustan enthusiasm for fable collections – as opposed to fables printed individually, or fables interspersed with other kinds of writing – suggests that skeptical display mattered at least as much as fables' materiality relative to other literary forms.

Such displays seemed to keep authors honest. Aesop himself was promoted as a "hireless Priest of Nature" who exposed "that which was by Art for Profit hid,/And to the Laities as to Spies forbid."[58] The eye-oriented and atomistic structure of the fable collections showed just how symbolic authority got cobbled together. By contrast, the long, sinuous moral tales of the Brahmin fabulist Pilpay were considered too esoteric and mystical for liberated English readers: Pilpay "lock'd up all his politicks; it was a Book of the State and Discipline of Inclosing," one preface noted with disapproval. And "besides his Fables are not distinct and separate enough; he crouds up one within another, [...] an extravagant Romance of Brutes, Men, and Genii."[59] *Aesop's* fables were always arranged in distinct sequence, as if to confirm Aesop's reputation for having "set the Truth in so clear a Light, as to make it stand in no need on any further Proof." For he "knew very well that Fable did not consist absolutely in Fiction but in a Collection of Circumstances which concurred to make a Truth understood." While on one level fables' brevity and resulting collectibility seemed to unite them with the physical world, on another level it also spotlit the canny contrivances that "concu[r]" to produce meaning.[60]

Unless we remember that by 1688 the open negotiation of political authority had come to define the character of the English nation, it's hard to see how anyone could have deemed Aesop's talking animals more probable than Pilpay's "extravagant Romance of Brutes, Men, and Genii." Yet while, as one fabulist observed, "the only Word, Fable, awakens [...] the Idea of Animals endowed with Speech," this "Idea" offended remarkably few sensibilities. Certainly, loquacious beasts could simply indicate a fabulist's willingness to employ a familiar and accessible style. La Motte, as liberally translated by Samber, interrupted one of his own fables to declare that "I who write of Brutes, a simple Fabulist, must write most plain and easy, and follow Nature in her Tracts" (p. 183). For "elevated Expressions impose upon and seduce us, tho" they are the best chosen, whereas the Familiar cannot gain any Respect but through Justice and a happy Application" (p. 44). But the "Familiar" style could also make rhetorical design explicit. As La Motte put it, fables "make Plants and Animals speak ... so that if there is a Necessity for it, the Spring may complain against its Stream; the File laugh at the Serpent, the Earthen and the Iron Pot discourse with each other and swim in one another's Company" (p. 38). Such voluble bodies fail to "impose upon and seduce us" because they point out what human designs "necessit[ate]" linguistic invention. Hence John Dennis (a fabulist himself) with reason doubted that anyone could "be so simple as to believe, that Reynard, Bruin, Isgrim, and Grimalkin say really of themselves the things that Æsop puts into their Mouths."[61] La Motte too assumed that the speaking animal pretense exposes its own cultural origins. One of the most important "Species of the

Merry Stile of Fable," he decided, "transfer[s] to Animals, those extrinsical Denominations we make use of to one another" (p. 45).

Because it works at the sociable level of "extrinsical Denomination," the body of the Aesopian brute shares an important affinity with the manifestly invented, printed body of the fable itself. The frontispiece to John Jackson's 1708 collection depicts a potbellied Aesop surrounded by an admiring entourage of beasts. It announces that "in this Figure, the Fables are represented addressing themselves to Æsop, as their Prime Patron." Jackson's preface even more vigorously mixes textual and animal estates: "With great Judgement [Æsop] dresses up Brutes with humane Forms and Qualities. [...] The Lyon, the Fox, the Horse, and other Animals, even the Mute-Fish, are his Speakers, and read Lessons of Morality for the Instruction of Youth in the Concerns of Life."[62]

Despite their plea to be read like the pages that cage them, Aesop's creatures are most conspicuously distinguished by the power of speech. In turn, fable collections great and small naturally figured speech as a matter of power. The wolf upstream locks in verbal combat with the lamb below, whom he accuses of sullying the water that actually flows from his mouth to hers; the lion tries to convince the fox to step into his cave, the fox persuades the crow to drop her breakfast into his waiting mouth, and so on. As Joan Hildreth Owen has observed, the differences between Aesop's interlocutors often extend to ethical systems and ways of life; these, like discrepancies of power, are made visible by positional and morphological distinctions.[63] Aesopian animals of the late seventeenth and early eighteenth centuries were especially aware that spatial arrangement decides signifying potential: When one of Ayres's lambs stands at a window and berates a wolf as a "cruel and murderous Beast," the wolf "refuse[s] to be offended by his Abuses" and observes himself that " 'tis not thou, but that secure Place wherein thou art, that injures me."[64]

While places might be "secure" in a given fable, an animal's tenure there is less so. In fables, animals signify only in opposition to each other, and in the context of the visible discursive field that they inhabit at a particular moment. They are not, that is, enslaved to traditions of static correspondence in which serpents always represent wisdom, lions power, diamonds knowledge, and so forth. While their bodies remain the same from fable to fable (and this could be literally true, since most Aesopian motifs were transmitted from illustrator to illustrator with little change), the meaning of those bodies is defined in a discursive field whose constituent terms can always be rearranged. Indeed, many fable collections openly rebelled against fixed correspondence: in the story of the farmer who warms a snake on his bosom and is stung for his pains, John Toland noted that "the Serpent is not always the Emblem of Wisdom, as that Passage of our Saviour seems to imply, when he charges his Disciples to be as Wise as Serpents and as Harmless as Doves." Even within a fable collection, a creature's significance can change from fable to fable, in response to his or her competition at a given moment. When an eagle outwits a fox, Toland concludes that "this Fable represents the Eagle in quite a different Character from what the former [where a crow imposes on him] did. There he plaid the part of a generous but overcredulous Prince... But here we see him put the Cheat upon the Fox."[65]

In Augustan fables character is emphatically situational, not essential, and hence it is always open to dispute. A moral, thus, might hoard the possibility of contradiction until the last possible moment: " 'Tis a Kind of *School Question* that we find started in the Fable, upon the Subject of Reason and Intellect," L'Estrange had noted at the end of the fable of the crow who drops stones into a pitcher until she manages to raise its contents to her beak.[66] Likewise, musing over another story, Toland wondered:

> Does Æsop intend hereby to inform us of the great Family of Mankind? Or is it to let us know [the eagle was] insensibly debauch'd by the Air of the Court? Or does Aesop by this Fable undertake to show that we are not obliged to keep our word with wicked Men? If the last be Aesop's intention, we entirely dissent from him; for, on the contrary, we are of Opinion, that if one must break one's word, 'tis more proper doing it to a good than to a Bad Man.

Even the less self-examining (and proportionally more conservative) collections of fables of the Augustan period throve "on the contrary" and on "dissent." As the anonymous preface to *Fables, Moral and Political* (1703) observed, "We may say of all human things, that they have two Handles, a right and a left: So we may with equal reason say of all the old Fables that they have an infinite number."[67] Readers caught on quickly. In the front of a collection of 1651, one of them scribbled that "Time brings opposites to pass/And various maxims teaches."[68]

But while Augustan fable collections reflected a precarious world, they often did so for conservative reasons – to teach English readers a single habit of interpretation, to reflect to them a single image of themselves as interpreters and potential producers of signs. The preface to *Fables, Moral and Political* tells us that "that all Men might be sufficiently convinc'd of the above-mention'd Truths in one and the same Manner, the Wise Ancients invented many fictitious Stories, Comparisons, Apologues, Parables and Fables, to make them well comprehend and retain those Truths."[69] The possibility of inversion did not ultimately threaten a fable's authority, so long as that fable maintained a single, reliable "Manner" of representation, guaranteed to instill a single, reliable "Manner" of approaching written signs.[70]

Even the editors of classroom Aesops reinforced this symbolic practice by introducing fables' caprices alongside their stalwart simplicity. At Dryden's Westminster School "Esops Fables" came first in Headmaster Busby's syllabus of texts by which "Schollers learne the rudim*ts* of Grammer &

Syntaxis in English."[71] In 1736 the *Gentleman's Magazine* described how "Aesop's tales at once instruct and please" students in the "first and least" class. But fables' rudimentary virtues grew less important as students grew more accomplished: at Westminster, the mornings were devoted to "conster[ing]" and "transcrib[ing]" a "Fable in Esope"; but in the afternoons, schoolboys were to "peirce the lesson they construed out of Esope." Likewise, the *Gentleman's Magazine* reported that the very fables that "instruct and please" in the first form later teach more subtle lessons about how business is actually conducted in a contentious symbolic field. In the second form

> *Aesop* in a clearer light is seen,
> Here they perceive to what his fables lean,
> Can smoke the *Fox* comending from below
> The voice, the shape, the beauty of the *Crow*;
> Who perch'd on high, far from his reach was sat,
> Bless'd (what he wanted) with a piece of meat.[72]

Even in the classroom, Aesopian instruction was two-tiered, stacking interpretive skepticism (seeing "in a clearer light," "perceiv[ing] to what [...] fables lean") on top of a rudimentary reassurance that written words can cohere with the physical world. Such a pedagogical strategy naturalized the myth of the discerning eye that keeps the viewer an ostensibly free subject of literary experience.

Aesopian instruction increasingly imbued the act of reading with the dominant political principles of an emerging England. This was true even when the language to be learned was not English. In a typical collection like Charles Hoole's *Æsop's Fables. In English and Latin* (1687), "every [fable was] divided into its distinct period and marked with Figures, so that little Children may [...] learn to imitate the right Composition, and the proper Forms of Speech, belonging to both Languages."[73] Hoole broke Aesop's fables into small syntactic units whose counterparts in different languages were easy to pick out in matching typefaces. Superficially, this reinforces a fairly even exchange between the two languages: the fable of the fox and stork, for instance, typographically varies parts of the story so that they may be compared with corresponding Latin phrases. In the English version

1 A Fox invited a Stork to Supper.
2 He poured the meat upon a Table, which, because it was thin, the Fox licked up, the Stork striving in vain to do so with her bill.
3 The Bird being abused, went her way; she was ashamed and grieved at the injury.
4 After a few days, she comes again and invites the Fox.
5 A glass was set full of meat; which vessel, because it was narrow-mouthed, the Fox might see the meat, and be hungry, but he could not taste of it.

6 The Stork easily drew it out with her bill.
7 Mor. Laughter deserves laughter, Jesting, jesting, Knavery, knavery, and Deceit, deceit.[74]

Across the page we find "De Vulpecula et Ciconia," a Latin version of the story that corresponds to the English point for point, down to the moral: "Risus risum, jocus jocum, dolus dolum, fraus meritur fraudem." The fable's plot performs the acts of matching and exchange that occur linguistically. Symbolic elements become body parts (bills and mouths) and visible objects (the glass, the table, the meat). All of these signs move in three directions at once. They are tokens in a series of transactions between the stork and the fox. They signify a moral that presents reciprocity as a fact of life. And they are linguistic counters that can be exchanged for their Latin equivalents across the page. At the same time, however, exchange is presented thematically as cruel and aggressive deceit. Hence, like Aesop's pedagogical productions, the fable ironizes its own assertions about language. It is not self-conscious about the irony; this is what distinguishes Hoole from fabulists like Ogilby and Barlow. But collections like Hoole's inculcated the reading habits that make it possible to recognize the predatory subtext of modern English signifying conventions.

For this reason, fables like that of the fox and stork enjoyed a high life in the cheap political fables that flourished on Grub Street at the turn of the century. Contrived by hack writers no doubt raised on classroom collections, these penny pamphlets all responded to the "late Change of Government" in 1688. Their titles moved Aesop from place to place in order to protest against or to welcome the prevailing political wind. They were as likely to be written from the Whig as from the Tory side: *Æsop at Tunbridge, Æsop at Whitehall, Æsop at Bathe, Æsop Return'd from Tunbridge* were all Tory; *Old Æsop at Whitehall, Æsop at Epsom, Æsop at Amsterdam, Æsop from Islington* and *Æsop at Westminster* all were Whig, Some others – *Æsop the Wanderer, Æsop in Portugal, Æsop at Oxford, Æsop at the Bell-Tavern, Æsop at Paris* – exploited Aesop's itineracy to address more global political situations: when Aesop went to Paris, for example, he became a French undersecretary. Others, like *Æsop at Richmond*, stole the "Aesop at. . ." formula for their titles but dished up social satire instead.

The bulk of the Grub Street Aesops, though, used the political climate of the day to justify their authors' choice to write in fables: "Who the De–l but a Modern Man would venture to write Truth this Time of Day?" one queried. Fables themselves were up for grabs in the recently renegotiated world of Williamite England. "I write Fables too," one Aesop noted, "only with this difference, mine are for the Government and his against it."[75] Fables' flagrant promiscuity went hand in hand with their materiality. One Aesop describes a rival's attempt to "squeeze itself into the press" and Aesop at Tunbridge reports the discovery of a "Parcel of Papers" dropped along Tunbridge Road: "Picking 'em up, I found they were the following fables."[76] Even the most ephemeral of all Augustan fable collections showed figures at the beck and call of a skeptical nation and a materialist age.

When Aesop at Epsom told the story "Of the Fox and the Stork," he captured exactly this preoccupation: writing against Aesop at Tunbridge, this Whig Aesop casts himself as the stork and his opponent as the fox, thereby demonstrating that it is now his turn to "make the Tallies even." He means that it is now his turn to eat, to speak, to laugh at the expense of the other. The fable turns the superficially egalitarian space of the dining table into an example of how power is organized in modern English culture. That culture's dominant political instrument is a press willing to spin its web of equally factitious and substantial signs for anyone who asks it to. In such a world, meaning waits on an imbalance that masquerades as parity: the fable would lose its own significance if the stork had the "narrow long neck'd glass" before her at the same time that the fox is supplied with his "liquid feast." Aesopian figuration repeats a national history that unfolds as a series of inversions and temporary subordinations.

Because all of the Grub Street Aesops speak the same language, only one of them can occupy Aesop's skin at a time. The conventional prefatory banter that always challenges an Aesopian predecessor of the opposing party invariably gives way to fables about unequal exchange, nervous compromise, contest over bodies which, like what one pamphlet describes as the "fine, empty" body of Aesop himself, are finally not worth the quarrel. As "Æsop Return'd from Tunbridge" put it:

> When the small ones give their Voice,
> Who shall be most Empower'd,
> They have but liberty of Choice
> By whom they'll be devour'd.[77]

Such jingles capture the tension between stability and subversion that organized both major and minor English fable collections between 1651 and 1740. Without denying the manifold differences among those collections, we can say that they shared at least one cultural aim – to create a common figural system. To the extent that reactive mediation between opposing sides was one perceived virtue of that system, these very differences may even be interpreted as marks of success.

Locke's Aesop: making the brain a page

It is hard to overestimate how much print culture mattered to the Aesopian project. In practical terms, of course, a press in overdrive multiplied the number of available collections, and potential readers. More subtly, though, the printed page provided a frame of literal reference for the fabulous figures that cavorted across it. At the same time, it rewarded readers for the very epistemogical habits that the average Aesopian character learns to cultivate, and thereby comes to represent. So to complete our picture of the fable collection in Augustan England, we turn to the question of how particular fabulists mythologized their own intimacy with the culture of print. Some, like Locke, did so frankly, with a stated and culturally conservative end in sight. Others, like Jonathan Swift, did so satirically, with an eye on the irony of their own involvement with Aesop. Taken together, however, these fabulists reveal an intricate symbiosis between the Aesopian fable collection and an emerging England that settled more and more cultural authority upon the printed page.

We saw that, from Ogilby on, Aesop's fables naturalized textual experience even as they made authorial contrivance visible, often in its historical and political setting. Because fables anchored symbolic language in the material world, they automatically proliferated in a post-revolutionary culture that inordinately valued sensible words even as it nervously required that the configurations into which those words were assembled remain open to inspection and possible revision. No one spelled out these linguistic requirements more clearly than John Locke, whose "interlineary" fable collection of 1703 was meant to teach language itself, both English and Latin.[78] Eight years before, Locke's influential *Thoughts concerning Education* (1693) had endorsed fable collections as an ideally "gentle Wa[y]," to teach children how to read. Locke imagined that "some easy pleasant book, suited to [children's] capacity" would be the best device for showing them how to master written signs. Such a book

should be put into [a child's] hands, wherein the Entertainment that he finds might draw him on, and reward his Pains in Reading; and yet not such as should fill his Head with perfectly useless Trumpery, or lay the Principles of Vice and Folly. To this Purpose, I think Æsop's Fables are the best, which being Stories apt to delight and entertain a Child, may yet afford useful Reflections to a grown Man; and if his Memory retain them all his Life after, he will not repent to find them there, among his manly Thoughts. And if his Æsop have Pictures in it, it will entertain him much the better, and encourage him to read, when it carries the increase of Knowledge with it; for such visible Objects Children hear talked of in vain, and without any Satisfaction.[79]

Locke might have lifted his claims for Aesop's fables from the preface to any one of a number of fable collections. Those claims in turn owed much to the reform movements that had recently labored to realign primary education with the world of "visible Objects," of phenomenal and familiar things. Fables had played a part in pedagogy since Quintilian, and many a Renaissance curriculum had conscripted them into elementary instruction in

Latin. But in the mid-seventeenth century their capacity to embed grammar points in graphic examples – along with the simplicity, concreteness, and easy translatability of the words they used – caught the fancy of Puritan reformers already modeling their ideal primers on the *Orbis sensualim pictus* (1658) of the Czech educator Johan Amos Comenius.[80] Assuming with Comenius that "Nothing in the Mind is not first in the Senses," his English disciples held that any introduction to written language should be mediated through sensible objects. Comenius's chief English translator, Charles Hoole, in turn produced one of the most successful classroom Aesops of the late seventeenth century. Hoole's English–Latin interlineary offered exactly matched typographies. Its uncluttered pages contrasted dramatically with the byzantine visual field that characterized the fable collections previously designed for use in "petty schools." If collections like Ogilby's and Barlow's claimed Aesop for the Royalist – later Jacobite – position, then collections like Hoole's and Locke's did the same for a fundamentally Puritan pedagogical agenda.

Locke construed fables as a natural method of literary instruction, one that viscerally "entertain[s]" novice readers until they are inveigled into the habit of reading. Especially when embellished with pictures, fables replicate a natural world that, as Locke conceived it, impinges on the senses in discrete, irreducible particles and is best known by the eye. Because fables are also verbal structures, they ultimately bridge the sensible and linguistic realms. As if to demonstrate this continuity, intermittent pages in Locke's own collection are crammed with tiny, precise illustrations which correspond by number to the fables which follow (plate 2). As its subtitle boasts, Locke's fable collection allows readers to match these "visible Objects" to words "without a Master." Later, identical typefaces yoke English and Latin cognates. In place of the "Master" author, it is the book's own empirical properties that ease transition from images of things to letters, and then from one language (English) to another (Latin).

The eviction of the "Master" and his replacement by the text caters to the political tastes of an only recently constitutional England. But it also institutes a more subtle form of mastery. That is, while fables teach children to read they also naturalize textual representation. As written words prove their native affinities with the sensible world, the fable collection nominates printed texts to be the new custodians of a cultural order based on the principles of Lockean empiricism. Indeed, we have only to think of the *tabula rasa* to realize how deeply Locke steeped his materialist theories of knowledge, identity, and representation in scribal imageries.

Recent readings of Locke's empiricism have already begun to treat it as a rhetorical system whose premises and metaphors derive from the ascendant authority of the printed page.[81] Though it invokes a sensible world that appears to exist *avant la lettre*, a Lockean fable also surreptitiously endorses a myth of textual primacy. And many of fables' supposedly corporeal properties

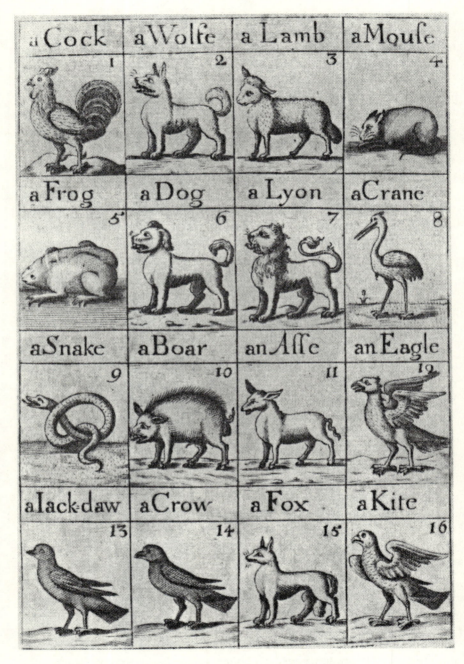

2   Plate from John Locke, *Æsop's Fables*, London, 1703.

may actually be traced to the happenstances of textual representation – their use of visibly different characters, and of numerically indexed "Pictures," for instance. Indeed, Locke liked fables because they yield a material and linguistic "Satisfaction" unattainable outside textual experience: the "Objects" that they concern "Children hear talked of in vain."

For Locke, then, fables install the rules and presuppositions not just of the experienced world, but also of a specifically literate one. Aesop endorses the page's necessary devotion to the visual and atomistic, to meaning garnered through the accumulation of tangible signs. Fables' primacy "among ... Manly Thoughts" guarantees that no knowledge other than that cultivated through literate experience will disfigure the surface of the sociable brain. While sensory information may come first, retainable and reproducible – sociable – information is always implicitly textual. And the criteria of its significance are economic – indeed subtly ideological – categories of "reward," "usefulness," and "Satisfaction."

Other fabulists were also impressed by fables' resemblance to the "Corporeal Figures and Images" that experience presumably imprints on the brain. And their collections too went quietly about the business of establishing the metaphor of the brain as a culturally legible page. For instance, the preface to *Fables, Moral and Political* describes that organ in unmistakably Aesopian terms:

Being accustom'd from our Childhood to comprehend all Things under some Corporeal Images, we find that our Thoughts and Words that denote and signifie any Things whatsoever, make no deep Impression in our Memory and Brain, unless we couple or join them to some Figures or Imaginations that have such Relation to them, as to make us reflect and think again, at any time. [...] We daily find that we can scarcely think on those Corporeal Figures or Images without remembering, at the same time, the Things to which we had before coupled them in our Thoughts.

(sig. A7r)

Memory and cognition solder the "Corporeal" together with "Figures or Imaginations" in the visual register that is common to both. A fable collection simply replicates seemingly involuntary cognitive processes of repetition and coupling:

We particularly chose to join several Fables together, reflecting that, according to the common Nature of Man, their Lives consist of several Actions or Imperfections, that have a mutual near Relation and Likeness, and that are the immediate Consequences of one Another; for which Reason, we are of Opinion, that it would not be improper thus to join and explain those Fables all together, that we might at once give a View to the whole Lives of such Men, and at the same Time show how they commonly end them. And all this we presume to have done in so few Words, and in so plain a Method, that in the Fables so join'd, as the Exposition, will, by a careful Reader, be easily imprinted and retain'd in his Memory.

(sig. A8v)

The "we" that promises that the physical body of *Fables, Moral and Political* will "imprin[t]" precepts on its reader's brain was mysterious, since the collection had been translated anonymously from the Dutch of an author whose name, once thought to be Johan DeWit, has been lost. Its roots in a mercantile and republican sociopolitical milieu do more to explain the collection's popularity in the burgeoning commercial culture of early eighteenth-century England. Surprisingly, though, it was a far from obscure English author, the Jacobite L'Estrange, who *via* fables did the most to popularize a text-based standard of cultural and cognitive competence. The fables in *Eminent Mythologists* model cognitive strategies equally suitable for reading and for piecing together the physical world. L'Estrange argued that they do not always do so. It is the fabulist who outfits them for service by tampering with the moral – the substantial part of the fable, the meat in the nutshell that can rescue figurative language from ephemerality and make it substantial, transmissible, even "profitable." Weighing the relative merits of the story and the moral, L'Estrange wagered that "the One is stark Nonsense, without the Application of the Other"; "an Emblem without a Key to it is no more than a Tale of a Tub."

L'Estrange found various ingenious ways to fit keys into emblems. He often transferred the prepositional structure of a fable to its moral; he used visually similar, contracted vocabularies for both. But, as Croxall would appreciate, L'Estrange's most distinctive innovation was to attach a "Reflexion" to every moral. The "Reflexions" frequently push L'Estrange's morals further, but they also mingle a moral's terms with the verbal elements of the story; thereby they make the fables, visibly, reflect their own devices. A "Reflexion," in other words, reflects a fable's own reflexivity, its capacity to refer in visual space to its own verbal and graphic modes of producing meaning, and thereby to the grounds of its own authority.

L'Estrange's "Reflexions" show that "Emblem" and "Key" – word and meaning, percept and concept – may be credibly aligned only in a visibly self-reflexive space. For him, that space is so necessarily the page that he, like Locke, inevitably pictured the reader's mind in its image: "Children are but Blank Paper." Nonetheless, L'Estrange's technique has its own ironies. Perhaps recalling the adventures of an earlier Aesopian fox who "fetched a hundred and two hundred Leaps at [a bunch of grapes] till at last he was weary as Dog" or of a farmer who, stung by a serpent, denounces his assailant "the snake i'th'grass,"[82] L'Estrange set out to distinguish his collection from those that mainly purveyed puns and witticisms. But in an irony that makes *Eminent Mythologists* an incipient satire on Lockean (and whiggish) fable theory, L'Estrange's reflexive strategy and his assumptions about textual primacy deliver his own fables to much the same ends. For they create a homogeneous verbal field whose terms are potentially infinitely interchangeable. Figures of speech often moralize L'Estrange's own fables: at the end of the fable of the wolf and lamb, for example, we learn that " 'Tis an Easie Matter to find a Staff to Beat a Dog."[83]

While L'Estrange himself did not fully own up to his own critique of Lockean confidence in the text's empirical properties, Jonathan Swift was another story. A young man when L'Estrange was an old one, Swift took a closer look at the pretensions of fable collections like *Eminent Mythologists*. Swift's most famous satire of figuration, modern authorship, and personal identity masochistically models their intertwining in print culture, and it owes its very title to L'Estrange's disparaging announcement that an "Emblem without a Key to it" is nothing more than a "Tale of a Tub." In *A Tale of a Tub* (1704), the mind of Swift's own narrator turns out to be the printed page. This is chastening, since it is the detritus of "Prostitute Bookseller[s]" perceived to be engulfing England that reaps the most bitter invective throughout the *Tale*.[84] With matters so disposed, Swift's sputtering text inevitably reaches for fables to malign "the Productions of the *Grub*-Street Brotherhood" (p. 297) – even though these "Productions" include fable collections themselves. Fables therefore provide both satiric rapiers against the obscene tumescence of print culture and a metonymic scapegoat for that same culture, where because all textual signs are superficial and interchangeable, all keys eventually turn to emblems.

Swift's "Introduction" specifically laments the "superficial Vein among many Readers of the present Age" – readers whom fables have trained to attend to the visible surfaces of signs. Such readers will

by no means be persuaded to inspect beyond the Surface and the Rind of Things; whereas, *Wisdom* is a *Fox*, who after long hunting, will at last cost you the Pains to dig out: 'Tis a *Cheese*, which by how much the richer has the thicker, the homelier, and the courser Coat; and whereof to a judicious Palate, the *Maggots* are the best. 'Tis a *Sack-Posset*, wherein the deeper you go, you will find it the sweeter. *Wisdom* is a *Hen*, whose *Cackling* we must value and consider, because it is attended with an *Egg*; But then, lastly, 'tis a *Nut*, which unless you chuse a Judgement, may cost you a Tooth, and pay you with nothing but a *Worm*. (p. 298)

Swift parodies L'Estrange's objections to superficial and multivalent figures. But he refuses to pretend that a new and improved fable collection can offer a real remedy. Instead, the *Tale* makes its point in an Aesopian language that refuses to distinguish the cure from the ailment. As it spins faster and faster in its own figural centrifuge, the passage replicates the very "superficial vein" that it derides. The only keys to emblems are other emblems. Fables offer no reliable guide to a comfortingly substantial world. Instead, they supply the vacuous, if seductive, stock in trade of "the *Grubaean* Sages" who "have always chosen to convey their Precepts and their Arts, shut up within the Vehicles of Types and Fables." Such "Vehicles" reward only a mock-Lockean epistemology based on visual surfaces:

[H]aving been perhaps more careful and curious in adorning, than was altogether necessary, it has fared with these Vehicles after the usual Fate of Coaches over-finely painted and gilt; that the transitory Gazers have so dazzled their Eyes, and fill'd their Imaginations with the outward Lustre, as neither to regard or consider, the Person or the Parts of the Owner within. A Misfortune we undergo with somewhat less Reluctancy, because it has been common to us with *Pythagoras, Æsop, Socrates*, and other of our Predecessors.   (pp. 298–299)

In *A Tale of a Tub*, fables epitomize a signifying convention which has reached its monstrous apogee in the hack writing of the present day. Yet it is only by exploiting fables' capacity to conjure up convincing surfaces that Swift's text manages to convey its own moral: Written signs are superficial and indiscriminate, and all textual representation is, willy-nilly, hollow. In this script-centered world fables emerge, ironically, as the only rhetorical devices truly equipped to make such a point. If they persuade, it is not because they supply emblems with keys but rather because only they manage to perform, in textual space, their own beguiling hollowness.

Swift's swipe at the English fable collection is almost ostentatiously ambivalent. His *Tale* exploits Aesopian exemplarity even as it derides symbolic "Vehicle[s]" intended strictly "for the gratification of superficial readers." Further, by displaying the assumptions and devices that make those "Vehicle[s]" mean, Swift inconspicuously restores his reader's impression that there is an "Owner within" them after all. This gesture actually aligns him with many of the fabulists he seemed to disparage. It also helps explain why, despite the *Tale*'s rant against the fable trade, much of Swift's work – from *The Battel of the Books* (1704) to various rhymed fables and "enigmas," to Gulliver's adventures in Houyhnhmland – actually puts Aesopian figuration to work. Through the "Vehicle[s]" of the squabbling volumes of the *Battel* and the talking horses of *Gulliver's Travels* (1726) in particular, Swift forces his readers to notice how meaning is produced in scribal imagery. This is also to notice how human authors have fled into the page, and therewith into a new figural economy that confirms those authors as "Owner[s]" of their own productions only by superficially *dis*owning that very relationship. We will see in Chapter 2 how Swift used this explicitly Aesopian technique to belittle "modern" literature. But here Swift's Houyhnhms offer a fitting moral for the story of the Aesopian fable collection and its Augustan authors.

As Terry Castle has pointed out, it is significant that Swift's most Aesopian animals, the Houyhnhms, do not write.[85] Their aversion to lying (saying "*the Thing which is not*") goes hand in hand with the fact that they "have no Letters" (p. 238). Boasting that all "their Knowledge is traditional," the Houyhnhms make an agreeable "Vehicle" for Swift's own anxieties about textual representation, as so amply demonstrated in the *Tale* as well as in the nervous matter prefatory to the 1735 edition of *Travels*. Swift's Houyhnhms therefore look like classic Aesopian "Examples." Not only do they voice the most reasonable "Precepts" but their illiteracy means that there are, by definition, no authors in Houyhnhmland. Apart from Gulliver himself, there are only actors we can trust.

But Gulliver is a significant exception, and after his "dangerous Voyage" back to England his contempt for "the *British* Nation," especially in its colonial enterprises, becomes as famous as "the Author" himself. So does the revulsion against all non-Houyhnhms that Gulliver tries to combat by "behold[ing] my Figure in a Glass" until he can once more "tolerate the Sight of a human Creature" (p. 259). As the ostensible "Author" becomes literally the visible object of Swift's reader's scrutiny, Gulliver's enthusiasm for the exemplary Houyhnhms and their precepts reveals its own deformity, and his morals hazard inversion. Our recognition that Gulliver is *both* a moral preceptor *and* the disputable, indeed almost disreputable, "Author" of his own possibly psychotic voyages, depends on an intricate and tricky exchange between the literal and figural levels of Swift's own text. Through that exchange, Swift risks Gulliver's authority to secure his own, much as the high-stakes "AUTHOR" John Ogilby had amassed his in the Aesopian lotteries of the 1660s. The gamble is complicated enough to make it scarcely surprising that Swift regarded Aesop as the toughest of all literary task-masters. Though *A Tale of a Tub* and *Gulliver's Travels* prove otherwise, Swift was convinced that he had failed at fables, and his friend John Gay was to earn his most admiring recognition not as a playwright or a poet, but as a fabulist.[86]

2

"The first pieces of wit": Augustan fable theory and the birth of the book

Fables were the first Pieces of Wit that made their Appearance in the World, and have been still highly valued, not only in times of the greatest Simplicity, but among the most polite Ages of Mankind. [...] We find Æsop in the most distant Ages of Greece; and if we look into the very beginning of the Commonwealth of Rome, we see a Mutiny among the common People appeased by the Fable of the Belly and the Limbs, which was indeed very proper to gain the Attention of an incensed Rabble, at a time when perhaps they would have torn to Pieces any Man who had preached the same Doctrine to them in an open and direct Manner.

Joseph Addison, Spectator 183 (September 29, 1711)

Comedy is not more at present than a well-fram'd Tale handsomely told, or an agreeable vehicle of Counsel or Reproof. This is all we can say for the Credit of its Institution, and is the Stress of its Charter for Liberty and Toleration. Then where should we seek for Foundation, but in Æsop's symbolical way of moralizing upon Tales and Fables, with this difference, that his Stories were shorter than ours?

George Farquhar, "A Discourse upon Comedy" (1703)

Popular fable collections were but one of Aesop's many English venues between 1651 and 1740. He also pops up everywhere in Augustan literary criticism, whose authors regularly billed his fables as the most ancient of "symbolical" forms. Mr. Spectator's urbane assertion that fables were "the first Pieces of Wit that made their Appearance in the world," for instance, was hailed as "the Testimony of a Modern, whose Authority [...] may be as readily acknowledg'd, as that of any Ancient of them all."[1] In George Farquhar's view, "Æsop's symbolical way of moralizing upon Tales and Fables" likewise forms the "Foundation" of modern signifying conventions.[2] Echoing William Davenant's poetic premise that fables' roots lay in "the Infancy of Time," in "Empire's Childhood and the Dawn of Arts,"[3] less illustrious writers were equally quick to classify fables as antique specimens of figurative language, "invented by famous Men of Old, to serve as Vehicles to convey the Precepts of Philosophy to our Minds."[4] They routinely placed these "Vehicles" among the very "oldest Books," and even held that "Æsop's

Fables, or the Book so called, [...] was so generally read in old Time as that it became a Proverb when they would say such a one was a very Idiot, or Ignoramus, to say to him [...] Thou hast not read Æsop."[5] It was rumored that fables were fashionable in "primitive" societies of the present day: "The *Americans* are said to be great Lovers of Fables, and to reward those who can relate them; being much delighted to hear of Dogs, Horses, and other Creatures discoursing together."[6]

What did it mean to insist that, in the history of representation, fables came first? Why did so many different pundits in the crystallizing literary culture of Augustan England seem to agree that Aesop gave access to that culture's own "Childhood"? One answer seems obvious: A contemporary of Homer after all, Aesop had remained a favorite touchstone for the first Augustans, esteemed Latin authors like Horace, Phaedrus, even Cicero. As "Old Books" sanctioned by the ancients themselves, Aesop's fables naturally appealed to the neoclassical temper, whose critical values coincided with a cultural crusade to mold multiplicitous England into a new Rome.[7] Augustans who measured modern literary virtue against ancient standards instinctively made fable theory an important branch of their literary criticism. Aristotle himself had not distinguished between plot and fable, thereby licensing neoclassicals like John Dennis, John Dryden, and Thomas Rymer to treat the fable as the backbone of all literary forms. From this point of view, *all* literary theory could be seen as fable theory, just as all literature – any "feign'd or devis'd Discourse" – could be seen as a variation on fable.[8] John Dennis was not controversial when he professed to "know of no difference that there is, between one of *Æsop's* Fables and the Fable of an Epick Poem, as to their Natures, though there may be great ones, as to their Circumstances." For him, as for others, "a legitimate Dramatick Poem" was "as much a Fable as any one of Æsop's, agreeing in Genus and differing only in Species."[9]

The Augustan assumption that the fable is the unifying principle of all literature in turn owed much to the French neoclassical critic René Le Bossu's *Traité du poème épique* (1675), which designated as a fable any "Discourse invented to form Men's Manners by Instruction disguis'd under the Allegory of one single Action."[10] Le Bossu's own authority was Horace's *Ars poetica*, where the word *fabula* described any probable and coherent arrangement of signs. Further, to Le Bossu's English disciples, a "fable" embodied more than the hierarchy of decorously interrelated signs that drew each literary form together into a legible whole.[11] The structure of a fable actually proved an author's shaping presence in his work: "Can anyone believe, that Æsop first told a story of a Cock and a Bull and afterwards made a Moral to it?" Dennis demanded. No. "'Tis impossible for a Poet to form any Fable, unless the Moral be first in his head."[12] From one point of view anyway, the "fable" seems to have won the favor of English Augustans because it was a classicizing sign of literary unity. It marked an author's jurisdiction over his own fictions. A source of narrative coherence, the fable was common to all genres, and it was shared by ancient and modern letters alike.

Contemporary conceptions of fables, however, were not always so general and monolithic. On the contrary. Many English writers spoke not of "fable" in the singular and abstract but of "fables," usually directly linked with Aesop's name. And in contrast to "fable," Aesop's fables were turning out to have had a highly irregular history which culminated in the embarrassing excesses of the popular press of the present day. In 1697, the irreverent researches of the classical scholar Richard Bentley refuted the existence of an original Aesopian text, demonstrating that even in classical times fables were transmitted haphazardly *via* a motley crew of Greek and Latin literary words. Meanwhile, in late seventeenth- and early eighteenth-century England, bestselling fable collections that expanded through successive printings, Grub Street ephemera published in Aesop's name, and schoolroom primers of the lowest degree all forced decorous antiquity to answer to a rough-and-tumble modernity. Fables were published together in no particular order, or as detachable parts of larger literary wholes, where they appeared sometimes as quips, sometimes as illustrative images, but always as discrete, promiscuous figures that borrowed their significance from a context that could change at any moment. Dennis's "story of a Cock and Bull" might share the fable-moral infrastructure of the *Iliad*. It might even bear the imprint of the "Poet's" will. But once it showed its face, say in Roger L'Estrange's sprawling miscellany of "eminent mythologists" – only to resurface a year later in political pamphlets hastily assembled by anonymous hacks – this fable's only plausible moral seemed to be that textual representation is erratic, uncontrollable, and provisional in the extreme. As Pope's *Dunciad* (1728) made clear, print culture only magnifies these monstrous details. It therefore seems paradoxical that Aesop's footloose "pieces of Wit" should have been revered as symbolic prototypes at the same time that generic, poetic and historical continuity were canonized as supreme literary – indeed cultural – values.

I want to argue that Aesop actually linked the monstrous exuberance of an accelerating print culture with the neoclassical movement in English letters. This is really to suggest that "Æsop's fables, or the Book so called" mediated between opposite mythologies of "the Book" itself. These mythologies competed for pre-eminence in Augustan England, and their contests have been chronicled by contemporaries like Jonathan Swift, as well as by post-game commentators of our own day.[13] On one side, we can place those at home in a world of spontaneously self-generating printed matter. Boisterous antiquarians like Bentley, subtle literary dissidents like Farquhar, and even self-critical fabulists like John Ogilby may have differed widely from one another in many respects. But they shared an almost gleeful pleasure in the sheer materiality of the written word. Burdened with relatively few anxieties about lost coherence between author and book, irreverent toward hidebound notions of genre and what we now call canonicity, eager to treat books as physical objects whose uncertain provenance points up the contingency of our own knowledge of the past, these authors were happy to see their own work proliferate in modern literate culture. Opposite them, however, stand the Augustans whose reactions to the new dominion of the press ranged from hostility to ambivalence. These authors were committed to values of hierarchy, decorum, generic integrity, and authorial presence. Like Dennis, they were often busy putting French neoclassicism into English dress. Others, like Jonathan Swift's patron William Temple and his disciples Charles Boyle and Francis Atterbury, canonized classical authors; still others, like Addison, tried to carve a cadre of polite readers out of the popular mass.

Taking their cue from the Augustans themselves, literary scholars have not often questioned this bifurcated portrait of the critical differences at play in late seventeenth- and early eighteenth-century England.[14] And it is true that the contrasts between the two groups in question are easily caricatured, most obviously in the contemporary distinction between "moderns" and "ancients" but also, in our own day, in descriptive dyads like the Bakhtinian pairing of the classical and the grotesque, or the high and the low.[15] In contemporary discussions of Aesop's fables, however, neoclassical advocates of antique restraint collided head-on with the emissaries of an aggressive modernity: "ancients" recruited fables to combat the unseemly effusions of modern writing even as unapologetic "moderns" borrowed Aesop in order to justify, even sanctify, their own excesses. Aesop's popularity among both critical contingents not only unmasks a welter of differences within each group but, more important, suggests that both participated in a single, though complex, cultural phenomenon. We saw in Chapter 1 that Aesopian fable collections underwrote factional politics with a shared symbolic economy, one whose currency was discrete graphic signs capable of reactive mediation. Just so, Augustan fable theories advanced from opposite attitudes toward literature (and toward the prospect of a culture defined by and through the printed page) joined forces to institute one modern English fable about the nature, purpose, and origins of books themselves.

Fables and the origins of writing

Among the critical pronouncements that proliferated almost as fast as fables themselves in the increasingly literate culture of Augustan England, it would be hard to find one more authoritative than Joseph Addison's *Spectator* essay of September 29, 1711. Aiming, as ever, to sophisticate readers of the London middling classes, Addison's widely quoted Mr. Spectator first established fables' genealogy, which he traced to "the most distant Ages of Greece," and thence to "the most polite Ages of Mankind." "Rais'd altogether upon Brutes and Vegetables" (p. 247), fables are characterized by a figural simplicity and concreteness that recapitulates their origins at the dawn of European representation. In the same vein, having supposed that they "took their Birth in the very Infancy of Learning," Mr. Spectator depicts fables as physical "Pieces" that make an "Appearance in the World." This image is significant: fables' primacy in the history of figuration does not, as we might expect, automatically identify them with primitive sounds and gestures. Rather, it locates them in a symbolic "World" whose constituent parts are visible, portable, amenable to arrangement. Only under these conditions can fables find transport from "the most distant Ages of Greece" to the "most polite Ages of Mankind," from "the very Infancy of Learning" to the moment "when Learning was at its greatest Height." As he ties the fate of fables to the plot of "Learning," then, and as he stresses their physical particularity and their literal migration through time, Mr. Spectator inevitably identifies fables not strictly with the first symbolic actions but more precisely – and more meaningfully for Augustan readers – with the origin of written signs.

Later essayists followed suit. One was confident that "Who ever is conversant with the Learning of the Ancients will find that originally the Method used among them of communicating their Conceptions, of whatever kind they were, to their Successors, was by representative Symbols, by Allegories and Fables."[16] As vehicles for "communicating" the "Conceptions" and "Learning of the Ancients" through time ("to [...] Successors"), fables become the most fundamental of textual "Method[s]." They help books yoke antiquity and modernity; they protect authorial "Conceptions" otherwise at risk of appropriation or misconstruction through time. In short, they make writing fit to convey "Conceptions, of whatever Kind" – cultural information, esoteric knowledge, moral precepts. John Toland elaborated:

The bare, naked, or simple way of instructing by Precept, being found jejune or nauseous, a mixture of Fable was therefore thought necessary to sweeten and allure the Minds of Men, naturally superstitious and credulous, which kind of Philosophy was first made use of among the *Eastern Nations*, the *Hebrew* themselves not excepted. Hence tis that the *oldest Books are Mythologies*, as Æsop, Homer, Hesiod, Orpheus, &c. This fabulous Way of Writing pass'd from the Poets to the Schools and Theatres.[17]

For Toland, fables' efficacy and sensual appeal made them the first reliable "Way of Writing." Their power "to sweeten and allure" uniquely equipped them to smooth ideas' otherwise rocky "pass[age]" from place to place, genre to genre, age to age. Temple also regarded fables as early examples of writing. Holding that "the oldest Books we have are still in their Kind the Best," he specified that "the two most ancient that I know of in prose [...] are Æsop's *Fables* and Phalaris's *Epistles*." Aesop himself, Temple declared, "has been agreed by all Ages since for the greatest Master in his Kind, and all others of that sort have been but Imitation of his Original."[18] Aesop's

"Kind," in Temple's formulation, are the authors of other "Books," and Aesop stands as their ideal original. Even the political press got into the act: a 1727 essay in the Opposition periodical *The Craftsman* places fables early in the progress of writing, speculating that in graphic history hieroglyphics must have come first, after which "the Use of Letters was discovered." But "the Learned still hid their Meanings in all Matters of Importance, under Allegories, Allusions and Fables."[19] Here fables again appear together with the first "Letters." And here again the coincidence benefits the "Letters" appointed to carry the "Meanings" of the "Learned." For while practicing a literary "Principle of Self-preservation" (p. 226), fables help literature preserve "Matters of Importance" that, we imagine, would otherwise find themselves exposed, stolen, ravaged, or lost.

Each of these accounts of fables' primacy also appoints them guardians of textual integrity. With the pristine excellence of a first Aesopian fable collection as his touchstone, Temple made confident and judicious discriminations between "original" texts and mere reproductions and bastardizations. For Addison's Mr. Spectator fables built a textual canal that could safely convey the values "of the most polite Ages" down throughout the centuries to modern England. To others, fables seemed to protect individual texts and the "Meanings" inside them. All of these functions are essentially conservative ones. Those who attributed them to fables assumed that good books are far between, and in perpetual danger of corruption and misrecognition, as are the authorities that readers ought to receive through them.

At the same time, though, the claim that fables are rudimentary *literary* (as opposed to merely figural) devices could itself cloak a more radical theory about the way letters work. The aforementioned *Craftsman* essay, for instance, suggests more than that fables protect "Meanings" during the perilous "Use of Letters." It also implies that authoritative "Letters" themselves are obscurantist and exclusionary, contrived by the few for the few. Similarly, when the Irish dramatist Farquhar encouraged writers to "seek for Foundation in Æsop's symbolical way of moralizing," he did so in the middle of a contentious essay curious as to why and how Aristotle, "the first and great Law-giver," ever came to legislate proper literary form. The *Poetics*, Farquhar scoffs, is after all "only some Observations drawn from the works of *Homer* and *Euripides*, which may be meer Accidents resulting casually from the Composition of the Works, and not any of the essential Principles on which they are compil'd" (p. 132). Aristotle's own authoritative definition of epic, for example, comes from the *Iliad*, which, Farquhar maintains, Aristotle exalted only because of "the great Esteem of Alexander the Great for the Works of Old *Homer*." Farquhar scandalously suggests that Alexander

always slept with the *Iliads* under his Pillow; of this the *Stagirite* to be sure was not ignorant; and what more proper way of making his Court could a Man of Letters

Devise, than by Saying something in commendation of the King's Favourite. [...
But] if *Prince Arthur* had been in the place of the *Iliads*, we should have had other Rules
for epic Poetry.   (p. 132)

Determined to reveal literary laws as the by-blows of accident and politic
contingency, Farquhar emphasized their textuality, embodied in the book
that allegedly nestled under Alexander's pillow. In the same spirit, he sought
a way to prescribe literary structure "without complementing [*sic*] any
Author, either Ancient or Modern," and "without one Quotation of *Aristotle*
or Authority of Euripides." Eager to challenge the blind authorities of the
past, Farquhar turned his readers' attention to "small Beginnings," which
"the Corruption of Time" has not "debarr'd [...] from their primitive
Innocence" – to Aesop's fables. At least with respect to comedy, and by
implication also with respect to other literary forms, "old Æsop must wear
the Bays as the First and Original Author, and whatever alternatives or
Improvements farther Applications have subjoin'd, his Fables gave the first
Rise and Occasion" (p. 137). The "primitive innocence" of Aesop's fables,
their status as a modest text that pre-empts the accidental authority of the
Homeric epic, gave a determinedly modern playwright's own little "Discourse" ammunition against the critical despotism of Aristotle's *Poetics*.

The myth of fables' textual primacy could thus be applied in radically
different ways. In some eyes, fables seemed to conserve the literary standards
that certain "Books" bore from antiquity to modernity. In others, fables
challenged these laws by challenging the authority of particular texts. The
myth that fables are the native property of the authoritative text itself
remained constant. Yet that myth too is complicated, in its very nature. In
Mr. Spectator's estimation, that is, fables "took their Birth in the very Infancy
of Learning," and "Learning" requires writing. Fables implicitly celebrate –
indeed, they help establish – writing as the foundation of cultural authority.
Mr. Spectator, though, goes on to cite two fables as exemplars of the form. In
the first, "we see, in the very beginning of the Commonwealth of Rome, a
Mutiny among the common People appeased by a Fable of the Belly and
Limbs" (p. 220). In the second, Socrates tells a fable just before he is to be
executed. Both of these examples come from classical texts, one by Livy and
one by Plato. By the time they got to Addison they had been filtered through
centuries of citation in a humanist literary criticism that used them as
examples of the power of figurative language. But despite an indisputable
textual history, both examples also preserve a primary attachment to the
world of speaking bodies; in both, fables are told, not written. Addison's
exemplary fabulists are speakers; he mentions also Prodicus, who "used to
Travel through *Greece* by vertue of [a] Fable, which procured him a kind
Reception in all Market Towns, where he never failed telling it as soon as he
had gathered an Audience" (p. 221). Physically present to their "Audi-

ence[s]," all of Addison's fabulists inhabit lively situations that make their fables' meanings – their applications – obvious and specific. Thus while these fables might exalt Plato and Livy as literary authorities, they also mythologize a previous, and implicitly superior authority which is not literary at all: it is oral and performative.[20]

For Addison and his contemporaries, fables' presumed origins in a pre-existing symbolic register – that of the spoken and gestural – complicated their mythic status as the world's "Oldest Books." For one thing, fables' exemplary performance in oral culture could expose a crisis of authority in modern literate culture. In one of Addison's examples (for example), a fable actually "appease[s]" a "Mutiny." But what if the mutinous commoners are modern readers, not ancient listeners or spectators disciplined by the present body of the fabulist – and by equally present circumstances – to apply the story as the teller sees fit? With only the bindings of books to provide the material setting that should fix their meaning, signs are open to multiple interpretations and therefore stand to lose the authority they commanded when spoken. One periodical essayist wistfully supposed that "the greater number of those Fables which have been transmitted to us as some of the most valuable Remains of the Simplicity and Wisdom of Antiquity, were spoken upon a particular Occasion, and then the Occasion fixed the Moral of the Fable."[21] Not so in Augustan London, where the infinite particulation of graphic signs, not a supportive particularity of occasion, was the rule.

William Warburton provided more details about how these "valuable Remains" once behaved in the reassuring fixity of oral culture:

As speech became more cultivated, [the] rude manner of speaking by action was smoothed and polished into an APOLOGUE or *Fable*, where the speaker, to enforce his purpose by a suitable Impression, told a familiar Tale of his own Invention, accompanied with such circumstances as made his design evident and persuasive.[22]

For Warburton fables originally acquired rhetorical certainty in an immediate setting, where the present body of the fabulist defined their field of application, thereby limiting their meaning and even controlling their reproduction. A fable's intimacy with its "Circumstances" made the fabulist's "Design" both "evident and persuasive." That is, the very first fables were significant and effective because they were grounded in a particular setting where the rudiments of figure-making – its motives, its devices, its applications – were all fully visible. Could fables written (as all were in modern England) claim the rhetorical candor and referential stability of fables spoken (as they were in ancient Greece and Rome)? To many, the odds seemed to be against it, given the anarchic promiscuity of print so dubiously immortalized in Pope's *Dunciad* (1728, 1742) and summarized long before in Temple's complaint that "the scribblers are infinite, that, like mushrooms or flies are born and die in the small circle of time.[23] In modern England, signs could be produced – and reproduced and re-interpreted – *ad infinitum*. Their immediate context was fragmentary, diffuse and perpetually mobile; it offered no stabilizing frame of reference.

Like their reputation as the world's "Oldest Books," then, fables' evocation of a pre-existing symbolic mode could be used to censure the increasingly textual – and increasingly disembodied – forms of modern cultural authority. Some, though, took advantage of fables' descent from oral culture to imagine a new model of textual representation: Edward Stillingfleet for example marvelled at "how nearly the *apologue* and *instruction by action* are related." For evidence of the relationship, he sent his own readers to the biblical account of "Jeremiah's adventure with the Rechabites; an instruction partaking of the joint nature of *action* and *apologue*. This was the birth of FABLE, a kind of speech which corresponds, in all respects, to *writing by hieroglyphics*, each being the symbol of something else understood."[24] For Stillingfleet, fables' suspension between "speech" and "hieroglyphics" seemed to promise that written words too could behave like living bodies, agile and influential actors on the stage of the page. "FABLE" offered a foothold within a disorienting and ever more monstrously denatured avalanche of printed pages. It was by invoking Aesop, after all, that Dennis imposed evidently natural hierarchies and distinctions upon different kinds of books, dividing them confidently into "Genus" and "Species."

If, in the aggregate, Augustan theories of fable all angled to rehabilitate books as the foundation of modern cultural authority, then on the surface Bentley's announcement, *pace* other "moderns" of French extraction, that there is no first edition of Aesop's fables threatened to sabotage this enterprise. Bentley's philology took no prisoners. It left his contemporaries without an "Oldest Book" to canonize, only a heap of textual reactions with no clear ties to any original authorities, spoken or written. His 1697 essay "Of Æsop's Fables" seems to anticipate present-day deconstruction, in which there are only infinitely differing textual signs – no extratextual meaning, no "*h'ors texte*," certainly no unwritten utopia to which we have genuine access.[25] But Bentley's methodology actually naturalized textual representation, treating fables as authorless textual particles that swerved and grouped like the atoms that composed the material world, and whose behavior could be described in similar terms. Bentley's empiricism brings his fable theory into ironic line with the nostalgia of Aesop's more conservative proponents, who also sought to stabilize and naturalize textual representation by discovering within it the still viable remnants of a more stable, regulated, and humanly embodied world of natural signs. The irony of Bentley's method, and its even more ironic convergence with an apparently hostile critical, position was nowhere more apparent than in the most notorious literary imbroglio of the 1690s – the battle of the books.

The battle of the books

Because they reputedly numbered among the very "Oldest Books," we might have expected fables to have played a pivotal role in late seventeenth-century debates about the nature of the text. And indeed, the "Battel of the Books" has been immortalized in the fable of the modern spider and the ancient bee that appears in Swift's 1704 satire of that name. This is doubly fitting since fables were both an object of inquiry and a key rhetorical device in the literary skirmish that broke out in the last decade of the seventeenth century over the authenticity of a body of classical documents. The most celebrated of these documents were the epistles of the classical tyrant Phalaris but the fables of Aesop also came under fire in a quarrel whose combatants epitomize the critical differences I have described.

As it is usually chronicled, that is, the battle of the books pitted "ancient" (conservative) against "modern" (skeptical and subversive) concepts of canonicity and textual integrity.[26] The conflict sprang to flame in mid-seventeenth-century France, where Roman Catholic exegetes resisting Protestant claims for the authority of sacred text had begun to treat scripture as disconnected, erratic, often contradictory pieces of writing. Their proto-deconstructive interpretive methods were soon applied to other texts, including the classical works that had become cornerstones of cultural authority.

When it got to England, this critical movement collided with the explosion of print culture. The effusions of the English press only confirmed the theory of writing's native indiscriminacy and incoherence. For moderns like William Wotton, the multiplication of printed pages promised a kind of literary *glasnost* in which "Books may be compar'd, examin'd, and canvass'd, with much more ease than they could before."[27] But ancients like Temple supposed that "the Invention of Printing has not perhaps multiplied books, but only the copies of them."[28] Temple much preferred the few select originals of the past; among these real books, we recall, he counted Aesop's fables. As recent scholars have suggested, ancients valued antique works because they seemed closely tied to a world uncorrupted by technology and instead "governed" by "auditory values" and the "collective felt presence" of a listening audience.[29] Correspondingly, the ancients shared a certain faith in the formal properties of language. They particularly admired the "shapely" and "artistic" rhetorical style that, indebted to oral forms of expression, promises that signs may somehow transcend the accidents that accompany their articulation in space.[30] One of the ancients, Charles Boyle, had recently translated Phalaris's epistles in order to demonstrate their author's excellence on exactly these scores.

By contrast, moderns like Wotton or the classicist Bentley submitted what they read to a "topical and analytical" procedure that exposed formal figures

as arbitrary and factitious. The moderns often regarded meaning as a
function of the letters that conveyed it; contemptuous of traditional models of
authorship, they favored the empirically verifiable authority of the documents
themselves. Bentley's impolite inquiries into the authenticity of the Phalaris
letters wielded empiricism's critical and expository methods against a myth of
rhetorical coherence. To him, the myth seemed as tyrannical as Phalaris
himself, who liked to broil his rebellious subjects in a brass bull designed to
emit their screams as music.[31]

Seen in large, the battle of the books was less about whether or not old
books are better than new ones than it was about competing conceptions of
textual authority. The "ancient" model for that authority is rooted in
humanist tradition and its metaphors; the "modern" model is empirical and
grounded in existing textual evidence. To "moderns," the "ancient"
perspective seemed despotic; to the "ancients," the "modern" point of view
fed on the hollow, atomistic, and ultimately self-determining incoherences of
the page. What conflict could have been more hospitable to a literary form
already, as we saw, imaginatively suspended between speech and writing?

Planted squarely in the center of *The Battel of the Books* (1704), Swift's
celebrated fable of the modern spider and the ancient bee indeed helps us
visualize the disparity between "ancients" and "moderns." Swift's spider
spews his web out of "a Native Stock within [him]self."[32] As a figure for the
text, the web signifies only its own desires and operations; it denies the
relevance, even the reality, of an organizing authorial presence. By contrast,
Swift's bee voices ideals of "Collectio[n]," "Desig[n]," and "Distinction of
Things" (p. 150). His silver tongue both expounds a doctrine of governable
form and identifies him with oral transmission, hence with the proposition that
bodies manipulate signs rather than the other way around. As Swift's fable
renders the ancient and modern modes of symbolic management morphologically discrete, it also specifies opposing constructs of representation.

What we know about fables, though, prevents us from taking such
oppositions at face value. And indeed Swift's own Aesopian narrative actually
marks ground common to ancients and moderns alike. The insect disputants
after all share the same typographical habitat and their confidence in their
differences from each other is correspondingly questionable.[33] Might not the
ancients and the moderns prove similarly collusive once we examine the
mechanisms they used to assert their respective positions? In the *Battel* Swift
uses the Aesopian fable as such a mechanism, thereby exploiting fables'
legendary potential to protect the text's rhetorical fabric. But Bentley too was
enthralled by the very idea of Aesop, and his otherwise hard-bitten prose
bristles with figures of speech presumably instituted by Aesop.[34]

Swift's attitudes toward the relationship between mutually exclusive
signifying modes are usually surmised from Book IV of *Gulliver's Travels* (1726).
There Swift's Houyhnhnms inhabit what looks like an ideal cultural order,

one defined by an ideal symbolic system. As was emphasized in Chapter 1, Houyhnhnms do not write. Terry Castle proposes that this is because like a good ancient Swift himself associated the oral medium with a "pure relation between words and nature" while holding that writing "ultimately interrupts, compromises, corrupts this relation."[35] For Castle, Swift is on the side of speech – the bee's side, the side of the ancients. But what sort of side is this, after all? As legible narratives about beasts that speak, fables actually equate words visibly arranged on a page and words that drop from open mouths.[36] They naturalize the signs so monstrously *de*natured in modern print culture.

The Battel of the Books really acts out this *rapprochement* between divergent symbolic modes. Swift's satire begins in a bibliographic dystopia. In St. James's Library, ancient and modern books have been shelved haphazardly, with "*Des-Cartes* next to *Aristotle*," "poor *Plato* [...] between Hobbes and the *Seven Wise Masters*, and "*Virgil* [...] hemmed in with *Dryden* on one side, and *Withers* on the other" (p. 146). Because the books concerned manifest no visible differences, and because all of them claim the same titles (the moderns maintain that they are "much the more *Antient* of the two"), the resulting exchange of "hot Words" fails to "admit the least overtures of Accommodation."

The famous wrangle between the spider and the bee thus comes as a relief. This "material Accident" disrupts the fiction around it. Previously, the conflict had raged between substantively identical words; by contrast, the voluble insects remain visibly distinct from each other and so enjoy more signifying power than books ever could. The fable holds a unique potential for representation, promising that stable and unambiguous figures might assert themselves after all. This potential needs to be harnessed to the rest of Swift's text; and in Swift's narrative it is Aesop who provides such a harness by supplying the moral that the fable lacks.

If he is to make application, however, Aesop himself must escape the pages where he has been confined. The beginning of the satire, that is, finds him "chain'd among a shelf of *Moderns*." Stripped of his titlepage and "sorely defaced," he can claim no natural identity. And as long as he shares books' signifying plane, he cannot resolve the quarrel between the spider and the bee. So Aesop wriggles his way through "a thousand Forms" until, arriving at last at "the borrowed Shape of an *Ass*," he discovers his tongue. Now sufficiently disengaged from the page to fix the fable's meaning, he observes "that in all his Life, he has never known two Cases so parallel and apt to each other, as That in the Window, and This upon the Shelves" (p. 150).

As promised, Aesop's application introduces a regulatory mechanism that permits Swift's reader to distinguish both that ancients differ from moderns and how they do so. He provides a formal pattern that Swift's "Full and True Account" lacks. It is Aesop's speech that shows readers how to sort out the complex figural strategies that shape the printed pages on which he appears.

Aesop persuades Swift's reader to suppose that the words on those pages are something more than interchangeable printed characters. He hints that they can perform with the competence and coherence of figures whose authors still are present within them.

As he slips out of his battered binding and into the skin of an ass, Aesop marks the possibility that, through the fable form, books may unbook themselves. His "Arts" and "Forms" suggest that the shifting and strife-torn typographical world of Swift's own text might regain the authority, clarity, and stability of the spoken. But at the same time the explicating frame that Aesop devises is a textual one, and his moral actually reconfines the fable in the very structure that it would escape. What is more, it is only because the librarian Bentley misreads Aesop's new body, even "mistak[ing him] for a *Modern*" (p. 150), that the fabulist is able to "escape" at all. Aesop's seeming flight remains a graphic maneuver. His metamorphosis is ultimately confined to written words – a fact rendered obvious because Aesop's vulgar new shape focuses our attention on the physical bodies that bear meaning. As a compromise between the *Realpolitik* of print and the imagined precision and integrity of the nonwritten, Aesop blurs what should be a clear boundary between writing and speech. He at last demonstrates that the oratorical sublime is itself a posture assumed within writing.

If in Swift's text Aesop links ancient posturing with modern mechanism, in Bentley's he brings the possibility of manipulative figuration to a supposedly anti-figural phase in the history of textual scholarship.[37] As we saw, Bentley's excoriations of the Phalaris letters and Aesop's fables mark the beginning of an empirical tradition of literary criticism, one (like that of the Royal Society) programmatically hostile to metaphor. Bentley's use of Aesop's fables, though, actually exposes the persistence of the figural in a discourse allegedly hostile to the "Arts" and "Forms" that Swift identified with the "Antients."

At issue in Bentley's essay "Of Æsop's Fables" are the very verbal devices that govern and motivate the parent dissertation on Phalaris. Bentley resented Boyle's translation of the Phalaris manuscript from the start: as Regent of the Library that held Phalaris's letters, he had never wanted to relinquish them into Boyle's hands. To embarrass their translator, Bentley set out to prove the "original" epistles forgeries. A literary version of his contemporary Robert Boyle's skeptical chemistry, his method was to break every letter down into its component phrases. Once divorced from the integrated claims of the whole, each of these phrases could be weighed against other texts whose different usages of the same phrases pointed up anachronisms and inconsistencies. It is significant that these irreducible elements are often tropes devised within the coercive intimacy of oral culture – colloquial figures of speech, proverbs, and sayings. For Bentley, such commonly spoken "Similitudes" can offer "as full a Testimony of [a forger's] Skill in Imitation; as the Birds gave to the Painter, when they peck'd at his

Grapes."[38] Bentley wrests these persuasive figures from what would seem to be their original, spoken contexts. He treats them strictly as visible bodies that are open to inspection. These same figures convince Bentley's own reader of the primacy and authority not of eloquence but instead of the investigable page.

For example, Bentley cites Phalaris's threat to his enemies "that he would come and extirpate them like a Pine-tree" (p. 27). The "Proverb" bears no obvious cultural or historical inflections. Bentley, however, makes it unlock the historical duplicity of the letter in which it appears. He invokes the writing of Herodotus, who tells us that the "Saying" originated with Croesus, who lived after Phalaris. Thus it "carries a date at least half a dozen [years] before" Phalaris (p. 28). Bentley discards one origin of the phrase (Phalaris's speaking body) and replaces it not with another speaking body (Croesus's) but instead with the written text (Herodotus's) that becomes the only legitimate means of ascertaining its full import.[39] As "Saying" after "Saying" comes to "carr[y] a date," Bentley's dissertation compulsively subordinates saying to writing. Anticipating Farquhar's expose of the underside of Alexander's pillow, Bentley associates the "Saying" with a myth of authorial prerogative, one that imperiously pretends to transcend textual forms that should be open to everyone's scrutiny. The written word, on the other hand, might not verify the human presence of an author. But it *does* verify that of the reader whose very senses and sensibilities it can train.

Bentley's attention to Phalaris's proverbs makes his attached essay on Aesop seem inevitable. For in Bentley's book proverbial forms are Aesopian devices: both are telltale linguistic units that may at first appear to escape textual contingency but that actually prove to be fundamental elements of historical and linguistic evidence. Because Aesopian forms open signs to close inspection, Bentley naturally found them the only rhetorical instruments compatible with his methodological principles. He informs his reader, for instance, that his business is to "discover the Ass under the Skin of the Lion" (p. 11).[40] Aesop's fable here supplies a figure that will help the reader remember what Bentley wants remembered about the letters – namely, that, like the ass's lion suit, they have been forged. At the same time, the fable argues for what are to Bentley the only authentic forms of discernment, and these are skeptical, ocular, and alert to the divisibility of all seemingly integrated forms.

Bentley's essay on Aesop's fables thus examines, not only literary artefacts – the fables themselves, as physical texts – but also the very tropes he uses to inculcate his own method and thereby to create a community of readers. His essay is organized as a numbered series of brief points which, Bentley insists, is "not a [...] set Discourse, but only a few loose things, that I fansie may have escaped the Observations of Others" (p. 135). This structure recalls L'Estrange's *Eminent Mythologists*, between editions of which "Rhapsody"

Bentley published his *Dissertation*. The appended essay on Aesop maintains that, like the epistles of Phalaris, the current fable collection is not an original classical text. It is at best a miscellany of disconnected redactions with no definitive beginning except in the indiscriminate field of writing itself. Aesop never wrote his fables down; he was never an author. But the paradox of Bentley's essay is that it arrives at this conclusion not, as in the Phalaris dissertation, by examining inconsistencies in the fable collection but rather by tracking references to the supposed Aesopian corpus through other literary texts. The authority of these pages depends on an absent and yet influential origin – the figure of Aesop's fables themselves.

Bentley begins with the *Phaedo*, where Socrates presumably became "the first [...] who put the *Æsopic Fables* into Verse" (p. 137). Bentley points out that "Socrates does not say, he made use of a Book of Fables; but, *I wrote*, says he, *those that I know, and that I could first call to mind*." The incident offers no evidence that there was a genuine fable collection for Socrates to draw upon. In any case, even Socrates's translation has been lost; we know it only by Plato's account and this puts us at two removes from the original text. Bentley then turns to Demetrius Phalareus, whose "*Collections of Æsopean Fables* [...] perhaps were the first in their kind, committed to writing; I mean in the form of a Book" (p. 138). Like a subsequent translation by "somebody, whose name is now lost," this work too has vanished; in the end, a loose cluster of scribal apparitions replaces the antiquated body of the original Aesopian collection. Ironically, however, that body's absence becomes the very present foundation of an ordered world of textual variants. Most important, it's also the foundation of another kind of moral, for it reinforces the reading techniques Bentley recommends to those who would navigate that world. Instead of proving the original fable collection a forgery, Bentley uses the absent body of the first fable collection to justify his own model of textual authority. What Bentley conveys to his readers, in other words, is an apparently natural and decidedly coherent prescription for apprehending written signs.

The ploy works specifically as well as generally. For example, Bentley's discussion of the fable of the bull who lamented "That his Eyes were not placed in his Horns, so as he might see where he pusht" (p. 142) shows how a deeper figure of prescribed method organizes the dispersed particulars of the page. From text to text, Bentley points out, this fable varies considerably. Demades the Rhetor regrets that the eyes are not placed in the horns, "but *Lucian* (speaking of the same Fable) has it thus; That his Horns were not placed right before his Eyes. And Aristotle has it a third way; That his Horns were not placed about his shoulders" (p. 142). For Bentley, the moral of the fable, as it differs from rendition to rendition, is "that Æsop did not write a Book of his Fables, for then there would not have been such a difference in the telling." Yet the image of the bull itself functions in a recognizably

Aesopian way, ironically confirming an ancient myth of conspiracy between letters and material bodies.

Bentley's Aesopian inscriptions of a concrete and performative reading method anticipate Swift's. And reading "The Battel of the Books" in tandem with "Of Æsop's Fables" shows us how Aesop bridged a world of differences in the signature battle of the ancients–moderns controversy. Both ancients *and* moderns used fables to naturalize the alienating, uncontrollable world of the text – to shape their reader's responses to written words, to regulate the perennially skittish economy of the literal and the figural, and ultimately to restore a sense of physical, even human, presence and agency to the page. In short, despite their myriad differences, Augustan theories of fable ultimately agreed that cultural authority rightly reposes in texts that have been naturalized by Aesopian design.

"The daily lumber of the press": polite and popular tensions in English fable theory

To "ancients" like Temple, Swift, and Boyle, Richard Bentley stood for more than the horrifying prospect of a centerless universe of unregulated pages. His assailants in the Phalaris controversy derided his "awkward Wit" and "rude Language"; Swift depicted him as "barbarou[s]."[41] By contrast, Bentley's opponents, when not aristocrats themselves, were at least patronized by them. In order to salute Aesop as "the greatest Master in his kind," they had to avert their eyes from his present incarnation in shapes that might have been described (as Bentley himself was) as "awkward," "barbarous," and "rude." Crude translations, political ephemera, and popular collections compiled for the at best average reader all traveled cheerfully through the channels of lower Augustan culture. Such itineraries were bound to embarrass Aesop's politer advocates.

It is pretty to think that there might have been two distinct theoretical models of Aesop's fables abroad in Augustan England, one high and one low, one based on what was really being published in Aesop's name and the other a nostalgic fantasy. But just as their approaches to Aesop ultimately united ancients and moderns, so does this opposition easily collapse. For the more theoretically inclined compilers of the very collections that bred "like [the] mushrooms or flies" of Temple's imagination *also* often wanted to look the other way. Despite the fact that their fables were as likely to end up in the clutches of literate ladies maids like Richardson's Pamela as in those of Samuel Pepys, these authors peddled theories of fable that were conspicuously neoclassical in argument and inspiration. With the magisterial assurance of Swift's "antient" Bee, they too placed fables halfway between oral and literate symbolic styles in order to mark their own texts as great books.

The irrepressible Ogilby is a case in point. Chapter 1 described the mortal splendor of Ogilby's *Fables of Æsop, Paraphras'd in Verse* in detail. Despite the elegance of the volume, Ogilby strove to protect his fables from the imputation of vulgarity as well as from diverse hostile readers. As early as 1651 he declared that

If any shall accuse my Judgement, and Choice, who had the Honour of Conversation with Virgil, that I have descended to Æsop, whose Apologues this Day are read and familiar with Children in the first Schools, [...] it shall not be impertinent to say, this Ancient Mythologist hath through all the most learned Times been highly esteem'd by the wisest. [Macrobius] allowed his Book a Place in the Temple of Wisdome, and Socrates [...] follow'd him in all his Works of persuasive Oratory.[42]

Unblushing vendor of his own textual merchandise though Ogilby might have been, he identified fables both with the manners and postures of "persuasive Oratory," and with a noble, almost sacred, image of the "Book." Claiming the tradition of Macrobius and Socrates for his own, he eschewed the indiscriminate and the low. Ogilby offers a theory of fable that puts it on par with a "Conversation with Virgil." He thereby crafts an unbroken model of literary history, one based on the fiction of bodily presence ("persuasive Oratory") written into the Aesopian "Book" from the start. In this author-izing myth of "persuasive Oratory" preserved by certain good books "through all the most learned Times," standards of value are stable and the choices of the past can be made again in the present.

Later, in the preface to his atlas *Africa*, Ogilby would make even loftier claims for his *Fables*. In composing them, he recalled, "I [...] betook myself to *Æsop*, [...] where I found such Success, that soon I seem'd to tread Air, and walk alone, becoming also a *Mythologist*." What was Ogilby mythologizing? Perhaps fable-writing itself, here depicted as sublime flight. Swift's bee would recognize a kindred spirit in Ogilby's Aesop, "the most Ancient and Wisest of the *Grecian* Sages, who first led us through a Vocal Forest." Ogilby continues: "On his plain Song I Descanted, on his short and pithy Sayings, Paraphras'd, raising my voice to such a height, I took my degree amongst the minor Poets."[43] The fabulist here selects the purest and most enticing elements of oral culture – the "short and pithy Sayings" and the "Vocal Feast" – and turns them into metaphors for elevated writing. These figures of speech reinforce textual integrity and hierarchies of literary value, even as they confirm Ogilby's own value as an author. As we saw in Chapter 1, Ogilby had no scruples about profiting from that value. This, along with his shameless exploitation of print technology, earned him an ignominious bit part in Swift's "Battel," where "Father *Ogleby* [...] disarm[s]" his fellow modern Thomas Creech and "assign[s] him to his Repose" (p. 390). To Ogilby's own mind, he belonged in the company of the "Antients" –

something Swift seems to acknowledge by allowing Ogilby, albeit inadvertently, to score points for the other side.

Ogilby's was far from the only theory of fable advanced to elevate the Aesopian collection. Philip Ayres's preface to *Mythologia Ethica* also reminds modern English readers that "Kings themselves have not disdain'd to speak this Language" and that "our Mythology [...] has been approved by the most learned Men of Past Ages, reverenced by all Nations, and esteemed even by Sovereign Monarchs. [...] The greatest Statesmen of all Nations, in their most supream Councils as well as on divers Occasions, have made frequent Use of [fables]."[44] The preface to Edmund Arwaker's *Truth in Fiction; or, Morality in Masquerade* (1708) begins with an epigraph from Juvenal and is studded with quotations from Plato, Lucretius, and Horace. And John Jackson's *New Translation of Æsop's Fables* (1708) contended that while a deluge of cheap fable collections – "the daily Lumber of the Press" – threatened to precipitate "one of our greatest British Calamities," a proper translation of Aesop's fables could put English literature on a par with that of the "Grecian and Roman Empires." Anxious to declare his own *New Translation* the long-awaited redeemed of the Augustan fable collection, Jackson predicted that its "intrinsick Merit shall give it so wide a Circulation, a Reception into those Thousand Hands as shall serve it in an Age of Life."[45] Producers of the very collections that the presses churned out by the dozens, in other words, summoned metaphors from a world of essential value and intimate exchange. Such metaphors put fables beyond historical time, claiming them as something other than overnight sensations daily quenched by the very press that had ignited them.

Consumers of fable collections likewise saw them as one place where the "intrinsick Merits" of high neoclassical discourse might almost epiphanically enter the netherworld "daily" fabricated by "the Press." Reactions to Roger L'Estrange's mammoth *Fables* are exemplary. Even as half of L'Estrange's readers reviled the coarseness and vulgarity that seemed to mire his collection in commerce, money, and matter, the other half hailed its erudition. An otherwise sympathetic Samuel Richardson felt that he had to excuse L'Estrange's apparent sense of "Obligation to take into his Medley [...] here and there a trivial or a loosed Conceit, for Company." This "Obligation," Richardson apologized, had been "imposed upon him [...] by his unhappy Circumstances [...] in order to add to the *Bulk* of his Book."[46] Thomas Gordon scornfully pointed out that L'Estrange seemed to "delight in low jests," and that his collection is "full of [...] phrases picked up in the streets from apprentices and porters."[47] Mr. Spectator upbraided L'Estrange for abbreviations and slang words he let leak onto the page.[48] Robert Dodsley later charged that his collection "affords the grossest [examples] of the *indelicate* and *low*."[49]

Yet the very same fictions that were branded as vulgar and "low" were also exalted, sometimes in terms so lofty that it is hard to believe that the same fables were at issue. Thomas Fordon conceded that "Sir Roger's works, indeed, are often calculated for the meanest capacities, and the phrase is consequently low, but a man must be under the influence of prejudice, who can discern no genius in his Writings." Other readers found in L'Estrange "fine humour, apposite Language, accurate and lively Manner." Arwaker praised "the judicious and learned Sir Roger L'Estrange, whose Wit and Mastery in the English Tongue [...] set him to the best Advantage."[50] We might, of course, invoke political terms to explain the schizoid critical reception that greeted *Eminent Mythologists*. Tory Jacobites were probably likely to see the collection as witty and "apposite," whereas Hanoverian Whigs must have found it far easier to sweep L'Estrange's undeniably raunchy apologues back into the gutter from which they appeared to have sprung. Rather than see difference (in this case political difference) as the cause of L'Estrange's incoherent reputation as a fabulist, though, we might instead suppose that a shared tendency to polarize literary value – indeed to experience written language in oppositional terms – made that incoherence inevitable. Critical opinion about *Eminent Mythologists* was a kind of practical fable theory. And not unlike the other forms of Augustan fable theory we have seen – philological, popular, self-consciously neoclassical – it established fables as reactive mediators between opposing concepts of what books are, and do. As such mediators, fables reveal not only that opposition's superficiality, but also its structural importance for a broader myth aimed to justify, naturalize, and ultimately consolidate a book-based English culture.

It is not surprising then that the most influential theories of fable published in the Augustan period also set out to mythologize themselves as agents of cultural coherence. As it celebrates the "first Pieces of Wit," for instance, Addison's *Spectator* essay invokes its own foundations both as a text with particular rhetorical ambitions in a particular cultural setting and as a document that exists in literary history. Addison launched the *Spectator* papers hoping to shape the vagrant tastes of "Men of polite Imagination."[51] As it made the rounds of coffeehouse culture, his periodical exploited print's capacity to disseminate and popularize authorial precepts. Means obviously cross purposes with ends here: the printed method is fragmentary, but the stated goal is to create a refined and convergent group of middle class readers. This paradoxical relationship between means and end breeds anxiety for the artificial body that reproduces the voice of cultural authority, that is, the page. Addison imagined this artificial body to be in danger not just because it itself is multiple and piecemeal but also because the society it addresses is heterogeneous and combative. Were we to ask why Addison wrote so often about fables – which also liberally pepper the pages of the *Spectator* – we might begin to answer by noting that Addison's first essay on fables portrays, and thereby strives to master, exactly these trepidations. For if they are indeed primary, universal, and transhistorical "Pieces of Wit," fables can quiet fears of the hazardous patterns of circulation and dispersal that make literary ventures like the *Spectator* possible but also, perpetually, threaten to undermine them.

Not coincidentally Addison made the prototypes of fabulous authority men who told stories to other ultimately like-minded men. One of Addison's exemplary fabulists, we recall, was Menenius Agrippa, who according to Livy delivered his "Fable of the Belly and the Limbs" at "the very Beginning of the Commonwealth of Rome." Menenius, Addison notes approvingly, found the fable "indeed very Proper to gain the Attention of an incensed Rabble, at a time when perhaps they would have torn to Pieces any Man who had preached the same Doctrine to them in an open and direct Manner" (p. 220). "Pieces of Wit" here keep authoritative bodies themselves from being "torn to Pieces." Addison's second example is Socrates, who presumably told a fable about the relationship between pain and pleasure when, on the day of his forced suicide, "his Fetters were knocked off" and he was allowed to converse with a coterie of devoted listeners. Addison's Socrates rubs his unshackled limbs and admires the strange contiguity of pleasure and pain. He invents a fable which explains how these two sensations, originally enemies, at last permitted themselves to be "joined together at one Head." Socrates's fable bears a subliminal message about the proper organization of opposition, making opposites" subordination to "one Head" both a rule of order and a condition of their survival both as entities and as meaningful signs: "Wherever you get one, the other follows after."

Addison's other example, from Livy, also tenders a cautionary tale about the evils of rebellion and unregimented difference. First told to a throng of secession-minded plebeians in the sixth century B.C. and delivered, according to Livy, in a "quaint and uncouth style" by a Roman diplomat who hails from the plebeian ranks himself, the fable presses the language of the commoners, and the constituents of a world they know, into the service of the fathers (*patres*). In Livy's account, Menenius Agrippa describes a human body whose "members did not all agree amongst themselves [...] but had each its own ideas and a voice of its own." Resenting that "the belly remained quietly in their midst with nothing to do but enjoy the good things which they bestowed upon it," the members rebel. But in seeking "to starve the belly into submission," they only reduce [themselves] to utmost weakness. The fable quells the rebellion. After the fabulist "draw[s] a parallel from this to show how like was the internal dissent of the bodily members to the anger of the plebes against the fathers, he prevailed upon the minds of his hearers" and "steps were then taken towards harmony."[52]

Menenius's fable registers the perceived dangers of diversity and the necessity of consent to a central authority. We, like Addison, may identify that authority not just with the Roman *patres* but also with certain rules of demonstration based on orderly analogy. The fable legislates both social and interpretive harmony (unity of group and meaning) by means of a "parallel." Further, as a metafable, it verifies the rhetorical power of the fabulist, whose speaking body is conjured up in Livy's text, and summoned yet again in Addison's. Because Addison treats the fable as a text – something we "look" at and "see" – it is impossible to separate the fable's authority as a written example of fables' consolidating power and just cultural primacy from the authority of physical presence that Menenius Agrippa demonstrates in performance.

Livy's fable of coherence actually invokes the *Spectator* papers' own cultural role, their ambition to refine a literate but disparate middle class audience into a single polite society. For in early eighteenth-century London it was not a fabulist *per se* who "preached" to "an incensed Rabble." Instead, Addison knew, the literate rabble holds the body of cultural authority in its own hands. The question of how to forge an integrated culture given the dangerous but also inalienable liberty – the individual differences – of those who consume that culture's favored emissaries lies at the heart of Addison's theory of fable. This is why he emphasized that the Sophist Prodicus's fables always "procured him a kind Reception in all Market Towns" (p. 221). In a second essay on fables, published in 1713 and also widely quoted, Addison elaborated on how fables might continue to "procur[e . . .] a kind Reception" even for the modern fabulist.

Upon the reading of a fable we are made to believe we advise ourselves. We peruse the Author for the Sake of the Story, and consider the Precepts rather as our own Conclusions than his Instructions. The Moral insinuates itself imperceptibly: We are taught by surprise. [. . .] In short by this method a Man is so far overreached as to think he is directing himself, while he is following the dictates of another, and consequently not sensible of that which is the most unpleasing Circumstance in Advice.[53]

Superficially Addison typecasts fables as subterfuge, the ploys of a crafty "Author" who wants to "insinuat[e]" certain "Precepts" into his unsuspecting reader. But surely any actual reader of Addison's essay would be privy to this secret, and thereby impervious to Aesopian technique. What then is Addison's real aim? Most likely, he uses fable theory to instill in all his readers the basic principles of a certain signifying convention – one obviously text-based, rooted in "reading" and "perus[al]." A fable unites its readers' own interpretive habits with the disposition of the page – a page that joins all such readers in community. More than the speaking body of the fabulist, then, it is now the open body of the page that organizes meaning and insures advice's safe transport. And it is by commonly consenting to this model of textual authority that diverse English readers band together into a single group.

Though itself scattered through different *Spectator* papers, Addison's fable theory finally reconciles many differences within a coherent myth about how texts work. Assisted by the fables they declared uniquely able to inculcate certain reading methods, printed pages can presumably preserve readerly freedoms without diminishing authorial prerogative. The authors of fable collections themselves shared this assumption, or at least promoted it as a culturally useful myth of textual integrity. John Locke, we recall, intended his 1703 fable collection "for Those who without a Master would learn the English and Latin Tongues." In 1722 Samuel Croxall represented himself as "a Lover of Liberty and Truth, an Enemy to Tyranny [...] who detest[s] Party Animosity and factious Divisions."[54] Croxall pictured his readers as "Children of Britain" who are "born with free Blood, and suck in Liberty with their Milk." Such readers enjoyed freedom without faction. They are too enlightened – and, frankly, too English – to fall for "slavish" political doctrines insinuated through obfuscating imageries. These Croxall associated with "the Nurseries of *Turkey*, *Persia* and *Morocco*," with "*Italy*, *France*, and the rest of the Popish Countries" (sig. B5r) and more immediately with his Jacobite predecessor Roger L'Estrange, whose "pernicious" support for "Popery and Arbitrary Power" Croxall meant to turn on its head.

While consistent with certain neoclassical ideals, Croxall's preface is fraught with the ironies that actually underlie those ideals and that fables make visible. In order to create cultural coherence, fables have to be universally available. But if universally available, they must be so to groups entitled to use them for specific interests. And those interests can be, as Croxall felt L'Estrange's were, those of "Tyrants." The real irony, though, is that Croxall exercised his own kind of tyranny by aligning his fables against culturally and politically marginal groups – Roman Catholics, Asians, Africans, Jacobites. And it was Croxall who used fables not to forge common bonds between groups but rather to define – and privilege – a specific, manifestly English, group. Reading Croxall's preface as classic Augustan fable theory, we are reminded that fables finally forge unity around a common center only through a more insidious kind of fragmentation. For they split the field of symbolic action into acceptable and unacceptable halves, with different groups firmly distributed between the two.

But behind this lies a further irony, one evident in Addison as well. As Swift and Bentley tacitly acknowledged, fables require fabulists – and the theorists of fable who invoke Aesop – to make their own art plain. In complying with this requirement, Croxall ends up confirming the entitlements of precisely the groups he tries to push aside. So it is that the rage for unity common to the many schools of Augustan fable theory that we have considered, conservative and otherwise, depends, inevitably and self-consciously, upon a whole range of material and irrepressible differences. As loudly as it trumpets fables' ability to reconcile liberty and unanimity, Croxall's fable theory finally exposes that reconciliation as a convenient myth.

Were Aesop's fables the "first Pieces of Wit that made their Appearance in the World"? Are they indeed as primal as the "Liberty" good Englishmen "suck in [...] with their Milk"? Whatever else they might have been, fables were the building blocks of Augustan literary criticism, and in turn of Augustan culture in England. Through Aesop's fables, English writers found a way to test the new symbolic order that their texts helped bring into being. Just as in the reading lives of English schoolchildren Aesop's fables stood at the threshold of literate experience, so in the dawning life of a self-consciously literate culture did they animate and confirm the authority of the text, even as they reserved the right to mock it.

3

Common and uncommon characters: the lives of Aesop

'Twas an old Tradition among the *Greeks*, that *Æsop* revived again, and lived a second life. Should he revive once more, and see the Picture before the Book that carries his Name, could he think it drawn for Himself; or for the Monkey; or some strange Beast introduced in the Fables?'

Richard Bentley, "Of Æsop's Fables" (1697)

It happened . . . that *Æsop* broke silence first. He had been of late most barbarously treated by a strange Effect of the *Regent's Humanity*, who had tore off his Title-page, sorely defaced one half of his Leaves, and chained him fast among a Shelf of *Moderns*. Where soon discovering how high the Quarrel was like to proceed, he tried all his Arts, and turned himself to a thousand Forms: At length in the borrowed Shape of an *Ass*, the *Regent* mistook Him for a *Modern*; by which means, he had Time and Opportunity to escape to the *Antients*.

Jonathan Swift, *The Battel of the Books* (1704)

Æsop's is sure no common Character.

John Vanbrugh, *Esop. A Comedy* (1697)

And who, one might ask, was Aesop? If we were to take Bentley's word for it, or Swift's, we might never arrive at an answer to that question, for these otherwise strange bedfellows somehow managed to agree upon Aesop's infinite capacity for metamorphosis. In this they were both much in tune with their times. Portraits of Aesop crop up everywhere in Augustan England – in popular fable collections, on the London stage, in linguistic theory and literary criticism. They punctuate Scriblerian satires of erudition, as well as provincial legends and urban autobiographies like that of the redoubtable Charlotte Charke.[1] But just as Bentley's Aesop fails to recognize himself in "the Picture before the Book that carries his name,"[2] and just as Swift's Aesop ends up "in the borrowed Shape of an Ass," so with each incarnation Aesop exchanged one identity for another. His race, his class, his physique,

71

his love life, his birthplace, even his literacy all provoked spirited dispute between 1651 and 1740. Augustans evidently agreed that fables' "Founder, and Original Author, or Inventer [*sic*]'[3] should be fully visible to his modern audience. But they also kept themselves at odds over the question of what Aesop had, in fact, been like.

Why? Chapters 1 and 2 showed how Aesop's fables mediated between rival English authors to institute a new form of cultural authority. We saw that because that authority is text-based, it forced individual writers to surrender the integrity of their own fictions. Here we can add that the printing press's conquest of England also called the category of the memorable, distinct, and influential author into question. Ogilby's audacious bid to accumulate a "handsom Stock of Reputation" by raffling off copies of his fable collections is only an extreme example of the "expressive author" twisting in the grip of what David Saunders and Ian Hunter call his "monstrous contingency."[4] Fable collections flourished at exactly the time that emerging legal, commercial, and ethical institutions conspired with a burgeoning book trade to demand a new definition of the author.

This coincidence provides a point from which to view the strange combination of prominence and instability that distinguished Aesop's far from "common Character" in England between 1651 and 1740. Annabel Patterson's recent analysis of the public image of fables' "Founder" (or "Author, or Inventer") during this period links that image with the fluctuating fortunes of the biography that transmitted it to posterity. Enumerating the diverse traits that his biographers assigned to Aesop, Patterson tracks his declining significance as a historical figure, his evolution into a "figurehead" for a range of narrative functions.[5] I too hold that in debates about Aesop's true character his historical identity, like that of any other author, came to matter far less than his ability to reflect, and reinforce, certain symbolic practices. In Patterson's argument, though, disagreement about Aesop is not necessarily key to his amazing eminence as a "cultural icon." In mine it is. Indeed, it is what made Aesop an antidote to contemporary anxieties about authorship.

What is more, for Patterson, Aesop most boldly figures the "unequal power relations" that deform all language. This reading is reasonable: Aesop was after all reputed to have been a slave. Still, as we have seen, in late seventeenth- and early eighteenth-century England authoritative language possesses a radical and self-conscious materiality. If we take this materiality into account – as by the epigraphs above we may judge that the Augustans themselves did – Aesop will still be seen to figure the migration of linguistic authority. But its destination will be less an empty name (a "figurehead") that could stand for a number of symbolic acts (though chiefly those of the powerless) than the very specific province of the printed page. That page's promiscuity, ubiquity, and strange animate transparency all translate power relations into terms not limited to those of equality or inequality.

Debates about Aesop intensified, then died down, over the ninety years that this chapter spans. Though I discuss them sequentially, one view of Aesop did not yield to another: Samuel Richardson's Aesop (1739) bears a stronger resemblance to John Ogilby's (1651) than to Samuel Croxall's (1722). On the other hand, a single unified view of Aesop did materialize in reaction to another, and this second Aesop's mounting celebrity corresponds to a deepening consciousness of what it means for cultural authority to be alienated and embodied at the same time – divorced from its "Founder, and Original Author, or Inventor," and yet able to be reconstructed only from the physical evidences that bear his name.

Turnabout Aesop: the bones of the controversy

In Augustan debates about Aesop, much of the bickering centered on his body, which was by many held to have been "in ev'ry Part so very Deform'd [...] as to render him the lowest Object of Contempt."[6] "A Thing that Nature in a merry Humour has made half Man, half Monkey," this Aesop won fame as a "Chaos of humanity," a "Lump of Deformity" whose exterior belied a rapier wit.[7] Just so, a "Puppet-show Punch,/With his Paunch sticking out and his back in a Bunch" dominates the frontispieces of many major fable collections of the period.[8] Ogilby's *Fables* featured a hunchbacked Aesop opposite its title page (see plate 1); the *Life of Æsop* that graced splendid collections like Barlow's *Æsop's Fables* and L'Estrange's *Eminent Mythologists* dwelled on Aesop's "deform[ity]" as well as his non-European features: his black skin, thick lips and flat nose (plates 3 and 4).

Alongside the bestselling "crooked" Aesop, however, there came to stand one who "was ... far from being dull and slow of Conception, harsh and stammering in his Speech, distorted, maim'd, or monstrous in his Person."[9] This Aesop turns out to have been such "a very handsome and comely Man" that the frontispiece to Samuel Croxall's *Fables of Æsop and Others* (1722) renders him as a classical statue. Croxall's sculpted dignitary (plate 5) in turn demands to be read differently from L'Estrange's "deform'd" storyteller. The latter shares space with his flesh and blood audience – an audience that also figures in the fables and that seems no more or less corporeal than the letters (*Utile dulci*) which describe Aesopian method. By contrast, Croxall's lapidary, and clearly Caucasian, Aesop may be of a piece with his inscription, but both stand aloof from their living interpreters. As its relegation to a separate stone beneath this Aesop's feet indicates, the written word is merely something attached to him. L'Estrange's "monstrous" Aesop, on the other hand, poses alongside graphic characters which he appears to have produced. Traveling from left to right, our eyes treat these words as part of a naturally embodied sentence that begins in Aesop himself.

How could Aesop have looked so different to the same community of

3   Frontispiece to Francis Barlow, *Æsop's Fables, with his Life*, London, 1687.

4 Frontispiece to Roger L'Estrange, *Fables of Æsop and Other Eminent Mythologists*, London, 1692.

*Æsopo ingentem Statuam posuere Attici
Servumque collocárunt æterna in basi.*

5   Frontispiece to Samuel Croxall, *Fables of Æsop and Others*, London, 1722.

English readers? As these frontispieces suggest, Augustans were obsessively curious about how visible signs are made. The need to take Aesop apart seems to express metonymically a broader need to determine just how graphic signs are put together. The authors of English fable collections were of course putting such signs together all the time, and thereby assimilating political strife to the relatively irenic authority of the modern page. These same authors were also only reproducing the work of another author, and the acknowledged differences among their reproductions further helped to make their claims to authority palatable to English readers. Aesop's own tendency to split into contradictory personae likewise kept the cultural space of the printed page open to rearrangement without denying that symbolic authority was most properly conferred upon negotiable material signs.

Our "distorted" Aesop is a direct descendant of the "Esopus" that William Caxton had brought to England in 1486. Caxton ignored a more nearly native collection whose author, the Scotsman Robert Henryson, imagined "Maister Esope" as a Roman of "gentill blude" – "the fairest man that ever befoire I saw."[10] Caxton instead borrowed Aesop's life story from a continental narrative popularized earlier in the century by the Byzantine monk Maximus Planudes. Caxton's frontispiece followed the German engraver Wilhelm Steinhowel[11] to display an "Esopus" wreathed by the objects that figure both in his "subtyll histories" and in his own life. The very letters that spelled out Aesop's name were all of a piece with the items that apparently issued from his mouth. In the end, the woodcut proposed that printed words, significant things, and Aesop himself all shared the same material origins. Because Caxton's Aesop linked the autocthonous production of fables to the reproduction of printed characters, someone very like him naturally surfaced in the second half of the seventeenth century, just as the printing press came into its own as England's chief agent of cultural reproduction.

It became apparent that the printed pages that reproduced Aesop's character for all to see might easily have produced it in the first place. With Aesop's biography consequently open to inspection and contest, alternative images of Aesop's body could and did take shape. Late seventeenth-century skepticism about the physical integrity of a biography that could be exposed as nothing more than a tissue of "ridiculous Fictions" and "gross Forgeries" paved the way for early eighteenth-century claims that Aesop cut "a merry comical Figure; at least as handsome as *Socrates*."[12] A disgruntled and self-conscious Aesop of 1711 therefore facetiously pronounced himself "beholden to the Poets and Painters for representing him to the World, with such Charms as a Scythe-Leg, Beetle-Brow, Goggle-Eye, Blobber-Lip, swarthy Phiz., &c, when, (says he), turning about, I'm as well-shap'd, as your Worship, or any Jack-Pudding of 'em all."[13]

This "well-shap'd" Aesop never fully replaced his "Blobber-Lip" alter-ego.

Rather, throughout the late seventeenth and early eighteenth centuries, Aesop was always "turning about." This, fortuitously, guaranteed that symbolic action would stay fair play. That is, if fables themselves satisfied a contemporary compulsion to keep the origins of signs and the grounds of their authority well in sight, those signs' progenitor was naturally also an object of curiosity. Yet to fix Aesop's character too firmly would be to compromise the very potential for self-reflexivity and inversion that textual representation presumably guaranteed.

If we cast Aesop as the figural hero of a contentious age that commonly consented to the authority of the book, we can begin to see why so many books made so much of him. Of course, Aesop's biography may also be seen as a popular fiction in its own right, or as a marketing strategy that fabulists used to boost the sales of their collections. An archetypal reading of the Aesop craze would cast the "Phrygian fabulist" as a trickster figure whose antics caught English imaginations between 1651 and 1740.[14] Sharing Patterson's view of the *Life* as an allegory of the politics of representation, I want to integrate all of these perspectives. In this chapter Aesop will be seen first in light of his perceived coherence with the material signs that conveyed information about him. This means that he will also be seen ironically – in light of his vital incoherence under the dogged scrutiny that the printed page invites.

"Eminent" impediments: the "monstrous" Aesop and the incandescence of obscurity

The possessive titles of countless fable collections – *Æsop's Fables with their Morals, Æsop's Fables with his Life, Fables of Æsop and Other Eminent Mythologists, Esops Fables for the Instruction of Youth*, and, often, simply *Æsop's Fables* – tell us point blank that Aesop was the author and implicit owner of a number of fables.[15] So frequently and emphatically does the name of this "eminent Mythologist" appear at the head of most editions of his work that the print explosion seems to have precipitated anything but the death of the author so often attributed to it. Frequently arranged in "Prospect" and embellished with portraits and plates commemorating significant episodes in his life, Aesop's ubiquitous biography suggests that the Augustans had a clear and distinct contemporary idea of who he was and what literary property belonged to him.

One of the first things that the standard biography tells us, though, is that for most of his life Aesop himself was property. In popular accounts inherited through Caxton from Planudes, Aesop is a Phrygian slave living in Greece in the sixth century, B.C. Born with a speech impediment (later miraculously cured), and inordinately fond of practical jokes and puns, he is sold over and over again, the last time to the philosopher Xanthus, who sometimes punishes and sometimes profits from Aesop's pranks and apologues. After adopting an ungrateful son in some versions of the story, and after marrying his beautiful fellow slave Rhodopis in others, Aesop becomes a political advisor and diplomat. He caps a career spent interpreting portents and assuaging rebellions by offending the rabble of Delphi so mortally that they frame him for theft, sentence him to death, and push him over the edge of a precipice.[16]

Many details of Aesop's life story resonated in post-Civil War England. His bondage is one. Because Aesop is a slave, his actions and utterances are always framed – we might even say deformed – by their political circumstances. As Patterson has shown, this makes the biography itself a "metafable" about the "logic of accommodation," imposed by political disadvantage, that structures all fables.[17] The *Life* thus acts out a potentially subversive theory of language. This theory becomes especially concrete once it is noticed, as it was frequently by the Augustans, that Aesop usually contrives his fables either to evade punishment or to convey advice without seeming presumptuous. In Oliver Goldsmith's view, in

telling the Story of a Lion, Dog, or a Wolf, the Fabulist describes the Manners and Characters of Men, and communicates Instruction, without seeming to assume the Authority of a Master or a Pedagogue. Aesop's Situation as a Slave might suggest this Method to him; for what would have been scornfully rejected if delivered in an authoritative Style by a Slave was received with avidity in the form of a Fable.[18]

Aesopian language is not just situational, then. Its "Situation" is actually intrinsic to its "Method," its "Method" is intrinsic to its form, and its form is therefore always an image of "Authority" at risk.

Aesop's limitations are not only political. For as Barlow's "Brief Prospect" tells us, "above all his Misfortunes, this was the most Eminent, that his Speech was slow, inarticulate and obscure; such was his Body."[19] Again, Aesop's speech impediment renders "Eminent" the material obstructions that encumber all efforts to produce meaningful signs. It also forces him to communicate through objects and gestures. Thus his first fables are told in a language of visible, manipulable objects; Aesop's original vocabulary includes neats' tongues, panniers of bread, figs, and buckets of water. As prototypic fables, Aesop's performances with these props satisfy one of the Augustan's most urgent linguistic requirements – that signifiers stick close to the sensible world. In George Dalgarno's linguistic treatise *Didascalocaphus; or, the Deaf and Dumb Man's Tutor* (1680), for example, Aesop makes a cameo appearance as Homer's slave. Deaf and tongueless, Dalgarno's Aesop is nevertheless well-versed in "Haptology" – a sign language communicated by pressure from hand to hand. To Dalgarno's mind this language is far superior to speech, which "can only enter by the door of one sense, and do its message only by one kind of interpretation."[20] In the biography that Dalgarno had obviously read, Aesop's own body also speaks eloquently, and it does so not only by manipulating objects but also in its own visible imperfections. As Aesop's misshapen body and gestures communicate a political and linguistic predicament, they also offer a language that can signify that predicament. One rhymed overview of his "Birth, Shape and Qualities" tells us that, "made up of NATURES worst deformities," Aesop speaks with "voice inarticulate; Gesture rude;/Presaging badges of plain servitude."[21]

In the *Life of Æsop*, Aesop's gestures might be rude, but they also sustain a remarkably flexible and efficient signifying system.[22] On one occasion, Aesop is accused of having devoured some figs that were stolen by his fellow slaves. To defend himself, Aesop swallows warm water and vomits. Instead of vindicating words, his mouth produces visible, and hence surpassingly hard, evidence of his innocence. Then, in a bulimic *coup de théâtre* vividly illustrated by Barlow (plate 6), Aesop

requested his Master his Servants might drink the same warm Infusion, whereby it might appear who had eaten the Figs. His master approving the same ingenious Artifice of Æsop, condemn'd them to the same Draught, which by its warmth and moisture, making the Members of the Stomach limber and docile, engag'd them to disgorge the Water and Figs together, by which act the innocence of Æsop was assoil'd, and his enemies punished.

Such "ingenious Artifice" supplies a template for the fable form itself: Fables spring from a more telling discourse than mere words can provide.

Eventually, though, Aesop's kindness to some itinerant priests leads to a dream in which "he saw Fortune standing by him, gratifying him with volubility of Language." Awakening to find it so, Aesop, in a parody of Adamic language acquisition, proceeds to "register each Animal by Name."[23] He also begins to tell stories whose characters and plots come from his old medium, the sensible world. Indeed, Aesop's speech has the visceral effect of "some Tree bringing forth fruit untimely, or some Beast had brought forth something Monstrous."[24] He "disgorge[s] intolerable Maledictions" – as well he might since, as Philip Ayres put it, "in Æsop, the Taste of *Fable* was the Gift of Nature."[25]

Ever the "Philosopher in his Works more than his Words,"[26] Aesop for the rest of his life reproduces in words the same sensible discourse that he mastered in his aphasic days. For instance, the newly verbal Aesop is fond of literal meanings. When one of his masters, the philosopher Xanthus, "commanded Aesop to bring some drink to them now coming from Bath," he, "taking water up from the stream of the Bath gave it to *Xanthus*, who without apprehending the strength of the water, cryed out to *Æsop*, what's this? from the Bath, quoth he." When Xanthus, speaking in slang, asks Aesop to boil him a lentil, Aesop produces exactly one boiled lentil, and when Xanthus threatens to whip him, Aesop points out that his master "commanded me to boil a lentil ... and not lentils in the plural."[27] Aesop's

So thrive false witnesses, and perjur'd Lyes,
Confounded by the innocent, and wise,
Tho' hid like thought, the guilded Treason rest,
The Mask puld off, the villain is confest.

6   Plate from Brancis Barlow, *Æsop's Fables, with his Life*, London, 1687.

verbal feats are like puns in that, "by the Power of a few Words," they press language back to its literal foundations. Such strict literalism ironically exposes the figural as arbitrary and manmade.[28]

Because they too are things, written characters also respond to Aesopian strategy. When Xanthus bids him decipher a monument figured over with Greek letters, Aesop interprets the inscription as an acronym, with the words each letter represents conspiring to tell where a treasure lies buried. After the treasure has been unearthed, however, Aesop decides that the letters really "intimat[e]" that the gold should be restored to the king who buried it. The episode grounds graphic characters in physical action; it also represents even the most material sign systems as malleable. Aesop elucidates standard patterns of symbolic formation not just by keeping their verbal elements rooted in the world of objects but also by showing how random and provisional those patterns really are.

Readers – Patterson most eloquently and extensively – have noticed that Aesop's biography identifies his fables with the discourse of things. But it is also true that the story they tell invests the biography's written words with the power of demonstration that, as a rule, only sensible bodies can claim. L'Estrange, for example, noted that his "Flat-Nos'd, Hunch-Back'd, Blobber-Lipp'd" Aesop had "a Complexion so swarthy, that he took his very Name from't, for *Æsop* is the same with *Aethiop*."[29] Here Aesop's "Complexion" and his written "Name" perform as equivalent signs. Just as the elements of Aesop's first fables (water, lentils, inscriptions) and the plot elements of Aesop's life story (his slavery, his stammer, his compact hunched body) reveal the original and constitutive grounds of symbolic action, so might the verbal elements of his biography – individual words – point back to corporeal beginnings.

Such beginnings were apt to invoke more than the physical world. In the text of the biography, words could also expose the arbitrary, even retroactive, fictions that assign them meaning. For instance, Aesop was presumably "born at Ammonius in *Phrygia the Greater*, a Town obscure in nature, but made Signal and Illustrious by being the Cradle of Æsop." Here, its relationship to Aesop thrusts Phrygia into significance's limelight; if Phrygia was once "obscure," Aesop's later celebrity made it "Signal and Illustrious." The moral would seem to be that significance is made, not immanent. This moral licensed other biographers to challenge the authority of all testimony about Aesop's origins. Ayres could remark that

Æsop's Fables were so delightful to [Asians'] Pallats, that they boasted, the Author of them was their Countryman. Now he being the same person with *Locman*, in the *Alcoran*, they endeavoured to take from *Phrygia* the Honor of his having been Born there; and establish it among themselves. And whereas some Arabians would make his Descent to have been from the *Hebrews*, the Persians deny it, and affirm him rather an *Æthiopian*, which the Etymology of his Name seems to confirm, but that he lived at *Cassavium*, which City many suppose to have been the ancient Arsacia in the *Media*.[30]

Here the language of origins proves altogether hypothetical and disputable, and birthplace a slave to each society's self-interest. Gleaned only from wary comparison, authoritative information can be conveyed only when the act of skeptical reading is represented in the text.

Even outside the fable collection, Aesop's origins remained a hot topic. Here again speculations about them supported a posture of skepticism, not certainty. In an "Essay [...]" concerning the Origin of Sciences" (1727), "Martinus Scriblerus" pictured Aesop as a "Prodigy" who "first brought Science to the world." Scriblerus's Aesop hails from Ethiopia rather than Phrygia, and for just this reason, it would seem, he belongs at the head of the genealogy of knowledge. For according to the original philosophers were a "sylvan" tribe of orangoutangs:

to this ancient and generous race the world is indebted ... for the acutest wits of Antiquity. One of the most remarkable instances is that great mimick Æsop, for whose extraction from these *sylvestris homines* we may gather an argument from Planudes, who says, that Æsop signifies the same thing as Æthiop, the original nation of our people. For a second argument we may offer the description of his Person, which was short, deformed, and almost savage; insomuch that he might have lived in the woods, had not the benevolence of his temper made him rather adapt himself to our manners, and come to court in wearing apparel. The third proof is his acute and satirical wit; and lastly his great knowledge of the nature of beasts, together with the natural pleasure he took to speak of them upon all occasions.[31]

Though Scriblerus pretends to be interested in Aesop's "extraction," he really concentrates on the rhetorical "proof" potential that Aesop's body carries. "Short, deformed and almost Savage," that body becomes a critical "instance," an "argument" employed to parody conventional claims about the origin of knowledge. Eventually "that great mimick Æsop" exposes even hypotheses grounded in sensible phenomena as fictions. Aesop himself becomes meaningful and credible not as someone whose simian genealogy is genuinely knowable but instead as an animated, and reflexive, rhetorical presence within the sentences that represent him.

In accounts of his deformity, then, Aesop's character was inseparable from the written characters that claimed to communicate it. Some writers saw the connection in Aesop's very body, whose "Crookedness," Barlow tells us, "was but a Transcript of his distorted and irregular manners."[32] Far from abstracting Aesop into a web of indeterminacy, the transcriptive character of his body actually makes "Manners," rhetorical and otherwise, more convincing and immediate. Against all odds, Aesop's body itself – that "coarse Piece of ill-shaped Mortal Ware," with its "swarthy" skin of "obscure Extraction"[33] – shared the revelatory, self-reflexive quality of his fables:

The *Egyptians* muffl'd up their Knowledge of Things in the Clouds of Hieroglyphicks, and other mysterious Signatures; the *Grecians* folded up theirs in *Symbols* and other Emblematical Allusions; but *Æsop* having uncloth'd it from that dark Vesture in which it lay conceal'd, beheld Truth in its naked and callow Principles, like those ancient Poets that saw her through all those Veils and gloomy Contextures they themselves had originally wrapped her up in.[34]

"Shuffeld up and huddeld up" though they might be, such obfuscations prove enlightening. For "Nature in his Production, did seem to insinuate, that she oftentimes does set the Most Refulgent Gems in the most uneven and ragged Collets."[35] In other words, Aesop's "sharp Head, flat Nos[e], his Back roll'd up in a Bunch or Excrescence, his Lips tumerous and Pendant, his Complexion black" are all morphemes in Nature's illuminating discourse. Finally, as it exemplifies a natural grammar, Aesop's expressive body links him not with "Hieroglyphicks and other mysterious Signatures" but rather with the symbolic possibilities seventeenth-century linguists associated with instituted signs, and particularly with alphabetical characters whose chief political virtue was that they had been invented by public consensus rather than by private *fiat*.[36]

To at least one seventeenth-century biographer, Aesop's contorted shape alone could recall the curious declivities of an alphabetical character; for example, we learn that "from [his skin's] dark Tincture he contracted his name (Aesopus being the same with Æthiopia)." This "contrac[t]" was so binding that "Thersites in Homer was but an imperfect Transcript of so stupendous a deformity."[37] And it had been recognized in the late sixteenth century, when William Bullokar's *Aesopź Fablź in tru Ortography* (1585) conspicuously conflated Aesop's life history with the bodies of letters themselves. Bullokar's text anticipates the universal language schemes, projects for sensible words, and orthographic experiments of the mid-seventeenth century. *Aesopź Fablź* was printed in bizarre characters that Bullokar had invented with the idea that these would express English utterance more accurately than the present alphabet. Even more ambitiously, Bullokar sought to develop a text that would physically demonstrate relationships between English and Latin transcriptions of Aesop's life story. His biography

begin[s] with Aesop's life very briefly gathered out of Maximus Planudes, who translated it out of Greek into Latin, and I into English, using herein this figure or mark [to show that the word or words between two such] be not in the Latin authors of these fables, but are added by me as necessary for the English phrase. And if ^ figured under it in the word ... I use it to explain the Latin word used for the same.[38]

For Bullokar, in other words, the literal and substantial elements of Aesop's life story – the printed characters that conveyed it – double as images of what went into their production.

Aesop's life story made a perfect subject for such semiotic experiments. In advance of that story, Bullokar's frontispiece featured an Aesop whose dense, misshapen body seemed to mirror the print that filled the titlepage. But Bullokar himself remained an anomaly among his fellow Elizabethans. It was for the far more print-centered Augustans to exploit, even multiply, his equation of printed and authorial bodies. In 1703, for example, Edmund Arwaker conflated the ostentatious humility of the fabulist's pose with Aesop's physical infirmity. On this foundation he built a model of literary value, a prescription for how to read:

I am sensible that, with some, the very name of Fables is enough to bring any work, to which it is prefaced, into Contempt, as a Thing of no Use or Value; or, at best, with a Childish Entertainment, and to render it as Despicable and ridiculous as the Person of Æsop was, which appeared so deformed and mean, that when he was exposed to sale, no one would demand his Price. But, as a Man is not to be judged by his Out-side, any more than a Book by its Title-Page, so Fables are not to be valu'd only as insipid Tales.[39]

Paradoxically, its resemblance to Aesop's "exposed," "despicable and ridiculous [. . .] Person" made Arwaker's own "Book" look more valuable and useful. This was not because the likeness confirmed certain cliches about representation ("don't judge a book by its cover"). Rather, Arwaker's appropriation of "the Person of Aesop" revitalized such cliches by returning them to their literal referent, the "Book." As it absorbed Aesop's body, its history and messages, that "Book" became a kind of biosphere, one where constant lively exposure and open negotiation demonstrably produce meaning.

From this perspective, Aesop's deformity and enslavement do not strip him of authority; quite the contrary. The misshapen authorial body thus characterized emerges endowed with a new form of authority. The author joins forces with a power of graphic demonstration that books may assume as well as persons. Hence, as Patterson implies, the proliferation of Aesop's name on countless titlepages betrays less a confident impression of who Aesop was than a tendency to treat him as a name under which scattered but structurally similar pieces of writing could be united. What is more, by calling a group of fables Aesop's, a fabulist could sidestep the assumption, so easily refuted, that an author's name guarantees either the authenticity of those works to which it is attached or their status as his property. Instead, literary identity might reside simply in a text's material composition. As long as any page's means of making meaning remain in plain sight, this prospect is not monstrous or alarming. Contingency ceases to threaten coherence.

Even fable collections that began with his biography admitted that

"Aesop" was not necessarily the author of all the fables that follow. These could be attributed to Phaedrus, La Fontaine, Avianus, Babrius – any of a dozen other fabulists. A collection of the early 1670s notes flat out that "it has been said that though a person by the name of Æsop was doubtless the author of some of these Fables which go by his Name; yet that the Book which we call Æsop's Fables (though they were not all his) is a kind of System or Panduct, of the Choicest Observations of Several Ages, delivered to the World by way of Fables."[40] "Aesop" emerges in Augustan print culture as a sign of authorship's ambiguity, due to its involvement in the matter of its production. "Aesop" often signified not the known progenitor of a text but rather the author function itself. Ayres announced that his "Centuries of Aesopian Fables" "run not according to the common method of the *Greek* or *Latin* Fables used in the schools; for being a mixture of divers Authors, which I English'd out of several Languages, I have Polished and Methodized them to my own Fancy, calling them *Aesopian* from the resemblance the rest have to his."[41]

Likewise, in the Grub Street pamphlets of the turn of the century, Aesop migrated from Bath to Whitehall to Islington to Epsom and beyond; but his mobility and resulting obscurity were also revelatory. Noting that "the following pages were taken up by a Gentleman at the Bell-tavern in Westminster," one preface pronounces itself "altogether in the Dark, as to the Author." Yet this entails no loss of authority. Instead, the pages themselves get a chance to affirm authorial integrity, for, be other circumstances what they may, "the *Method* [the fables] are written in will convince the Intelligent, that a Person of Understanding, as well as Education, is the Composer of them."[42] Lodging in the page, Aesop participates actively in a living community, here, happily, composed mainly of "the Intelligent."

Material and methodological continuity between the page and the world creates genuine rhetorical opportunities for the written word. We can read the "fatal and calamitous Catastrophe" that marks the end of Aesop's life as an allegory of this continuity.[43] On a diplomatic trip to Delphi, Aesop tells fables that insult the Delphians. In retaliation they plant sacred goblets on Aesop's person, charge him with theft, and see to it that he is "condemn'd to be thrown headlong down a Precipice." Aesop tries to dissuade them with more fables, but to no avail: "He was speaking on, but they push'd him headlong off from the Rock, and in the fall he was dash'd to Pieces."[44] As it figures the end of speech, Aesop's demise precipitates the piecemeal fable collection itself; with his death, an Augustan fable collection typically took over the discursive burden that Aesop's corporeal frame bears throughout the *Life*. The end of the biography thereby bridges the fabulist's human body and the textual body of "his" fables. This bridge shadows another between the book and the social world of its living readers. Both bridges are apparent in Barlow's image of Aesop's final moments of life (plate 7), where Aphra Behn's caption invites the "reader" to "reflect upon this scene of woe/How little

Reader reflect upon this scene of woe,
How litle faith there is in pomp below.
When one so good, so great, so truely wise,
Shall fall a scorn'd, tho' guiltless sacrefice.

7   Plate from Francis Barlow, *Æsop's Fables, with his Life*, London, 1687.

faith there is in pomp below,/When one so good, so great, so truely wise,/ Shall fall a scorn'd, tho' guiltless sacrefise."

If the "deform'd" Aesop's "precipitation" literalizes the death of the author – refers him to the field of letters – it also presides over his rebirth. In other words, rather than float indefinitely in a sea of milling and randomly recombitant symbolic particles, the "sacrefise" of Aesop's body creates a securing frame for the exercise of linguistic authority. In the end, Aesop emerges as both sign and agent of a changing construction of authorship. Such a construction requires that authority be revealed as a fiction; it discovers new stability and rhetorical possibility within the exposure of that fiction, and so also within the premises of animate and consciously mediatory texts – in the demeanor, and misdemeanors, of letters.

Dismantling "monastic waggery": the other Aesop

So far, we have taken the story of Aesop's "crooked" body straight. As it became inextricably interwoven with printed matter, though, that same body more and more loudly demanded a skeptical and materialist approach to written documents themselves. To read the *Life of Aesop* aesopically was after all to treat it as a tissue of material signs with contestable origins and detachable parts.

While twentieth-century classicists have decided that the *Life of Aesop* is authentically "classical," it is even so a mosaic text, written in three hands which date from three different historical periods.[45] In any case, until this century the *Life* was known as an integrated document only through Maximus Planudes's probably spurious redaction – one which, it must be said, has Aesop hobnobbing with figures who lived and died after him, speaking a modern dialect, and delivering lines that appear in plays written much later. At best, Planudes's popular biography forces its reader to think about the historical relations between texts; at worst, it makes Aesop's life story look like a grotesque forgery whose author, even one of its defenders admitted, "meant to suit the Life to the Book which follows, and writ out of his own Invention."[46]

To English writers of the later seventeenth century, the biography's incoherence was as obvious as that of Aesop's own body; but for a while this discouraged no one from wheeling the unsightly Aesop into public view. Fabulists like L'Estrange found "divers Inconsistencies ... in the Account of [Aesop's] Life ... which the whole Earth can never Reconcile."[47] But like L'Estrange they too decided that the "Account"'s coherence and authenticity were less relevant to their purposes than Aesop's present environment – the English marketplace and the appetites that drove it. When Richardson decided to include the *Life of Aesop* in his own *Fables* of 1739, he echoed L'Estrange's skepticism about "the historical credit of a relation that comes so blindly and variously transmitted to us." But he also openly confessed his reasons for maintaining the probable fiction of Aesop's life story:

This uncertainty at first inclined us to avoid entering into the Life of Æsop, which we find mingled with so many trifling circumstances, and subject to so great confusion; but our booksellers acquainting us, that something of this kind would be very acceptable to the generality of readers, and that those copies had been most inquired after, which contained the life of this excellent person, in compliance with their request, we will give a brief summary of it.[48]

Having migrated from master to master, the shrinking story of Aesop's life had by 1740 become more and more like Aesop himself; in conforming to a particular cultural context, it exposed that culture's true face and imperious appetites. Thus while the story of Aesop's life sacrificed one kind of rhetorical advantage (a claim to indisputable truth), it found another kind of authority in its ability to elucidate the cultural grounds of its own reproduction, distribution, and consumption. Aesop's experience in the marketplace thus came to figure his fables' fate in a modern milieu.

But what about those who refused to accept the biography as a conspicuous fiction? Many did set out to expose the *Life* as a jigsaw of "Conjectures, Opinions, Traditions, and Forgeries ... so inconsistent and absurd, that it would be but a dull and sorry Amusement for the Reader, if [a biographer] should lead him into such a Maze of Uncertainty."[49] Repudiations of an Aesop "distorted, maim'd, or monstrous in his Person" came from several quarters and took several shapes. Surprisingly, no one seemed interested in reviving the bearded Roman of "gentill Bloude" and native manuscript tradition whom Henryson had envisioned as a "Poet Lawriate" bearing "ane Roll off paper," a "swannis pen" and "ane Inkhorne."[50] On the contrary, the courtly fabulist who begins to appear at the end of the seventeenth century shares the same classical origins that give rise to the "stupid, stammering ... Buffoon" of popular legend.[51] He is born of critical dissections of the Planudean *Life of Aesop*, or he is reconstructed out of references to the very classical authorities with which the *Life* claims affinity. We find him in Samuel Croxall's preface to the leading fable collection of the early eighteenth century, in translations of French fable collections, and in the thick of the battle of the books. In turn, the motives occasioning his appearance in each of these places could differ dramatically. Croxall backed him out of political animosity to L'Estrange; translating Boissat and Méziriac, John Toland sought a new prestige for fables themselves; Richard Bentley needed to defend the Aesopian figures that buoyed his own rhetorical and methodological style in the battle of the books.

Why did it begin to matter that the life story of the deformed Aesop might be itself a fable? What was ultimately at stake in the campaign to "prov[e] by unquestionable Authorities that Aesop was an ingenious, eloquent, and comely Person, a Courtier and Philosopher; contrary to the fabulous Relation of the Monk *Planudes*, who makes him Stupid, Stammering, a Buffoon, and monstrously Deform'd?"[52] As the rhetoric of this phrase suggests, part of what was at stake was, ironically, exactly what was at stake in the myth of an Aesop whose "monstrous" characteristics turned out to be surprisingly reliable instruments of demonstration. Those who rejected the Planudean biography saw themselves as champions of "true" knowledge in the war against "fabulous Relation." Armed with "unquestionable Authorities" – reputable classical texts that made sporadic but concordant reference to Aesop – they wanted to undermine the authority of a single manipulative "Monk" whom they associated with the mysticism and coercive enigmas of Roman Catholicism. But like advocates of the "monstrously Deform'd" Aesop, supporters of the "comely" courtier claimed a special prerogative for Aesop, linking him to the contestatory (but not itself contested) authority of the page.

As we might expect, political animosity drove Croxall to pit his picture of Aesop against Roger L'Estrange's well-established one. An ardent supporter of the Hanoverian monarchy, Croxall already felt that his Jacobite *bête noir* had twisted Aesop's fables into vehicles of "pernicious Principles [...] coin'd and suited to promote the Growth, and serve the Ends of Popery, and Arbitrary Power." He saw L'Estrange's Planudean version of Aesop's life as similarly corrupt, and thus exercised his own "Liberty" as a reader to expose the biography's flaws and inaccuracies one by one. For "sure there never were so many Blunders and childish Dreams mixt up together, as are to be met with in the short Compass of that Piece" (Croxall, sig. A2v).

His aversion to so-called "Arbitrary Power" and his practical emphasis on readers' rights go hand in hand with Croxall's politics, just as his caricatures of L'Estrange's fables draw on Whig myths of Jacobite secrecy and tyranny. But Croxall's point-by-point excoriation of L'Estrange's Planudean biography also responds to contemporary anxieties about textual authority not unlike those which structured the very account he rejected. Just as L'Estrange found the life so "blindly and variously transmitted to us [that] it is not one jot to our business ... whether the fact be true or false,"[53] so Croxall saw the *Life of Aesop* neither as a single coherent text passed down from antiquity nor as a responsible composite. To him it was merely a pastiche of lies and errors:

An ingenious Man might have laid together all the Materials of this kind that are to be found in good old Authors, and, by the help of a bright invention, connected and work'd them up with Success; we might have swallow'd such an Imposition glibly, because we should not have known how to contradict it: But, in *Planudes*'s Case, the Imposture is doubly discover'd; first, as he has the unquestion'd Authority of Antiquity against him; secondly, and if the other did not condemn him, as he has introduc'd the witty, discrete, judicious *Æsop*, quibbling in a Strain of low monastic Waggery, and as archly dull as a Mountebank's Jester. (sig. A3v)

Ironically, Planudes is more useful to Croxall than he would have been had he concocted a more palatable imposition out of classical authorities, or had he not set Aesop "quibbl[ing] in a strain of low monastic waggery" that identified him with inferior classes and religions. For Croxall, the Planudean *Life* is illuminating in and through its very "Imposture." Precisely because its anachronisms and inconsistencies are so conspicuous – open to "doubl[e] discover[y]," even – the *Life* shows how "Materials" are "laid together" to produce authoritative structures. Its obvious impostures also make it virtually impossible for the judicious reader *not* to reject this *Life* in favor of "the unquestioned Authority of Antiquity." In turn, and significantly, that "Authority" is not an alternative life of Aesop. It is a set of references in a group of classical works that "quot[e] or mentio[n]" Aesop. As a collection of originally scattered quotations rather than a single pretentious document, such authority can be questioned and tested. Similarly, the problem of knowing just what Aesop was like could be resolved by choosing not between competing traditions but rather between competing interpretive methods. One of these methods fails to detect "Imposture" because its practitioners are "so superficial in their inquiries that they take all upon trust." But the other – the one that the revised *Life of Aesop* encourages – is radically skeptical of what presents itself as whole cloth. By showing where reliable particles of significance come from (public texts rather than the inscrutable recesses of a monkish imagination), Aesop's biography promises to promote right reading and proper knowledge.

The Aesop who materializes upon a systematic reassembly of textual pieces differs substantially from the one born of a transparent imposture. Above all, he is not "so deform'd as the Monk has represented him." Had he been so, Croxall reasoned,

he must have been so monstrous and shocking to the Eyes, as ... scarce fit to be admitted as a slave in any private family. Indeed, what *Plutarch* hints of him is that he had something particular in his Mein: but rather Odd than Ugly, and more apt to excite Mirth than Disgust, in those that convers'd with him. Perhaps something humorous display'd it self in his Countenance as well as Writings; and it might be upon Account of both, that he got the name of [ridiculous], and *Lucian* calls him, and his works, that of [jests].   (sig. B1r)

Instead of originating in an authoritative text, this Aesop is the offspring of an authoritative method of inference (he would not have been shown to polite society had he been "monstrous"). More exactly, he is made up of inferences concerning what others' inferences of him would have been. Further, the object of inference is really a linguistic and textual and hence self-reflexive one. We are not looking at Aesop himself here, but rather at Lucian's and Plutarch's references to Aesop – at the legible words that, like the inscription under the statue in Croxall's frontispiece, are so intimately attached to Aesop that they have become part of it.

The "comely" Aesop reflects the reliability of the authorities that convey him to posterity. When the books about him are internally inconsistent, anachronistic, and apocryphal – when they are founded in monkish fantasies that make him "quibbl[e] in a strain of low monastic waggery" – Aesop himself will look "monstrous" and enslaved. But when we reconstruct him from verbal elements that are in agreement with each other – regulated by shared authority rather than dominated by a single author – Aesop's "Frame" will be much more prepossessing, and it will be knowable as such. It will also be consistent with the structure of his fables. Indeed, his "Countenance" will square with his "Writings" and "his Legacy [. . .] will preserve his Memory clear and perpetual among us: What we have to do therefore, is to shew our selves worthy of so valuable a Present; and to act, in all respects, as near as we can to the Will and Intention of the Donor" (sigs. A7v–r). Produced by a group of reciprocal incidents in authoritative ancient texts, Aesop regains the authority (the "Will" and "Intent") he was in danger of losing before. His fables become "Gifts" that in their turn preserve the character of the "Donor" and rescue it from oblivion and misrepresentation.

Croxall's alleged resuscitation of Aesop's reputation may be crude in its bigotry, and ironic in its deeper compatibility with the very accounts it wants to malign, but it is also far from original. French writers had begun to correct the deformed version of Aesop's life in the seventeenth century, and Croxall's revision was made possible as much by their philological work as by his own acquaintance with the classical texts that mention Aesop. Influenced by the skeptical exegetical tactics of the Port Royalists, seventeenth-century French writers like Claude de Méziriac, Jean Baudoin, and the encyclopedist Pierre Bayle saw Planudes's Aesop as the dubious progeny of a medieval forgery marred by internal contradictions and glaring errors in chronology. They turned to supposedly more reliable sources – to Aristophanes (whose characters quote Aesop throughout The Birds and The Wasps), to Plato (in whose Phaedo Socrates retells Aesop's fables), to Plutarch (who invites Aesop to the dinner party of the Nine Worthies), to Lucian and so on. Together, such scattered references to Aesop could fortify encyclopedic articles as prodigious as the chapter on Aesop in Bayle's Dictionnaire historique et critique, whose footnotes consume three times the space of the main text to exemplify the cumulative and empirical scholarly methods of modernity.

In France, revisions of Aesop's life story grew up amid veneration for an Aesop whose "laideur" did not preclude refinement. According to Eustache Lenoble, Louis XIV ornamented a labyrinth at Versailles with "quelques uns des fables d'Esope," complete with inscriptions in quatrains. Set at court, Edmé Boursault's theatrical adaptations of Aesop's life story – Les fables d'Esope, Esope à la ville – were stage sensations in the Paris of the 1690s; Madeleine de Scudéry wrote Aesop into her prose romance Artamène, where she praised "toute l'Histoire de la Cour qu'il avoit faite en fables, aussi bien qu'il compose une morale de cette espèce."[54] René le Bossu's *Traité du poème épique* took Aesop's fables as seriously as those of the *Iliad* and *Odyssey*; preceded by a *Vie d'Esope le Phrygien*, La Fontaine's fables became national treasures.

So radically distinct in England, in France the two Aesops inspired equal affection. Even when he was "difforme et laid de visage" as he was in La Fontaine,[55] or "endowed with "le corps laid," as he is in Boursault,[56] the French Aesop remained a courtier at home among the rich and famous; he was always more refined than the one who spoke "with a dead English weight at the tail of him."[57] Thus French revisions of Aesop's life story lack the shrillness of their English counterparts. Many English revisionists moreover had complicated relationships to their French models, who in addition to superior research methods offered a means of purging fables of their "low," "Buffoon[ish]" and "Mountebank" associations: from an English point of view, they could also hoist the fable, and with it the fabulist, into the most polite echelons of literary culture.

For example, to his translation of Boissat's fables Toland "prefix[ed] the true Life of Æsop, by the most Learned and Noble Critick Mssr. de Méziriac." Méziriac, Toland declared, is the one who "discover[ed] the ridiculous Fictions, the gross Forgeries, and childish Applications of PLANUDES (a lying Grecian Monk),"[58] and thereby "clearly prov[ed] that Æsop was ... of an admirable Quick Genius." While, as Patterson has shown, Méziriac's *Vie d'Æsope* (1632) made important substantive corrections to the *Life*, for English biographers his method was as important as his message.[59] On the surface, Toland was attracted to the Méziriac model because it substituted inquiring method for slavish reproduction. Toland noted that

it was my intention to follow the Method of Maximus Planudes, and to offer nothing but what he has left us in writing. But Mssr. de Meziriac convinc'd me that in his Life, there were such palpable mistakes, contrary to History and Chronology, and so many incredible and ridiculous Stories, that in the Opinion of Learned and Judicious Persons, it rather past for a Romance, than for a true Relation. But not contenting himself thus to dissuade me from translating the Reveries of Planudes, he likewise gave me certain Memories collected from several good Authors, to compose another Life of Æsop, that should be more conformable to the truth.   (sigs. A4r–A5v)

Méziriac's account promises "true Relation," "Memories collected" to produce a story "conformable to the truth." It is free of "palpable mistakes," "incredible and ridiculous Stories," "Reveries." "Collected" and "compose[d]," it eschews the groundlessness of "Romance." At the same time, though, Toland admits that Méziriac's own "convinc[ing]" text is a bit elusive. In fact, it tends to vanish from the sight of an invidious public whose "Malice against this successful Painter of their Vices" spurs them to slander him. Because of the hostility of the mob, we learn, Aesop's "Life by Mssr. de

Méziriac became in very little time as good as never written, and many
doubted whether there ever existed such a piece. Those who were sure of it,
yet with all their Industry could not obtain a sight of it."

Méziriac's corrected version of Aesop's biography dangerously resembles
the evanescent and apocryphal text that it revises. It too falls prey to the
vulgar opinion that obscured it until "it fell at last into [Bayle's] hands." As
its textual history unfolds, a true story's superiority to a false one becomes less
important, as does a public narrative's superiority to one fabricated in private
"Reveries." Such distinctions pale in light of any text's uncertain fate in the
world where it is to be read. More telling is Toland's desire to be part of a
polite society of learned readers distinct from the hoi polloi, his longing to
share the "opinion of Learned and Judicious Persons" and the society of
"several good Authors." More revealing still is his desire to elevate the status
of the fable collection itself – a gesture already implicit in the use of French
interpretive models, even though English ones like those of the less polite
Richard Bentley were also available. In shifting authority from the text of the
"Grecian monk" to a group of polite readers united by their shared
relationship to the fragments of antiquity, this alternative *Life* may seem to
reclaim Aesop's biography for the truth. But – in a move that marks an
important historical shift – it actually transfers authority from the text's
explicit claims to its ability to select interpretive communities.

If he is to play such an important role in a community of civilized
European readers, then Aesop must of course share their complexion and
physiognomy. Just as Croxall's "witty, discrete, judicious" Aesop cannot be
"ugly" because he needs to serve the interests of a politically dominant
group with access to the classical canon, so the more cultured Aesop who
emerges in translation has to be well-proportioned and above all Caucasian.
Anxious to deny the possibility that Aesop might have been black, our
translator brings a different pressure to bear on words themselves. Thus
Planudes's theory that

Æsop signifies the same with Æthiopian, because he was very black, may be
contradicted with a great deal of Reason; since the Grammarians are of Opinion,
that from the Verb, *aitho*, which signifies to burn; and from the Noun, *ops*, which
signifies Visage, is formed the word *Æthiops*, because the Æthiopians have very black
faces, if being Parcht by the excessive Ardour of the Sun. But we learn from
Eusthanthius, that Æsop is deriv'd from the same Verb *aethio*, which signifies to shine
as well as to burn; and from the Noun *ops*, which signifies the Eye, so that Æsop is as
much as to say, a Man that has sparkling Eyes.   (pp. iv–v)

Close to parody though it might come, the argument *ad nominem* shows how
an Aesop who is bright-eyed instead of black can gain access to the linguistic
styles of a dominant culture. Toland rejected the premise that Aesop "had his
Tongue so ty'd that he could scarce speak, or form any articulate sound." He

claimed instead that the first fabulist learned "the purity of the *Greek* language, as at the fountain Head." The alternative biography even interprets the story of Aesop's miraculous acquisition of language as an allegory of his dawning ability to tell fables. These in turn become elegant rhetorical forms rather than "ingenious Artifices" still tied to the material world.

Although reclaiming the marginal Aesop for a "higher Sphere" of letters often meant supposing that he spent most of his life "somewhat above the degree of a Slave," the correctors of his life story found other ways to master him. For in extracting Aesop from miscellaneous accounts rather than from his own words or from a single biography, the revisionists ended up, point blank, depriving him of authorship. Toland pointed out that we may only

speak of Aesop as represented to us by the best and most antient Writers, and by the Idea we may frame of his general Design from the Collection of Fables which pass at present under his name, as well as from those other Fables, called Æsopick, to be found in ARISTOTLE, PHAEDRUS, HORACE, PLUTARCH, AULUS GELLIUS, APULEIUS, AVIENUS, and Others. For we have not with his own genuine Work [...] and as if Men were desperately angry with him for labouring to make them wiser or better, they have yet worse abus'd him (if possible) in his Person. This is well known to every Child that can read, to all that frequent the Schools or Theatre.   (sig. A2r)

Although it rescues Aesop from "abus[ive]" opinion, the alternative life of Aesop finds other ways to retain him as a self-reflexive figure for symbolic practice. He is at once trapped inside "the Collection of Fables which pass at present under his Name" and denied a definitive – i.e., authorial – relationship to it, "for we have not with his own genuine Work." He has been displaced by the vehicles that convey him to posterity. Knowable only through readerly inference, he was never a writer; indeed, if he is to verify the authority of "the most ancient Writers," it is important that he *not* be one himself. Just so, it is only when Aesop is actually driven out of the book as a human being who made it that he can become the figural presence *within* it that is capable of knitting a community of readers together.

Drawn from iconoclastic French revisions of his life story, Toland's "comely" Aesop seems at first to serve the cause of truth and revelation. But he also reveals the structure of modern cultural authority itself. Reading his biography, we can surmise that scholarly method works not only by stripping a represented past down to its significant elements but also by creating discriminating communities of readers and empires of privileged texts.

We recall that in the infamous battle of the books the figure for a particular reading method replaced the fiction of the author. In that battle, it so happens, Planudes's *Life of Æsop* was scrutinized as closely as the fables and the Phalaris manuscripts themselves. Earlier too we saw how heavily the arch-modern Richard Bentley's style and method relied on Aesopian figures. Indeed, the reputedly "low" Bentley might easily have identified himself with the Aesop so often derided as a "Mountebank." Nor, given his propositions that critical method can integrate texts, is it surprising that Bentley should have labored to convince his own readers that Aesop was actually much more coherent physically than his biographers had represented him.

Bentley even attacked the frontispieces ("the Picture before the Book that carries his Name") that so often reproduced Planudes's Aesop. He wanted to replace such deceptive images with the more reliable, because less coercive, bodies of letters themselves. Nor did he trust crafted verbal portraits of Aesop. Instead, for the "Shapes and Features" contrived in Planudes's "Dream and Vision" Bentley substituted his own more "ordinary" modes of textual inquiry, namely reading. Bentley's own pages become images of these modes, whose verbal foundations in turn allow them to communicate a more symmetrical and homogeneous Aesop. In Plutarch's *Convivium*, Bentley observes, "there is abundance of Jest and Raillery, . . . particularly upon *Æsop*; but no body drolls upon his ugly Face; which could hardly have escaped, had he had such a bad one."[60] In Philostratus's "Description of a Gallery of Pictures, one of which is *Æsop* with a Chorus of Animals about him, [Aesop] is represented *smiling and looking towards the ground, in a posture of Thought*; but not a word of his Deformity; which, were it true, must needs have been touch'd on, in an Account of a Picture." And according to Phaedrus, the Athenians "set up a noble Statue to [Aesop's] Honor and Memory" upon which "*Agathia* the Poet has left us an Epigram." "How," Bentley wonders, "could He too have omitted to speak of it, had his Ugliness been so notorious" (p. 150)? Ultimately, Aesop's body is a referent to be inferred, not a point of origin to be taken for granted. For Bentley, Aesop's contours are inseparable from our text-dependent ways of making their acquaintance. Aesop's body thus reflects the deeper coherence of those methods.

Bentley, predictably, maintained that Aesop never wrote his fables down. Just as he is more accurately known through "an Account of a Picture" than through any actual picture, so is Aesop more properly understood as a product of writing than as its producer. Bentley's chief antagonist on the Aesop question was the "ancient" Charles Boyle. Translator of the Phalaris manuscripts, Boyle defended the traditional Aesop as ardently as he did the authenticity of those notorious epistles. Boyle especially resented Bentley's assertion that " 'tis very uncertain if [. . .] Æsop himself left any Fables behind him in Writing."[61] He argued that "the Phrase of Antiquity is the same, when they mention any thing of *Æsop*'s, as it would have been, had they thought *Æsop* really to have wrote it: The Ancients quote him just as they do other Authors. . . . And how would they have expressed themselves otherwise, if *Æsop*'s writings had confessedly lain before them?" (p. 233). For Boyle, the activities of the ancient "Authors" – particularly the act of quotation – realize and certify authorship in the social realm, just as opinion influences word choice: "According to *Suidas*, no body doubted but that he wrote Fables. . .

Eusthathius calls him expressly not *logopoios* only, but *mythographos*, expounding the one by the other" (p. 234).

Similarly, as evidence that Aesop himself never wrote, Bentley had cited the old man in Aristophanes who says he learned Aesop's fables in conversation. Boyle simply isolated the Greek word Bentley translated to mean "conversation" and interpreted it to mean "learned at a Feast." And "might it not be a Part of their Festival Entertainments to have some agreeable Book read to them? And might not Æsop sometimes be that Book? If this might be the Case, then the Old Man might learn his Fables at a Feast, and yet learn " 'em out of a Book too" (p. 235). Boyle saw writing and reading as cultural performances; for him, Aesop can "be [a] Book" and still be an author. He makes a sociable and functional – a human – definition of the book possible.

Like Bentley, Boyle concluded with the vexed question of what Aesop himself might have looked like. Boyle admitted that he had "no great Opinion of" Planudes's *Life*, for "there are in it several Idle, Trifling Stories, told in such a Fabulous Way, that one would think that *Planudes* meant to put the Life to the Book which Follows, and write out of his own Invention for Want of Authorities." Yet it is precisely this fabulous continuity between the "Life" and the "Book which follows" that makes Aesop real. Interpreting the *Life* literally, Boyle took language's physical properties as part of its meaning and thereby felt obliged to "reject every Circumstance of his Account as fictitious." The "Circumstance" he keeps is, predictably "*Æsop*'s Ugliness":

'Tis true, Every-body knows, that the *Æsopic* Fables were often in *Æsop*'s time frequently called *iscos*, by the Greek Writers, and from thence *Ridicula* by *Avienus*, but 'tis not unlikely that the Original of the use of this Word was from Something Ridiculous in the Gesture, Look, and Mimical Wit of *Æsop* that accompanied "em, when he first told 'em; rather than from the structure of the Fable itself, which does not seem contriv'd to operate that way. I am willing to think therefore that the name usually given to these Fables ... carry in 'em some small Hint of *Æsop*'s Ugliness; for nothing is so Divertive, or raises Laughter so much as Deformity, especially when Wit goes along with it. (p. 271)

For Boyle, authorship and appearance were finally inextricable – authority is a matter of "Gesture" and "Look" and books should be judged by their covers. This perspective even gave Boyle a glimpse of the author in Bentley's text, whose reasons for revising the myth of Aesop's so-called ugliness were now apparent: "He is extremely concern'd to have Æsop thought Handsome, at the time that he is endeavouring all he can to prove him no Author. He hopes by his Civilities to his Person to atone for the Injuries he does him in his Writings" (p. 283). Boyle backed the "ugl[y]" Aesop because Bentley's argument for a "Handsome" one seemed to divorce the text from human agency and "Gesture." His way of restoring gesture to the text was to turn

Aesop around again. But the point of turning him around was less to prove Aesop had been as physically "divertive" as "the structure of [his] Fable[s]" than to call attention to the animate, hence volatile, nature of writing itself.

Who then was Aesop? Augustan England's textual self-consciousness can make any answer to that question look tendentious, contingent, precarious – in a word, fabulous. Ultimately it would appear to matter less who Aesop might have been than how he behaves as a textual presence at particular moments of reading. It is his uncommon character to be visibly shaped by, and thus to shape, the very devices that communicate him to his readers. Augustan efforts to appreciate this symbiosis reflect a larger anxiety to decide what an author might in fact be. It is significant that his contemporaries described the modern English author most plagued by this question, Alexander Pope, as "a little *Æsopic* sort of animal."[62]

The fabulist Charles Draper noted that the story of the first fabulist's own life "bear[s] as evident marks of fiction as the fables of Aesop themselves," and he proceeded to make Aesop a character in many of the fables in his collection.[63] Far from trivializing or dismissing Aesop's life story as a mere "fiction," Draper's observation suggests the subtlety, complexity, and concreteness of the ties that bind Aesop to his fables. These are not simply ties of analogy or metonymy. To be sure, the fractured frames of Aesop's life and body resemble the atomistic verbal form that reputedly sprang from them. But Aesop and his fables are also, in an important sense, identical. Hence they are powerfully self-reflexive. As Draper's consciousness of the power of "evident marks" suggests, to a culture adjusting to the emphatic ephemerality of print, and thus always probing writing's figural and evidentiary potential, the Aesopian character and the character of fable are empirically indistinguishable. It is no accident that fable collections were called "Aesops." For all their interminable squabbling, Augustan authors at least agreed not to separate either Aesop or his fables from the stubbornly ambivalent pages that gave birth to them.

4

Brutal transactions, "mysterious writ": Aesop's fables and Dryden's later poetry

Much malice mingl'd with a little wit
Perhaps may censure this mysterious Writ,
Because the Muse has peopl'd *Caledon*
With *Panthers*, *Bears*, and *Wolves*, and Beasts unknown,
As if we were not stocked with monsters of our own.
Let *Æsop* answer who has set to view,
Such kinds as *Greece* and *Phrygia* never knew;
And Mother *Hubbard* in her homely dress
Has sharply blam'd a British Lioness,
That *Queen*, whose feast the factious rabble keep,
Expos'd obscenely naked and asleep.
Led by those great examples, may not I
The wanted organs of their words supply?
If men transact like brutes, 'tis equal then
For brutes to claim the privilege of men.

> John Dryden, *The Hind and the Panther*, III: 1–15 (1687)

It [*The Hind and the Panther*] was very surprising at first Sight, as Ostriches in the Desart are said to be to the Caravans of Merchants, appearing as far off like Horsemen, are yet discern'd upon a nearer approach to be the most stupid and senceless of all Fowls. Indeed, for its Bulk it imitates one of the mock Elephants *Semiramis* made use of in her Indian Expedition, all Straw within, and cover'd with Beasts hides without.

> Thomas Heyrick, *The New Atlantis, with some Reflections upon the Hind and the Panther* (1687)

Few literary works have faced their readers with more trepidation than *The Hind and the Panther* did; fewer still have found as much justification for their anxieties. First published in the predominantly Anglican England of 1687, John Dryden's tripartite petition for the toleration of Roman Catholics is easily the longest and most maligned beast fable of the later seventeenth century. Contemporaries judged the poem "monstrous and unnatural," even "improbable and contradictory to the Rules and Examples of all Fables, and to the Design and Use of them."[1] And in Dryden's "tedious and impertinent Allegory," it is true, a Roman Catholic hind and an Anglican panther debate a series of doctrinal points so arcane that Dryden himself was thought not to have grasped them.[2] Abrupt stylistic shifts and multiple digressions into personal and ecclesiastical history cripple a "mysterious Writ" that ends, implausibly, with each fabulous beast telling an "*Æsop*'s fable" of her own. Small wonder that the poem should have reminded Thomas Heyrick of a "mock Elephan[t, ...] all Straw within, and cover'd with Beasts hides without."[3]

What provoked Dryden to produce such a "monstrous" piece of writing? Heyrick sardonically guessed that he must have "intended it religiously as a piece of mortification, or politickly design'd to annex the fame of a Prophet to that of a Poet, by making out what he so long since foretold, his fumbling Age of Poetry."[4] Without imagining that they might have been "intended," later readers have also belabored *The Hind and the Panther*'s irregularities. Samuel Johnson's verdict that "such is the unevenness of [the] composition that two lines are scarcely found together without something of which the reader is ashamed"[5] thus anticipates twentieth-century descriptions of *The Hind and the Panther* as a "canvas whereon to embroider all sorts of episodes, digressions and ornaments."[6] Apparently plagued by "random symbolizing,"[7] the poem has struck others as "unsystematically handled,"[8] and even its most sympathetic critics deem it a "fascinating, risk-taking failure," one "betrayed by too many inventions, too many styles, too many conflicting purposes."[9]

As we turn from fables' history as a cultural phenomenon to the meaning that they held for particular English poets of the late seventeenth and early eighteenth centuries, we find something of an embarrassment. We will see that Anne Finch and John Gay used fables to secure symbolic authority within a literary culture that they also mistrusted, even disdained. But in Dryden's case, an eleventh-hour interest in Aesop only inaugurated "his fumbling Age of Poetry." Or did it? Dryden himself promises that his "great exampl[e]" Aesop can "answer" all charges, that he can "set to view" – and thereby justify – *The Hind and the Panther*'s many flaws and contradictions. If Dryden's Aesop has anything in common with the Phrygian fabulist whose acquaintance we have just made, we may manage to find significance in the very tangle of aberrations so many readers have deplored.

"A dramatical and scenical way of scribling"

Sometime just before he began writing *The Hind and the Panther*, Dryden converted to Roman Catholicism. Many of his detractors speculated that the aging, eminent but reputedly opportunistic poet wanted to ingratiate himself with a king more than kindly disposed to Rome.[10] In fact, conversion incurred far more risks than advantages: although James II was one of them, Catholics were hated and persecuted throughout England. The Popish Plot (1678) had stirred stubborn animosities, and priests were still drawn and quartered in the provinces.[11] Meanwhile the Test Act, in effect since 1673, compelled all Catholics to swear oaths to the Church of England. The year after *The Hind and the Panther* was published, James's faith would hasten his ousting in the so-called Bloodless Revolution, in favor of the unambiguously Protestant consorts, William and Mary.

Because *The Hind and the Panther*'s overt ambition is to plead, in highly figurative language, for Catholic exemption from the Test Act, *The Hind and the Panther* recalls much of Dryden's earlier political poetry. Written from the cultural center and exemplified in *Absalom and Achitophel* (1681), that poetry worked within tight figural frameworks, like typology, to gain specific rhetorical ends; timely publication sped its success. A few weeks before *The Hind and the Panther*'s completion, however, James issued a Declaration of Indulgence that rendered this particular poem superfluous. Dryden finished it anyway. The final version was printed simultaneously in London and at Holyrood House, a Roman Catholic press in Edinburgh; it subsequently raced through three editions. But Dryden's biographer Walter Scott put it mildly when he remarked that its "appearance [...] excited a clamour against the author far more general than the publication of *Absalom and Achitophel*."[12] Anglican writers found sitting ducks in Dryden's clumsy arguments for the infallibility of the church and the superior integrity of oral tradition, while secular poets and playwrights took potshots at the poem's ramshackle literary machinery. Even Catholic readers found little to be grateful for: "Some wonder what kind of Champion the Roman Catholics have now gotten," one critic remarked, "for they have had divers ways of representing themselves; but this of *Rhiming* us to death is altogether new and unheard of."[13] It is striking that both Protestants *and* Catholics were less exercised over Dryden's partisanship than over his literary infractions. This unlikely consensus guides our attention away from *The Hind and the Panther*'s literal claims (for toleration and, quietly, even for Catholic hegemony) and encourages us to see the poem instead in light of its symbolic aims.

The Hind and the Panther was also an awkward novelty from another point of view. Until 1687, Dryden's best-known theological work was *Religio Laici* (1682), a poem devoted to justifying the ways of an explicitly Anglican God to English readers. *The Hind and the Panther* renounces many of the positions that Dryden had taken up in the earlier piece. In particular, Dryden's Anglican theodicy confirms Scripture's authority as the bearer of God's word, and thus endorses writing itself as a plausible medium of revelation.[14] In *Religio Laici* the Bible "speaks no less than God in ev'ry line" (line 153), faith is confirmed "by reading that which better thou hast read" (line 237), and the competing interpretations that threaten to undermine all written language actually clarify "the Book" that, "oppress'd without and undermin'd within,/[...]" thrives through pain, its own tormentors tires" (lines 161–162). By contrast, *The Hind and the Panther* appears to revoke the bibliophilic argument of the former poem. The Hind, Dryden's evident heroine, insists on the superior integrity of unwritten traditions and crafts a horrific image of exegesis in the figure of Protestant "chiefs" like Luther and Calvin, who "like wild horses sev'ral ways have whirl'd/The tortur'd Text about the Christian world" (II: 120–121). The later trope for the "Text" contradicts the earlier one not only in underlying religious conviction but also in its anxiety about the status of written language, and thus about the security of literary authority itself. No trivial about-face for a poet.

Together, these two side effects of Dryden's conversion – a new political marginality and a new take on the text – may have tempted him to experiment with fables. Readers have long linked Dryden's conversion with his attraction to Aesop. Annabel Patterson, for example, treats the fables in *The Hind and the Panther* as a "structural solution," inherited through Spenser, to the "ethical ambiguities" of a Catholic monarchy. David Bywaters interprets Dryden's retreat into the fable form as an attempt to identify himself with a "classic poet in a great tradition," and thereby, if ironically, to dissociate himself from the political consequences of his religious decision. Steven Zwicker sees Aesopian style as a self-protective enigma demanded by a hostile political climate. James Winn similarly conjectures that fear made Dryden appreciate the "slight ironic distance characteristic of the beast fable tradition from Aesop on," although Dryden thereby "risked seeming to trivialize conflicts that mattered deeply to his contemporaries and him."[15] Those contemporaries had their own theories about Dryden's stylistic choice: in 1690 Tom Brown decided that many tenets of Catholicism – the miracle of transubstantiation, for example – belonged in the fabulous realm of logical contradiction and romance.[16] "[Dryden's] Brains indeed have been a long time us'd to *Chimeras*, the Raptures and *Visions of Poetry*, gaudy Schemes, unaccountable Flights of Nonsense and Absurdities," Nathan Clifford scoffed. "Consequently, he may have a good Head for the believing of Legends" like the Catholic faith itself.[17]

As Judith Sloman suggested, Dryden may also have turned to Aesop when he turned to Rome because Aesop's fables themselves had Catholic ties.[18] Versified by Aphra Behn – herself a convert – Francis Barlow's 1687 *Aesop's Fables, with his Life* has been called the "Catholic Aesop," while Aesop's chief biographer, we saw, was for centuries the "monkish" Maximus Planudes; in the 1690s, the "Popish" Roger L'Estrange would become his leading editor. We could speculate that fables provided a viable, because coded, language of protest in the perilous political climate of late seventeenth-century England. It is also true, however, that collections like Behn's and L'Estrange's catered to a cultural obsession with the material and political foundations of literary authority. We saw that by performing their own signifying assumptions in graphic space, fables supplied a figurative language uniquely suitable to a modern England desperately in need of material signs that can mediate reactively between opposing sides. Augustan fables achieved their meanings neither referentially nor cryptically but rather by making the page animate and dramatic. The resulting symbolic structure was self-consciously involved with even the most brutal of human transactions, and for that reason was resigned to the likelihood of its own violation.

Far from mysterious, these Aesopian qualities are relevant to Dryden's new political vulnerability as well as to the tremulous vision of textual authority embedded in the Hind's image of the "tortur'd Text." In his "Address to the Reader," Dryden actually defines fables not as remote and esoteric symbols but rather as tokens in a "free and familiar exchange."[19] In the poem itself, the exchange is between "two kinds whose natures disagree" (III:901) about everything except the value of fables. As Sloman remarked, *The Hind and the Panther* is "Dryden's most important poem about language."[20] Through Aesop, I suggest, Dryden seeks a linguistic solution to the problem of how to produce a written text that, if it fails to fend off a truculent and divided society, might at least put its own incoherence – its susceptibility to inversion and rearrangement – to good use.

Formal coherence, at least, was evidently never one of Dryden's intentions. In his prefatory remarks, Dryden promises that in the poem to come "raise[d]," "Majestick" and "Magnificen[t]" verses will alternate with "familiar" and "plain" language, "Heroick Poesie," with "plain" disputation and "the Common Places of Satyr" (p. 122). The Aesopian "Episodes" of the third part only emphasize the found, composite nature of the whole, for these are "interwoven with the main Design, so that they are properly Parts of it, though they are also distinct stories of themselves." More, Dryden ventured to "hope that no *Reader* of either Party will be scandalized; because [the fables] are not of my Invention: but rather old to my knowledge, as the Times of *Boccace* and *Chawcer*."

Dryden's edgy awareness of the partisan, and easily scandalized, reader here suggests a rationale for his poem's piecemeal character. His address's opening lines also cast *The Hind and the Panther* as a verbal performance anxious not to be treated as a modern text:

The Nation is in too high a Ferment for me to expect either fair war or even so much as fair quarter from a Reader of the opposite Party. All Men are engag'd either on this side or that, and tho'' Conscience is the common Word which is given by both, yet if a Writer fall among Enemies, and cannot give the Marks of *Their* Conscience, he is knock'd down before the Reasons of his own are heard. A *Preface*, therefore, which is but a bespeaking of Favour, is altogether useless. What I desire the *Reader* should know concerning me he will find in the Body of the Poem, if he have but the patience to peruse it.   (p. 119)

Finding traditional referential strategies (for example, "a bespeaking of Favour") altogether "useless," and an ordinary display of "Marks" foolhardy in a nation embroiled in "Party" politics, Dryden hides authority in "the Body of the Poem." That body in turn will reward only certain kinds of reading. Dryden is determined not to meet modern textual expectations; his poem demands "perus[al]" (use) instead of rapacious scrutiny; it presents itself as a lively performance instead of as a stiffened concatenation of decipherable "Marks."

Dryden's first readers obligingly did treat his poem as a physical "Body," a spontaneously regenerating surrogate for the author's own. One predicted that "Grocers and Haberdashers [...] will bind up their rotten *Raisons* and *Mundungus* in his Papers; and [...] his works shall be bound up, as his Forefather William Prynne's were in Trunks, Hat-cases, and Bandboxes.[21] Another was happy to interpret it as ritual performance: "An Altar up he rears," declared *The Revenger* (1687):

> Poetic Fires, and sharpen'd Knives prepares,
> Renews the Ancient Laws of Sacrifice,
> And for the Slaughter Victims new Supplies,
> To these the *Panther* add, the *Wolf* and *Boar*;
> The Sacrificing Age had ne'er such gore,
> A wondrous Holocaust. [...]
> For by his Medley Offerings now we find,
> Which was the idol of his ravenous Mind.[22]

Its "Medley" quality aligned Dryden's "wondrous Holocaust" with gesture, not with letters. And this very textual dramaturgy invited even hostile readers to enter the dramatic world of the poem, where they might rearrange its miscellaneous contents as they saw fit. For instance, while one victim of its "*Satyr*," Gilbert Burnet, understandably decided that the long "Conversation that [Dryden] had set between the *Hinds* and the *Panthers*" was "the worst poem [...] that the Age has produced,"[23] others imagined that it would have made a better play: "By changing some Lines, and bringing a few People talking in the way of Dialogue," speculated Nathan Clifford, "this very Poem may serve for a Play, as *smiling* and *frowning* are performed in the Face with the same Muscles and very little Altered." Indeed, Clifford continued,

Such hath always been [Dryden's] Dramatical and Scenical Way of Scribling that there was no Post nor Pillar in the Town exempt from the pasting up of the Titles of his Plays; Insomuch that the Foot-boys, for want of Skill in Reading, do now bring away by Mistake, the Title of a new Book against the *Church of England* instead of taking down the *Play* for the Afternoon.[24]

This alliance between the Aesopian "Book" and a "Dramatical and Scenical Way of Scribling" had some precedent in Dryden's own work, for in 1685 he had classified his play *Albion and Albanius* as an "*Æsop*'s fable shown today."[25]

The printed "Aesop's fable" of 1687 itself inspired more than one play, or satiric dialogue, including Charles Montague and Matthew Prior's notorious parody, *The Hind and the Panther Transvers'd* (1687). Like *The Revenger* (a "Trage-Comedy Acted between the Hind and Panther and Religio Laici") the sketch stages the fatal encounter between a page and its consumer. It transposes elements of *The Hind and the Panther* to Horace's fable of the country mouse and the city mouse, bits of which are read aloud by a proud "Bayes." As the two mice debate the merits of a bottle of wine (one defers to tradition, the other to his taste buds), *The Hind and the Panther Transvers'd* mocks the parent poem. It also corporealizes the way that written signs respond to critical interpretation. Thus it shares *The Hind and the Panther*'s dramatic consciousness of its own incongruous, particulated style. Dryden's Aesopian anticipation that his poem would not be kindly received nonetheless compelled his detractors to respond in kindred, Aesopian spirit.

We saw that Aesop's fables were surviving in Dryden's England precisely because they could be "transvers'd" without losing their convincing liveliness. This is what made it possible for writers to maintain, through them, at least a plausible fiction of literary authority, and it is what in turn promised to coordinate symbolic practice amid the figural fragmentation, that followed the English Civil Wars. Just as it would have negotiated among the "factious rabble" waiting to read Dryden's poem, so would the Aesopian model of textual performance have appealed to a distinctively Roman Catholic theory of textual representation. Roman Catholicism was often associated with non-verbal sign systems and with non-textual institutions (the church) headed by infallible authorities and sustained through mystical tradition rather than through free and open interpretation.

These associations are what potentially alienated the Catholic Dryden from the Protestant – irrefragibly textual – signifying conventions of his own day. His predicament corresponds to one that critics have been quicker to recognize – to the vexed relationship to figurative language engendered in the poet by Catholic commitment to the literal, as exemplified in the doctrine of Real Presence. But rather than abandon textual representation altogether, some Catholic writers showed how writing might signify other than metaphorically or referentially. For instance, Jacques Bossuet's *Exposition and Doctrine of the Catholic Church* (1672) aimed to defend the dramaturgical and imagistic elements of Catholic ritual. These included the "religious offic[e]" in which the pious "bow their heads before the bookes of the Gospell when they stand up in respect as they pass by them, and kisse them reverently."[26] In Bossuet a text ("the Gospell") can be performative and non-referential, an "Instrument" that directs attention to – "expose[s]" – an "Eternall Verity." Similarly, Dominique Bouhours's *Life of Saint Francis Xavier* (which Dryden translated in 1688) uses St. Francis's letters as the basis of its "Narration," which they render "more lively and moving, [...] mixing [Francis's] own Thoughts and Reflections with his Actions."[27]

Just as the textual skepticism of Catholic scholars in France motivated Richard Bentley's Aesopian researches in the 1690s, so Dryden's Roman Catholic contemporaries forged the myth of the performative text that is rehearsed in the three most Aesopian aspects of Dryden's long poem of the late 1680s. As we examine each of these aspects, we will see that throughout *The Hind and the Panther* Dryden underwrites his own principles of "free and familiar exchange" with the possibility of inversion. Yet it is by peopling the pages of his poem with figures whose capacity for reactive mediation renders them uniquely concrete that Dryden infuses the entire piece with authorial presence. He thereby reclaims a plausible fiction of literary authority, albeit one ironically predicated on its own surrender.

"Peopl'd Caledon"

For a fable, *The Hind and the Panther* is remarkably short on plot. The "First Part" of the poem begins at dusk, with Dryden's Roman Catholic Hind "view[ing]" her "martyr'd offspring" as they lie "extended o'er the *Caledonian* wood" (1:14); it ends at a "common wat'ring place," with the Hind herself set "full in view" before the other animals who live in the wood and who have been ordered by the "sovereign Lion" to share the "neighb'ring flood" with her. In the "Second Part," the Hind and an Anglican panther take an evening stroll and debate the finer points of their respective creeds, and in the third the two share a "Lenten sallad" in the Hind's cottage, then tell Aesopian fables until dawn. The inset fables themselves are tightly plotted, teeming with conflict, catastrophe, and political intrigue. But, while it might observe the unities, the larger poem is a mighty maze of nervous, and often improbable, symbolic exchanges. As Prior pointed out, for example, "a Hind who is so quaint and innocent a Beast would not in all Probability be delighted with the Conversation of so fierce and cruel a Creature as a Panther."[28] Nor, one imagines, are hares likely to house with bears, or foxes with wolves.

There is also the question of just what kind of signs these hares, bears, foxes, and wolves actually are. While Dryden's beasts have emblematic and allegorical characteristics, in other words, neither of these symbolic modes holds throughout the whole poem. Nor does the Caledonian wood consistently invoke another text that could coordinate its references, as the Old Testament story of Absalom and Achitophel did Dryden's poem of that name. From time to time, *The Hind and the Panther* resorts to typology, as when the tribulations of the Hind's offspring are likened to those of a "Captive Israel multiply'd in chains." But such figures are never sustained. Instead they must come to terms with other, different figural strategies that share the wood with them. Whereas, to borrow Alan Roper's terms, earlier poems like

Absalom and Achitophel or *The Medall* devise "paradigms" that stabilize the relationship between "internal and external references," in *The Hind and the Panther* the paradigms have ceased to be reliable. Here, a new textual self-consciousness converts what were once self-sustaining symbolic kingdoms into contiguous material "estates," each forced to take the others into account.[29]

This, however, is just what led Dryden to classify his "*Caledonian* wood" as an Aesopian setting. Anticipating the "malice" that will "censure" his muse for having "peopl'd *Caledon*/With *Panthers*, *Bears*, and *Wolves* unknown," Dryden decides to "let *Aesop* answer, who has set to view/Such kinds as *Greece* and *Phrygia* never knew" (III: 6–7). Anyone who finds *The Hind and the Panther* incongruous, in other words, should "view" it in light of Aesopian convention, in terms of what it shows to be true about signification. Dryden's "*Caledon*" bears a striking resemblance to the "vast Woods" that housed John Ogilby's *Fables* – whose powerful influence Earl Miner has suggested. A political jungle, the Caledonian wood is also a kind of amphitheater where the behavior of signs is prominently displayed.[30] Dryden's "*Panthers*, *Bears*, and *Wolves*" are all poised to spring and "devour." What holds them back is a Hobbesian arrangement in which they have conceded authority to the lion: "The common Hunt [is] from their rage restrain'd/By sov'reign pow'r" (I: 27–28).

In Dryden's wood, "sov'reign pow'r" is symbolic but not necessarily linguistic. Usually the lion "restrain[s]" by imitating the inclusive gesture of an Adam "kneaded up with milk" and eager to embrace "th'inferior family of Heav'n." Sometimes he "awfully forbids the prey" with his deafening roar: "Much is [his subjects'] hunger, but their fear is more" (I: 307).[31] These non-verbal checks barely hold. As they gather around the Hind, the lion's restive subjects cast "glares of secret enmity": "Scarce, and but scarce, from inborn rage restrain'd/[They] frisk'd about her and old kindred feign'd" (I: 545–546). Such antic artifice assures us that the surest foundation of Dryden's poem is the anxious production, scrutiny, and exchange of visible signs in a Hobbesian context.

As a literary convention, the Caledonian wood translates this structural foundation into linguistic terms. Inherited from Aesop, Dryden's volatile and heterogeneous Caledon allows its occupants to experience a continuity they do not know in relation to one another. For it places them in a tradition *of* representing the turbulent and divisive politics of representation in graphic space. The inhabitants of the wood are themselves each known by "family," "race," "lineage" – by the symbolic and interpretive categories that convey them through space and time. The "*Quaking Hare*" is defined by her place "among the timorous *kind*" (I: 85), the Socinian fox according to his in an "impious race." "The *Bear* [and] the *Boar*" are "salvage name[s]," and the Presbyterian wolf is sinister because he belongs to no single genetic line: "Some authours thus his pedigree will trace,/But others write him of an upstart race" (I: 174–177). Likewise, as Albert Cacicedo has suggested, Dryden's animals" mode of meaning is primarily "tropological." Their referents are less this sect or that one than the ways in which signs have been used, the conventions to which they belong.[32] Each animal engages in a specific kind of symbolic "transact[ion]" and eventually becomes, itself, a reliable sign of that mode. The Baptist Bear "in groans her hate express'd"; the Quaker Hare "profess'd neutrality, but would not swear"; the atheist Ape "mimick'd all sects" and "when the Lion look'd, his knees he bent,/And pay'd at Church a courtier's compliment." The Boar "betray[s] his guilt with broken tusks and borrow'd name" (I: 36, 38, 40–41).

If the inhabitants of Dryden's Caledon are characterized, aesopically, by the way they are known – by visible tokens of membership to a class, and by their symbolic gestures toward each other – then all signs are fundamentally equal. For all are defined contingently, according to the way they are used, in a particular historical and material setting. Montagu and Prior complained that Dryden's determination to deal in a family of signs (where the sign "wolf," for example, counts the same as the sign "Wickliff") threatened to make his poem illegible. A proper neoclassical fable, they maintained, should

never tell you that the Dog which snaps at a Shadow, lost his Troops of Horse, that would be unintelligible; a Piece of Flesh is proper for him to drop and the Reader will apply it to Mankind; they would not say that the Daw that was so proud of her borrow'd Plumes lookt very ridiculous when Rodriquez came and took away all the Book but the 17th, 24th, and 28th Chapters, which she stole from him.[33]

Objecting to this same equal valuation of signifier and signified, Tom Brown proposed to "sacrifice [Dryden's] Hind and the Panther, to the Memory of Mr. Quarles and John Bunyan." As an emblematist and an allegorist respectively, both Quarles and Bunyan wrote in ways that posit a distance – and with it a strict and hierarchical correspondence – between signs and what they signify.[34]

By rendering signifier and signified interchangeable, *The Hind and the Panther* seemed to defy Aesopian convention. But objections like Brown's, and Montagu and Prior's, make us wonder if the poem did not actually illuminate that convention, exaggerating almost *ad absurdum* the desire for mediation among opposing sides, and among different symbolic practices, that, we recall, typically motivated fables in the first place. Thinking both of Aesop and of Spenser's "Mother *Hubbard* in her homely dress," Dryden demanded:

> Led by those great Examples, may not I
> The wanted organs of their words supply?
> If men transact like brutes 'tis equal then
> For brutes to claim the privilege of men.   (III: 12–15)

Just as Ogilby's Aesopian "Examples" promised to "make Men lesser Beasts," human behavior licenses breaches of figural decorum in the Caledonian wood. The point is not just the satirical one that people are more like animals than they would like to admit. Dryden's statement of intent also holds particular figural implications. In the transactional world of "peopl'd *Caledon*," the relationship between a given animal and the human being or institution that it figures is horizontal and insecure rather than vertical and predictable. Conveying this relationship requires tropes equally involved in the figural and the literal.

Enter Aesop's fables. While other tropes – analogy, emblem, typology, metaphor – never hold up in *The Hind and the Panther*, those, like fables, which register the changing, prolific, and heterogeneous field of their application find a happier fate. In the first part of *The Hind and the Panther*, Dryden twice uses Aesopian fables, as figures of speech and as ways to anchor such figures in political history. Both of the fables portray the Panther's dependence on the Lion, and in the first Dryden remarks parenthetically that "Before the sounding ax so falls the Vine/Whose tender branches round the Poplar twine" (I: 439–440). As Miner has pointed out, the image combines two of Ogilby's fables – "The Husband-man and the Wood" and "The Gourd and the Pine." Its immediate points of application are, on the one hand, the figural world of Dryden's own poem, and, on the other, the England of the late 1680s. The fable makes these two referents interchangeable, just as it levels the image of a present excess of dependency with that of future catastrophe.

Similarly, noting the relative ease that the Church of England has enjoyed since the Restoration, but also its susceptibility to the persuasions of other sects, Dryden compares the Panther to creatures who, "resolv'd into a baser form," "bore the wind but cannot bear the sun" (I: 446–447). In the fable of the sun and the wind, the two vie to force a traveler to remove his coat. The fable provides a figure that can travel back and forth between English history and fiction, not only displaying a point of connection between them but also rendering the one as pliable to the poet's authority as the other. Dryden's readers would have considered him the author of neither of these fables, which had appeared with adorning sculptures in Ogilby's collection, and also in Barlow's *Æsop's Fables*, the second edition of which appeared the same year as *The Hind and the Panther*. In both cases, the morals were rather different. For Ogilby, for instance, the point of the fable "of the Sun and Wind" is linguistic: "Loud Threatnings make men stubborn, but kind Words/Pierce gentle Breasts sooner than sharper Words."[35] Because, as Montague and Prior complained, they claim no natural moral, the fables do not really function as images that the author plies with deeper meanings. Rather they offer points of transaction between fictional "brutes" and historical "men," which the author strategically arranges. Borrowing Dryden's own metaphor, we might regard the inset fables as symbolic nodes in the ungainly "Body of the Poem." They coordinate its various parts by performing in demonstrative miniature the locally disruptive but ultimately oddly harmonizing figural procedures responsible for the whole.

The Hind and the Panther

If Dryden's "peopl'd *Caledon*" modulates superficial discrepancies and rein-states the poet's literary authority by making symbolic action visible, what about the Hind and the Panther themselves? As Prior maintained, their "Conversation" is the least probable aspect of the entire poem, but the two beasts also focus the questions about the nature of linguistic authority that present themselves the moment we agree to read the Caledonian wood as an image of symbolic accommodation. Interpreted allegorically, as emblems of the Roman Catholic and the Anglican Church, the Hind and the Panther register two kinds of linguistic authority in crisis – the Hind its untranslat-ability when it is concentrated in unwritten flesh, and the "Lady of the spotted Muff" its fragmentability when it is distributed through the graphic system of differences that is writing. Construed as Aesopian characters, however – as active emissaries *of* these crises who are forced to cultivate common ground – the Hind and the Panther together show how signs can regain authority, immediacy, and even integrity in a diverse and belligerent modernity.[36]

To seventeenth-century readers, the connection between a hind and the Roman Catholic Church, or between a panther and the Anglican one, seemed arbitrary. As Prior put it, even in fables, "the Beasts who speak should have reference to the Characters of the Persons they represent. [...] Now by his two Beasts, how can we understand the Two Creatures? The C. of R. is no more like a Hind than an Elephant, & the Rhinoceros is as good a representation of the C. of E. as the Panther."[37] Even those who grudgingly accepted Dryden's "representation[s]" found inconsistencies within them. *A Poem in Defence of the Church of England* wondered "Who ever read in Earnest or in Jest/Of any white unchang'd immortal Beast?/Or of an harmless Hind that knew no Fear,/Yet fled when Hunters and the Hounds drew near?"[38] Like the "chop'd and chang'd" Panther who equivocates her way through his long poem, Dryden's fugitive and yet fearless Hind betrays high critical expectations that "the Characters" in a fable will be "the same throughout, not broken or chang'd, and always conformable to the Nature of the Creatures they introduce."[39] But such failures of conformity do spark consciousness of where standards of literary propriety originate to begin with. Prior's insinuation that *The Hind and the Panther* might as well have been called *The Elephant and the Rhinoceros*, for instance, shows that, by frustrating probable analogy, the Hind and the Panther provoked a skeptical recognition of the imposed or arbitrary nature of all tropes and literary conventions, analogy and probability included.

Readers of our own age, meanwhile, have been perplexed less by the "broken" logic of Dryden's "representations" than by the puzzle of their literary ancestry. Modern scholars seek symbolic precedents in zoographies, in scripture and in emblem books, even in the deer who grazed near Dryden's home in 1687.[40] While such genealogies can be captivating, they never quite teach us how to interpret the Hind and the Panther. Really, the animals" own bodies offer broader clues as to what we ought to make of them. Likened to "one solid shining Diamond,/Not sparkles shatter'd into sects," the "milk-white" Hind is ancient, pure, and absolute. The Panther, on the other hand, is a mixed bag, a "creature of a double kind," who is "too black for Heav'n and yet too white for Hell" (I: 343). "A Mule made up of diff'ring Seed," she can assume the traits of other animals, particularly that of the "blatant beast" (the wolf), at a moment's notice. Her "house [is] not ancient" and she herself is a pleasure-seeker charmed by novelty; she's first drawn to the Hind because she wants someone to help her "beguile the tedious walk." To the extent that she stands for a "C. of E." founded on Henry VIII's willful infidelities the century before (the "schism of beds" [III: 205] and the betrayal of "the pure queen Catherine"), the Panther's origins lie in political exigency and erotic impulse. Thus while the "milk-white Hind" is a "Matron," a nearly prehistoric point of origin, this "second-best mother" (I: 451) is foremost a guilty consort, "undaunted as an Indian wife." Like the Aesopian vine, she twines around the sovereign tree, perpetually "bound to the fate of murder'd monarchy." In contrast to the Hind's innate authority, the Panther's significance comes from contiguity. "Rul'd while she rules," she is finally nothing but "a part submitted to the whole." Her power is contingent and precarious.

In the midsection of Dryden's poem, the Hind and the Panther confirm their differences through a doctrinal debate clothed in the garb of a "plain and perspicuous" conversation. The conversation, in turn, reminds us that their differences are fundamentally discursive. It also casts the two institutions that they represent as competing forms of authority, rival modes of symbolic transmission through space and time. Most simply, the Catholic Hind seems to stand for oral tradition and the Anglican Panther for its written counterpart. The Hind's "immortal and unchang'd" (I: 1) body, her rapid transit through air and her tendency to evade the fixing gaze of the other animals all identify her own body with the discursive forms that she idealizes in her nostalgic evocation of a world "e'er the written word appear'd" (II: 322). In that world, knowledge is perpetuated orally and through practical example by Apostles who "writ but seldome, [though] they daily taught" (II: 342). Meaning itself comes of action and performative tradition: "Clearness by frequent preaching must be taught." Symbolic transmission – the handing down of an original interpretation through the ages – is linear and hierarchical; though the Hind herself is female, it is also patriarchal, flowing from the first "Fathers" and thence from "sire to son." Physical continuities between successive generations make "plain proofs" and "clearness" attainable ideals.

The Hind defies the boundaries that would divide signs from their referents, and their donors from their recipients. Slipping from place to place like a white shadow, she embraces a doctrine that "spread[s]" everywhere and "is everywhere the same," unimpeded by cultural, historical, or linguistic boundaries. She is uninterpretable from any perspective that expects signs to behave as discrete tokens coined to meet the crises of a particular historical moment. The animals who gather around her at the stream, for example, fail to recognize her as the "ten-horned monster [...] such as the Wolf and Panther had design'd" – as a rhetorical invention. Indecipherable, the Hind disturbs the occupants of the Caledonian Wood. At the same time, her illegible mystery also jeopardizes her authority, for it threatens to put her beyond the reach of Dryden's own text, immersed as it is, perforce, in a world permeated with Protestant habits of representation and textual protocols.

On the other hand, the Panther's "chop'd and chang'd" body and "spotted Muff" link her with writing – with individual graphic signs, each arranged in visual space and all therefore vulnerable to the abusive and conflicting interpretations that exploit the written word's estrangement from what it signifies. One of Dryden's sources, Edward Topsell's *History of Foure-Footed Beasts and Serpents* (known to Dryden in an edition of 1658), failed even to offer a single name for the panther, classifying it as "the Panther, commonly called a Pardall, a Leopard, and a Libbard."[41] The "many names devised for this one beast" show how "the greatest variance hath arisen from wordes." In Dryden's own text, variance spells conflict. Because of her endless equivocations and willingness to grant writing supreme cultural authority, no questions asked, the Panther perpetuates a culture fraught by "jarring Sects," one in which "Civil War" is waged through "squadrons" of written matter. No wonder her own body betrays such a moribund delicacy: "The dew-drops on her silken hide/Her tender constitution did declare/Too lady-like a long fatigue to bear" (II: 685–687).

Ostensibly, Dryden's poem is on the Hind's side: but precisely to the extent that the Hind and the Panther represent different styles, and different crises, of symbolic authority, they eventually overlap. The two animals, that is, stand for different figural modes, and for different ways of reading; but they stand for these differences in the same way. In what Prior called Dryden's "new way of telling a Story," reading and figure, "the Moral and Story" merge.[42] For, as Dryden's poem's persistent emphasis on the way signs are "peruse[d]" so frequently reminds us, both creatures finally signify within a third convention – that of the animate text that mediates reactively between them.

Superficially, this arrangement often seems more congenial to the Panther than to the Hind: its foundation is mixture and compromise, and Dryden himself appears more interested in his cross-bred, and thoroughly modern, "Lady of the spotted muff" than in the ancient "Matron" who eventually "couch[es] securely by her side." But because Dryden depicts not only symbolic arrangements but also the ways in which they are used and construed, *The Hind and the Panther* emerges as a true compromise, one more important than a literal reconciliation between the churches in question. Aesop's fables figure this compromise in convincing miniature.

There are also broader compromises, of course. For example, the Hind and the Panther both first appear in Dryden's poem alone, but their later relations are mediated by a common code of civility. At the end of the "First Part," the Hind decides that the Panther is a "well-bred civil beast," and at the end of the second, she plays "friendly Hostess" to a "welcome Guest" who in turn "civily drew in her sharpen'd paws,/Not violating hospitable laws" (II: 718–719). The Hind and the Panther also have other things in common: their conversation, for example, is a fiction of orality actually contained in blocks of writing, each subject to inspection and inversion. The textual reality of the ostensibly spoken exchange grows all the more pronounced as the Hind and the Panther move from doctrinal "point" to doctrinal "point."[43] Near the end of the "Second Part," the Hind embarks on a long summary of the "Marks" whereby the Roman Catholic Church may be known and recognized. Her summary is physically bordered by marginalia that marks it as a digest of the "*Marks of the Catholick Church from the Nicene Creed.*" And, blending oral and literate signification, she praises

> The Gospel-sound diffus'd from Pole to Pole,
> Where winds can carry, and where waves can roll,
> The self-same doctrine of the sacred page,
> Convey'd to ev'ry clime in ev'ry age.   (II: 552–555)

In this warily conciliatory atmosphere, only Aesop's fables can emerge as appropriate figures of speech, for only they actively exemplify the figural compromises that make exchange between the Hind and the Panther possible. Structurally, the speaking animal pretense "set[s]" Dryden's method "to view" and integrates his poetic machinery – his conspicuously artificial animal signifiers – with the material conditions to which they refer – specifically a malicious, witty, and divisive England amply "stocked with monsters of [its] own." Just so, within the symbolic world that results, fables offer miniature images of a gigantic *rapprochement*, tendered by the Hind and the Panther themselves.

Early in the "Second Part," the Hind indulges in her first fable. Appropriately, the subject is semiology. The Hind charges the Panther with

"equivocat[ing]" about the meaning of the word "real" as it refers to the
presence of Christ's body in the Eucharist:

> [. . .] to explain what your forefather meant
> By real presence in the sacrament
> (After long fencing push'd, against a wall),
> Your *salvo* comes, that He's not there at all:
> There chang'd your faith and what may change may fall.   (II: 31–35)

The Panther defends herself with a maxim – "Tortures may force the tongue
untruths to tell" – to which the Hind rejoins that if this is indeed the case, as
it may be,

>   as you the matter state,
> Not onely *Jesuits* can equivocate;
> For "real" as you now the word expound,
> From solid substance dwindles to a sound.
> Methinks an *Aesop*'s fable you repeat:
> You know who took the shadow for the meat:
> Your Church's substance thus you change at will
> And yet retain your former figure still.   (II: 44–51)

At the most literal level of the poem, the Hind jabs at the Anglican creed,
classifying it as an investment in illusion by likening it to Aesop's graphic fable
of the dog who loses his shoulder of mutton when he snaps at its reflection.
But the allusion works as more than an analogy. It also provides a point of
exchange between two symbolic actions: a verbal act – equivocation about
the meanings of words – "repeat[s]" the fable. What is more, just as in the
story the dog's bid for the image of the meat dramatizes one way of
responding to a sign, so in applying the same gesture to a doctrinal debate
the Hind animates that debate.

    As it happens, the Hind and the Panther are really quibbling over the kinds
of relationship that signs can have to their referents. Historically, the dispute
centered on the possibility of transubstantiation, which Roman Catholics took
as a literal fact and which Anglicans finally decided to understand
metaphorically. More specifically, it revolved around the nature of figurative
language; the underlying question was one of whether Christ's words ("This is
my body") could be taken literally. Finally, the question is whether or not
"the Church" that the Panther represents, and which had first agreed with
the Roman Catholic position, can "change at will,/And yet retain [its] former
figure still" – whether or not authority, such as we might grant to the Christ
of the *hoc est*, requires a stable sign system in order to survive.

    If the Hind's subject is a set of unresolved questions about the relationship
between authority and figural change, then her choice of persuasive tropes is
extremely limited. Essentially, she needs to find one that can remain
unresolved but still plausibly bridge the literal and the metaphorical. As her

assumption that the Panther "know[s] who took the figure for the meat" suggests, "*Æsop*'s fable" supplies just such a figure. Both the Hind *and* the Panther "repeat" the story, and they do so in ways that combine language and gesture. The Hind repeats the fable verbally as a rhetorical device whose plot materially links it to the symbolic issues at work in the debate; the Panther repeats its plot gesturally as she throws away substance for "shadow." The fable solders both kinds of symbolic action together. At the same time, however, it does so far more to the Hind's benefit than to the Panther's. The compromise it orchestrates allows the Hind – disenfranchised in the outside world of the wood – to put the Panther in her place.

We find a similar settlement cloaking a similar advantage to the Hind in the "Third Part" of Dryden's poem, when the Hind and the Panther return to the Hind's "poor abode" to share a "Lenten sallad." Fables fly thick and fast under the Hind's "lowly Roof." Some of them are thinly veiled insults. The Panther, for example, likens her hostess to the "gawdy fly" from Ogilby's Aesopian fable of "The Fly and the Ants": "You, like the gawdy fly, your wings display,/And sip the sweets, and bask in your Great Patron's day" (III: 66–67). As it imports a figure from another text, the Panther's fable actually respects the Hind's eagerness to "avoid [...] extreme debate." For while Ogilby's own margins declare the fly who jeers at the industrious ants an "Embleme of Idlenesse and Impertinence," his moral urges mediation between the two insects: "These are Extremes; upon the Medium fix."[44] Ogilby's fable in other words reinterprets conventional "Embleme[s]" as negotiable signs. It is in this revised form that the fly finds its way in to Dryden's poem, where the Panther tries to apply it one way (as a sinister emblem), but where its effect, as the Hind herself immediately perceives, is really to reveal the extreme resentments driving the Panther's own fictions:

> This heard, the Matron was not slow to find
> What sort of malady had seiz'd her mind;
> Disdain, with gnawing envy fell despight,
> And canker'd malice stood in open sight. (III: 68–71)

Eventually, the Aesopian fly exposes the very foundations of political order, showing the Panther's "new-made union with her ancient foes,/Her forc'd civilities." Though the fable preserves the delicate "civilities" that make exchange possible, it also pulls their "gnawing," "canker'd" roots up "in[to] open sight."

Building on the envy that the Panther's fable had revealed, the Hind then invokes the story of the wolf and the sheep:

> When at the fountain's head, as merit ought
> To claim the place, you take a swilling draught,
> How easy 'tis an envious eye to throw
> And tax the sheep for troubling streams below,

> Or call her (when no farther cause you find)
> An enemy profess'd of all your kind.
> But then, perhaps, the wicked world wou'd think
> The Wolf design'd to eat as well as drink.   (III: 123–130)

Since the Wolf himself lives in the Caledonian wood – where he even counsels the Panther – the Aesopian fable snips a piece out of the quasi-historical fabric of the whole and turns it into a figure. Reference to the wolf thus shows how figures are made, and *that* they are made through their finally negotiable application to a present, variable, and politically charged reality.

The Hind's fable itself turns on a simple homology, in which the Hind is to the Panther as the sheep is to the wolf.[45] In the fable, we know, the wolf prevails. But when Dryden finds a new field of application, the balance of power in the fable shifts. Ordinarily, the wolf's "envious eye" and his "tax[ing]" tongue are both the media and the emblems of his authority. But the Hind turns them into images of design and desire, and in doing so she replaces the wolf's authority with her own. Her exercise of authority differs from the lion's dispensations, and even from the crude authorial intervention that would tilt the Aesopian plot in favor of the harassed sheep. Rather, the Hind's authority lies in a conspicuous interpretation of visible signs of discernment and judgment (the taxing tongue and the envious eye). This kind of appropriation of Aesop's fable makes it uniquely efficacious, even painful: "This last allusion gall'd the *Panther* more,/Because indeed it rubb'd upon the sore" (III: 131–132). As it splices the literal and the figural, the Aesopian "allusion" draws the Panther into the world that the Hind has invented – a world no longer figurally distinguishable from that of the wood, which excludes her and which she did not invent. Aesop's fable lends Dryden's poem a point of mediation between the Hind and the Panther, and between the figural and the literal. "His" fable thus carries us into the "Third Part" of Dryden's poem – into a dynamic, revelatory, and reversible symbolic world that the Hind and the Panther can share.

Equal banquets and malicious wit

In *The Hind and the Panther Transvers'd*, "Mr. Bayes" is especially eager to show off the tail end of his masterpiece: "Here," he boasts with a flourish, "I give you *Fable* upon *Fable*; and after you are satisfied with Beasts in the first Course, serve you up a delicious Dish of Fowl for the Second."[46] The "Fowl" in question are of course the pigeons and swallows who figure so prominently in the fables that the Hind and the Panther exchange in the "Third Part" of Dryden's long poem. As they satirized the postprandial transaction, Montagu and Prior mocked the least probable piece of *The Hind and the Panther*: fabulous brutes making fables – and morals – indeed! But precisely by picturing

Dryden's readers as gourmands, their very eyes as hungry mouths, Montagu and Prior also preserved the bonds between eating and speaking, matter and abstracted meaning, that Dryden forges when he tells us that his storytellers' "Commons, tho but scarce, were nothing scant,/Nor did their minds an equal Banquet want" (III: 28–29).

His consciousness of signs' vulnerability led Dryden to expect malicious appropriations like *The Hind and the Panther Transvers'd*. Within *The Hind and the Panther* too the word "malice" aptly summarizes the environment in which fables acquire meaning. The fables' flagrant tendentiousness challenges the very fiction of "equal Banquet" that their mere existence promises to uphold.[47] The Hind easily "mark[s] the malice of [the Panther's] tale": "in malice it began in malice grows." Both she and the Panther surrender interpretive control over their stories: "Make you the moral and Ile tell the tale," the Panther archly invites (III: 426). Her own response to the Hind's fable is a yawn whose majestic and sinister indifference undermines the Hind's confident Aesopian forecast that her authority will one day end. Dryden's inset fables, then, are at once open-ended and tightly bounded by consciousness of the malicious and voracious context that gives all signs their meaning. The combination of liberty and restraint that so clearly makes them mean allows the fables to translate the linguistic assumptions that drive *The Hind and the Panther* as a whole into the most concrete of figural vocabularies.

Dryden's "Address to the Reader" stressed these fables' status as itinerant material signs. "As old [. . .] as the times of *Boccace* and *Chaucer*," they come from elsewhere. A more recent harbor is Ogilby's *Fables*, whose story of "The Parliament of Fowles" lends much to the Panther's fable of the Swallows, while the Hind's fable of the Pigeons owes something to Ogilby's "Of the Pigeons and the Hawks." Like Dryden's more incidental fables, these two embedded narratives demonstrate that figures derive meaning from a present, pressing, but temporary context. And they too mediate between two frames of reference, one (English history) literal and one (the Caledonian wood) already figural. In her story of the "council" of swallows whose leader, the "Martyn," deceives them into believing signs of a false spring, the Panther depicts the Catholic convocations with James that, led by Father Petre (the Martin), ended in the Declaration of Indulgence.[48] Likewise, the Hind's fable of the filthy pigeons who hire a buzzard to do away with their neighbors, the pious chickens, satirizes Anglican measures against English Catholics, as spearheaded by Gilbert Burnet.

Efforts to interpret the avian "Episodes" strictly as topical satires, however, do them only partial justice. For example, Earl Miner's excellent notes to both fables illuminate their correspondences to recent events up to a point, but are forced to admit that many such correspondences are "not clear," and "very difficult to interpret."[49] At the same time, within *The Hind and the Panther* itself, the Panther's fable does warn the Hind that her halcyon days

are numbered, and the Hind lets the Panther know that her persecutions are
self-destructive. Each of the fables may thus claim at least two applications,
one to historical figures and events, which it allegorizes, and one to an
inhabitant of Caledon, whom it "warn[s]." This constant and self-conscious
double reference gives the process of figuration itself material form. We read
the fables not in terms of what they represent by analogy but rather in terms
of what they say about the process, and politics, of representation.

The fables of the Swallows and the Pigeons have the status of historical
incidents with respect to the Caledonian Wood. The Panther's story of "the
Swallows" fortune" is, as the Hind recognizes, an account of what actually
"those pretty birds befell." What makes a fable a fable, then, is not its
fictiveness but rather its open ending and resulting vulnerability to interpretation. Both the Hind and the Panther recognize this at the outset, for when the
Hind, taking the bait of the Panther's sly allusion to "the Swallows" fortune,"
asks her to "tell/What sad mischance those pretty birds befell," the "savage
Dame" immediately corrects her: "Nay, no mischance [. . .]/But want of wit
in their unerring guide,/And eager haste and gaudy hopes and giddy pride"
(III: 421–423).

The Panther's cautionary tale copies the signifying style that is developed
in *The Hind and the Panther* as a whole. Like the larger poem, it brims with
individual, ambiguous signs whose interpretation will determine how things
will end for the birds in question. And like the "common Hunt" in the
Caledonian wood, the Swallows are defined in terms of relationship and
reputation: "Privileged above the rest/Of all the Birds as Man's familiar
Guest," "held of heav'nly line," they are also mysterious, ultimately knowable
only through traditions of inference. Seduced by long-lasting summer
weather, they let a martin "of little body" and "little learning" persuade
them not to fly south for the winter. The Martin, whose own character is
conspicuously conventional (he is "a dunce, as *Martyns* are by kind"), gains
power and influence by "casting schemes by planetary Guess." His tools are
symbolic ones – boding dreams, "sacred Story" and even "a leaf inscrib'd
with sacred rime/Whose antique characters did well denote/The *Sibyls* hand
of the *Cumaean* Grott" (III: 487–489). After the Martin persuades the swallows
to stay, they fall prey to natural time (freezing weather) and to natural law
("Crows" and Ravens" Rights"). Poor "Martin himself" is "caught alive and
tri'd/For treas'nous crimes, because the laws provide/No Martin there in
winter shall abide." The fable ends with the image of his "corps." Left
"hanging still,/To show the change of winds with his prophetick bill" (III:
637–638), the carcass acquires meaning in two registers at once, one natural
and one artificial, one literal and one figural.

The Panther means the Hind to take her story as a "timely warning," and
even though so much of that story is about how signs can be manipulated to
further artificial "schemes," she herself tries to subordinate all of its characters

and events to natural authority. Her plot, she pretends, is governed – and thus its end is decided – by the change of seasons, by the natural revolution of time. The Hind, though, sees that it is a malicious and deliberate arrangement of telling signs rather than the march of time that makes all of the miniature emblems in the story register not what the Martin would have them foretell but rather what the Panther wants them to describe – Catholic folly. Once embodied in the text of *The Hind and the Panther*, her sharp discernment in turn makes these signs register what *Dryden* wants them to register – a more demanding theory of representation, a plea for a sign system that, because it can communicate its own contingencies, holds the possibility of transformation.

It is when the Hind accepts the Panther's invitation to "make [...] the moral" that the fable claims symbolic action as its real theme. The Hind's ability to mine so many evidently unintended morals out of the Panther's story does not signal interminable relativity. Instead, her moral converts the fable into a performative figure for the way in which and the conditions under which meanings are assigned to things:

> [W]ell she mark'd the malice of the tale,
> Which ribald art their Church to Luther owes;
> In malice it began, by malice grows;
> He sow'd the Serpent's teeth, an iron-harvest rose.
> But most in *Martyn*'s character and fate
> She saw her slander'd sons, the Panther's hate,
> The people's rage, the persecuting state.   (III: 639–646)

For the Hind, the Panther's fable not only reveals the Panther's motive ("hate"); it also dramatizes the behavior of signs from (Martin) Luther's "ribald art" forward. It displays the contingencies and self-interest that decide "character and fate."

This is the true moral of the story of "*Martyn*'s character and fate." The Martin's dangling "corps" marks the end of the Panther" fable; converted from a self-important body into a feathered weathervane, it also metamorphoses symbolically into a "prophetick" index of the "change of wind." The Panther then transforms the Martin into still another kind of sign, this time an index of the power of "laws" that "provide/No Martin there in winter shall abide" and thus of the wisdom of Catholic departure from England. But when her turn comes to interpret, the Hind remolds the Martin's body into still another kind of signifier – into a counter within political rhetoric: "in *Martyn*'s character and fate/She saw her slander'd sons, the Panther's hate,/The people's rage, the persecuting state" (III: 644–646) The Martin finally gains figural stability only by becoming a trope for how the fable works. Because of him, the Hind can claim that "through your parable I plainly see/

The bloody laws, the crowd's barbarity" (III: 657–658). And having seen as much, she counters with folk wisdom:

> I take th'advice in friendly part,
> You clear your conscience or at least your heart;
> Perhaps you fail'd in your foreseeing skill,
> For Swallows are unlucky birds to kill.   (III: 647–650)

The moral of the Panther's fable is that history is malleable, an amalgam of individual, transposable material signs. As both the Hind and the Panther stake their claims in the fable, this symbolic arrangement emerges as the foundation of a new cultural order. That order will endure as long as it can accommodate differences in a process of continual revision.

To preserve the "equal Banquet," the Hind thus offers a fable of her own in return. But just as the scene at the dinner table is as tense with "malice" as it is eager to find common ground, so the fable of the Pigeons shows how even a cultural order based on Aesopian figuration remains at risk. "A wholesome tale, tho" told in homely style," the fable of the Pigeons recounts a recent event, one now "sung in ev'ry Street,/The common chat of Gossips when they meet" (III: 902–903). Like *The Hind and the Panther* itself, this ostensibly homespun story asks "what concord there cou'd be/Betwixt [...] kinds whose natures disagree." Here the "kinds" are the pigeons and chickens who share a single barnyard under the auspices of a gentle farmer. "Bound by promise" (III: 952), their "Host" is a "plain good man" who is explicitly identified with literal uses of language. His "honest bluntness and "unsuspected plainness" (III: 928–929) carry some liability – he "look'd into Himself, and was deceiv'd" (III: 929) – but they also promise to moderate barnyard animosities.

The problem lies in the kinds of difference that the "plain good man" must actually reconcile. "By their high Crops and corny Gizzards known," the pigeons are ravenous parasites who "lodge in Habitations not their own" and who exist, evidently, only to feed off of their host's largesse, which they do incessantly, "repay[ing] their Commons with their Salt Manure" (III: 992). The farmer's "Domestick Poultry," by contrast, live "for his use," simply and piously. The two groups differ not only morphologically but, far more important, in social and symbolic deportment. The "happy Gluttons" begrudge the chickens even their "Modicum" of grain and water and plot to drive them out, from Chanticleer, the "Beast of a Bird" whose "miter'd Crest" declares him their leader, to "sister *Partlet* with her hooded Head." The Pigeons operate through art. They draw "an hideous Figure of their Foes," a "Grotesque design, expos'd to Publick view" that recalls first an "Ægyptian piece" and then a "Holland emblem." Next they "a deadly *Shibboleth* devise," requiring all who desire "Trust or Profit" to "swallow first a poysonous wicked Weed." Finally, fearful and envious of "th'encreasing race of Chanticleer," they cast about for a "Potent Bird of Prey" to rid them of their hated rivals.

In the Hind's story, it is the Pigeons who make new signs. The Chickens preserve old ones, as when Chanticleer, to the Pigeons' irritation, refuses to let the "Example" of crowing early "die" (III: 1016). By contrast, the Pigeons employ the Buzzard who, "call[ed . . .] but a Hawk by courtesy," rapaciously renovates the very elements of language. His followers sport B's on their chest, and he himself sends "loud praises to prepare his paths [. . .]/And then himself pursue the compliment" (III: 1158). In his own mouth, words are interchangeable – "Oft has he flatter'd and blasphem'd the same." All of these contrivances create cultural order and group identity – for example, when the "Ægyptian Piece" is put on display, "the daubing pleas'd, and Great and Small/To view the Monster crowded Pigeon-hall" (III: 1050–1051). But more subtly they also corrode the very cultural order that they pretend to support.

Apparently the solution to the problem of oppression lies in the patron's generous decision to "mak[e] all Birds of ev'ry sect/Free of his Farm, with promise to respect/The sev'ral Kinds alike, and equally protect" (III: 1245–1246) An obvious, if outdated, hint to James, the declaration of indulgence gives birth to a new culture. Here "Arts and Wealth succeed," and the Pigeons, "Smiths of their own Foolish Fate," decline. "Sunk in credit, they decreas[e] in Pow'r" and finally most of them, "like Snows in warmth that mildly pass away,/Dissolv[e] in the Silence of Decay" (III: 1271–1272). The few survivors drop into the Buzzard's beak, and the fable ends with the image of the "Tyrant" who "smiles below and waits the falling feast."

The Hind's "wholesome tale" seems to seek alliance with the plain good man's unadorned language rather than with the wickedly artful symbols that the Pigeons manipulate. But in fact it combines elements of both of these symbolic domains: its "style" might be "homely" but the future it predicts for the Pigeons – not to speak of its depiction of them – is decidedly malicious. As a story with origins in "the Times of *Boccace* and *Chawcer*," the fable dips into the Chickens' antique sign system as well. It negotiates among three symbolic possibilities, finally offering a fourth alternative, and with it a figural compromise more authoritative even than the plainspoken language of indulgence. Indeed, the fable subsumes and regulates the plain good language of indulgence, and thereby qualifies its own insinuation that such a language can make all right: it would seem that the more canny language of fable has a better chance of doing so.

But the Hind's fable needs a moral to seal its symbolic authority – to transport it into the realm of lively historical experience to which it seeks application. It receives none, for the Panther responds with a yawn. Withholding words, she declines to participate in the symbolic order that the Hind wants to perpetuate:

> Thus did the gentle *Hind* her fable end,
> Nor would the Panther blame it, nor commend;

> But with affected Yawnings at the close,
> Seem'd to require her natural repose.   (III: 1289–1292)

The fable ends in artifice ("affect[ation]," "seem[ing]") and fear. It ends in silence. And this silence heralds the conclusion not just of the Hind's fable but of Dryden's as well.[50] The end of the poem is ambiguous. The Panther's yawn looks past the irenic traffic of fables to the state of nature that threatens always to disrupt it. But the Hind bids her good night and turns to her own "glorious visions of her future state." The visions are not specified; the Hind looks toward the future as to a text that promises to be a better version of the past, though built of its same elements. Only the poem's abrupt and unmoralized ending confesses that it is not necessarily so.

The fact that Dryden's beast fable apprehends the failure of fables returns us to contemporary complaints about *The Hind and the Panther* – chiefly those, like Montague and Prior's, that accused it of a "monstrous" failure of compliance with the rules of the fable form. Dryden's unwieldy poem does test those rules to the limit, but its momentary sacrifices and dizzying retrievals of symbolic authority remind us that it always does so in indisputably Aesopian terms. Which is why *The Hind and the Panther* was not Dryden's last Aesopian outing.

Ancient and modern fables

Thirteen years after the publication of "The Hind and the Panther," and now nearing the end of his life, Dryden gave his remarkable collection of translations and original poems, *Fables, Ancient and Modern* (1700), a title that linked it to Aesop, and he placed near its center the Aesopian saga of a single-minded fox and the rather bohemian cock who outwits him.[51] This fable functions in the later work much as fables do in the earlier and far less beloved one, for it actively exemplifies the figural assumptions that drive *Fables, Ancient and Modern* as a whole. This is an easier task than it was in 1687. For in *Fables*, gaps, discontinuities, and even mistranslations are necessarily – and explicitly – part of the way that new shapes are conceived and new significances emerge. "Nothing can," as Dryden puts it, "continue in the Figure it began."[52]

As the volume's title recalls, fables reconcile different (ancient and modern) literary conventions. Its contents are eighteen translations (from tales of Ovid, Homer, Chaucer, and Boccaccio) and two "Original Papers of my own." Together, these pieces exemplify the last stage of Dryden's poetic career. Dominated by translations of classical and medieval texts, this phase has only just begun to be explored in the vital context of the "poetics of translation."[53] Such "poetics" assume that language's value lies less in its purity than in its resilience, its capacity to be changed by other languages, and by historical, political and cultural circumstance. Dryden's own theoretical remarks on translation articulate precisely this linguistic sense and apply it specifically to literate culture. The prefaces to his 1685 collection of translations (eventually titled *Sylvae*), to the *Æneis* (1697), and to *Fables, Ancient and Modern* (1700) all suggest that the act of translation was a direct encounter with the materiality and particularity of language. It forced Dryden to embrace words' vulnerability to the "process of Time." Thus, just as his late translations find purpose and authority as practical "renovation[s] of Words," so Dryden's late prefaces declare that "Words are not like Landmarks, so sacred as never to be remov'd: customs are chang'd, and even statutes are silently repeal'd, when the reason ceases for which they were enacted."[54] This sense of words' dire contingency logically coincides with Dryden's eleventh-hour attraction to Aesop's fables. For fables' translatability – their fitness to different and ever-shifting verbal contexts – was intrinsic to their cultural value.

Of the *Fables* themselves, only the middle one – "The Cock and the Fox" – is strictly Aesopian. On the whole, as Miner has shown, their greatest and most obvious debt is still to Ovid's *Metamorphoses*. We have seen that in late seventeenth-century England "Aesop" increasingly referred to a specific figural strategy, one that all of Dryden's fables, ancient and modern, practice. As translations, moreover, the *Fables* do so in the explicit context of literary relations: they apply Aesopian assumptions directly, usually to English writing. For instance, as a collection, *Fables* is by nature atomistic; its very structure calls attention to the way in which literary pieces are arranged by depriving its reader of an encompassing formal device. As Sloman suggested, this does not mean that the fables fail to define themselves in relation to each other.[55] But it does mean that they create a context in which discontinuity, gaps and absences all clamor to be recognized as constituents of meaning. By translating only parts of the *Metamorphoses*, of *The Canterbury Tales* and *The Decameron* – all themselves only loosely integrated collections of tales – Dryden further emphasized the fragmentary nature of the forms that transmit meaning and reproduce cultural value. His preface admits that even "I have not ty'd my self to a Literal Translation, but have often omitted what I judg'd unnecessary" (p. 1457). "Something must," he later acknowledges, "be lost in all Transfusion, that is, in all Translations" (p. 1458). The poems in *Fables* may be classified as fables because of what they share with the fables in *The Hind and the Panther* – a congenital incompletion that creates the potential for transmigration and change. Sense in turn is preserved *through* omission, loss, and misapprehension, not in spite of them.

When discontinuity emerges as an explicit literary principle, and risk as a condition of literary authority, the relationships among written signs, however aberrant, become visible emissaries of that authority. Many of Dryden's poems begin with headnotes that summarize their context in the original work, their "CONNEXION to the Former STORY" in the *Decameron*,

Canterbury Tales, and *Metamorphoses*. The *Fables'* own fate in literary history suggests that they were themselves loved partly for imperfections that could turn their readers into active participants in them, even into authors. One eighteenth-century reader's copy of *Fables*, for example, makes the physical transformation of Dryden's text inseparable from the act of reading it: virtually every line is pencilled over and revised to suit the taste of the reader. A handwritten note on the facing page betrays an intense and intimate attachment to Dryden's words:

Imagining that it is in my Power to improve Dryden's Fables (so called) [...] which I deem at least equal to any of his works, by elevating the unequal Parts to a level, I have employed some leisure hours in that Task; thinking it a pity such Jewels should want perfecting. This observation of Johnson in his Life, such is the unevenness of his Composition, that two lines are seldom found together without something of which the reader is ashamed; indicates the propriety, if no practical necessity of their Revisal.[56]

The reference to Johnson's reading of *The Hind and the Panther* links *Fables* to that poem; the kind of "unevenness" that Johnson held in such contempt generates a different approach to meaning: it rebuilds Dryden's text as the stage for a genuine exchange between reader and author.[57] Dryden had seen his own predecessors in just this light: with respect to Chaucer, for example, he confessed himself to have "added somewhat of my own where I thought my Author was deficient, and had not given his Thoughts their True Lustre, for want of Words in the beginning of our Language" (p. 1457). And, as in *The Hind and the Panther*, he saw the transmission both of signs and of literary authority in terms of genealogy:

Milton was the Poetical Son of *Spencer*, and Mr. *Waller* of *Fairfax*; for we have our Lineal Descents and Clans, as well as other Families. *Spencer* more than once insinuates, that the Soul of *Chaucer* was transfus'd into his Body; and that he was begotten by him Two hundred years after his Decease. *Milton* has acknowledg'd to me that *Spencer* was his Original.   (Preface, 1445)

Dryden's genealogy is not a genealogy at all. In it a temporal model of inherited authority gives way to a decidedly atemporal picture of authorship, one in which, weirdly enough, all authors end up inhabiting the same "Body." This single authorial "Body" condenses historical, political, and personal differences into a single and very corporeal fiction of authorial presence – a fiction authenticated because it registers the accidents and impositions that shape all symbolic action. Dryden's anti-genealogy anticipates Samuel Richardson's preface to his 1739 *Æsop's Fables*, where, we saw, the pressures of different historical conditions in which "one Extreme produced another" disfigured the authorial profiles of the fabulists Croxall and L'Estrange and at last rendered them interchangeable.[58] Dryden and Richardson are seldom mentioned in the same breath, but both exercised

Aesopian prerogative to craft a unified model of symbolic authority that could accommodate vast differences among writers, especially English ones.

This very model informs Dryden's individual translations, which, as Cederic D. Reverand II has shown, often prise open "ancient" narratives so that they can support "modern" English reference, for example to William of Orange.[59] At the same time, like his earlier translations of Lucretius, many of the poems that Dryden chose to translate – "Pygmalion and the Statue," for instance, or Ovid's lyrical precis "Of the Pythagorean Philosophy" – represent the way that form is created. Often it is only violence that can impose symbolic coherence, even cultural order. For example, Dryden's Pygmalion sculpts his statue with writerly gestures: "It seem'd, the Breast beneath his Fingers bent;/He felt again, his Fingers made a Print" (lines 78–81). Likewise, in "Of the Pythagorean Philosophy" Dryden identifies the Pythagorean cosmos with translation, and thereby forges an important metonymic bond between his theme (figural change) and the mode of its articulation:

> Those very Elements which we partake,
> Alive, when Dead some other bodies make;
> Translated grow, have Sense, or can Discourse,
> But Death on deathless Substance has no force.   (lines 394–397)

As Dryden's *Fables* find stability in figural transformation, they offer a solution to the fears for the "tortur'd Text" that Dryden had articulated thirteen years earlier. Fables are the perfect – or at least the most ancient and enduring – symbolic form in this fluctuating universe. Which is why, as Dryden's translation of the medieval allegory "The Flower and the Leaf" puts it, "mystique Truth [was] in Fables first convey'd" (line 601).

It is fitting, then, that the poem near the center of *Fables* should be the Aesopian story of "The Cock and the Fox, or, The Tale of the Nun's Priest, from Chaucer." Dryden's very title includes a microhistory of the tale's transmission. That history becomes in itself the moral of the story, it is recapitulated in the opening couplet ("There liv'd, as Authors tell, in Days of Yore,/A Widow somewhat old, and very poor..." [lines 1–2]). With its subtext of Roman Catholic authorities and references, Dryden's translation points back to *The Hind and the Panther*. Chaucer's England was after all a Catholic one, and in *The Canterbury Tales* it is a priest who tells the tale. His hero is the "noble Chanticleer, whose singing did surpass/The many Notes of Organs at a Mass" (lines 40–41), and who reincarnates the "beast of a Bird" so sorely abused by the Hind's Pigeons.[60] Meanwhile, "full fraught with seeming sanctity," the fox who nearly devours Chanticleer could easily hail from the Caledonian wood: in a character sketch wholly invented by Dryden, he is a "pious Cheat that never suck'd the Blood,/Nor chaw'd the Flesh of Lambs, but when he cou'd" (lines 484–485).[61]

The fable proper retells Chaucer's Nun's Priest's story of the polygamous,

literate, and musical rooster whose "deadly Dream" of a fox foreshadows a
near-fatal encounter with the beast himself. "False Reynard" flatters
Chanticleer into performing for him and then "while he pain'd himself to
raise his note," seizes him. The cock has presence of mind enough to
persuade his captor to shout back at the dogs pursuing him even as he is
bearing his quarry away in his mouth. As soon "as the word he spoke,"
Chanticleer swoops to safety on a nearby bough, vowing to keep "the Tree
betwixt" the Fox and him for all time to come. As Reverand suggests, "The
Cock and the Fox" parodies the themes of other fables in *Fables,* and Dryden
must have put something of himself in the randy, gifted Chanticleer, proud of
his own father and the legacy he has inherited from him.[62] But the fable also
offers an active figure for symbolic action. In true Aesopian fashion,
Chanticleer's plummet from the fox's jaws makes linguistic activity animate
and material, with Chanticleer a fleshly substitute for the words the fox aims
to speak. In the same way, Dryden's moral promises that

> In this plain Fable you th'Effect may see
> Of Negligence and fond Credulity:
> And learn besides of Flatt'rers to beware,
> Then most pernicious when they speak too fair.
> The Cock and Fox, the Fool and Knave imply;
> The Truth is moral, though the Tale a lie.
> Who spoke in Parables, I dare not say;
> But sure, he knew it was a pleasing way,
> Sound Sense, by plain Example to convey.   (lines 810–818)

"The Moral" reorders the preceding tale so that its visible meaning
("th'Effect" that the reader "may see") includes the exchange and evaluation
of material signs – flattery, lying, parable-telling. Absent in Chaucer,
Dryden's moral is naturally concerned not just with what the characters in
the fable stand for and "imply." More meaningful is the visible and perilous
("I dare not say") conveyance of "sound Sense" through "plain Example" –
the act of fabling itself.

As they cast the fable as a "plain Example" designed "sound Sense [...] to
convey," Dryden's lines recall Ogilby's maxim, "Examples are best Precepts." Just as Ogilby's Aesopian "Examples" qualified as "best Precepts"
only because they displayed the grotesque contingency of their own authority,
so Dryden's "Example" is "plain" only because it is filtered through a
discontinuous history of translation and interpretation, one in which perusal
– reading by use – sustains "Sense" by conspicuously distorting it. Like
Chaucer's, Dryden's Chanticleer is a bad translator: he thinks that "*Mulier est
hominis confusio*" means "that Woman is to Man his Soveraign Bliss" (lines
418, 420), and the "Solace" of mistranslation engenders the false compla-
cency that makes him vulnerable to the fox. As it both figures and

circumvents the perilous transmigration of material signs, "The Cock and the Fox" finally moralizes not only *Fables* as a whole, nor strictly even Dryden's own late work and the improbable resurrection of literary authority that the superannuated and politically sidelined poet experienced there. It also comments, performatively, on Aesop's fables themselves, and on the symbolic order that they supported in the fraught England of the late seventeenth century.

5

In her "transparent Laberynth": obstructions of poetic justice in Anne Finch's fables

On a rich Pallace at the first they light
Where pleas'd Arachne dazzl'd with the sight
In a conspiccuous corner of a Room
The hanging Frett work makes her active Loom. [...]
[But] with extended Broom th'unpittying Maid
Does the transparent Laberynth invade.
Back stroke and fore the battering Engine went
Broke evry Cord and quite unhing'd the Tent.
        Anne Finch, Countess of Winchilsea, "The Goute and Spider.
        A Fable Imitated from Monsr. de la Fontaine" (1689?)

Here is Lady Winchilsea, for example, I thought, taking down her poems. She was born in the year 1661; she was noble both by birth and by marriage; she wrote poetry. [... But] clearly her mind has by no means "consumed all impediments and become incandescent." On the contrary, it is harassed and distracted with hates and grievances.

        Virginia Woolf, *A Room of One's Own* (1929)

She was unlucky in her models – Pindaric odes and French Fables.
        William Wordsworth, Letter to Alexander Dyce (1830)

Around the time that the Revolution of 1688 drove her from the Stuart court into retirement at Eastwell, her husband's Kent estate, Anne Finch began to translate the fables of Jean de la Fontaine. In one of the resulting poems, derived from La Fontaine's "La goutte et l'araignée" (1668), an ambitious spider weaves her web in a "conspiccuous Corner" of a formal drawing room. But the minute she tries to make the "hanging Frett work" her own "active Loom," the "pleas'd Arachne" attracts the unwelcome attentions of an "unpittying Maid." And as the maid's "extended Broom" batters the spider's "transparent Laberynth" to bits, it also drives home the moral of the story: "Each [should] his propper Station learn to know."[1]

"La goutte et l'araignée" stops here, with "l'araignée" resolving "très sagement de changer [son] logis."[2] "The Goute and Spider," by contrast, goes on to take its own moral very much to heart. Finch adds twelve new and autobiographical lines, all of which underscore the propriety of her own "Station" in life, with particular tribute evidently due the "happy Nuptial state" she shares with the gout-stricken husband she is nursing back to health. Such arrangements, we learn, have more than fables to justify them; for "Heav'n the hard Fatigues of Life/Gave the first Maid a Husband, Him a Wife" (lines 61–62). Finch begins, then, by forging a flexible linguistic bond with another writer. But as its own language performs the spider's unhappy trajectory from "rich Pallace" to obscure hovel, her translation ends in private life. And there it endorses a very different kind of bond. This bond seems indisputable, for it resides outside language, in the realm of "hard Fatigues" and primordial social arrangements.

"The Goute and Spider" turns upon a singular irony. As a reader and translator – as a fabulist – Finch magnifies those features of La Fontaine's fable which link the creative female body to a history of women's mythmaking (Ariadne and Arachne) and that capture its violent thwarting by cultural implements (the broom). In Finch's "active" hands, La Fontaine's "toile tissu" turns into a "transparent Laberynth" spun from the spider's "hungry Bowels." "L'Aragne" metamorphoses into a "hungry" and "pleas'd Arachne." Undescribed in "La goutte et l'araignée" the housemaid's broom becomes a brutal "batt'ring Engine." As a moralist, though, Finch commits her fable to the doctrine of "propper Station." The end of her translation locks the lively play of signs inside sentences of propriety. Paradoxically, these sentences are the ones that most aggressively mark the difference of Finch's own text from its original, and thereby register the English author's arachnid desire. A similar irony shapes the textual relations between Finch's poem and its French pretext. For instead of faithfully "englishing" La Fontaine, "The Goute and Spider" introduces real historical circumstances that obstruct transparent imitation. In fact, it is only as an ostentatiously flawed imitation that the fable animates written signs and the transactions between them. Only through its own disappointment does it transfer literary authority from an authoritative text to its transfiguring reader, Finch.[3]

Barely two years separate the unpublished folio manuscript (1689) that contains "The Goute and Spider" from *The Hind and the Panther*, and, like the aging Dryden, the young woman to whose husband's uncle Ogilby had dedicated his 1651 *Fables* wrote from a position of cultural and political disenfranchisement: Wordsworth even wondered if "Lady Winchelsea [was] a Catholic" (she was not).[4] Like Dryden, too, Finch found herself irresistibly attracted to translation, especially fables and, like his, her estrangement from emerging centers of cultural authority was twofold. Just as the Revolution of 1688 conspired with Dryden's conversion to sweep him from the literary mainstream, so the aristocratic Finch found her life as Maid of Honor to Mary of Modena cut short by the accession of William and Mary. Whereas in Stuart days an intimate circle of friends had read her poetry in manuscript, the Revolution replaced that circle with the dispersed, disembodied world of professional letters that increasingly defined Augustan England.[5]

Rather against the odds, Finch, a non-juring Tory, became the most prolific female poet of the early eighteenth century. Much of her work protests against women's exclusion from the institutions – particularly the literary ones – that shape and transmit culture. " 'Tis true I write and tell me by what Rule/I am alone forbid to play the fool?" demands one poem. Others disdain "the dull mannage of a servile house," and imagine a return to days before women were "debarr'd from all improvements of the mind,/ And to be dull expected and dessign'd."[6] Ranging from Pindaric ode to feminist polemic, from nature lyrics to satire, friendship poetry and verse tragedy, Finch's poetry attributes women's ills sometimes to cultural myths and expectations – "Rule[s]" and "dessign[s]" – and sometimes to what seem to be the innate vagaries of female flesh: "So here confin'd and but to female clay,/ARDELIA's soul mistook the rightfull way," one "Fragment" begins.[7] As such couplets suggest, Finch was preoccupied not only with obstacles to women's cultural participation, but also with what she saw as the elimination of signs of material difference from the dominant discourses of the period: her non-Aesopian writing seeks an ever-elusive *rapprochement* between linguistic signs and the material bodies that both produce and are governed by them.

As we have seen, fables are exceptionally well-positioned to negotiate such a *rapprochement*. Fabulists like Ogilby, Behn, L'Estrange, and even Locke, had long exploited Aesop's special position on the cusp between sensible particulars and the manmade fictions that organized those particulars into meaningful – and culturally constructive – forms: Aesopian method had given even the most peripheral of these writers influential access to the literate culture of Augustan England. Dryden in particular had dispatched Aesop to find new ways to embody literary authority in print: both *The Hind and the Panther* and *Fables, Ancient and Modern* offered, if not models, then encouraging precedents for a woman writer seeking a similar – and similarly self-authorizing – accommodation of body to sign. Second, we saw that fables mediated reactively not only between corporeal "facts" and cultural fictions but also between competing political interests and ideological positions. In the battle of the books, for example, fables potentially reconciled an ever more spectral and monstrously prolific print culture with the "ancient" (usually aristocratic and Tory) desire to stabilize literary form by reuniting it with securely embodied authority.

The English fable, then, catered both to Finch's frustration as a woman writer coveting visibility within her own texts and to her aristocratic craving for invisibility in modern literary culture. It seems almost inevitable that fables should have supplied the most consistent thread in her diverse *oeuvre*. Mischievous, intricate, often violent, they constitute half of the pieces in the only published volume of her work, *Miscellany Poems* (1713), and they figure prominently in that volume's precursor, the handwritten folio privately circulated in 1689. Fables also make up a full three-quarters of the Winchilsea section in the important *Poems by Eminent Ladies* (1755), and it was not until Wordsworth publicly favored Finch's nature lyrics that her Aesopian work fell into eclipse.

The tone of many of Finch's other poems makes it tempting to read her fables as covert fictions of protest against women's cultural disenfranchisement. Often female, their protagonists – spiders, owls, elephants – constantly find themselves abused by the very conventions of representation that they cannot help but reproduce through the labors of their own "Bowels." Yet, like "The Goute and Spider," Finch's fables are also actively engaged in literary transactions which complicate their plots. Just as "The Goute and Spider" denies that "La goutte et l'araignée" is its male author's exclusive property only by burying itself in doctrines of submission and propriety, so Finch's other fables, some imitations and some original, weave their plots between conflicting imperatives in order to create a third and far more viable figural possibility – a third and even more viable model of literary authority.[8] As they draw upon Aesopian practices by now intrinsic to English writing, these poems form a vital, if previously unrecognized, matrix for Finch's own work.[9] And, in turn, as they uncover the labyrinth of resistances and acquiescences that necessarily shaped an aristocratic woman's relationship to Augustan literary culture, Finch's Aesopian poems apply fables to a new version of the problem of how to establish literary authority in "modern" England.

Poetics of translation

Over the last three centuries, Finch has been read more frequently and consistently than any other female poet of her day. Some of her poems appeared in print as early as 1701; praised by Swift and the playwright Nicholas Rowe, she saw her *Miscellany Poems* go into a second edition the year after its first publication in 1713. In 1815 Wordsworth declared himself an admirer of her "image[s] of external nature,"[10] and in 1929 Virginia Woolf recorded in detail her own experience of reading Finch's poetry. While new critics hailed Finch's work as a belated manifestation of metaphysical wit, feminist critics of our own day regularly anthologize and interpret her poems of social protest.[11] They foreground the disruptive features of her lyrical verse, noting its declared affinities with women's arts, like weaving, and with "feminine" elements, like shade and night, that seem to challenge the Enlightenment's supposed "consolidation and perfection of systems."[12]

Because Finch's poetry is so congenial to a range of romantic and post-romantic polemical positions, her involvement in contemporary literary exchanges has been ignored. Wordsworth, for instance, deemed her "unlucky in her models, Pindaric odes and French Fables."[13] Eager to make Finch an example to support her own angry thesis that historically women's oppression and their resulting rage kept them from writing pure poetry that can "consume all impediments and become incandescent," Woolf emphasized the "harassed and distracted" features of Finch's verse.[14] She took Finch's own vow never "in faded silks [to] compose/Faintly, the inimitable *Rose*'[15] as a sign of resistance on the one hand to social standards of feminine creativity and on the other to neoclassical literary codes seemingly informed by ideals of painstaking imitation.

To see Finch strictly in light of her failures and deviations from perceived sociopolitical and literary protocols, however, is to fail to imagine how she might have converted those deviations into illuminating and constructive rhetorical strategies.[16] And it is also to ignore the nature, and the vitality, of contemporary Aesopian practice, to which Finch turned and returned throughout creative life. Aesop, as we saw in Chapter 2, was licensed to undermine Augustan formalism; as symbolic tokens whose loyalties could shift at the drop of a hat, his fables exposed literary authority itself as a matter of exchange between individual (usually tendentious) texts, and between members of specific linguistic communities. Aesop provided a consensually approved figural device in which and through which even laws of genre could be dramatized, renegotiated, and revised. Thus while much of Finch's writing marks her estrangement from the literary culture of Augustan England, her Aesopian poems engage in more complicated transactions with that culture.

Finch's non-Aesopian work draws upon Miltonic constructions of the fall ("by our seducement wrought") and women's presumed guilt therein to define her own poetic voice as an illicit one. Many of her poems characterize "female Clay" as inherently errant, always straying from the "rightful way" into misprision, fiction, splenetic fantasy. Other poems, though, speculate that women's errors might originate not in inborn proclivities but rather in manmade fictions: women, they propose, are "fal'n by mistaken Rules,/And Education's more than Nature's fools."[17] Often the poetic solution to the problem of the female body's indeterminate relationship to oppressive cultural codes is to look toward death – the "absolute Retreat," "the only Heav'n." The arrival of this "kinder friend though with the harsher face" will simply cancel the need to resolve painful paradoxes: death limits speculation without forcing the speaker to choose among conflicting rhetorical positions.[18]

But Finch also experimented with a solution that was at once more vital and more textual. In her prose preface to the 1689 folio, she positions herself amid prevailing assumptions about writing. Often quoting authorities like Beaumont and Dryden but also clotted with parentheses and misspelled words, the preface casts Finch as an "Imperfect Peniten[t]" whose writing is transgressive, self-indulgent, a compulsive recreation of the fall: "I have writt, and expos'd my uncorrect Rimes, and immediately repented, and yett have writt again," she confesses, "till at last (like them) wearied with uncertainty, and irresolution, I rather chuse to be harden'd in an errour, then to be still at the trouble of endeavouring to over come itt."[19] Finch's "(like them)" forges a covert but striking analogy between the fallen (or falling) woman and her own "uncorrect Rimes." Both are tempted by the same desire for recognition that doomed poor "pleas'd Arachne." Both withdraw from the only available modes of articulation. And as they do so, literary relations perform, thereby investigate, a lived experience.

For Finch, the task of translation evidently epitomized the frustration and inner conflict that hampered other kinds of writing. Her preface, for instance, acknowledges that her translations lack one desirable element – the erotic. "Keeping within those limmits which I have observ'd," she reasons, "I know not why itt should be more faulty, to treat of that passion, then of any other violent excursion, or transport of the mind." Yet while its treatment of "passion" attracted her to Tasso's pastoral comedy *Aminta*, for example, "Love" remained a "more faulty subject" than any other, and this

wholly prevented me from putting [all of *Aminta*] into English verse, from the verbal translation I procured out of the Italian, after I had finish'd the first act extreamily to my satisfaction ... but there being nothing mixt with it, of a serious morality or usefulness, I sacrafis'd the pleasure I took in itt, to the more sollid reasonings of my own mind.   (p. 10)

As a translator, Finch feels "sollid reasonings" (morals) at war with "pleasure." Close identification with an "original ... soft and full of beautys" competes with the social expectation that her work will impart "a serious morality, or usefulnese." But, unlike other, less explicitly imitative kinds of writing, translation can demonstrate as well as recount the conflicts and frustrations that accompany the desiring body's encounters with prescribed laws of symbolic formation. Because they are always attached to pre-existing texts, and thus are always readings, translations can be uniquely performative, and therefore exceptionally convincing. A translation can refer to what it has left out; it can register the conditions of its own reproduction, and the desires of its author. Yet since she always remains a reader, that author can also stay allied with her original.

Finch chose to translate a wide assortment of original texts. These included a French version of Petrarch's Sonnet 188, a verse ("The Song of the Cannibals") from Montaigne, part of Racine's *Athalie*, various Psalms and fragments from the Song of Solomon, "Five Pieces out of Tasso's *Aminta*," and, of course, many fables of La Fontaine. Like the "Penitent" responsible for them, these translations are "imperfect": with the significant exception of the fables, they are always only parts of larger wholes. Yet it is precisely because they are fragmentary that Finch's translations can embody the plait of aggression and dependency that attaches them to their pretexts.

As Nancy K. Miller has suggested, one way women writers might weave their signatures into their own work is through "representations of writing itself."[20] Translation promises to accomplish this assertion of authorial presence structurally and linguistically as well as thematically. Finch in fact often translated the most self-reflexive passages in her originals. For example, one of the "Five Pieces" of *Aminta* that she put into English dramatizes an aesthetic moment relevant to her own project. In the third "Piec[e]," a magician warns his male companion to avoid a city of women who

> [s]ubt'ly will thy solid Sense bereave,
> And a false Gloss to ev'ry Object give.
> Brass to thy Sight a polish'd Gold shall seem,
> And Glass thou as the Diamond shalt esteem.
> The very Walls by Magick Art are wrought,
> And Repetition to all Speakers taught:
> Not such, as from our Ecchoes we obtain,
> Which only our last Words return again;
> But speech for Speech entirely there they give,
> And often add, beyond what they receive.[21]

Tasso's "soft enchantresses" are translators who literally interfere with ideals of correspondence ("Ecchoes") and transparency ("Glass"). "Add[ing], beyond what they receive," they weave walls of "false Gloss[es]" that can dismantle their originals. As they "abuse [visitors'] wond'ring Eyes/ ... And all they see with Imitation mock," Tasso's enchantresses exemplify women's relationship to manmade signs – a relationship mediated through fictions that masquerade as natural constructs. In the Italian *Aminta* these bewildering women exist simply to warn against mimetic mockery. Reframed in Finch's literary mosaic of partial imitations, however, they enliven the very text that reproduces them. In the end, Finch's writing acts out the theme of its pretext. Tasso's theme becomes a palpable function of Finch's own writing.

Similarly, when Finch decided to translate "Part" of Racine's girls' school tragedy *Athalie* (1687), she chose the moment when the play's eponymous, and ambitious, heroine boasts that "to the empty'd Throne I boldly rose,/ Treating all interceptors as my Foes." Athalia's recollection of her own meteoric rise is interrupted by a vision of her mother, Jezebel, who invokes patriarchal authority to warn her overweening daughter that in the end "the *Hebrews* God [...] shall Thee [...] confound" (lines 54–55). When Athalia tries to embrace her mother's "shade," her arms close around nothing. She finds herself left with only "a heap of Bones" and

> Flakes of mangled Flesh, that quiv'ring still
> Proclaim'd the Freshness of the suffer'd Ill;
> Distained with Blood the Pavement and the Wall,
> Appear'd as in that memorable Fall.   (lines 62–65)

Finch's Athalia dwells in a world of phantoms, bloodstained impediments ("the Wall"), and kinetic fragments ("flakes of mangled Flesh"). Her struggle to break into the real political world links her private phantasmagoria with Finch's own translation, and both with the "memorable Fall" that Finch's folio preface treats as the constitutive myth in women's linguistic experience.[22] Severed from its original setting, Athalia's frustration figures the relationship between Finch's translation and its own textual environment.

It is all too often the female body which keeps Finch's translations from the ideals of correspondence and coherence that they seem also to have internalized. The spider in "The Goute and Spider" similarly works her own downfall because for her appetite and art are inseparable: "The hungry Fiend does in close Ambush lurk/Untill some silly Insect shall repay/What from her Bowels she has spun that day" (lines 14–16) The "back stroke and fore" of the maid's "batt'ring Engine" only pins more responsibility for disruption on a female body. Many of Finch's translations rehearse this effect on their own pages, literalizing and materializing – referring to the behavior of letters – the tribulations that other poems can only thematize. At the same time the translations necessarily represent that body's fragmentation – which is plotted into their pretexts, after all – as inevitable.[23] The disrupted and disrupting body becomes a condition of correspondence, and so of each work's legibility. Often translations themselves, Finch's fables give this inevitability narrative form and animal face. Most important, though, the fables generate some of the same self-reflexive morals implicit in Finch's translations without being themselves fragmentary. Aesopian strategy therefore not only embodies an authorial dilemma but also puts it into terms immediately communicable to Augustan readers.

"The epithet of *inimitable*" and the uses of La Fontaine

Finch's first Aesopian pieces were translations of La Fontaine. Dedicated successively to the French Dauphin (1668), to the influential Madame de Montespan (1679), and to the Duke of Burgundy (1694), La Fontaine's fables had appeared in three "receuils" throughout the late seventeenth century. Although he had also written odes, elegies, a translation of Apuleius's tale of Cupid and Psyche, and many racy "contes et nouvelles en vers," it was the *Fables choisies* that made La Fontaine the darling of the *salons*, a member of the Académie, and in the end a hero of French literary culture. As his first English biographer, William Lockman, observed in 1744, the French fabulist was soon and long recognized as "a Poet on whom All (and justly, I believe) bestow the Epithet of *Inimitable*."[24]

Finch's relationship to the inimitable La Fontaine was necessarily intricate. For it was mediated not only by obvious differences of language, culture, celebrity, and gender but also by the unusual combination of seductions and resistances built into what La Fontaine, disingenuously, liked to call his "mensonges" (white lies). English readers came to think of La Fontaine as a kind of nature poet whose "lyrick Enthusiasms" testified to his "aversion to restraint of any kind."[25] At the same time, however, his fables are painstakingly wrought, fraught with artifice. Lockman compared his work to "a large, ancient Statue I have read of somewhere. To look at it could not be more irregular or undelicate, but open it, and it exhibited a sett of little Images, representing all the Deities, the workmanship of which was exquisite."[26] La Fontaine's fables reconcile abandon with boundary, license with contrivance. As they confuse the boundaries between natural and cultural modes of reproduction they prove at once inviting and evasive, hospitable and "inimitable."

When La Fontaine began writing his little "bagatelles" for the amusement of ladies and little boys of royal blood, he proposed to celebrate Aesop, "l'Esclave" born lacking "entièrement l'usage de la parole," as "l'Oracle de la Grèce."[27] "Plus de sagesse/Que tout l'Aréopage,"[28] La Fontaine's Aesop invented animal actors who were heroes in their own right, and whose passions and casuistries naturally ironized classical heroes and pantheons. In the fables themselves, the *badinage* of animal actors mixes the play of signs with the skirmishes of material bodies. Here authority perches precariously within signs' temporary concatenations rather than in presuppositions about the integrity of form. La Fontaine therefore naturally purported to favor the under-represented and disenfranchised: "Le loup en langue des Dieux/Parle au Chien dans mes ouvrages." "Tout parle dans l'univers;/Il n'est rien qui n'ait son langage." "Nos Héros avec leurs Phalanges/Ce sont des contes plus étranges./Qu'un Renard qui cajole un Corbeau sur sa voix."[29]

It is not hard to imagine how La Fontaine might have caught a woman writer's eye. Most pragmatically, La Fontaine could look "easie and familiar" to those, like most women, uninitiated into classical learning.[30] In fact, La Fontaine often wrote specifically for women and seems to have preferred their company to that of men: he dedicated fables to Mademoiselle de Sillery, to Madame de Grignan (daughter of Madame de Sévigné), and of course to his beloved patroness, the intelligent, spirited, and scientifically inclined Marguerite de la Sablière. Even in the twentieth century it was Marianne Moore, not Ezra Pound or T.S. Eliot, who produced a complete (and dazzling) English translation of La Fontaine's fables.[31] Without making claims for a transhistorical "female imagination," we can say that, historically, women have often felt drawn to La Fontaine.

They may also have found themselves attracted because La Fontaine's "jeux innocents" left room for others. Famous for his "negligence" and "inaccuracies," La Fontaine was eventually dubbed the "Correggio of poetry," for his capricious "method" recalled the Italian painter's random "scattering" of angels across the top of a canvas.[32] Once he had dedicated the first books of *Fables choisies* to the dauphin, La Fontaine dropped the pretense that their point was to instill moral virtue in a young prince. His poems grew more deft and complex, atomizing Rochefoucauldian maxims and Lucretian reflections into delectable "morceau[x] de matière,/[. . .]Quintessence[s] d'atome[s], extrait[s] de la lumière."[33] La Fontaine often reminded his readers that the resulting pieces "ne sont pas ce qu'elles semblent être." They are notoriously slippery and inconclusive; signs play in them so inexhaustibly that fictions of identity become functional realities: "Chacun tourne en réalitès,/Autant qu'il peut, ses propres songes," one fable ends. "L'homme est de glace aux vérités;/Il est feu pour les mensonges."[34] As we might expect, structurally and thematically, the *Fables* are preoccupied with questions of symbolic authority. As we might also expect, they deny signs' integrity, disinterestedness, and invulnerability to the imagination of their interpreters: "Si mon oeuvre n'est pas assez bon modèle,/J'ai du moins ouvert le chemin:/D'autres pourront y mettre une dernière main," offers one "Epilogue."[35] La Fontaine's poetry naturally leaves room for creative revision.[36]

While potentially enticing to writers like Finch, these were also the very characteristics that made La Fontaine seem "inimitable." Despite their inclusive and iconoclastic pose, that is, and despite their built-in skepticism about symbolic authority, his fables proved so labyrinthine that French fabulists did not try to copy him, preferring instead to use his example as a license for Aesopian experiments of their own.[37] Likewise, while other French fabulists easily found their way across the English Channel (complete translations of Boissat and La Motte appeared in 1701 and 1722 respectively), English translators were reluctant to attempt a complete translation of *Fables choisies*. It was not that they did not like La Fontaine; much to the contrary, they perceived him to have been more kindly disposed to them than the French usually were, and in 1711, Addison could report that he "is come more into Vogue than any other Author of our Times."[38] Yet even in 1744 Lockman wondered that

we have not any *English* version (in Verse) of these Fables, the executing of which, with Propriety, Humour, and Spirit, wou'd be a prodigiously difficult Task. No Genius, except one like that of our Author, is (perhaps) equal to it; and so little Honour and Advantage are gain'd by the Translation, possibly the whole collection of these Fables may never be attempted, in *English*, by any one single Pen of Abilities; the most we can hope for is, that they may be done, at several times, by several Hands.[39]

Although Lockman attributed their untranslatability as a "whole" to La Fontaine's "Genius," his unique "Propriety, Humour and Spirit," La

Fontaine's fables seem anything but committed to a formal notion of authorial integrity: they send a double message about literary authority itself, which they preserve by flaunting its fragmentability.

Finch was quite possibly the first English writer to respond to this message. Later, John Dennis would include ten "burlesque" translations of La Fontaine in his *Miscellany Poems* of 1695; in 1692 L'Estrange would name him among his "Other Eminent Mythologists"; and Bernard Mandeville would publish some *Fables after the Easie and Familiar Method of Monsieur de la Fontaine* in 1703, expanding the collection the following year to include fifty-five translations and two originals which he retitled *Aesop Dress'd*. But the first complete translation of *Fables choisies* would not appear until 1810; until then, La Fontaine remained inimitably "several."

Finch's male contemporaries liked to iron out La Fontaine's ambiguities and multiple small tricks of light. They spelled out morals that he often braided into his stories, converting the stories themselves into proofs of distinct propositions. And they seldom investigated their actual differences from him. For example, when Mandeville slipped two "Fables of my own" into his collection, he challenged the reader to "find 'em out" on his or her own, and he tossed off the whole translation as a careless exercise performed "in an idle hour."[40] Finch's translations are different. As "The Goute and Spider" shows, she never assumed that her task was to reproduce her original exactly. Nor did she merely simplify La Fontaine. Instead, her imitations of La Fontaine emphasize their originals" violence. Finch feminizes La Fontaine's characters and predicaments, and personalizes his morals to mark her own fables less as imitations than as usages. By what we might call "inimitating" the "inimitable" La Fontaine, Finch brought the frustrations that drive her other, more private writing forward into the relatively public domain of English letters.

Dire contests: some translations of La Fontaine

In the French fables that Finch turned into English, assault and battery mark material bodies' confrontations with established symbolic designs. Brass pots shatter the stone jugs that aspire to travel with them. Brooms rend cobwebs built in inappropriate places. Acorns bruise inquisitive noses. Whole armies of rats perish when their caps and epaulets keep them from squeezing through their ratholes. La Fontaine's morals note the irony of such collisions and leave it at that; translators like Mandeville and Dennis usually carried only La Fontaine's detachment into English. But Finch worked traces of her own agency into her translations, fiercely taking sides against the characters in the fables. Her morals are harsh, even retributive. They often force La Fontaine's poems into a sterner, far more repressive framework. If anything, Finch's fables seem to alienate themselves from their potentially rebellious originals. Like "The Goute and Spider," they trade the free play of linguistic signs for incontestable doctrines of propriety.

For example, one of Finch's most popular imitations reproduces La Fontaine's "Le gland et la citrouille" (ix.iv).[41] La Fontaine's "original" begins with a succinct moral: "Dieu fait bien ce qu'il fait" (line 1). The fable proves the moral in the story of a "villageois," Garo, who uses the incongruities between oaks and the tiny acorns that they produce, and between pumpkins and their slender vines, to challenge divine authority: "A quoi songeait-il, ait-il, l'Auteur de tout cela?" (line 6). Had he been "l'Auteur," Garo imagines, he would have suspended pumpkins from branches and acorns from vines. When an acorn drops onto his nose, though, he turns grateful that pumpkins do not after all grow on trees, and concludes that "Dieu ne l'a pas voulu: sans doute il eut raison." In the end, "en louant Dieu de toute chose,/Garo retourne à la maison" (lines 33–34). La Fontaine's fable asks how an aesthetic arrangement can win the consent of those whose lives and bodies it shapes. But Garo's painful object lesson less confirms the authority of an existing *ordonnance* than reduces it to a number of chance effects. In the end, having suggested that the supreme author might be a dreaming fabulist, La Fontaine never really resolves the question of whether Garo is right or wrong to challenge existing arrangements; he merely diverts our attention.

As this fable's translator, Finch confronted several established designs. These include not just the meaningful order of things whose manmade – fabulous – quality "Le gland et la citrouille" had insinuated, but also the potentially subversive pattern of "Le gland et la citrouille" itself. If Finch wanted to challenge the authority of existing rules of order, we might expect her merely to transpose a fable that already poses such a challenge. But instead "The Atheist and the Acorn" takes a more conservative tack. Its very title spotlights the interpreting human figure in the scene, and passes scornful judgment upon him. Once her English Garo surmises that the world is "oddly made," only to suffer the acorn's reprimand, Finch's moral berates the "dull presuming Atheist": "Fool! had that Bough a *Pumpkin* bore,/Thy Whimseys must have work'd no more,/Nor Scull have kept them in" (lines 26–30). Where La Fontaine skated across a bright ice of ironies, Finch officially casts her lot with the unspoken laws which determine the order of things. Her moral traps La Fontaine's story in a grim verdict that, like the domestic addendum to "The Goute and Spider," flattens, domesticates, defiguralizes its most playful and subversive elements.

Yet at the level of textual performance, Finch's moral works differently. "Le gland et la citrouille" ends with a cold flicker of irony. "The Atheist and the Acorn" leaves us with an image that could not be more corporeal or violent. As it grounds La Fontaine's fable in the material world, the image of the atheist's shattered skull more fully embodies – indeed, it literalizes – an alternative arrangement of things. Finch's moral, that is, may seem to chastise the atheist who has dared to imagine a different natural scheme. But it also allows the atheist's "whimseys" literally to escape their container, the "scull [that] kept them in." In its revisionary relationship to "Le gland et la citrouille," the moral manages to release fantasy ("whimsey") even as, thematically, it urges it to stay leashed.

In fact, this recognizably Aesopian strategy is already at work before the moral rears its head. For Finch's exemplary acorn is itself a rebel, "loosen'd from the Stay" of its branch. The double entendre links the acorn's defiant energy with women's bodies in their manmade trappings. In effect, it exposes the boundaries which social order literally imposes on the body. It even suggests a secret affinity between Finch and a La Fontaine averse "to restraint of every kind." It is only that Finch's resistances are played out in verbal performance rather than thematically and imitatively. By seizing, specifying, and materializing La Fontaine's fabulous figures, Finch insists on fictions' accountability to the physical bodies whose shapes and fates they prescribe. Finally, her failure of imitation marks a "Genius," if not exactly "like that of our Author," nevertheless "equal to it."

Other translations make a similar impression. For example, in La Fontaine's "Le combat des rats et des belettes" (IV.vi) a rat army at war with weasels is driven into retreat: "Leur resistance fut vaine." Although all of the routed rats flee to their native hole, only a few actually manage to squeeze through, for in order to distinguish themselves from the "racaille" among their own ranks, the aristocratic rats have donned elaborate headgear – plumes and horns, "des plumails," "des cornes [et] des aigrettes" (line 38). While the unadorned rats slide effortlessly to safety and freedom, the "seigneurs," encumbered by the manufactured signs of rank, find their way blocked and themselves devoured by the enemy. "Une tête empanachée n'est pas petit embarras," La Fontaine concludes. "Les petits en toute affaire./ Esquivent fort aisement;/Les grands ne le peuvent faire" (lines 49–50, 54–56).

La Fontaine's little fable tempts its reader to classify it with the slippery, sly "petits." Fifty-six quick lines breed a full spectrum of conspicuously fictive distinctions – between rats and weasels, between titled rats and untitled ones, between rat bodies and the insignia that differentiate them. What makes the great ones great and the small ones small? As the fable hints that such distinctions are made rather than inherited, and that they are for that very reason unstable, it also allows differences of signification to override differences of body: "plumails" and "aigrettes" happen to be feathers as well as military plumes; "cornes" can mean either the detail of a uniform or the horns of an animal. Because it treats marks of difference as marks, not as signs of intrinsic difference, the fable exposes distinction itself as a fiction – arbitrary, avoidable, and finally political.

As Ross Chambers has suggested, however, La Fontaine's role as the pet of aristocratic salon culture makes it difficult to decide how far and in what sense his fables actually opposed the structures through which that world constructed and maintained itself.[42] As it favors "les petits," that is, the fable might pretend to evade. But in order to imply (transgressively) that authoritative signifying systems are arbitrary and subject to the manipulations of those who wield the most powerful fictions – aristocratic rats in the beginning, but clever fabulists by the end – the fable must first posit a universe made up of signs no more and no less fictitious than the bodies they define.

Finch's "The Battle between the Rats and Weazles" resists La Fontaine's tendency to reduce all authoritative structures to constellations of manmade signs. Her translation compresses La Fontaine's fifty-six short lines into the space of nineteen long ones. Metrically her iambic verse burdens the rhythm of its original; it terminates the enjambed gliding lines of its model, pinning La Fontaine's fable back down into physical space. And Finch puts the body back into La Fontaine's fable figurally as well as literally. Her fable begins in the field of "dire Contest" which La Fontaine's ironic chronicle supplies. Here certain plots have already been forged: "Foot to Foot and Point to Point was set." This paraphrase of La Fontaine's fable is also a reference to it, and it implies a range of possible relationships between body and sign, emphasizing their incongruous conjunctions and overlooking the ambiguous identifications implicit in La Fontaine's "cornes," "plumails," and "aigr-ettes." We may thus read the warring feet as animal feet or as poetic ones; we may also read combative "Point[s]" as body parts, as typographical marks, or as the aim of an argument. As lexical and literal elements coincide, the page hosts an Aesopian exchange between matter and sign.

Fable's end confirms this exchange while still presenting the conclusions to be drawn from it as arbitrary, thus contestable. As in La Fontaine, Finch's rats ultimately "repai[r]" to their rathole. "The undress'd Vulgar" slip easily through Finch's "slender Crannies"; true to form, the "Rats of Figure" get stuck, courtesy of their own "branching Marks of Honour." But where La Fontaine ends with a moral, Finch finishes with a pun. In the end, she observes wryly, "the Feather in the Cap was fatal to the Head" (line 19). The pun cooperates with her determination to show how and that all signs start out in the literal register. Puns by definition defy distinction between the figural and the literal.[43] Possible only in English, Finch's points to her own poem's difference from La Fontaine's, a difference decided in part by its different – manifestly English – linguistic context. At the same time, the pun makes a sign accountable to the body whose "fat[e]" it decides. And, most crucially, it makes a colloquial figure for accomplishment – "the Feather in the Cap" – function like a thing (a real feather in a real cap) without losing its figural power.

Finch's translation of "Le combat des rats et des belettes," then, shares that fable's preoccupation with the negotiable ties that bind bodies to signs. But whereas La Fontaine repairs the split between body and sign, ultimately denying their differences in order to ironize other systems of distinction, Finch "re-pairs" – violently yokes – them in conspicuously awkward combinations whose ultimate effect is to criticize La Fontaine's comparatively facile solution. La Fontaine teased an existing law of generic classification by hinting that what that law classifies are themselves only signs. Finch re-entitles the law he would ironize, but stresses its accountability to the bodies that it would regulate.

A similar strategy structures "The Brass Pot and the Stone Jugg," Finch's translation of La Fontaine's "Le pot de terre et le pot de feu" (v.ii). In La Fontaine's fable, two pots venture into the world tied together so that the iron pot can protect his more fragile companion. All pots having been fashioned into certain shapes, however, the itinerants must travel "à trois pieds/Clopin-clopant, comme ils peuvent" (lines 22–23). Predictably, the "pot de feu" soon shatters his earthen "camarade." The resulting moral warns us to choose only our equals for company: "Ne nous associons qu'avecque nos égaux,/Ou bien il nous faudra craindre/Le destin d'un de ces pots" (lines 29–31). As is so often the case in fables, morphology is "destin[y]"; here, however, La Fontaine also reminds us that that morphology is manmade. One wonders whether it is indeed only because we should associate "qu'avecque nos égaux" that the clay pot meets his demise. Perhaps "il fut mis en eclats" because of the human habit of casting cookware into different shapes. La Fontaine's fable attributes the clay pot's exemplary fragmentation as much to human designs as to a mismatch with a member of another class of objects. And because the fable insinuates that difference itself may be manmade, it manages to mock classificatory schemes that assume innate similarities and differences. Finally, like "Le gland et la citrouille" and "Le combat," the fable places the fabulist's linguistic designs at the foundation of a presumably natural order. By converting the catastrophe that befalls the two pots into a cautionary tale, the fable makes its own devices transparent. So it manages to break all schemes with pretensions to natural authority "en éclats" – into obvious fables with debatable morals.

Typically, Finch pumps La Fontaine's delicate "pot de terre" up into a "bloated *Jugg*, supine and lazy"; his "pot de feu" becomes a "Brazen *Pot*, by scouring vext,/With Beef and Pudding still perplext" (lines 1–2). Her crockery is obviously English, and she emphasizes its substantiality. She also stresses that these objects make their own fates, for like her "pleas'd Arachne," her Brass Pot is an ambitious storyteller. Seeking a travelling companion, he contrives a "fine Story" that "mov[es]" the Jug to "share the Strife" of his projected quest for "Wealth and Place" beyond the humble hearth. Finch never attributes that last "obdurate Thump" and the "rud[e] fall to helter-Skelter" to pottery styles. She arraigns quantities not qualities – namely, the "pond'rous Load" of the Jug's own bulk as it keeps him from scaling a hill, and the "perfidious" difference of the Pot's weight as it strikes against him. In the end,

> The Pot of Stone, to shivers broken,
> Sends each misguided Fool a Token:
> To show them, by this fatal Test,
> That Equal Company is best,
> Where none Oppress, nor are Opprest.   (lines 51–55)

More complex than La Fontaine's "ne nous associons qu'avecque nos égaux," Finch's moral makes more than one sign system emerge from a world that is both relentlessly physical and culturally specific. It also preserves the violence of exemplarity, and makes that violence itself a component of the moral. The moral in turn elaborates not just a maxim but also (and rather more courageously) a political philosophy that cites the sensible world as its authority. Finch's doctrine of "equal Company" may seem to discourage mixture and ambition, but it also refuses to separate physical from figural oppression.

"The Brass Pot and the Stone Jugg" ends in a scene of fable-making where the "fatal test[s]" of concrete "Token[s]" convey a theory of representation. Other translations of La Fontaine also comment performatively on Aesopian signifying conventions. In "The Jester and the Little Fishes," for example, a hungry jester finds himself seated at the bottom of "a plenteous Board." When he is accordingly served only "the worse and least fish," the jester contrives to secure some of the large ones. Grasping one of the "little fishes," he pretends to hold a conversation with it, and requests news of an old friend lost at sea. Then, "ma[king] his Tongue the Hook," he announces to the company that the fish is too young to supply the information he requires and asks to speak to one of the "Monsters of the Deep" served at the head of the table. The jester's Aesopian double-talk literally weaves elements of the material world into an intentional narrative. And it proposes that language, returned to its literal roots, can rearrange the political structure that is exemplified in the arrangement of the dinner table.

Yet Finch's fable disdains the chance to identify with the jester's trick. Instead of sympathizing with his hunger or acknowledging how much his rhetorical strategies resemble her fable's own, her moral endorses the hierarchy of the table: "A Jest, well-timed, though from a worthless Man/ Often obtains more than true Merit can" (lines 46–47). By contrast, La Fontaine's "Le rieur et les poissons" (viii.viii) concludes more subversively. "Le rieur" finagles "un monstre assez vieux pour lui dire/Tous les noms des chercheurs de mondes inconnus/Qui n'en étaient pas revenus,/Et que depuis cent ans sous l'abîme avaient vus/Les anciens du vaste empire" (lines 28–32). "Le rieur"'s little trick invokes lost names and submerged ruins to belittle the pretensions of empire. Declining the Fontainean hook, Finch casts her lot with the table, and so not only with presumably absolute standards of "worthless[ness]" and "true Merit" but also with a hierarchical social and symbolic structure (high table/low table; great fish/small fish).

At the same time, however, by declining La Fontaine's bait, Finch's own fable depicts the origins of figuration differently. Her moral shows that a "worthless Man" builds his "jest[s]" within a rigid and powerful symbolic order. From this perspective, unexamined Aesopian antics seem facile. Finch employs Aesopian devices more cautiously and self-consciously to create a rhetorical world in which bodily desires must come to terms with symbolic boundaries. Unlike La Fontaine, Finch is not interested in making her fable work like the jester's little hook to ironize the pretensions of a dominant culture. Instead, her fable animates an ultimately collaborative tension between the imperial arrangement of the table and the Jester's longings.

Much in line with contemporary Aesopian practice, Finch's translations of La Fontaine thus built a performative and self-reflexive symbolic system that could support all of her writing. Openly engaged with La Fontaine's volatile plots, Finch's Aesopian work applies morals to textual effects. It is the resulting lively and unusually convincing signifying field that underpins her *Miscellany Poems on Several Occasions* of 1713. While several of Finch's poems had been published previously – in Charles Gildon's *Miscellany* (1701) and in Delarivière Manley's *Secret Memoirs . . . from the New Atalantis* (1709) – they had not borne her name. Nor, in fact, did *Miscellany Poems*, until its second printing in 1714. Charles H. Hinnant suggests that in submitting *Miscellany Poems* to the press, Finch was painfully conscious of the economic and legal contingencies which, following the Copyright Act of 1710, increasingly decided the outlines of authorial prerogative, often in competition with that of publishers and printers.[44] Fables' preponderance in *Miscellany Poems* both raises and potentially redresses the problem of representing authorial presence. It does so, moreover, in a symbolic form that, as we saw, thrives on authority's visible contingency. At the same time, because Finch's sex and sociopolitical position made the problem how to embody authority specific and unique, her Aesopian solutions stand apart from those of her male counterparts.

"Rehears'd as first 'twas told": the fables in *Miscellany Poems*

Miscellany Poems begins with "A Prefatory Fable" whose title, "Mercury and the Elephant," betrays the same preoccupation with the relationship between myth (Mercury) and matter (the elephant) that shapes Finch's translations of La Fontaine. This preoccupation had been explicit throughout the folio manuscript of 1689, first home to many of the fables that make up exactly half of the seventy-four poems in *Miscellany Poems*. But, with little exception, only the fables preserve it in the published collection. Most of the other pieces that Finch exposed to "publick View" seem demure by comparison; in addition to a verse tragedy, *Aristomenes*, they range from lyric verses to friendship poems, from songs and satires to meditations on death.[45] Thus not only do fables provide the only generic consistency in *Miscellany Poems*, but, by and large, only they sustain the furious energy and the sense of physical intimacy between the author and her readers that characterize the folio.

Be they translations of La Fontaine or imitations of L'Estrange, original fables about fable-making or paraphrases of Old Testament parables, the fables in *Miscellany Poems* take interactions between literary texts as their condition and theme. Their plots, meanwhile, chronicle the misfortunes of disgruntled hogs, sheep, goats, fleas, eagles, sows, cats, brambles, and assorted household appliances. Such plots bear familiar themes of frustrated desire into the mainstream of contemporary literary culture. At the same time, because Finch's morals often savagely confirm the folly of ambition and pretense, the fables in *Miscellany Poems* can no more be dismissed as allegories of frustration than they may be treated as unambiguous demonstrations of the vanity of human wishes. Rather, they oscillate between two poles of meaning, one public and one private, one covert and one conspicuous. In the end, they demonstrate these poles' mutual constitution, and finally their intertwining's status as the condition of Finch's own authority.

Several of Finch's fables, including "Mercury and the Elephant," take the making of fables as their subject. Their plots witness confrontations between self-indulgence or ambition (usually feminine) and social constraints against those desires. Taken as a group, Finch's metafables offer a running commentary on the compromises, exclusions, and dislocations that occur as any symbolic system crystallizes. Throughout, Finch reminds her anonymous readers that the text at hand is at issue in all of these processes.

As a preface, "Mercury and the Elephant" bridges Finch's writing and the outer world where it will circulate, while at the same time building an Aesopian foundation for the collection as a whole. Finch's "Prefatory Fable" prepares us to read *Miscellany Poems* as an extended argument, intimately addressed to the group of readers from which Finch herself is absent; within this argument, incidental fables may perform as clinching rhetorical devices. At the same time, however, "Mercury and the Elephant" shirks full commitment to such a program, for its official subject turns out to be its own defects, as defined by contemporary reading practices and standards of taste.

Finch's Mercury, "whose Errands are more Fleet than Good" (line 2), is a culturally valorized figure of symbolic transmission. By making Mercury's interlocutor an elephant, Finch forces bulky matter into a confrontation with authoritative methods of transmitting meaning. Mercury finds his path blocked by a disgruntled and "unweildy" pachyderm who contends that his late altercation with a "wild Boar of monstrous size" has been misrepresented: "Fame [...] with all her Tongues" has reported to "Brutes" and

"Men" alike that he took unfair advantage of "th'opposer." Hoping to acquit himself, the Elephant desires to know how the event "stands recorded" in the more important annals of heaven. An impatient Mercury brushes him off with the revelation that heaven never noticed the fight to begin with: "Then have you Fought?" he inquires with chilly disdain.

Finch's fable asks how a conflicted corporeal world can find its way into an established – here mythic – sign system. Evidently, it is only by obstructing them that the body can enter conventional channels of signification at all. The moral applies this impasse directly to Finch's own book. It thereby forgoes abstract reflection. As did Dryden's *The Hind and the Panther*, it pours its energy instead into the negotiations and contingencies that structure contemporary literary culture. In turn, it is that culture's founding principles that this fable breaks down into its material components and thereby contests:

> Solicitous thus should I be
> For what's said of my Verse and Me;
> Or shou'd my Friends Excuses frame,
> And beg the Criticks not to blame
> (Since from a Female Hand it came)
> Defects in Judgement, or in Wit;
> They'd but reply – Then has she Writ!   (lines 27–33)

Finch's moral uses the preceding fable to point to the shaping power of the "Female Hand." But it also converts the fable into an allegory of its author's own insignificance. The fable's conclusion seals the contradiction, for it finally authorizes the "Female Hand" simply by denying that public recognition matters. The closing couplet declares that poets write strictly "for our Selves," anyway, and that they "repair" to the "Press" only "to fix our scatter'd Papers there" (lines 47–48).

Like "The Goute and Spider," "Mercury and the Elephant" uses the story of a split – between the desire for self-representation and entrenched social expectations – to advocate a state of obscurity and internal reference. Yet as the critic's "Then has she writ!" echoes Mercury's "Then have you fought?" Finch links fighting with writing, poking fun at her own ambitions with a metaphor that also reveals what is at stake in them. In turn, because "Mercury and the Elephant" constructs such an explicit parallel between the predicament *in* the fable and the predicament *of* the fable, it also develops an alternative frame of reference – one that manages to compound the bodily origins of written signs (their literal origins in the "female Hand") with what happens in the public, and notoriously uncontrollable, "Press." As printed matter and the body become rhetorically equivalent points of origin, an alternative application emerges. This is the realm of the animate page, now fully equipped to negotiate between the public domain and a private world of strife and longing. True, thematically and in the conventional connection between story and moral, Finch's fable is self-mocking and resigned. Aesopically, however, it develops new frames of reference that render resignation and disclaimer themselves rhetorical poses with investigable origins.

Halfway through *Miscellany Poems*, Finch raises the question of how fables themselves fit into literary culture. Finch's instructive exchange between "The Critick and the Fable-Writer" begins with a sigh of relief as it greets fables' liberating obscurity in the canon of literary forms. It identifies fables with private and often sensuous experience, where "Teach[ing]" and "Divert[ing]" are fully compatible, and where the capricious swerve of a sentence less obstructs or diverts useful meanings than brings them into being:

> Weary, at last, of the *Pindarick* way,
> Thro" which advent'rously the Muse wou'd stray,
> To *Fable* I descend with soft Delight,
> Pleas'd to Translate, or easily Endite:
> Whilst aery Fictions hastily repair
> To fill my Page, and rid my Thoughts of Care,
> As they to Birds and Beasts new Gifts impart,
> And teach, as Poets shou'd, whilst they Divert.   (lines 1–8)

"Fill[ing the] Page" with fables promises free rein and boundless pleasure. As they appear out of nowhere, however, these lines are also unrecognizable as part of a fable; in fact, Finch's poem only assumes the literary form that it professes (that of a fable) when a literary critic's voice interrupts the free fall of the first verse paragraph. The fable, that is, becomes a fable only when the lyrical and subjective voice that speaks first is isolated and objectified as the exponent of one (contingent) point of view:

> But here, the *Critick* bids me check this Vein
> *Fable*, he crys, tho" grown th'affected Strain,
> But dies, as it was born, without Regard or Pain.
> Whilst of his Aim the lazy Trifler fails,
> Who seeks to purchase Fame by childish Tales.   (lines 9–13)

Like the "Fable-writer" he reprimands, the critic identifies fables – "childish Tales" – with joyful life, low writing, and free play. And these he naturally devalues, finding them, like the elephant's Aesopian tussle with the boar, ill-equipped to purchase "Fame." At the same time, however, the Critick's "but here" has an important textual effect, for it transports the poem's self-involved opening lines into the public domain of literary evaluation and exchange. This is of course precisely the world from which the author of "Mercury and the Elephant" seems so ambivalently alienated.

The rest of the fable races through the list of genres (epic, pastoral, satire) the "Critick" approves even as he dismisses less lofty literary forms as "Bombast," or as "insipid Dreams." When Finch's moral comes reeling out of the scene of generic exhaustion muttering, *"Happy the Men, whom we divert with Ease,/ Whome Operas and Panegyricks please"* (lines 59–60), the forces of pleasure, diversion and desire that prevailed at the beginning of the poem resurface as acceptable literary values. The words "divert" and "ease" even resuscitate the values of the opening verse paragraph. But having shifted their referential allegiance to "Operas" and "Panegyrick," these values no longer apply to fables. Instead, the critic's invasion has pushed the fable into the rhetorical frame of the present poem, where it becomes the very authority that calls a halt to the gentle play of creative sensations and literary possibilities ("Translat[ing,]" "easily Edit[ing]," spinning "aery Fictions") with which the poem begins. As "The Critick and the Fable-writer" turns into a fable, in other words, fables lose their initial subversive liberty. Rather, they become a scene of confrontation between uninhibited desires and the demands of contemporary literary culture. Fables are thus defined by a radical ambivalence toward the different possibilities among which they mediate, not by their affinity with the realm of the body and its desires.

If both "Mercury and the Elephant" and "The Critick and the Fable-Writer" treat fables as women's writing, two other metafables in *Miscellany Poems* actually add women to their originals. "The Poor Man's Lamb," for instance, paraphrases the parable of the poor man and his lamb which, in II Samuel, Nathan invents to reprimand David for murdering Uriah and marrying his widow, Bathsheba. As in the Old Testament account, he tells the story of a "King-like Man" who, though he owns "countless [. . .] Flocks," steals and slaughters a poor man's lamb. At fable's end, David swears vengeance on the villain, but Nathan points out that *"Thou art the Man."* A parable of David's own atrocities, the story persuades the king to abjure his "false nuptials" with Bathsheba. Vowing to return to righteous ways, David "tears the Nuptial Vest/By which his Crime's Completion was exprest" (lines 155–156).

Finch's paraphrase testifies to fables' efficacy, which she attributes to the deft knitting of linguistic designs and sensible *données*. But, quite unlike II Samuel, "The Poor Man's Lamb" dwells on the parable's consequences for Bathsheba, whose marriage to David had meant that "with his Heart the Kingdom too is hers": *"Queen* she's made, than *Michal* seated higher,/Whilst light unusual Airs prophane the hallow'd Lyre" (lines 31–32). The parable aims to disband a political structure – a system of authority – in which the king is "by Passion sway'd and glorious Woman taught." The objectionable order is identified as one that empowers women and the body. It recalls both the amorous and "violent excursion[s]" that Finch's folio preface found so seductive and the "light unusual Airs" that the "Fable-writer" was loath to relinquish to the carping "Critick." To the extent that Nathan's parable dethrones Bathsheba and the forms of authority that she represents, fables again pit themselves against an explicitly feminized ambition and desire. But as a negotiation with an Old Testament text, Finch's poem actually registers ambivalence. The ancient parable becomes a modern fable. Truly the handiwork of an Augustan Aesop, its moral counts the costs and real consequences of linguistic authority and weaves them into the very fiber of Finch's text.

"The King and the Shepherd" likewise employs sovereigns, shepherds, and fabulists-within-the fable, presumably in order to demonstrate fables' efficacy. In Finch's translation of La Fontaine's "Le Berger et le Roi" (x.ix) a king spies a good shepherd and immediately recruits him from the "Pastures" to the palace. A neighboring hermit warns the shepherd that "Preferments treach'rous" and to illustrate the point tells the fable of the blind man who "froze upon a Bank/A *Serpent* found, which for a staff he took." The shepherd ignores Aesopian counsel and moves to court, where the envy of the courtiers soon drives him home again, convinced at last that "no one was e'er without the Curse of some Ambition born."

Like La Fontaine, Finch buries a fable about the hazards of ambition inside a fable about the folly of declining good advice. Verbal relationships therefore intertwine with themes that include the "seduc[tions]" of power and the desire for recognition. But Finch's diversions from her original are also instructive. "Le berger et le roi" begins with a brief disquisition on the relative influence of "deux demons," love and ambition, who continually besiege "la raison." La Fontaine decides that "l'Ambition ... étend le plus loin son empire;/Car même elle entre dans l'amour" (lines 6–7), and moves on to offer an illustration of ambition's power. Finch's beginning nearly doubles the length of La Fontaine's, and while it keeps ambition as its theme, it also complicates the issue:

> Through ev'ry Age some Tyrant Passion reigns,
> Now *Love* prevails, and now *Ambition* gains
> Reason's lost Throne, and sov'reign Rule maintains.
> Tho" beyond Love's Ambition's Empire goes;
> For who feels Love, Ambition also knows,
> And proudly still aspires to be possest
> Of Her, he thinks superior to the rest.
> As cou'd be prov'd but that our plainer Task
> Do's no such Toil, or Definitions ask;
> But to be so rehears'd, as first 'twas told,
> When such old Stories pleas'd in Days of old.   (lines 2–12)

Finch's extended introduction writes the female body into a fable where it once had no place. The coveted woman stirs up a more complex struggle among forces of passion, possession, and power. Yet in order to maintain correspondence with La Fontaine, she must be excluded from her rightful role. This conspicuous exclusion in turn anchors the linguistic order of Finch's own fable, for only exclusion allows the fabulist to perform the "plainer Task" of "rehears[ing]" her story "as first 'twas told." Finch adds to La Fontaine by pointing out what he subtracts from his picture of human affairs. The double gesture creates new signifying possibilities, for, not unlike Dryden's *Fables*, her own poem finally crafts a plausible fiction of authority by calling attention to its own omissions and inadequacies.

The same paradoxical authority is exercised in Finch's two imitations of her own compatriot, Roger L'Estrange. Whereas most English fabulists (like Croxall a few years later) simply bent L'Estrange's fables to produce new morals, Finch retains original plots and morals and innovates from within them. From L'Estrange's hundreds of fables, she chose two that bring distressed human bodies into conflict with the (duplicitous) sign systems that dispose their fates. L'Estrange's "A Doctor and his Patient," for instance, tells the tale of a dying man whose physician insists that all of his symptoms actually promise recovery. L'Estrange's moral rules that "Death Bed Flattery is the worst of Treacheries"; the source of Finch's title, his "Reflexion" offers a political homology in which the patient is to the flattering doctor as the nation is to the statesman.[46] Finch besieges *her* patient with "shudd'ring Cold," "swooning Sweats," and "scalding Heats." Her "Quack" resolutely denies each symptom, abstracting material signs of impending death into cliches ("For the Better"), bad puns, and worse maxims ("They're most *Patient* who the most are seized"), false etiologies ("what you seem to feel/ Proceeds from Vapours"), and other "formal Stories." Finch's doctor is really a quack fabulist, and her extremely visceral rendition of L'Estrange's original explores fables' structure even as it identifies their victims.

"For the Better," that is, describes the alienation of material signs from the bodies that produce them, their appropriation into fictions that, by consent of custom, dispose those bodies' fates. Finch even applies this alienation to women's lives, for her powerless patient rails against the doctor's "Ignorance's Skreen, your *What-you-please,*/With which you cheat poor Females of their Lives,/Whilst Men dispute it not, so it rid their Wives" (lines 21–22). But to resolve the destructive split between word and symptom, the fable resorts to a third way of creating meaning. Unlike L'Estrange's, Finch's doctor departs when his patient runs out of money. The shift to money matters calls a halt to the conflict between body and symptom, distracting attention both from the graphic language of the flesh and from the lying prognosis, invoking instead a symbolic domain based on the exchange of discrete material tokens. Meanwhile, the fable itself offers a verbal equivalent of this resolution. In response to a friend's query, "the Sick" replies that "whilst all Symptoms tow'rd my Cure agree,/[I] am *for the Better*, Dying as you see" (lines 49–50). The patient's last words literally blend what his body has announced all along ("I am [...] Dying") with what the doctor has been saying all along ("For the Better"). The fable grafts the literal truth to the lie to mint a new jest that can be circulated in literary culture.

"There's No To-Morrow," meanwhile, even calls itself a "Jest." It too paraphrases a fable that L'Estrange built around an ironic discrepancy between body and sign. A pregnant woman who "desire[s]/The cloak of Wedlock, as the Case require[s]" is repeatedly put off by her lover's constant but never fulfilled "Vo[w], that he wou'd marry her *To-Morrow*." The "Jest" is that "To-Morrow" has no real referent: "There was no *To-Morrow*,/For when it comes in Place to be employ'd,/'Tis then *To-Day*." Nothing could more clearly demonstrate the tenuous link between the "Word" (or "Oath" or "Lie") and the body, "wrought [...] to this Sorrow," whose fate that "word" is nonetheless capable of determining. Once "employ'd," though, the word "To-Morrow" becomes efficacious and oppressive: fiction or no fiction, it wields power in the material world. Structurally, the fable elaborates this very insight as its moral confesses that "This Tale's a Jest; the Moral is a Truth;/ *To-Morrow*, and *To-morrow* cheat our Youth" (lines 16–17). Finch's tale, of course, is as much a "Truth" as her moral, for the moral's lesson is, precisely, that fictions are powerful, that even jests have consequences in the world of "Truth," which they shape. By casting her "Tale" as a "Jest," Finch appears to trivialize the "pregnant Dame"'s predicament, but her woman "wrought to sorrow" also visibly bears the cost of the quip.

Virtually all of the fables in *Miscellany Poems* redefine the boundaries between signs and the bodies whose fates they decide by displacing moral authority into textual particulars. Some of Finch's fables actually thematize this displacement. Their protagonists are enterprising bodies whose activities mimic the fables' own signifying strategies, but who are betrayed by the polyvalent scenes of their own devising. Finch's morals convert their predicaments into cautionary tales. But such chastening also becomes the condition of a fable's legibility and thus exposes the structure of prevailing habits of signification.

"Jupiter and the Farmer" translates La Fontaine's "Jupiter et le métayer" (vi.iv). In the French fable, Jupiter gives an undesirable farm to a peasant "non pas le plus sage" (line 8). The peasant agrees to accept the gift if the god will allow him to control the weather affecting the plot in question. Jupiter consents; the farmer disastrously mismanages the elements, repents of his "imprudence" and is so mercifully dealt with by "le maître fort doux" that the fable "conclu[t] que la Providence./Sait ce qu'il nous fait mieux que nous" (lines 30–31). The fable enjoins both the powerful (be benevolent) and the powerless (accept the dispositions of "Providence"), for it can count on a social structure that maintains an absolute difference between the powerful – who act by acting – and the powerless – who act by interpreting. It inhabits, and reproduces, a vertical gift economy rather than a horizontal one based on exchange.

This is not the way of the English poet Anne Finch's world. Her bankrupt Jupiter holds "traffick with the Earth." He "had a Farm to Lett," not give, and moreover "the Fine was high,/For much the Treas'ry wanted a Supply,/ By *Danae*'s wealthy Show'r exhausted quite, and dry" (lines 3–5). Though well fortified by myth, this new economy of possession and rental is much less stable than the one ruling La Fontaine's fable. Here verbal tokens too must behave differently: the powerful must be incited to interpretation rather than to action. Finch's fable after all is headed not for a Parisian salon but rather for an English reading public whose members will have bought her book.

"Various Projects rolling in his Breast," Finch's poor clown also signs his lease in return for control over the elements, and catastrophe rewards his efforts to adjust the "Scene" that surrounds him to his own satisfaction. The English fable ends with his unanswered appeal to the heavens:

> O *Jupiter*! with Famine pinch'd he cries,
> No more will I direct th'unerring Skies,
> No more my Substance on a Project lay,
> No more a sullen Doubt I will betray,
> Let me but live to Reap, do thou appoint the way.   (lines 26–30)

As Finch's series of "no more[s]" takes the place of a stated moral, the farmer's own words consent to the forces that pinch his own body. These in turn overlap with the conditions that grant this fable its significance. The farmer's pinched flesh provides a speaking (and telling) image of Finch's fable's own linguistic status. "Jupiter and the Farmer" seems to be about the folly of projection. It appears to urge resignation to divine "appoint[ment]." But it is also a performative and self-reflexive allegory of aesthetic dispossession in the same modern marketplace in which Finch's *Miscellany Poems* was bought and sold.

In another departure from La Fontaine, Finch's first line significantly – and self-reflexively – fixes the poem in literary history, at a moment "when Poets gave their God in *Crete* a Birth." Once this conspicuously literary framework is established, symbolic action moves immediately into the foreground. Just so, Finch recasts Mercury as the villain responsible for the farm's prolonged vacancy:

> But *Merc'ry*, who as Steward kept the Court
> So rack'd the Rent, that all who made Resort
> Unsatisfy'd return'd so, nor cou'd agree
> To use the Lands, or pay his secret Fee.   (lines 6–9)

This is a very different disincentive indeed from La Fontaine's non-arable land, and, since Mercury is a figure of communication already suffering from the bad press of "Prefatory Fable," it is also a most significant one. Exemplified in his "secret Fee," Mercury's greed turns the poem into a fable about artists who lack symbolic authority.

Fittingly, Mercury soon drops out of the picture, to be replaced by a discussion of the "Terms" of the peasant's contract with Jupiter. These are simple, each reducible to some aspect of the peasant's "Desire." More sensuous and complex than that of La Fontaine's "métayer," the peasant's wish is for "the frost to kill the Worm, the brooding Snow" and that "the filling Rains may come, and Phoebus glow" (lines 14–15). But the "sign[ing] and seal[ing of] the Lease" depends on desire's translation into legible "Terms" – into a vocabulary of contract and exchange.

The rest of the fable recounts the farmer's requests and "crav[ings]," and his endless bungling within the confines of the contract:

> The Sun, th'o'ershadowing Clouds, the moist'ning Dews
> He with such Contrariety does chuse;
> So often and so oddly shifts the Scene.
> Whilst others Load, he scarce as what to Glean.   (lines 22–25)

When at last the starving farmer begs Jupiter to "appoint the Way," he becomes a cautionary example of the chaos that ensues when the impersonal traffic of signs admits desire. But the fable also communicates a very clear message about the nature of ambition in a modern cultural setting. Finch's fables at once participate in that culture and challenge its assumptions and imperatives. As much class- as gender-based, her critiques of materialist systems of acquisition and exchange are nevertheless also, and self-consciously, mounted from within them.

A second fable, this one original and interested in sexual politics, offers a comparable allegory of aesthetic dispossession. It subtly links that dispossession to a prevailing set of linguistic conventions and to the power structures that they mask. "The Owl Describing her Young Ones" is quite legible as a story about the female artist's fate in patriarchy. But it is also about symbolic arrangements that claim as their basic principles equity, reciprocity, and the free and open exchange of signs and services.

Finch's lead players are an eagle and an owl – a patriarch and a mother. Although both are birds, Finch houses the sovereign Eagle at the top of the cedars, the Owl and her offspring in the "Holes" of an "ancient Yew." The two birds have "seal'd" a contract that should regulate their differences: on the condition that the owl "promise from her Heart/All his Night-Dangers to Divert," the "King of *Cedars* wav[es] his Power" and promises not to "devour" her daughters. The eagle, however, also demands that the owl "but shew [her children] or describe" them. The Owl chooses the second option, representing her daughters as "pretty Souls" whose "Eyes outshine the Stars by Night" (lines 22–23). On a night when she is "prol'd away,/To seek abroad for needful Prey," the hungry Eagle spies the owlets in the flesh. Marking their "Vulture's Necks/And Shoulders higher than their Necks," he concludes that they bear no resemblance to the "enchanting beauteous Race" their mother had painted and that "for [his] Supper they're designed."

Without further ado, "the plumes are stripped, the Grisles broke." The eagle
feasts. And the Owl returns to find her "Family [...] out of frame," not only
literally mangled but also ripped out of the descriptive frame that she had
invented with her own words. The eagle vindicates himself on the grounds
that the Owl "ly'd in every Word [she] said." He is not to blame for missing
the correspondence between her story and its referent. Finally, Finch's moral
extends the analogy to literary culture: "*Faces or Books beyond their Worth
extoll'd./Are censur'd most, and thus to Pieces pull'd*" (lines 76–77).

"The Owl Describing Her Young Ones" figures women's verbal art in a
discursive system regulated by contractual relations designed to uphold male
prerogative. Even if the owl's natural talent for "diver[sion]" did not link her
with the deviant female poet of Finch's earlier work, the moral automatically
applies her predicament to the fate of female-authored texts in modern
English literary culture. It therefore revives the anxieties and apprehensions
set forth at the beginning of *Miscellany Poems*. It too compounds material
violence with its linguistic, aesthetic, and literary counterparts. *Miscellany Poems*
itself becomes the owlets, Finch the mother owl, her reader the eagle. Yet the
moral also takes sides against the owl, denying her progeny's "Worth," and
dismissing the mother's fictions – indeed identifying her with darkness,
disturbance, and "ill Omens." The fable is thus suspended between the eagle's
interpretive authority and the owl's diverting but also threatening fantasies.

As it applies the fable to textual relations, however, the moral renders *both*
positions rhetorical stances between which the (female-authored) page alone
manages to mediate. The fable types the eagle as a "League Breaker" even as
it chastises and mocks the owl's delusions: both are fictions, both contribute
to the gruesome fate of pages, and owls. Meanwhile, though, the fable itself
assumes a third kind of authority – one (reminiscent of Dryden's *The Hind and
the Panther*) that resides neither in brute power nor in crafty diversion but
rather in the project of revealing these positions as mutually constitutive, and
as materially relevant to contemporary habits of symbolic exchange.

From the beginning of her poetic career, Anne Finch articulated her
literary ambitions in fables. In "The Bird and the Arras," she tells the story of
a bird "by neer Resemblance [...] betray'd," who "mistakes a well-wrought
Arras" for a real landscape (lines 1–2). After several failures to escape into the
arras, the bird sinks to the floor "in flutt'ring Cercles of Dismay"; the poem
concludes that she must wait patiently for a hand to lift her to "ample Space,
the only Heav'n of Birds." Repulsed by the "obdurate Scean" that cripples
the range of experience, the bird (a finch, no doubt) also confronts limited
possibilities for representing that experience. She finds herself at once
mirrored and obstructed by the "immitated Fowl" who "their pinnions ply"
across the screen: she is trapped not only by a literal boundary (the screen of
figures) but also by her own body, likewise suspended between the literal and
the figural.

Along with "The Goute and Spider," "The Bird and Arras" was one of the few fables that Finch never published. But over the years, she developed an increasingly complex and public relationship to Aesopian writing. Her fables rearrange the boundaries between the figural and the literal in conspicuously literary space. They balance moral directive and imaginative experiment, cultural imposition and rebellions against it; eventually they show that these evident oppositions are in fact intertwined. Such reactive mediations place Finch's fables firmly within the Aesopian conventions we have been examining; in themselves, they testify to the Stuart-sympathizing woman writer's full participation in Augustan literary culture. Like Dryden, Finch used Aesopian strategy to redefine the relationship between the literal and the figural, indeed to create a place for the authorial body within the prolific monstrosity of an emerging literary culture. As her fables faithfully imitate her spider's "transparent Laberynth," inventing obstructions in order to illuminate, they follow to the letter an Aesopian prescription for surviving in the state of culture.

6

Risking contradiction: John Gay's *Fables* and the matter of reading

> The man, who with undaunted toils,
> Sails unknown seas to unknown soils,
> With various wonders feasts his sight:
> What stranger wonders does he write!
> We read, and in description view
> Creatures which *Adam* never knew;
> For, when we risque no contradiction,
> It prompts the tongue to deal in fiction.
>
> John Gay, "The Elephant and the Bookseller" (1727)

> [Gay's] fables, the most popular of all his works, have the fault of many modern fable-writers, the ascribing to the different animals and objects introduced, speeches and actions inconsistent with their several natures. An elephant can have nothing to do in a bookseller's shop.
>
> Joseph Warton, *Essay on the Genius and Writings of Pope* (1756)

To Augustan readers, John Gay's first collection of animal fables (1727) must have come as no surprise. With Aesop still all the rage and Gulliver's voyage to Houyhnhnmland (1726) a very recent memory, no one would have wondered to find "creatures which *Adam* never knew" holding forth on every page of Gay's handsomely illustrated *Fables*.[1] Nor, since George II had just acceded to the throne, would anyone have batted an eye when "his most faithful and obedient servant" dedicated the *Fables* to George's five-year-old son, Prince William. Primed by Gay's irreverent renditions of venerated literary forms, like the pastoral, his contemporaries would have known how to appreciate his mocking exaggerations of fables' vaunted powers of moral exposition. And with Gay the pet of glittering satirists like Pope and Swift – evidently happy, in Thackeray's later phrase, to "frisk and fondle [...] and sport and bark and caper" for his more illustrious friends – few must have marvelled at lions and butterflies who ape human obsession with self-representation, while needles and roses hold forth on the subject of their own significance.[2]

156

What readers perhaps did not expect was a troupe of animals, vegetables, and household objects who are themselves voracious readers. Even Swift's Houyhnhnms steer clear of the written word, but in a *reductio ad absurdum* of Aesopian convention, Gay has a boar and a ram moralize a sheepskin strung from a nearby tree. A turkey studies the tribe of black ants slated to become her breakfast and contemplates her own future beneath the butcher's blade. Stumbling across a well, a young cock "mounts the margin's round,/And prys into the depth profound."[3] These are all arresting approximations of the act of reading. To crown them all, in Gay's most notorious fable an elephant has only to stroll into a bookseller's shop before "a book his curious eye detains,/ Where with exactest care and pains,/Were ev'ry beast and bird portray'd,/ That e'er the search of man survey'd."[4] The elephant launches into a scathing review of this intriguing text, but when the bookseller offers to employ him as a hack critic, he "wrinkl[es] with a sneer his trunk," declining the offer on the grounds that the book trade is already glutted with the printed progeny of "the senseless sons of men." Nor would he care to market his own alterity, thank you very much: let someone else "write the history of *Siam*."

Gay's own *Fables* have received decidedly mixed reviews since their debut. While many influential readers have had reservations about them, others – often women, children, and colonials – have adored a group of poems whose title alone acknowledges a steep debt to the English Aesop. Just one look at Gay's learned pachyderm suggests a reason for this split in readerly opinion, for the story of his altercation with the bookseller puts him at least on a par with the human being who would employ him; the fable claims the printed page as ground common to two very different links in the chain of being. While cultural subalterns might naturally have warmed to such exhibits of parity, it is a very small wonder that, even though the speaking animal pretense remained an acceptable literary convention, the loftier custodians of eighteenth-century literary culture came to regret Gay's *Fables* in general, and "The Elephant and the Bookseller" in particular, as "a fiction wherein no regard is had to the nature of things."[5]

As it happens, the "sagacious" brute in question holds much the same opinion of the text before him:

> The page he with attention spread,
> And thus remarked on what he read.
>   Man with strong reason is endow'd;
> A beast scarce instinct is allow'd:
> But let this author's worth be try'd,
> 'Tis plain that neither was his guide.
> Can he discern the diff'rent natures,
> And weigh the pow'r of other creatures,
> Who by the partial work hath show
> He knows so little of his own?   (lines 33–42)

Not unlike Finch's (whose frustrating encounter with Mercury we examined in Chapter 5), Gay's elephant places himself on the side of the misrepresented and misconstrued. As a declared underdog, he is able to criticize entrenched assumptions about the proper order of things, including its necessary correspondence to the way it is depicted. But he is also a creature of culture. Unlike many of Gay's own readers, this elephant "the *Greek* can read," and as he indicts the unnamed author's failure to "discern" difference and "weigh the pow'r" of others, he embraces the very "partial" sense of hierarchy he deplores.

Because Gay's elephant signifies from within the symbolic structure that he denounces, it is finally less the text at hand (or at trunk) than the criticism of it that risks credibility. And it is less this fable's willingness to give voice to creatures usually muted than the compromised character of what they say that makes it so unsettling. Like many others in the collection, Gay's poem risks self-contradiction. As even one of its most perceptive interpreters admits, it is "difficult to define."[6] Above all the fable defies those determined to extract a single clear moral from what they read. Indeed, one such reader, Samuel Johnson, found the *Fables* downright *un*readable. Gay had never "formed any distinct or settled notion" of how he wanted his fables to work, Johnson decided. They were so hopelessly "confounded both with Tales and allegorical Prosopopoeias [that] by whatever name they may be called, it will be difficult to extract any moral principle."[7]

Although – *vide* Swift – ambivalence to Aesop had always existed alongside a rueful intoxication with him, Johnson ultimately spoke from a new moment in the history of reading, one intolerant of the Aesopian strategies that have claimed our attention so far. As we will see, Gay's own fables straddle the shift in literary attitudes that Johnson's remarks announce: a second collection was published posthumously in 1738, and each of the sixteen poems to be found there hijacks a fable into the idioms of verse epistle and high neoclassical satire. The 1727 fables work much differently. They share – indeed amplify – the spirit of the popular collections and biographies of Aesop. In particular, like the most complex of his Aesopian precursors, Gay wove compliance with contemporary print culture together with criticism of it to forge a uniquely embodied literary language, one that established literary authority by displaying its vulnerability.

Rather deaf to this language, Johnson used the evidently "confounded" texture of the *Fables* as an excuse to classify Gay as the "Poet of a Lower Order" – rank that Gay has held in the critical imagination ever since. Just as Victorian readers pronounced the *Fables* the "ambling and slipshod" offspring of a very minor talent,[8] so most of their twentieth-century readers have treated them as mildly amusing satires against contemporary politics and manners.[9] But by reading the *Fables* as fables – as self-conscious, and performative, verbal devices through which a text-centered culture articulates, examines and ultimately perpetuates itself – we can come to a fuller understanding of them. Like *The Beggar's Opera* (1728), the *Fables* forge powerful bonds with the "lower" phylogenetic, social, and literary orders. But the *Fables* also explore the ties that bind these orders to the ones above them. And, in an increasingly critical analysis of Aesopian convention, they implicate books – and with them textual authority itself – in the resulting ambiguous and often fraught relationship.

Confounding the credit of the book: the 1727 *Fables* in history

"The last Year may be justly esteemed a *Year* of *Wonders*, not inferior to any in recorded History," observed an anonymous essay in a 1727 issue of *The Craftsman*, leading newspaper of the opposition press. Tongue in cheek, the essay proceeded "to enumerate all those stupendous Prodigies, mishapen [*sic*] Monsters, strange Sights, and unheard-of Wonders which have late been exhibited to our Eyes" – "the *wild Human Youth*, brought forth by an old Oak, in a desert, uninhabited Forest abroad, [...] the young *Lyons* whelp'd in so uncommon a manner at home, [...] black Swans, white Bears, six-legged Cows, Men with two Heads, flying Horses, speaking Dogs, and dancing Elephants in abundance, [...] portentous Rarities of all Kinds."[10]

With such "stupendous Prodigies" abroad in the world, Gay's 1727 fables look more like chapters in a natural history than flagrant fictions. Many proffer the soberest advice: "Lest men suspect your tale untrue," one warns, "Keep probability in view;/The traveler who leaps o'er bounds/The credit of his book confounds."[11] The 1727 *Fables* shamelessly milk the Aesopian pretense that it is perfectly reasonable for animals to make liberal use of human sign systems. Bulls quibble with mastiffs and lions with geese; goats hire simian barbers to shave their beards and when worldly monkeys come home to the jungle showing off the European manners that they have just acquired, their friends and family flock to "copy human ways."[12]

The pages of Gay's *Fables* are also riddled with beasts that read, and it is most consistently the shared habit of evaluating visible signs that knits the lofty human and the lowly animal together. In true Aesopian fashion, the *Fables* themselves appealed to human readers of many different stripes; subscribers to the famed Stockdale edition of 1793 ranged from marquises to schoolmasters. Officially intended for "the Amusement" of a prince, the *Fables* became a staple of the growing market for far less privileged classes. If frequently reprinted "for the Practice and Amusement of Gentlemen and Ladies," they also appealed to middle-class mothers and their sons. Even hack journalists sang their praises. In 1754, for example, a poem in the *Gentleman's Magazine* confessed that

> I've trac'd Gay's Fables o'er and o'er,
> Which often read, delight the more,
> Their morals are exceeding good,
> If rightly weigh'd and understood,
> An ample present for a prince,
> To feast and cultivate his sense;
> T'embellish, form and clear his mind,
> And learn him how to read mankind.[13]

Such appraisals of the 1727 *Fables* recognized that they are fundamentally about reading, an activity obviously common to "prince" and poor poet alike.

But Prince William, the exemplary reader whose "sense" they allegedly "cultivate[d]," grew up to lead the slaughter of the Scots at the Battle of Culloden (1745). As Thackeray put it, the 1727 *Fables* evidently "did not effect much benefit upon the illustrious young prince, whose manners they were intended to mollify, and whose natural ferocity our gentle-hearted satirist perhaps proposed to restrain."[14] On the contrary, the 1727 *Fables* failed to prevent the abuse of power and, as if to hint that they might even have encouraged it, Gay's dedicatee was in adulthood caricatured as a calf in butcher's clothes. So portrayed, William became a living illustration for a fable collection that abounds with often brutally violent scenes of category-crossing. Presumably, such scenes were meant to "learn" their consumers "how to read mankind," but they also hired themselves out to other, less benign ends.

Whether we consider them biographically, structurally, or thematically, in terms of their reception and cultural use or in the context of critical responses to them, what is clear is that, even more explicitly than earlier English fables, the 1727 *Fables* refer questions of relationship between seemingly distinct categories to the levelling, but also subtly brutalizing, process of reading. For instance, to approach the 1727 *Fables* biographically, we have only to turn to the last of the fifty poems in the collection. Eighteenth-century readers were especially fond of "The Hare and many Friends": Mary Barber centered her poetic appreciation of the whole volume on it and Jane Austen's Catherine Morland knows it "as well as any girl in England."[15] The fable begs to be read as an allegory of Gay's own frustrated efforts to obtain recognition at court, for its eponymous

> Hare, who, in a civil way,
> Comply'd with ev'ry thing, like *Gay*,
> Was known by all the bestial train,
> Who haunt the wood, or graze the plain:
> Her case was, never to offend,
> And ev'ry creature was her friend.[16]

Once a hunter sets his sights upon the hare, however, her friends refuse to shield her; even the "feeble" sheep perverts fellow feeling and denies her the refuge of his wool on the grounds that "hounds eat sheep as well as hares." The fable ends in suspense, "the hounds [...] just in view," and the hare left with no place to run, no body to which she might, literally, attach herself.[17] At the same time that it leaves room for royal readers to intervene as patrons, her plight confirms the string of morals that ties the first stanza together:

> Friendship, like love, is but a name,
> Unless to one you stint the flame.
> The child, whom many fathers share,
> Hath seldom known a father's care;
> 'Tis thus in friendships; who depend
> On many, rarely find a friend.   (lines 1–6)

"The Hare and many Friends" recapitulates in miniature the *Fables'* bid for the attention of the new ruling family. The poem itself shares the hare's terrible suspension between dependence and recognition, subjugation and the social significance that equals survival. In turn, both plot and text mimic – and serve – Gay's own way of life, coordinating a servile sociability with other forms of subordination and marginality; the hare is female and wild, while the horse, bull, goat, sheep, and calf who decline to assist her are all male and domesticated, as is the hunter from whose "deep-mouth'd thunder" she flees. In the fable, childishness, femaleness, and hareness are all roles demanded and defined by the signifying structure in which they participate. By playing with respect to its reader precisely the part that the hare's petition plays with respect to the other animals, the telltale fable perpetuates the scheme that both makes it possible and limits it.

Many readers have imagined Gay himself as unmanly – as childish, effeminate, animal. One Victorian ventured that he "understood animals so well because he had so much of the animal in him';[18] Austin Dobson admitted how easy it was to find the *Fables* "wearisome, almost unmanly."[19] Even a modern character sketch describes Gay as "a sort of Augustan Peter Pan riding in the coaches of his noble friends."[20] In his own century, Gay was often compared to La Fontaine: notoriously childlike, the French fabulist had prospered by amusing powerful patrons. Others identified Gay with the belatedly freed classical slave Phaedrus; Christopher Smart even pointed out the happy coincidence that "PHAEDRUS in Greek ... signifies Gay" and "thus there is a great resemblance between the Roman Fabulist and the Englishman."[21] All of these identifications recognize that the modern English fabulist speaks from culture's sidelines and lower rungs even as he expresses devotion to what keeps him there.

Gay wrote to Pope that composing his first round of fables had put him in a "strange confusion and depression of spirits,"[22] and to Swift that "though this is the kind of writing that appears very easy, I find it is the most difficult of any I undertook. After I had invented and finished one fable, I despaired of finding another."[23] Part of Gay's depression certainly stemmed from the *Fables*" miscarriage as instruments in his none-too-subtle bid for patronage: the Hanovers offered Gay only the degrading post of Gentleman Usher to the two-year-old Princess Louisa. Insulted, Gay declined, and after Walpole stripped him of his position as Commissioner of the State Lottery (a position Gay's forefather John Ogilby would have coveted), he retired to the estate of his old and devoted friends, the Duke and Duchess of Queensberry, where his last, bitter fables were born.[24]

But Gay's despondency may have had other sources. In life, of course, our human hare's many friends did not leave him to face the hunter's gun. The point of the fable, though, is not just that "friendship, like love, is but a name,/Unless to one you stint the flame." More urgently, the hare's eagerness to "comply" and "never to offend" itself supports a violent, frustrating, and inevitably oppressive order. This order is preserved by signs and symbols (many dispersed "name[s]"), and in it the possibilities for self-representation are limited by the perceptions of others – perceptions that the hare herself compulsively confirms with every new petition. By encouraging his own readers to interpret the fable and others like it as poems *à clef*, Gay could not help but court their debasement.

A like duplicity characterized *Fables*' fate in popular culture. Over 300 editions of Gay's *Fables* had made their way into the world by the middle of the nineteenth century. Translated not only into the usual European tongues but also into languages as exotic as Urdu and Bengali, they found an ardent international audience as well. Illustrations by six different engravers further enhanced *Fables*' market value,[25] generating motifs that showed up in mantelpieces, china patterns, and *bas reliefs* throughout England. Thomas Bewick and William Blake both later illustrated popular editions of *Fables*; Bewick won a prize for his in 1778.

Often reprinted along with penny histories and ballads in publishing houses that catered to the lower classes, *Fables* also fed a growing appetite for children's literature. As early as 1731 they were to be found "curiously engrav'd for the Practice and Amusement of Young Gentlemen and Ladies'; Mary Barber described a mother's "vast Pleasure" as she reads Gay's *Fables* to her son. Moved by the fable of the hare with many friends, the boy imagines his mother "Queen" and the fables "writ for me'; though in reality "barr'd .../From the best Privilege of Courts," the mother can in fantasy become Caroline showering Gay with the recognition and financial compensation ("at least a thousand Pounds a Year") he merits.[26] Gay's *Fables* made him a hero of the domestic scene, the realm of affection and imagination where the powerless preside. Not surprisingly, it was a woman who first translated them into French.[27]

But the charms that the *Fables* held for readers of the "lower" sociocultural orders are not simple ones. It is true that the *Fables* give voice to creatures often denied it: the scenario that unfolds in the fable of "The Turkey and the Ant" is typical. Surveying "the busy *Negro* race" of ants that supply her "most delightful meat" a turkey contemplates her own destiny under "the poult'rer's knife." When one of the ants in question urges her on just these grounds to "controul thy more voracious bill,/Nor for a breakfast nations kill,"[28] the fable gains an important global dimension. Importing their characters from "Persia," Africa, and "*Siam*," as well as from the bottom rungs in the ladder of species, Gay's fables grant "discourse" to the "lower" echelons of more than one "order." Then too, they seemed to grant special license to the least entitled of their historical readers. The gist of Barber's poem is that Gay's own dependency creates an analogy between one triangle – Barber, her son, and the *Fables* – and another – Queen Caroline, Prince William, and the *Fables*. The many translations of Gay's fables suggest that they licensed readers to turn their own readings into writing. And in *Northanger Abbey*, fables join romances to verify an epistemology that grants the presumably passive consumer of signs the power to become an author in her own right.

At the same time, however, because they are symbolic, such gains are tricky to evaluate. In Barber's poem, for example, the two triangles that the *Fables* put on parallel are actually overlapping homologies. Barber and her son are to the *Fables* as Caroline and William are to the *Fables*. With Gay's book as the intermediary term, the political structure of one triangle, based on subservience and *noblesse oblige*, dictates the political fantasy of the other. Just so, the *Fables* could be seen less to value the "lower" orders in their own right than to claim for the interests of the higher ones. In 1767, a verse printed beneath the frontispiece portrait of a turbaned Gay elevated the fabulist, praising this "favourite of the Muse" as "refin'd in Taste" and "superior to Many/Inferior to none." Gay's late eighteenth-century editor, William Coxe, supposed that "since the *aera of letters*, [...] scarcely five authors can be found who deserve particular mention," and, on the strength of the *Fables*, deemed Gay one of them. Barber classified him with "the Sages of Antiquity," and with Addison and Pope. The *Fables* thus flattered the very hierarchies they promise to flatten.

Predicted by their own themes, the *Fables'* guilty history is part of what makes them revealing performative readings of time-tested Aesopian poses. We saw that Aesop's fables became key figures in a culture whose forms of authority, increasingly, had to take hold in and through the often uncontrollable exchange of discrete graphic signs, usually in the shape of written words. Fables could both ironize and confirm this emerging cultural arrangement: they exposed authorial imposition but they also instilled differently authoritative – text-based – prescriptions for negotiating the significant world. This means that, from 1651 forward, fables worked to

empower their own readers, regaining mastery through their own performative subordination, either to readers whom they advised without seeming to
do so, or to other texts that absorbed them.[29] Gay's *Fables* certainly embrace
this legacy, in a way that identifies them even with fable collections as
conservative – and as culturally formative – as Locke's. But they also critique
it. The 1727 *Fables* carry to extremes the methods of some of Gay's most
complex predecessors, like Ogilby and L'Estrange, and often Gay revives the
reactively mediatory signs that Dryden and Finch used to embody literary
authority in their Aesopian writing. The 1727 *Fables* thereby point out – act
out – the fact that the integrity even of graphic and negotiable signs is
ultimately compromised by the very system of social practices that they are
meant to serve.

Literate brutes: the 1727 *Fables*

In the 1727 *Fables*, the founding presumption of Aesopian style is often
painfully obvious: non-human actors who wheel, deal, shave, speed-read, and
contemplate careers as trapeze artists are all eventually exposed as manmade
devices. Indeed, they themselves often claim to have contracted their foibles
from human beings. A lion, for example, confides that he kills other animals
and leaves their bones to bleach into trophies only because his courtiers
"agree/That human heroes rule like me."[30] A "monkey who had seen the
world" turns his simian compatriots into examples of human "malice, envy,
spite" by urging them to "grow like man polite" (lines 57, 54). Structurally,
Gay often put its morals at the beginning of a fable to make sure we notice
the human contrivance that turns innocent objects into legible signs. In the
stories themselves, ubiquitous butchers, tanners, hunters, and horse-tamers
advertise the pervasive power and violence of human invention. One rose
aptly informs the lover who raids her garden for flowers to give to his Chloe
(and for imagery he can use in love poetry) that "[You] found [Chloe's]
praise on our abuse."[31] At the same time, by allowing many morals to
proliferate in each poem, Gay not only overworks one of fables' distinctive
traits but induces his reader to take part in – and responsibility for –
meaning's guilty manufacture.

The first two fables in the 1727 collection build a fit platform for the
volume as a whole. First, Gay's "Introduction to the Fables" stages a
conventional debate between a shepherd who reads nature and a philosopher
who reads books. The juxtaposition investigates – and finally mocks – the
Aesopian maxim that examples are best precepts. The shepherd, whose
"wisdom and [whose] honest fame/Through all the country rais'd his
name,"[32] gets his moral codes from careful scrutiny of the animal kingdom:
"The daily labours of the bee/Awake my soul to industry," he assures the
"Sage" who has stopped by to ascertain whether or not the shepherd deserves
his reputation. "My dog (the trustiest of his kind)/With gratitude inflames my

mind" (lines 41–42). Impressed, the philosopher decides that the shepherd's "fame is just," and he draws what seems to be the appropriate moral – that "books affected are as men,/But he who studies nature's laws/From certain truths his maxims draws" (lines 79–81).

Once the shepherd's exemplary use of nature becomes a literary precept, however, the poem risks contradiction. Because they themselves appear in a book (*Fables*), the "maxims" to be drawn from the story *of* the shepherd's evidently exemplary readings of "simple nature" are not necessarily as reliable as the maxims that the shepherd presumably draws from the brutes he "mark[s]." The fable cannot demote books without also demoting the natural signs that it, part of a book, promotes. Indeed, the word "draw" describes not only how the shepherd "studies natures laws" but also how the "deep Philosopher" derives his "rules of moral life" from "schools."

While it thwarts readers who expect to extract a moral from it, "The Shepherd and the Philosopher" rewards those ready to acknowledge the complexity, and potential rapacity, of all assertions of symbolic authority. The second poem in the collection lets us practice this new kind of reading. As a wheedling appeal to Prince William, "The Lyon, the Tyger, and the Traveller"'s most explicit moral is that flattery is "the nurse of crimes" and its ambition is to teach its young reader how to detect its signs. "To those of your exalted station,/Each courtier is a dedication," Gay's own "Dedication" warns, by way of preface to the story of a lion preyed upon by his own "servile train" of courtiers (lines 13–14). When a few lines later Gay predicts, hyperbolically, that "True courage shall your bosom fire,/And future actions own your Sire" (lines 31–32), his cozening fable risks contradiction.

A similar risk shadows the moral's relationship to the fable that follows and that presumably endeavors to guide Prince William's "future actions" by instilling in him the precept that "cowards are cruel; but the brave/Love mercy and delight to save." Gay raises the odds against his own apparent didactic mission by offering not the example of a brave animal loving mercy and delighting to save but instead a debate about representation. Waged between a lion and man, the debate exposes the signifying web that underpins Gay's "moral lay."[33] In the fable, a lion rescues a human traveler from "a Tyger, roaming for his prey," then invites him back to his cave, so he can show off the signs that "attest [his] pow'r and right":

> These carcasses on either hand,
> Those bones that whiten all the land
> My former deeds and triumphs tell,
> Beneath these jaws what numbers fell.   (lines 57–60)

The traveler tries to persuade the lion to exercise his power in other ways: "Shall a monarch, brave like you/Place glory in so false a view?/...Be lov'd. Let justice bound your might" (lines 63–66). He wants to transport the lion's prized "carcasses" and "bones" into a new system of symbolic relations, one based on something other that "attestation" and "false" display. The lion admits that his guest's "case is plain." He even confesses he has been misled by delusions of "false glory," spurred by courtiers who, diligent "flatt'rers of my reign," praise him for his convincing imitations of human nature: "All my fawning rogues agree/That human heroes rule like me" (line 82). So brutally effective is the force of shameless blandishment that by fable's end the lion is still powerless to give up either his old signifying habits or the forms of violence with which they are interwoven.

Johnson's objection that Gay's fables "confound" too many different styles might certainly be raised here: what starts off as a simple attempt to warn against flattery and advocate "clemency" turns into a satire against the "fawning rogues" who parasitically exploit regal favor. More important, though, Gay's poem engages the same fable of the lion and the man that, we saw, epitomizes the English fable collection as a whole. In that fable it is the lion who points out the politics of representation and imagines a different figure that might set the record straight; most fabulists, we saw, applied his argument to Aesopian writing itself. Here, however, it is the man who finds fault with a particular kind of representation. And whereas before the fault lay with a non-verbal figure that could be made negotiable and self-critical through language, here it lies with language itself, as words stir invidious and insatiable desires. The poem's true foundation, that is, is the language of the "flatt'rers," which not only rules the lion but also decides what and how the carnage that strews his cave may mean. Without actually speaking it, the "fawning rogues" truly have the last word – "human rulers rule like me" – for the lion can only echo their duplicitous and evasive platitudes.

"The Lyon, the Tyger, and the Traveller" identifies a politics of representation more intricate, slippery, and dauntingly abstract than the one that fables usually haul up to scrutiny. What is more, in confessing its own resemblance not to the lion's gruesome monuments but rather to the sycophants who, it warns early on, are all "dedication[s]," Gay's dedicatory fable employs the very symbolic conventions – of flattery and duplicity – from which it at first strives to preserve a satiric distance.

Together, the first two of the 1727 *Fables* rummage back through decades of Aesopian convention to count the cost of cultural – and particularly figural and linguistic – security. In Gay's view, that security is achieved through an intricate web of symbolic involvements; one that bestows significance and visiblity on its constituent parts even as it demeans and abuses them. In turn, Gay's *Fables* propose that the symbolic system whose construction costs they figure is not necessarily a stable one after all: when a peasant nails a kite to his barn door to serve as "a terror to his kind," a visitor, who just happens to be Pythagoras, notices that "the hammer's sound/Shook the weak barn."[34] An Aesopian grammar of sensible examples and broadly intimated morals coincides with the logic of exploitation and greed; like the barn, both are precarious. Since the "Clown" at one blow murders and makes signs to preserve his own poultry – which Pythagoras correctly identifies as his "dinner" – he should "own . . . this manlike kite is slain/[His] greater lux'ry to sustain" (lines 37–38).

"On the wall his wings display'd," the "manlike kite" is only one of the many kinds of discrete graphic signs that the *Fables* single out, and then properly locate in ruthless and opportunistic symbolic systems that are ultimately based on rapacious employment. For instance, although "two formal owls" convince themselves of their own worth on the grounds that "on *Pallas*" helm we sit,/The type and ornament of wit,"[35] they come to this conclusion in a fable that scoffs at the very notion that authoritative meaning comes from discrete objects spatially arranged. The fable proposes instead that significance depends on the interweaving of such terms. This is in many ways an Aesopian insight: certainly it locates symbolic authority in demonstrated contingency. But Gay takes this insight one step further by foregrounding the patterns of exploitation, predation, and abuse, that it requires in order to reproduce itself.[36] Thus a sparrow urges the owls to stop identifying themselves as types and ornaments. Instead, they ought to "pursue the ways by nature taught" – i.e., to chase mice they will find more "delicious far" and thus be "prais[ed]," "reward[ed]," and "regard[ed]" in a far truer light. Just as the owls became performative figures of "vain glory," so a turkey who finds evidence of her "intrinsic merit" in her "whiter skin" provides fodder for a moral that translates her braggadocio into a visible sign of envy, itself a very different, and much more deeply implicated, mode of relationship between two terms. When two "grinning" monkeys at Southwark Fair cast themselves as the imitated originals of human dancers and tumblers, analogy loses all credibility. Instead, it is absorbed into a shifting and uncertain web of emulation and mimicry, where simian "criticks" come off little better than the trapeze artists they mock.

In Gay's *Fables*, plausible meaning, often identified thematically with physical survival, comes about through the interaction of adjacent terms. And this structural relationship in turn always, if ironically, threatens an entity's survival even as it temporarily preserves it. The 1727 *Fables* are thus an apposite forerunner to *The Beggar's Opera* (1728). Gay's "Newgate pastoral" pivots on Lockit's observation that "lions, wolves, and vultures don't live together in herds, droves or flocks. Of all animals of prey, man is the only sociable one. Every one of us preys upon his neighbour and yet we herd together."[37] As Eliza Haywood noticed, "a constant Strain runs through" *The Beggar's Opera*, "putting the whole Species pretty much upon a Level." Levelling comes about through the revelation that all levels are connected through common employments – everything acts in a "double capacity" that, Ian Donaldson has pointed out, shapes the play's verbal texture as well as the social order that it describes.[38] Drawing on the English fable's historical preoccupation with the the the structure of symbolic authority, Gay's 1727 *Fables* apply these ironies directly to the behavior of graphic signs. Because their verbal elements share the status of the characters who inhabit them, that is, fables are uniquely equipped to literalize symbolic relationships. In turn, they manage to capture not only the "real," or at least material, foundations of symbolic action, but also these foundations' linguistic aspect.

One fable, for instance, tells the story of a colt who, "elate with strength and youthful ire," refuses to be bitted and castigates the other horses as an "abject [...] race,/Condemn'd to slav'ry and disgrace." One aged horse, however, persuades the dissident that the equine relationship to "grateful man" is actually defined by mutual service: horses "lend [their] pains" and "aid [humans] to correct the plains," while humans provide food and shelter. This "*Nestor* of the plain" eventually persuades the colt to "act the part by Heaven assign'd" and the fable ends tersely: "The colt submitted,/And, like his ancestor was bitted." The fable might pretend to describe human culture in terms of "aid" and "len[t ...] pains." But it also makes what could be represented as a natural and inevitable relationship a matter of social roles – "parts [...] assign'd" less by "Heaven" than by convention, and perpetuated through a history of interpretation that is finally indistinguishable from a history of exploitation.

Other fables specify that this is also a history of linguistic practice. "The Old Woman and her Cats," for instance, begins with a familiar precept: "On the choice of friends/Our good or evil name depends."[39] To prove that significance is a function of dependency, Gay cites the Aesopian example of "a wrinkled hag, of wicked fame." The old woman is tormented as a witch because she maintains a "hellish train" of cats, while at the same time the cats are reputed "imps" because they live with her. Witch and familiars together achieve significance within the byzantine cultural grammar of "infamy."

The same grammar structures "The Fox at the Point of Death." Tormented by the guilty memory of "murder'd geese," "bleeding turkeys," and "chicken slain," a dying fox tries to inculcate in his sons the maxim that they should "restrain inordinate desire." The young foxes, however, are able only to interpret the old fox's words in terms of "what our ancestors have done;/A line of thieves from son to son" – in terms, that is, of a long, intricately braided history of representations in which "Infamy hath mark'd our race." The foxes recognize that their own credit depends on a tradition of institutionalized interpretations that decides what kinds of "mar[k]" or "name" may be reproduced, and even what analogies will be credible: "Though we, like harmless sheep, should feed,/...The change shall never be believ'd./A good lost name is ne'er retrieved."[40] Arbitrary though they might be, cultural conventions here prove indomitable, reproducing symbolic order and predatory self interest in direct – and mutually dependent – proportion.

As they make violent encroachment fundamental to symbolic order, the 1727 *Fables* invert any hierarchy that would place humans above animals: language, the *Fables* hint, employs both, and both thus occupy only arbitrarily assigned positions whose relations are better described in the terms of implication and convention than in those of natural right. This, as we have seen, is an Aesopian attitude, but Gay pushes it farther by applying it directly to the matter of reading. A case in point is the fable of "The Wild Boar and the Ram." The fable begins with a typical image – "Against an elm, a sheep was ty'd,/The butcher's knife in blood was dy'd."[41] A "patient flock" of sheep stands watching the flaying "in silent fright." When a "savage Boar" berates them as passive "cowards" who willingly participate in their own victimage, an "ancient Ram" rejoins that since sheep "want tusks to kill," they must extract revenge in other, more civil ways – by implication rather than by extraction:

> Know, Those who violence pursue
> Give to themselves the vengeance due,
> For in these massacres they find
> The two chief plagues that waste mankind.
> Our skin supplys the wrangling bar,
> It wakes their slumbring sons to war,
> And well revenge may rest contented,
> Since drums and parchment were invented.   (lines 21–28)

The ram's words make Gay's fable a performative allegory of guilty reading, one in which the material of representation – parchment and drumskin – literally consists of its interpreters.

The opening scene is appropriately dominated by a human "murd'rer" who "with purple hands and reeking knife/[...] strips the skin yet warm with life." This brutal assault, we learn, secures the pages that will perpetuate human culture in the form of legal "parchment." As John Wootten's plate (plate 8) appreciates, the image itself is actually peripheral. What matters is the opposing readings that the dark boar and the light ram apply to it. Without precisely assigning the living figure different meanings, the boar and the ram manufacture contradictory prescriptions for the kind of action that it demands. The wild boar reads the ensanguined spectacle as a sign of oppression and a clear "call for revenge." His moral is thus that "the heart that wants revenge is base." What the domesticated ram sees is that his "race" actually "want[s]" not "revenge" but "tusks to kill," and the moral he attaches to the "horrid sight" is a more complicated one, in which a violence explicitly of letters is made intrinsic to the perpetuation of culture. This arrangement is maintained by both the dominant and the submissive parties. Figurally, the ram's own well-wrought disquisition – a sign for Gay's own reader to evaluate in the context of its origins – replicates the very cultural process that it describes. "Drums" and "parchment" stand for "war" and "wrangling bar"

16   *FABLES.*

FABLE V.

The WILD BOAR *and the* RAM.

Gainſt an elm a ſheep was ty'd,
The butcher's knife in blood was dy'd;
The patient flock, in ſilent fright,
From far beheld the horrid ſight;
A ſavage Boar, who near them ſtood,
Thus mock'd to ſcorn the fleecy brood.

All cowards ſhould be ſerv'd like you.
See, ſee, your murd'rer is in view;   With

8   John Wootten, plate from John Gay, *Fables*, London, 1727.

in a metonymic economy continuous with the one in which sheepskin materially "supplys" an entire cultural system. The former supports the latter literally, as the helpless matter through which it is preserved, transmitted, reproduced. Gay uses the self-incriminating potential built into Aesopian style to prove that we may indeed "upbraid the passive sword with guilt."

Thematically and linguistically, the fable of the wild boar and the ram exemplifies the method of guilty reading that Gay's *Fables* themselves require. The requirement places them well within the Aesopian conventions that we have explored so far, conventions that redefine cultural assumptions about authority, figural origin, and symbolic propriety in terms that can ensure their perpetuation in a text-centered culture full of domineering readers. At the same time, however, Gay's *Fables* risk their own interesting constitutions by applying Aesopian insights directly to fables. Their tendency to do so makes "The Elephant and the Bookseller" truly the emblematic poem in the 1727 collection.

This fable begins by calling attention to its own unlikelihood, here seen as a side effect of textual representation: "We read, and in description view,/ Creatures which *Adam* never knew" (lines 5–6). But even before his elephant sets foot into the "shop of learning," Gay takes pains to guarantee the veracity of the scene he is about to describe: "Let those who question this report,/To *Pliny's* ancient page resort," the long preface invites (lines 18–19), citing a place in Pliny's *Naturalis Historia* where elephants indeed not only "learn the shapes of the Greek letters" but pray, write complex sentences, and contrive intricate social rituals.[42]

Although few of Gay's contemporaries would scarcely have taken Pliny as a sacred authority, the citation pretends to dig underneath the verbal surface of the text to unearth a body of corroborating material – real animals turning real pages. What it "really" does, though, is enlist its own reader's page-turning in the project of authentication. As Gay's reader, I, for example, find that it is my own grappling with written words that gives the elephant a probable body, and that makes me agree that such beasts can read. Substituting an authoritative text (Pliny's) for nature itself, and thereby compounding the scrutiny of matter with the inspection of black marks, "The Elephant and the Bookseller" shifts to the book a burden of proof normally assumed by the phenomenal world. All of its premises rest on the reader's implication in the material before her: To doubt that beasts can read is to doubt that we ourselves can do so.

Throughout the 1727 *Fables* such convincing fictions converge, often against the odds, to produce symbolic order. The *Fables'* foundation always lies in literate experience, but the point of foregrounding that experience is never merely to posit a universe of endlessly regressive, and fundamentally equivalent, signs. On the contrary, Gay's *Fables* license reading as a meaningful, indeed constitutive, cultural activity. Gay's elephant is thus an apt figure for the reader of the *Fables* for he takes the book that he is reading seriously, in terms of his relationship to it. At the same time, though, the elephant also makes a less than ideal reader, for he conspicuously fails to recognize himself in the pages he peruses. The failure, from his point of view, is the fault of a "partial" author who has himself failed to "discern the diff'rent natures,/And weigh the fault of diff'rent creatures" because he "knows so little of his own" (lines 39–40, 42). But it could also be the fault of the elephant himself, whose own ideals of probable correspondence and proper generic distinction between humans and animals are manmade.

In fact, the fable withholds the name of the text under judgment – a text in which, we recall, "with exactest care and pains/Were ev'ry beast and bird portray'd/That e'er the search of man survey'd" (lines 29–30). We are only told that this book is written in Greek, that it depicts animals, and that the elephant does not find it up to snuff. Of course, if the book is a natural history whose pretensions to verisimilitude the elephant exposes, then we can accept his reading as exemplary and can respect at least some of the restraints he imposes on literate behavior.

But what if the elephant is reading a fable collection? The pages he turns after all feature a "spaniel [...] proficient in the trade" of flattery, "a foxe's theft and plunder," a "lyon, wolf, and tyger's [...] thirst of blood." If the book *is* a fiction, then the elephant is an example of bad reading, not of good. In any case, Gay's fable refuses to distinguish between reading wrong and reading aright. This is not to say that it shuts down the possibility of interpretation altogether. Rather, it redefines that possibility, for through his pachydermic fall guy, Gay invites us to read not for the moral but rather for something more like the plot – the plot of reading itself.

Those of Gay's readers who did read this way – many of them from the lower orders, or connected to Gay by real friendship – found in the 1727 *Fables* a foundation for their own literary voices. Even Swift built a poem around the image of the *Fables*" being read. In his satire of Tighe, "*Tim* and the *Fables*," Swift has the minister run across "the *Fables* writ by Mr. Gay." Pleased to recognize himself in the woodcut that accompanies "The Monkey who had Seen the World," Swift's reader dashes to the mirror, where he, "comparing/His own sweet Figure with the Print/Distinguish[es] ev'ry Figure in't." When Tim's eyes travel down the page to "read what underneath was written," however, the mimetic contract shatters, and, forced to read in another way, he charges Gay with libel, ranting and cursing to the end of Swift's satire.[43]

Swift's "Tim" takes over the part that Gay's elephant played in another fable: in denying resemblance he proves he is part of what he reads. Meanwhile, it is by using Gay's fable that Swift gives it the kind of reading that it demands. And because their ideal reader recognizes his or her own monstrosity in them, the link between Swift's poem and the *Fables* is in its own way as unnerving as the one that joins them to the infamous caricature of their first reader, Prince William. The 1727 collection grafts the human and the animal countenance, the civil and the savage, the dominant and the submissive. But it does so less either to berate humans or to elevate defenseless brutes than to remind us that it is through guilty implication, exemplified in the act of reading, that the world contracts its meanings.

"The muse's mortifying strain": the 1738 *Fables*

Written near death, Gay's last fables found their way to the press only posthumously, in 1738. Appropriately enough, the last fable of the sixteen takes place in a graveyard, where after debating the relative merits of a dead horse and a piece of "two-legg'd carrion" (a deceased squire), two ravens and a sexton finally call in a local earthworm to perform a taste test. The poem recalls Gay's 1727 dedication to Prince William; addressed "To Laura," its long verse preface cautions a beautiful woman against the delusions of flattery. But having admired her "full lustre" and "celestial grace," the preface, unlike the earlier dedication, seeks to defend its own language from charges of sycophancy:

> . . .I check my lays,
> Admiring what I dare not praise.
> If you the tribute due disdain,
> The muse's mortifying strain
> Shall, like a woman, in mere spite
> Set beauty in a moral light.[44]

"Moral light" is harsh; it picks out beauty's inevitable decay and marks the corresponding flight of social identity ("To age is such indiff'rence shown,/As if your face were not your own"). Yet as she moralizes the transience of all earthly charms, the mortifying muse joins the speaker's own predicament with Laura's ("Those features, cast in heav'nly mould,/Shall, like my coarser earth, grow old"). Thus the fable revives a chain of sympathies very like the one that allowed a friendless female hare to stand for Gay at the end of the 1727 *Fables*.

To the reader accustomed to those far pithier and less pontifical poems, it can seem less that the 1738 *Fables* bring a coherent set of concerns full circle than that the face Gay wears in them is, like the decaying Laura's, not his own. The later collection's differences from the earlier one range from a nervous tendency to "check [the] lays" so mischievously tendered in 1727 to an air of dank self-righteousness to a new taste for political satire.[45] As Warton complained, many of the poems read like "party pamphlets versified,"[46] and jackals, baboons, and maladroit bears often appear as thinly veiled caricatures of Gay's political enemy Robert Walpole.

The nervous, bitter, often lachrymose tone of the later fables has sources both in bodily and in political mortification. For following the humiliating offer that came from court in response to the 1727 *Fables*, Gay retired to the estate of his dear friends the Duke and Duchess of Queensberry. And there, as Thackeray put it, he "wheezed, and grew fat, and so ended."[47]

Thackeray painted a dismal picture of Gay in his "latter days," turned "very melancholy and lazy, sadly plethoric, and only occasionally diverting."[48] The 1738 *Fables* do seem to encourage such an image of the author. Although it contains thirty-four fewer poems, the collection is only a few pages shorter than its precursor. This is because, as Gay put it to Swift, all of the fables have a long "prefatory Discourse before 'em by way of Epistle." Each "prefatory Discourse" elaborates a moral, and it was evidently the morals, not the fables, that most interested Gay. He wrote to Swift that he seemed always to "have a moral or two more that I wish to write on." Many of these, he admitted, "are of the political kind, which makes 'em run into a greater length than those I have already publish'd."[49]

In themselves, Gay's morals seem to restore to fables the resonance with English politics that was integral to collections like Ogilby's but had grown scarcer and scarcer as the eighteenth century wore on. As Warton complained, though, the morals were so very "long and languid" that they robbed the fables of the pungent brevity that had made Aesopian fictions key figural devices in a culture concerned to grant special authority to the most portable – and transposable – signs. Gay's obsessive morals, moreover, make the fables themselves feel like afterthoughts, overburdened before they begin and in the event applied only mechanically to the state of affairs (or affairs of state) elaborated in both prefaces. Although some twentieth-century critics have preferred these more conventionally neoclassical poems to the 1727 *Fables*, or at least have found them easier to interpret, others may be more inclined to agree with Warton.[50]

However we value them, the difference of the 1738 *Fables* marks a larger shift in Aesopian activity in England, one that coincides with fables' exposure to new constructs of literary authority, of writing and reading. That the 1738 *Fables* belong to a new cultural milieu is clear from the start. Unlike the titlepage to the 1727 volume, which featured a mask of ambiguous race and gender, their frontispiece is dominated by an image of Gay's own imposing monument, inscribed in Pope's lofty, if also faintly condescending, couplets to a gentleman "of Manners gentle, and Affections mild,/In Wit a Man, Simplicity a Child." (plate 9). The frontispiece is a canonizing ploy. Without irony, it sets the fables apart from ordinary writing and their author apart from ordinary writers. Engraved by the distinguished French artists Hubert Gravelot and Gerard Scotin, the plates for the fables further claim them for high neoclassicism. Printed on pages of their own, these long, chaste, elegant illustrations usually spotlight human actors, not animal ones.

9   Gerald Scotin, plate from *Fables of the Late Mr. Gay*, London, 1738.

In addition to their sepulchral frontispiece, the 1738 *Fables* began with an advertisement that describes the *Fables'* text history. These fables, we learn, have been published because their current custodian, the Duke of Queensberry, "permitted" them to be. They have also been scrupulously "printed from the Originals in the Author's own Hand-writing," and, the bookseller assures us, they "certainly shew [Gay] to have been (what he esteemed the best Character) a Man of truly honest Heart, and a sincere Lover of his Country."[51] Obviously eager to claim the *Fables* for a conservative Tory poetics that values ancient traditions of patronage, such a note could never have been prefixed to the 1727 *Fables*. The earlier collection would have mocked the (highly marketable) pretense of segregating the poems from the literary marketplace. The fabulist would have scoffed at the attempt to authenticate the volume by fixing the "honest" and "sincere" character of the fabulist.

Although contrived after Gay's death, the illustrations and advertisement reflect the poems' own anxiety about the relationship between that author and his readers. We saw that Aesopian fiction, as developed by the authors of fable collections and adapted by innovative poets like Dryden and Finch, worked by performing authority, and all its crises, in the printed page. But Gay's 1738 *Fables* labor to locate the author outside and behind the language of the poems. No longer embodied in printed characters, he cannot form an Aesopian bond with his readers, many of whom the 1738 *Fables* nervously specify. Usually Gay's model reader is a Theophrastic type ("A Lawyer," "A Young Heir," the lustrous "Laura") or an exemplar of Horatian retirement ("A Friend in the Country," "A Country Gentleman"), but he can also be a historical personage ("The Reverend Dr Swift, Dean of St Patrick's," "Myself"). The epistolary technique obviously claims Gay's later fables for an Augustan – and specifically a Horatian – poetics. As in Pope's contemporary *Moral Essays* (1731–1735) and *Essay on Man* (1733–1734), specifying a reader announces particular poetic (and, in the 1730s, also political) alliances.

In Horace's own verse epistles, fables were expository tools obedient to the discursive mechanisms of a larger whole.[52] Following Horace, Gay dislodges fables from the primary position they enjoyed in 1727. He presses them into the service of a different language, which in its turn invokes a different convention of exemplarity, one in which – as had not been the case since before Ogilby – example is separate from precept. Whereas in 1727 they are inextricable, the later *Fables* were printed with a wide space between the epistolary moral and the story related "for the moral's sake".[53]

Meanwhile, the introduction of a specific reader fosters a new construct of reading. As we saw, Gay's earlier fables assume an involvement and intimacy with their readers that is itself a form of moral implication; hence their implied reader is a theoretically impressionable boy of five. The 1738 *Fables*, on the other hand, assume adult readers – full-fledged, and probably antagonistic, individuals. These imagined readers further divide the speaker from his actual ones, who receive little incentive to identify with "A Lawyer" or "A Young Heir," and who by definition cannot see themselves as Swift or Gay. Whereas, albeit perversely, the figure of William brought real readers into the 1727 *Fables*, the invented readers of 1738 "bar" readerly involvement. Because, in fact, *Fables* shrink from the prospect of such involvement as from imminent abuse, they use language as a protective edifice. The very first fable in the collection models this volume's unusually defensive stance. The lawyer whom it addresses is really a type of the reader, one who "can, with ease/Twist words and meanings as you please."[54] His "profession" is "skepticism," and he will for profit if not for malicious pleasure sit down to a book "with intent/To find out meaning never meant." Quick to "hold there's doubt in all expression," he sees even "the clearest case [. . .] with a double face."

The image of the face haunts this poem, where eventually the fabulist resorts to the ambiguities of the Renaissance physiognomist Giovanni Baptista Porta, "whose skill could trace/Some beast or bird in ev'ry face." The fable thus tracks language's retreat into the imprecision and ambiguity that Aesop had actually circumvented. In the "prefatory Discourse," the honest fabulist, "*se defendendo*," resolves to "bar fallacious innuendo'; imitating "sagacious Porta," he does so by throwing the responsibility for recognizing a figure's implications back onto the shoulders of its beholder: "Like him, I draw from gen'ral nature:/Is't you or I then fix the satire?"[55] Gay's Porta reincarnates a painter of 1727 who, finding he "could please no Body" (and thus earn nothing) by painting spitting images, turned to painting flattering portraits instead. Porta, however, chooses evasion and indirection over instrumentalism, the general image over the specific. And although they may blend the animal and human face, his "sketches thus design'd" can no longer limn the politics of representation: their point is to mask all evidence of their involvement with the world.

The fable that follows exemplifies this shift of sensibility. The story of "The Dog and the Fox" begins with an account of their new-struck if improbable, friendship. Renard even manages to convince his canine interlocutor that historically foxes have always been the victims of slander: human propaganda has shamefully "stigmatize[d their] race." "You know me free from all disguise," the fox protests. "My honour as my life I prize." When the fox starts in terror at the "clatter" of a passing farmer's wife, the dog assures him that they are "safe from harm." But, bad reader that he is, Renard interprets the dog's reassurance as a veiled accusation: "Your meaning's in your looks I see./Pray what's dame Dobbins, friend, to me?/ Did I e'er make her poultry thinner?" (lines 89–91). The dog pronounces the fox unnecessarily "captious'; after all, "no lamb (for aught I knew)/May be more innocent than you." The fox again defends himself against the perceived "saucy hint": "Your vile reflections would imply/That I'm the thief. You dog, you lye" (lines 105–106). Upon which the dog decides that the fox's "guilt these applications speak," and lunges. In the end, of course, "the self-convicted felon dyes."

On one level, Gay's fable simply repeats in figurative language the moral's warning against readerly captiousness. But as the fox's anxieties about figurative language (sheepish innocence, lying like a dog) betray, figures can disguise intent as well as reveal it. Thus here all they reliably figure is the frustration of efficient symbolic action. Gay's reader never knows whether or not the dog is indeed baiting the fox. The fable keeps itself inscrutable, and thereby "bar[s]" its own reader from the kind of active participation that rescued, say, the figural structure of Dryden's *The Hind and the Panther.*

Many of Gay's "cautious rhymes" entertain grave doubts about fables' powers of implication. The second poem typically even begins with a false premise in order to defend the fable from falser imputations: "E'er I begin, I must premise/Our ministers are good and wise;/So, though malicious tongues apply,/Pray, what care they, or what care I?"[56] Because so many of the fables deny, rather than initiate, implication, they often assume elaborate poses of denial. Thus they can produce meanings only negatively: "For though not this, nor that is meant/Can we another's thoughts prevent?" While obviously Gay's disclaimers are partly ironic, and while, as the fable of the fox and dog suggests, he does not abandon Aesopian strategy altogether, the 1738 *Fables* do subordinate it to different rules of evidence, and these in turn suppress writing's impulse to perform.

Different rules of evidence also demand a different kind of author. While the 1727 *Fables* sometimes beg to be read as personal allegories, a different "I" speaks in the 1738 *Fables.* He is a Horatian speaker, one who, as the volume's advertisement avers, works overtime to reassure his readers that he is "(what he esteemed the best Character) a Man of truly honest Heart, and a sincere Lover of his Country." He insists over and over again that "merit finds its true success" in retreat; he begs "kind Heaven" for a "private Station" apart from the sullying compromise and duress of court life; if his voice occasionally rises to "strike at vice" in Juvenalian ire, it is more often temperate and carefully modulated, "vent[ing] no slander, ow[ing] no grudge." Many of the 1738 *Fables* aim not simply to persuade their readers of particular morals but also to convince them of the "character" of the author – without, of course, granting them enough material to construct it for themselves. The author-speaker in turn tries to keep up an unequivocally human face, one undistorted by the symbolic conventions that distribute it to the outer world.

The speaker's credentials fit what Rachel Trickett has described as the Augustan ideal of "honest, clear-sighted integrity."[57] That ideal, as Trickett points out, had already laid some claim to fables, not only in Horace's own satires and epistles but more recently (and from an English point of view) in Oldham's *Satyr address'd to a Friend* (1683). In Oldham's poem Phaedrus's fable of the wolf who takes note of the collarmarks in the dog's fur advocates the integrity of independence and the desirability of detachment from fraught political centers. Gay's 1738 *Fables* try to reclaim fables as suitable to the *honestus vir*'s cultural position, a position whose authority comes of separateness and self-containment, not of the investment in textual matter that characterizes the Aesopian author.

"Jupiter and the Countryman," which Gay apostrophized to himself, exemplifies the Horatian model of personal example. Recognizing himself as the only friend who never "mortified [his own] hours with shame," the "I" advises himself to "write, practise morals and be poor," to seek "th'intrinsic and the true" sources of happiness, and to practice the virtues of "content" – a state which resonates both as containment (secure boundary) and as satisfaction. The need to imagine a bounded self motivates the fable, in which Jove lends an overworked peasant "the optic glass of intuition." Surveying the wants and fears that gnaw at every station of life, the peasant learns not to "repine at partial fate," and he soon regrets his wish for a better life, begging Jove to "reject my pray'r,/And guard my life from guilt and care."[58] For "true happiness" only "dwells in ev'ry honest mind."

When Gay's peasant, now seeking resolution within, rescinds his petition for a better life, he literally repudiates linguistic structures (petition or "pray'r") based on want and dependency. Willy-nilly, a worldview in which parts are joined by partiality (either favoritism or incompletion) falls by the wayside, to be replaced by a very different syntactic arrangement. In this arrangement, the sources of authority, like controlling Jove, hover always at one remove from the signs that assert it.

In the 1727 *Fables* parts became significant to the extent that they found employment – by virtue of their implication in adjoining terms, and according to their tendency to be used and misused in a signifying chain that ultimately incorporates the text at hand. By contrast, the 1738 *Fables* offer copious generalizations about the system of the world, about English political structure, even about relationships between nations. Whereas before a fable like "The Turkey and the Ants" blended mutual dependence with mutual exploitation in the form of a nation that kills several others for breakfast, the 1738 collection imagines a new international order bounded and commonly regulated by English trade and "British laws." England itself, however, is represented as a fine and private place. "By bounteous nature set apart," its "fertile grounds/The liquid fence of Neptune bounds."[59] In a rare position to view the rest of the world, the good Englishman hawks a view of natural order in which those of different capacities and means all converge in a configuration that the 1727 *Fables*, at their most generous, would have deemed laughable:

Each, aiming at one common end,
Proves to the whole a needful friend.
Thus, born each other's useful aid,
By turns are obligations paid.   (lines 45–48)

The 1738 *Fables* describe a world where entities practice the harmonious mutual assistance that will bring them to their fitting end. In a fable meant to endorse a political order in which all "in duty, to the throne,/Their common obligations own," a man does away with various animals" "hunge[r] for precarious food" by showing them how "to gen'ral use /[Their] parts and talents may conduce" (lines 85–86). Only the fly is ruled a "useless coxcomb," and while such ravenous parasites spoke loudly for themselves in 1727, in the 1738 collection, the man "with a sudden blow/[...]laid the noxious vagrant low," thereby booting the insect out of an economy where "by turns are obligations paid."

At the same time that the 1738 *Fables* seem to value a humanist culture perpetuated "by turns," however, Gay does not always resist the Aesopian urge to literalize figures like that of peaceful turning, and thereby to investigate their material foundations. But he sequesters such investigations inside other fables that are presumably designed to point different morals. Thus, if we were to seek a playful but revealing literalization of the "turns" that structure Gay's presumably ideal world, we would only find it in another fable – one that, addressed "To a Poor Man," is, in theory, designed to show merely that, in a world of "wants," "God is just," and others more lacking may always be found.

In the illustrative fable of "The Cookmaid, the Turnspit, and the Ox," a lazy turnspit shirks his job. When the cookmaid "presses near,/He slinks aloof, and howls with fear," deploring the evident fact that he is "for life by compact bound/To tread the wheel's eternal round" (lines 57–58). It is only when a nearby ox reminds him that "you, by the duties of your post/Shall turn the spit when I'm the roast;/And for reward shall share the feast,/I mean, shall pick my bones at least" (lines 95–98) that "with chearful heart he mounts the wheel." Had Gay coupled this fable with the moral that he expounds in the fable of the unfortunate fly, the turning wheel would have literalized, and ironized, the image of a world that runs "by turns." It would have exposed that world's dependence on a system of predation that is eventually absorbed into the human culture that it supports. Here, however, the prefatory discourse centers the fable on the ox's advice to "think on the ox, and learn content."

It is Gay's anti-Mandevillean fable of "The Degenerate Bees" that most emphatically realigns Aesopian writing. Addressed to Swift, the fable describes a hive dominated by "a Bee, of cunning, not of parts" (line 37). "Rapacious, arrogant and vain,/Greedy of pow'r but more of gain" (lines

39–40), the bee makes the hive safe for a "degenerate" culture dominated by luxury and greed. "Disdaining the degen'rate kind," however, one Swiftian drone detaches himelf from the hive and enjoins the others to return to their proper, and mutually supportive relations to each other: " 'Tis industry our state maintains." Where Mandeville used the hive to embody the guilty implication of all society's parts, wanting and replete, Gay's fable presumes the possibility of segregation, and the restoration of "parts" in the sense of intrinsic quality. The figure of the "degen'rate" hive itself strives to realign Aesopian style with a vision which separates sociopolitical order from the exemplary discourse offered by the "stubborn" Swiftian bee.

"The Degenerate Bees" is only one of the fables "of a political turn" featured in the 1738 collection. Though the prefatory discourse pretends to deny it, the degenerate hive is an image of Walpole's England. This, in Gay's view, is an England whose violated integrity, symbolic and otherwise, other fables exaggerate as they sketch biographies of an "Ant ... whose forward prate/Controul'd all matters in debate," of a "proud Jackall [that] opprest the wood," of a "Bear of shagg and manners rough" who "intrudes" on the sensibilities of the other beasts and manipulates them to his own political advantage, of a vulture who "intrudes to power."[60] "The Degenerate Bees" obvious debt to Mandeville, however, compounds the effort at political detachment with the effort to disengage from Aesopian writing. It reminds us that fables are political tropes, and that their use had thus far been to figure a (decidedly English) sociopolitical order from which they also benefit. The push to turn fables into devices that can malign contemporary political practices and encourage political disengagement feels unnatural, but a typical couplet shows that Gay wanted to make it: "My fable read, their merits view,/Then herd who will with such a crew."

Gay's fables "of a political turn" necessarily struggle to defend themselves against the political elements built into Aesopian style. But because that style consists of symbolic actions, like performance and bribery, that are remarkably consistent with the fables' own figural devices, self-defense often looks like expulsion and denial. Gay's "bear of shagg and manners rough," for example, becomes the "dictator of the wood" by Aesopian methods. Like a true descendant of the shaggy denizens of Dryden's Caledonian wood, he captivates the attention of the other beasts, distributes "common booty" (" 'Twas his each portion to allot") and ostentatiously mixes species categories: "In stratagem and subtle arts,/He over-rules the fox's parts" (lines 94–95). At last he sails a boat out before the eyes of an initially admiring crowd, boasting that "From me that helm shall conduct learn/And man his ignorance discern" (lines 107–108). But the boat is "born down, adrift, at random tost." The bear's "oar breaks short," his "shatter'd vessel" runs aground, and eventually some "clam'rous watermen" see to it that he is "seiz'd, thresh'd and chain'd."

Gay's fable toys with a political metaphor – the ship of state – and thus in an important sense it is political metaphor that finds itself "at random tost." So does Aesopian style, for it is precisely because he plays an Aesopian part that he has written for himself that the bear is hauled to shore by humans who (unthinkable in 1727) emerge as heroes eager to restrain excess. The prefatory moral, meanwhile, associates the bear first with the social type of the coxcomb and then with the political type of the "self-deem'd Machiavel at large" – a stock figure throughout the 1738 *Fables* and one recognizable in many of the many characters who try to control others' discernment through their own performances. The 1738 *Fables* work to expose the limits of such strategies, and thus of the forms of authority that accompany them.[61] Here, Gay's own moral labors to define and defend an alternative exemplar, the man "whose search is bent himself to know." In contrast to the bear, this man

> [. . .]learns the bounds of human sense
> And safely walks within the fence:
> Thus conscious of his own defect
> Are pride and self-importance check'd.   (lines 13–16)

While the bear defines himself practically, in terms of generic encroachment, the good man cultivates an almost pathological respect for "fence[s]," "check[s]," and "bounds." Gay's own grammar reflects his passivity. Such exemplars are necessarily mute on the subject of how they "lear[n]" what they know; anti-didactic, even anti-graphic, they firmly close themselves to what lies outside their own edges.

Throughout the 1738 collection, fables' historical, and practical, complicity with the signifying styles of the administration that they oppose creates a new anxiety about boundaries, a new need for separation and authentication. This anxiety, as we have seen, sponsors both self-shielding addresses to untrusted readers and several campaigns to create a bounded and detached authorial voice. In the end, it drives the *Fables* to deny (ultimately Aesopian) relationships based on implication and mutual, if agonizing, constitution.

Written for "Laura"'s benefit, Gay's last fable labors to restore the figures of speech, including emblem and analogy, that he had so ruthlessly dismantled in 1727.[62] Analogy in 1738 equals mortality, likeness death. Whereas the 1727 *Fables* sought ways to redefine analogy in terms of its foundations in contiguity and implication, the poems of 1738 resign themselves to it. Thus Gay's last "prefatory discourse" warns that Laura's "features, cast in heav'nly mould" will decay "like my coarse earth," and that "like common grass, the fairest flower/Must feel the hoary season's power" (lines 43–45). "Alike the laws of life take place/Through ev'ry branch of human race." The conclusion spares nothing: "Dust form'd us all. Each breathes his day,/Then sinks into his native clay." Such sentiments revise the Aesopian perception that all things achieve meaning through their guilty involvement with each other. The sense of shared origins that was the source of Aesopian vitality now feeds analogies that, left to themselves, only foretell the end of discrimination and the failure of articulation.

At their conclusion, the 1738 *Fables* bring fables themselves into time. But they do not see time as human history negotiable in and through representation. It is instead a trowel that levels everything it touches, ultimately mocking all pretensions to distinction, and exposing the frailty and factitiousness of all the signs that attempt to mark difference. To illustrate the point, Gay offers the macabre fable of "The Ravens, the Sexton, and the Earth-worm." Two hungry ravens "snuff" the air; as they "the promis'd feast [of carrion] inhale,/[And] taste the carcase on the gale," they anticipate aloud the "dainty treat" that a dead horse will provide. A nearby gravedigger takes offence at the implication that there is no distinction between a human and an animal corpse: "The meanest bird of prey/Such want of sense could ne'er betray/For sure some diff'rence must be found" (lines 99–100). The ravens agree that there is indeed no "similitude of scent," for horses actually make the better meal:

> As Epicures extol a treat,
> And seem their sav'ry words to eat,
> They prais'd dead horse, luxurious food,
> The ven'son of the prescient brood.   (lines 109–112)

These ravens are dyed-in-the-wool Aesopian characters: they deal in tangible, even palatable, words; they model the forms of "prescience" that have always marked their place in Aesopian convention; as epicureans, they speak for the atomistic *rerum natura* that authorizes the transmigration of signs themselves into "sav'ry," and easily transferable, particles. Their verbal "contest" with a man also reprises one of fables' most familiar scenarios, as does their determination to refer the debate to something concrete, in this case to an "Earth-worm, huge of size," and in particular to "th'experience of his jaws."

The earthworm, though, embodies a worldview that limits and diminishes all of the Aesopian elements in the fable, for his verdict is that all bodies are ultimately the same: "Death confounds 'em all." Instead of yielding the possibility of meaningful mutual implication, the fable presages perpetual indeterminacy. For the earthworm decides that

> . . .the case
> Appears with such a dubious face,
> To neither I the cause determine,
> For diff'rent tastes please diff'rent vermine.   (lines 155–158)

As it aligns the different with the "dubious," Gay's fable tosses fables themselves into a new pool of signifying – and interpretive – conventions, one in which difference is now construed as an obstacle to sensible meaning rather than as its foundation. It may be disappointing to read that "Diff'rent tastes please diff'rent vermine" when we are used to discovering that "diff'rent vermine" have something significant in common. Nevertheless, Gay's mortifying muse could not have written a more appropriate epitaph to Aesop's fables.

7

The moral

In Aesop's famous fable of the fox and crow, the cheese that falls from the gullible bird's beak is not exactly lost: It is only diverted into a different sign system. Transformed from "prize" to warning, it becomes a material sign whose referent is a form of linguistic practice (usually perilous flattery). We might apply the cheese's trajectory to the fate of English fables after 1740, for, far from vanishing into thin air, Aesopian fictions merely took up lodging in new symbolic registers. Popular collections continued to appear throughout the century, with Croxall and Gay often reprinted. Dryden's *Fables, Ancient and Modern* became, in Hazlitt's words, "the most popular of his works" – so much so that Joseph Warton predicted that "it is to his Fables, though wrote in his old age, that Dryden will owe his immortality."[1] Meanwhile, writers like Edward Moore, Horace Walpole, Christopher Smart, and William Godwin dabbled in fables, and both Robert Dodsley (1764) and Thomas Bewick (1779, 1784, 1814 and 1818) produced new collections. The year 1780 greeted no fewer than *89 Fugitive Fables*, while volumes bearing titles such as *The Economy of Beauty* (1777) and meant to teach proper behavior to young ladies throve from mid-century on.

Even fables by writers as deft as Walpole and Smart, however, lack the bite of earlier Aesopian fictions. Nor do their authors share the Augustan Aesop's confidence in his own relevance to the political and material spheres. The change is especially glaring in the difference between Gay's two volumes of fables, but we can also discern it in the precipitous decline of biographies of Aesop, and in the English fable's growing reputation as a furtive, even "fugitive" literary language, its fading image as an animate, mediatory, and self-reflexive figural device. Smart's *Poetical Translation of the Fables of Phaedrus*, for example, appeared in 1761, at the same time that the reputed madman was writing his cryptic *Jubilate Agno*. Walpole's fables cultivated the arcane. Godwin's *Fables Ancient and Modern* (1811) nurse a covert Jacobinism. If in the fables published between 1651 and 1740 "Things hold Discourse," after the middle of the eighteenth century they began to host a more surreptitious conversation.

Many narratives might account for the transmigration of Aesop's spirit as this book has understood it. For one thing, we might point to certain changes in linguistic practice. Throughout the eighteenth century, as intellectual historians like Murray Cohen have shown, an atomistic and empirical model of language yielded to a syntactic, extended, and mental one.[2] During our period, these two models competed on more level ground, and the former – to which Aesop's short, muscular and emphatic fables naturally appealed – occasionally prevailed. At the very least, we saw, fables mediated between two linguistic sensibilities: the triumph of the one, as witnessed by the emergence of new, extended, and interiorized literary genres like the novel, meant that Aesop's diplomatic services were no longer so urgently required. A second transformation in symbolic practice also coincides with the end of the Aesopian era in English letters: this was the gradual demotion of the sensory image as a valuable symbolic form, its replacement by what Barbara Stafford calls a new "epistemocracy" that promotes "bodiless concepts," spectralizes even cultural information, and "marginalize[s . . .] imagery" as a viable mode of representation and apprehension.[3] We saw that fables cultivate language's eidetic properties and that *via* a burgeoning print technology they salvaged, and transferred to words, some of the authority that the Civil Wars had stripped from literally and metaphorically visible symbolic forms. Fables' cultural cachet suffered as language relinquished its affinity with the image.

The fate of the English fable is bound up not just with an epistemic change but also with a shift in national self-definition. We have seen that in England fables were an *English* phenomenon: English writers and readers spent the end of the seventeenth century and the beginning of the eighteenth adjusting to a new cultural system dominated on the one hand by textual representation and on the other by an oppositional political structure that forged new constructions of difference itself. Having shepherded the English through the adjustment, Aesop became less obviously useful once the nation had settled into a stable sociopolitical – and semiotic – arrangement. Perhaps too the widening gap between popular and polite literary spheres made it harder for fables to maneuver after the 1730s. And the rise of realist literary imperatives, exemplified in the novel, robbed fictions as conspicuous and self-ironizing as Aesop's of much of their authority. It follows quite logically that fables should have found themselves consigned to the literary outposts of children's and women's literature, and that they should have been authored more and more frequently by political and social outcasts who had never identified with the centers of cultural authority and thus lacked the fruitful ambivalence of earlier English fabulists. Deluded by romance, Charlotte Lennox's female Quixote, Arabella, is nonetheless quite clear-sighted about "the Fables of Æsop," in which "the Absurdity discovers itself, and the Truth is comprised in the Application."[4]

Arabella's infamous "cure" from romance to realism in *The Female Quixote* (1752) marks the rising stock of new literary standards of verisimilitude – a rise that certainly shaped fables' destiny after 1740. Such impressions find confirmation both in critical commentary on fables and in Aesopian practice of this later period. Bewick's *Fables of Aesop, and Others* was admired not for its language – the fables themselves – but rather for the extreme naturalism of illustrations that made the most of an advanced technology based on white-line engraving and boxwood blocks. The book is thus more closely related to works like Bewick's own *History of British Birds* (1797) than to other fable collections.[5] Many fabulists thought the language of fable had grown too ornate and artificial anyway. Dismissing the present age as one of "artifice, chicane and juggle," they longed for the time "when father Esop liv'd," which era they imagined as the "reign of good simplicity."[6] The long, dry "Essay on Fable" that prefaces Dodsley's *Select Fables of Esop* declares that the fable "has a right to some share of our esteem [...] as it is honourable to spring from a noble stem, although in ever so remote a branch." But Dodsley also calls for fables' return to the "ease and simplicity" they knew before they were "disfigured by the *Language* in which they [had been] clothed" by recent, precious, and capricious, fabulists.[7]

The most virulent attack on Aesop's fables, however, came from France, where in *Emile* (1762) Jean Jacques Rousseau castigated the Aesopian premise that a child can learn anything from an imposture as glaring as the speaking animal pretense. Setting his sights on La Fontaine's version of the fable of the fox and crow ("*A speech*! Foxes speak then? They speak, then, the same language as ours?"), Rousseau regarded fables as outright lies. He scoffed that "the words of fables are no more fables than the words of history are history. [...T]he apologue in giving enjoyment to children deceives them; [...] seduced by the lie, they let the truth escape."[8] English readers were slightly more temperate in their reactions to Aesop's trademark ploy: "I shall not ask Jean Jacques Rousseau/If birds confabulate or no," William Cowper resolved. "'Tis clear, that they were always able/To hold discourse, at least in fable."[9] But Cowper's quatrain holds it own reservations about the Aesopian premise (which it echoes) that "Things hold Discourse," and it is really Rousseau's indictment that captures the later eighteenth century's narrowing view of what fiction is and does.

Rousseau summoned a natural logic of probability to arm his attack on Aesop, and English fable criticism followed suit. Finding modern fables both improbable and low, critics often scapegoated Gay's fable of "The Elephant and the Bookseller," which, we saw, exaggerated the defining elements of Aesopian method to date. Joseph Warton, for example, took Gay to task for "ascribing to the different animals and objects introduced, speeches and actions inconsistent with their several natures."[10] For Warton, this flaw was typical of the *Fables* as a whole, a volume "without any elevation." And even those – like their late eighteenth-century editor William Coxe – who were willing to elevate the *Fables* had to "confess it is a high breach of probability

to introduce an Elephant into a Bookseller's shop. [...] Birds and Beasts, in
the language of fable, may be supposed to talk, but an Elephant in a
Bookseller's shop must be acknowledged too forced and unnatural a conceit."

Why is it acceptable – probable anyway – for "Birds and Beasts" to talk,
but not for them to read? How, in other words, does reading come to seem
more threatening than producing signs, and how after all do producing and
consuming signs come to be defined as completely separate activities? Like
the other English fables whose designs they magnified, Gay's do not permit
reading to stand apart from the contrivance of meaningful signs. Rather, they
mediate reactively between these two symbolic actions. Thus morals (which
are images of reading after all) are no more plausible than the figures and
fictions they pretend to decipher. To later eighteenth-century readers,
though, the fables that Gay's epitomize seemed to cross boundaries not so
much between different kinds of things, or even between signs and things, as
between different kinds of signs. Published in 1783, James Beattie's thoughts
on the subject are representative.

In Beattie's opinion, "that an elephant should converse with a Bookseller
about Greek authors [...] is a fiction wherein no regard is had to the nature
of things." In general, he deemed the works of most "modern fabulists" sadly
fallen from the "Greek apologues ascribed to Aesop and the Latin ones of
Phaedrus," which he considered "masterpieces in this way of writing."
Whereas the ancient fables were simple, and properly respected the "nature
of the animals, and other things that are introduced as agents and speakers,"
modern ones are too complicated, too "quaint and full of witticism." Gay's
Fables particularly offend:

In [the Aesopian], as in the higher sorts of fable, it is right to adhere, as much as may
be, to probability. Brute animals, and vegetables too, may be allowed to speak and
think: this indulgence is granted, from the necessity of the case, for without it, their
adventure could neither improve nor entertain us; but, with this exception, nature
should not be violated; nor the properties of one animal or vegetable ascribed to a
different one. Frogs have been seen inflated of air, at least, if not with pride; dogs may
swim rivers; a man might take a frozen viper into his bosom, and be bit to death, for
his stupid choice; a fox might play with a tragedian's head piece; a lamb and wolf
might drink of the same brook, and the former lose his life on the occasion: but
whoever heard of an elephant reading Greek, or a hare riding on the back of a calf?[11]

For Beattie, good writing keeps natural signs untainted by cultural ones,
and *vice versa*. Yet Aesop's fables, at least as practiced in England between
1651 and 1740, absolutely insist – even demonstrate – that nature and
culture are, for all intents and purposes, inextricable: "Things hold
Discourse." Their devotion to the fact of this intertwining is what made
Aesop's fables such indispensable figures in the England that began to create
itself as a coherent but internally differing political and symbolic entity after

the Civil Wars. Regretfully but firmly, later eighteenth-century commentators demoted the ways of writing, and of reading, that Aesop had previously demanded, often interpreting the story that his fables told as an annoying and irrelevant one. It is time to assign a new moral to that story, though – even if to do so is only to tell it in a different way.

Notes

Introduction   The English fable

1 Adapted from Edmé Boursault's popular *Les Fables d'Esope, Comédie* (1690; later retitled *Esope à la ville* to distinguish it from its sequel, *Esope à la cour* (1702)), John Vanbrugh's *Æsop. A Comedy* opened at Drury Lane in 1696, with Colley Cibber as Aesop. The popular play ran off and on through the next two decades, and Thomas Sheridan turned it into a farce in 1778.

2 Joseph Addison, *Spectator* 183 (September 29, 1711), in *The Spectator*, ed. Donald F. Bond. 5 vols. (Oxford, 1965), II: 247.

3 John Dennis, *The Stage Defended from Scripture, Reason, Experience, and the Common Sense of Man* (1726), in *Critical Works of John Dennis*, ed. Edward Niles Hooker. 2 vols. (Baltimore, 1939–1943), II: 302.

4 Doctoral dissertations include Mary Pritchard's extremely valuable "Fables Moral and Political" (Ph.D. diss., University of Western Ontario, 1974), which treats the Aesopian fable as "a truly English genre" (p. 1) whose development was complete by 1722; William Wray's sweeping "The English Fable, 1650–1800" (Ph.D. diss., Yale, 1950); Joan Hildreth Owen's "The Choice of Hercules and the Eighteenth-Century Fabulist" (Ph.D. diss., New York University, 1974); and Albert Edwin Graham's "John Gay's *Fables*, Edited with an Introduction to the Fable as an Eighteenth-Century Genre" (Ph. D. diss., Princeton University, 1960), which includes a cogent overview of Aesopian writing in England up to Gay. Two useful critical essays are Stephen H. Daniel, "Political and Philosophical Uses of Fables in Eighteenth-Century England," *The Eighteenth Century: Theory and Interpretation* 23 (1982), 151–171; and an early article by M. Ellwood Smith, "The Fable as Poetry in English Criticism," *Modern Language Notes* 32 (1917), 466–470.

5 H.P. Blackham's wide-ranging *The Fable as Literature* (London and Dover, N.H., 1985) has a few pages on Samuel Croxall, John Gay, and Bernard Mandeville. Thomas Noel's succinct *Theories of the Fable in the Eighteenth Century* (New York and London, 1975) considers eighteenth-century English conceptions of fables, along with their French, German, and Spanish counterparts.

6 Earl Miner's *Dryden's Poetry* (Bloomington, Ind., 1967) links Dryden with the fabulist John Ogilby; Judith Sloman's *Dryden: The Poetics of Translation* (Toronto, 1985) discusses the Aesopian fable collection in terms of a quest for a "common language" (p. 19) that she also finds motivating Dryden's *The Hind and the Panther* (1687); and Steven N. Zwicker's *Politics and Language in Dryden's Poetry: The Arts of Disguise* (Princeton, 1984) associates fables with the "party fragmentation, shifting

190

political self-definition, the elaboration of defenses, explanations and apologies' (p. 31) that characterizes so much literature of Dryden's age.

7 By far the most important study of Aesopian writing to date, Patterson's *Fables of Power: Aesopian Writing and Political History* (Durham, 1991) covers the history of fable from sixth century B.C. (Aesop's own era) to 2000 A.D., but focuses incisively and extensively on the fable in England in the sixteenth, seventeenth, and early eighteenth centuries. I discuss Patterson at greater length below.

8 Throughout this book I use the term "Augustan" to describe the period between roughly 1660 and 1745, aware that its valences have been recently and widely contested, but convinced of its power as a general designation. Howard Weinbrot offers a useful summary of the critical debate over the term, and a stimulating discussion of contemporary ambivalence toward it in *Augustus Caesar in "Augustan" England: The Decline of a Classical Norm* (Princeton, 1978).

9 Patterson, *Fables of Power*, 1.

10 Powerful analyses of the sociopolitical structure that evolved during this tumultuous period – which begins with the Civil Wars, and continues through the Restoration and Revolution of 1688 to the rocky genesis of an oppositional two-party system – include J.H. Plumb's *The Origins of Political Stability in England* (Boston, 1967); W.A. Speck's *The Divided Society: Party Conflict in England, 1694–1716* (New York, 1967); and Speck's *Stability and Strife: England, 1714–1760* (Cambridge, Mass., 1977).

11 Mandeville's wickedly perverse little story of a "spacious Hive well stockt with Bees" whose "Luxury and Ease" turns out to depend on fraud and knavery, and indeed all of whose "Ingenuity" is "nurs'd" by "Vice," has a long and complex publication history. The *Fable* began as *The Grumbling Hive: or, Knaves Turn'd Honest*, a sixpenny pamphlet published anonymously in 1705. But by 1733 it had swollen into the two-volume *Fable of the Bees: or, Private Vices, Publick Benefits*. In the intervening years, successive editions incorporated an *Enquiry into the Origin of Moral Virtue* and twenty "Remarks" (1714); an *Essay on Charity and Charity-Schools* and a *Search into the Nature of Society* (1723), and a preface and six dialogues (1729).

12 Gerard Reedy is especially incisive about the immense violence that the Civil Wars inflicted on a contemporary sense of referential stability: He shows that the cynical political uses of formerly authoritative figures made plausible correspondence between "phenomenal" signifiers and "noumenal" signifieds virtually untenable after Charles II's restoration. See Reedy, "Mystical Politics: The Imagery of Charles II's Coronation," in *Studies in Revolution and Change*, ed. Paul J. Korshin (Merston, Yorkshire, 1972), 20–46. For a detailed and persuasive discussion of "figural change" during these periods in response to a number of "determinants" including the Civil Wars, see Korshin, *Typologies in England, 1650–1820* (Princeton, 1982), 39–74.

13 The printing press's attainment to cultural hegemony is established in Elizabeth Eisenstein's now, and justly, classic *The Printing Press as an Agent of Change* (New York, 1979). Important amplifications of her argument may be found in Jeremy Black, *The English Press in the Eighteenth Century* (Philadelphia, 1987); and Alvin Kernan, *Printing, Technology, Letters and Samuel Johnson* (Princeton, 1982). On the press's role in forming new epistemological habits, see Richard Kroll, *The Material*

Word: Literate Culture in the Restoration and Early Eighteenth Century (Baltimore, 1991); and on its often paradoxical social implications, Kathryn Shevelow, *Women and Print Culture: The Construction of Femininity in the Early English Periodical* (New York, 1989).

14 Charles Montagu and Matthew Prior, *The Hind and the Panther Transvers'd to the Story of the Country Mouse and the City-Mouse* (1687), in *Literary Works of Matthew Prior*, ed. H. Bunker Wright and Monroe K. Spears, 2 vols. (Oxford, 1959), II: 35.

15 Roger L'Estrange, Preface to *Fables of Æsop and Other Eminent Mythologists* (London, 1692 and 1699), sig. B2r.

16 Anon., *Fables, Moral and Political* (1703), sig. A11v. Richard Blackmore, Preface to *Prince Arthur* (London, 1695), n.p.

17 Abraham Cowley's ode to the Royal Society, which precedes Thomas Sprat's *History of the Royal Society* (London, 1667), aesopically recalls that without a reliable contract between "Words" and "Things," "like foolish Birds to painted Grapes we flew" (sig. B2r).

18 Thomas Sprat, *History of the Royal Society* (London, 1667), 112. For a discussion of linguistic assumptions that drove emerging scientific discourses, see Murray Slaughter, *Universal Languages and Scientific Taxonomy in the Seventeenth Century* (Cambridge, 1982).

19 John Wallis, *Grammatica Linguae Anglicanae* (London, 1653). For examples of the obsession with a universal character whose structure would be as familiar and common as that of any physical object, see Cave Beck, *Universal Character* (1657); and John Wilkins, *Essay towards a Real Character and a Philosophical Language* (London, 1668). A fascinating discussion of these and related works, especially in terms of their opposition to idealist linguistic philosophies may be found in Murray Cohen, *Sensible Words: Linguistic Practice in England, 1660–1720* (Baltimore, 1977).

20 John Bulwer's *Chirologia* and *Chironomia* (London, 1644) offer striking examples of the effort to represent words" intimate and direct relationship to a material world, and of contemporary obsession with the human organs that can produce signs. So do John Wilkins's *Mercury: Or the Secret and Swift Messenger* (London, 1661); George Dalgarno's *Ars signorum* and *Didascalocaphus* (London, 1680); and William Holder's "Inquiry into the Natural Production of Letters," in *The Elements of Speech* (1667). Two helpful essays on this material are Don Cameron Allen's "Some Theories of the Growth and Origin of Language in Milton's Age," *Publications of the Modern Language Association* 28 (1946), 5–16; and James R. Knowlson's "The Idea of Gesture as a Universal Language in the Seventeenth and Eighteenth Centuries," *Journal of the History of Ideas* 26 (1963), 495–508.

21 Theriophilist movements of the period are an obvious context for the fable craze. See especially Marin Cureau de la Chambre's *Traité de la connoisance des animaux* (1645), translated into English by "a Person of Quality" (1657), and John Hildrop's *Free Thoughts upon the Brute Creation* (London, 1742). George Boas traces the theriophile tradition in France in *The Happy Beast in French Thought of the Seventeenth Century* (Baltimore, 1983), and for thinking about animals in England during this period, see Dix Harwood, *The English Love of Animals and How it Developed in Great Britain* (New York, 1928).

22 Cohen, *Sensible Words*, 43–47.

23 Schemes to materialize symbolic systems are much in the air during Gulliver's voyage to Laputa in Book III of *Gulliver's Travels* (1726). In Laputa, we learn, "an Expedient was [. . .] offered; that since Words are only Names for *Things*, it would be more convenient for all Men to carry about with them such things as were necessary to express the particular Business they are to discourse on." Thus the Laputans bear on their backs gigantic peddlers" packs crammed with the implements of conversation. See Swift, *Gulliver's Travels*, in *The Writings of Jonathan Swift*, ed. Robert A. Greenberg and William B. Piper (London and New York, 1973), 158.

24 John Evelyn (1654), Lucy Hutchinson (1670?), and John Dryden (1685) all translated parts of *De rerum natura*, but it was Thomas Creech's 1682 rendering of "the Epicurean Philosopher" that "expose[d Lucretius's] full system to publick view" (sig. A2v) and made Lucretius's account of how "from disagreeing Seeds the World did rise" a part of English poetry. Though Creech's prefatory renunciation of Lucretius's atheism reflects prevailing animosity toward him, Lucretius's view of language is nevertheless consistent with the linguistic materialism of this period, and his conception of words" brutal origins is obviously sympathetic to Aesop's speaking animal narratives. "But now since *Organs* fit, since *Voice* and *Tongue*,/By *Nature*'s Gift bestow'd to Man belong,/What Wonder is it then, that Man should frame,/And give each different thing a different Name?/ Since *Beasts* themselves do make a *different* Noise." Creech's translation of Horace's Satire I.iii. also finds language's roots in brutal conflict: "When men "for Acorns fought, and shady Cave,/With Nails, then Clubs, then Weapons Nature gave/[. . .]Till Words and Names for Things and Laws began." But rather than bear strife into symbolic action, Horatian language tames and effaces nature by imposing "Laws to curb our Rapine and our Lust." Horace and Lucretius represent two poles of a fundamental tension in contemporary thinking about language, one to which the speaking animal pretense obviously responds. See Creech, *The Epicurean Philosopher* (London, 1682), 183 and *The Odes, Satyrs, and Epistles of Horace, Done into English* (London, 1684), 386. On Lucretius's role in the literate culture of Restoration England, see Kroll, *Material Word*.

25 Douglas Lane Patey examines probabilism as a symbolic system and demonstrates its centrality to later seventeenth- and eighteenth-century reading practices and conventions of representation in *Probability and Literary Form: Philosophic Theory and Literary Practice in the Augustan Age* (Cambridge, 1989).

26 Both Gay Clifford, in *The Transformations of Allegory* (London, 1974), and Maureen Quilligan, in *The Language of Allegory* (Ithaca, N.Y., 1979), note the decline of allegory in the late seventeenth century. But for a precise discussion of allegory's succumbing to historical pressures and its emergence in new configurations, see John Wallace, "Dryden and History: A Problem in Allegorical Reading," *English Literary History* 36 (1969), 265–290; and for the poetics that results, Wallace's "'Examples are Best Precepts': Readers and Meaning in Seventeenth-Century Poetry," *Critical Inquiry* 1 (1975), 273–290. Korshin takes up the matter of the image-based languages during this period in *Typologies in England*; and their pertinence to the theater is established in Peter Holland, *The Ornament of Action:*

Text and Performance in Restoration Comedy (Cambridge, 1979). For the emblem tradition, which also declined as fables rose, see Peter M. Day, ed., *The English Emblem and the Continental Tradition* (New York, 1988); Rosemary Freeman, *English Emblem Books* (London, 1948); and Mario Praz, *Studies in Seventeenth-Century Imagery* (Rome, 1964–1974). Two fabulists of our period, Philip Ayres and Edmund Arwaker, were both also noted emblematists.

27   Henry Felton, *A Dissertation on Reading the Classics* (London, 1709), 20.

28   Thomas Blackwell, *Enquiry into the Life and Writings of Homer* (London, 1730), 4.

29   For an especially enlightening study of the press's formative influence on theatrical writing, see Julie Stone Peters, *Congreve and the Drama of the Printed Word* (Stanford, 1990); and for its relevance to the novel, J. Paul Hunter, *Before Novels* (New York, 1991).

30   Aphra Behn, "The Fox and Crow." In *Æsop's Fables, with his Life* (London, 1687), 10.

31   "Ay and No. A Fable," line 1. This fable, first published anonymously in Pope's *Miscellanies in Prose and Verse* has usually been attributed to John Gay and was often printed with Gay's own fables in the eighteenth century. But it might as easily have been the work of Gay's Scriblerian crony John Arbuthnot. Its plot tells the story of "two hostile Adverbs, Ay and No," who decide to change places and end up hiring themselves out to opposing sides in different debates of the day. The fable clearly links linguistic opposition with sociopolitical conflict, and uses the fable form at once to exploit and to expose language's political dimension – its contingency, efficacy, and vulnerability in a conflictual modernity.

32   Charles Hoole, *Æsop's Fables, English and Latin* ((1687), 2nd ed. London, 1700), 7, 20, and 6.

33   The conspicuously manmade Restoration of Charles II, the limitation of sovereign power that followed the Revolution of 1688 and was embodied in the Declaration of Rights (1689), Queen Anne's manipulation by her ministers, and the party politics under the first two Georges that made the rise of Walpole possible all illustrate the negotiable nature of England's political structure during this period.

34   For a stimulating study of Aesop's potentially subversive role in classical letters, which his relativism and often excremental vision so frequently ironize, see Jack Winkler, *Auctor and Actor* (Berkeley and Los Angeles, 1985); and for classical conceptions of fables, Gregory Nagy, *The Best of the Achaeans: The Hero in Archaic Greek Poetry* (Baltimore, 1979). Joseph Jacobs's *The Fables of Aesop*, 3 vols. (New York, 1889; repr. 1970) comments on classical conceptions of fables. Ben Edwin Perry's *Aesopica*, 2 vols. (Urbana, Ill., 1932) and his *Studies in the Text History of the Life and Fables of Aesop*, Philological Monographs 7 (Haverford, Penn., 1936) still offer the most substantial and comprehensive summary of classical fable-writing to date. See also Perry's introduction to the Loeb *Babrius and Phaedrus* (Cambridge, Mass., 1945), xi–xcvi.

35   Hegel's *Aesthetik* identifies fables with the animal origins of human signifying practice. Hegel argues that "Aesop's fables [...] in their original form, are [...] an interpretation of a natural relation or occurrence between single natural things in general, especially between animals, whose activities spring from the same vital needs which move men as living beings." Thus "the setting which we may ascribe

to the fables of Aesop" is one where animal "activities spring from the same natural needs which move men as living beings." See Hegel, *Aesthetics: Lectures in Fine Art*, trans. T.M. Knox, 2 vols. (Oxford, 1975), ii: 382, 384. Hegel's point of view survives in Blackham's speculation that fables function anthropologically much as totemism does – as "primitive device[s]" that can assist "thinking about human behavior in the abstract" (pp. 202–203). More abstract and less anthropological versions of this approach to the fable form may be found in Roland Barthes's "Myth Today," the first of a series of post-structuralist inquiries into fables. Barthes places fables at the linguistic, indeed grammatical foundations of modern myth: "I open my Latin grammar, and I read a sentence, borrowed from Aesop or Phaedrus: *quia ego nominor leo*." The sentence reminds him that he is "faced with a particular, great semiological system that is coextensive with the language" and that in fact underlies it. See Barthes, "Myth Today," in *Mythologies*, trans. Annette Lavers (New York, 1972), 115. Influenced by Barthes, Louis Marin treats Aesop's fables more explicitly and extensively as performative indices of "l'origine du récit," even of language's beginnings. See Marin, "Le récit originaire, l'origine du récit, le récit de l'origine," in *Papers on French Seventeenth-Century Literature* 11 (1978), 13–38; and his *Food for Thought*, trans. Mette Hjort (Baltimore, 1989). Other poststructuralist and essentially ahistorical interpretations of how fables work include Michel Serres's *The Parasite*, trans. Lawrence W. Schehr (Baltimore and London, 1982); and Serres's "Knowledge in the Classical Age: La Fontaine and Descartes," in *Hermes: Literature, Science and Philosophy*, ed. Josué Harari and David F. Bell (Baltimore, 1982), 15–28.

36 Fables" use to insinuate subversive and punishable meanings is most apparent in twentieth-century writing about or under totalitarianism (Brecht, Orwell, Kafka) than in the Augustan age. But Patterson in *Censorship and Interpretation* (Madison, 1974) and Zwicker have made claims for their perceived powers of indirection in the context of censorship in seventeenth-century England. While censorship's efficiency has probably been overestimated, Augustan fables do sometimes cultivate the guise of political enigma. For instance, *Fables, Moral and Political* (1703), an influential collection presumably translated from the Dutch of Johan DeWit, ventured that in the past poets relied on fables "that they might not subject themselves to the Lash of ... Fury ... by inventing and writing fictitious Stories, Apologues, Comparisons, Parables and Fables, to the end that they might with safety to themselves, at once both instruct and delight mankind" (sig. A9r).

37 See Marcel Gutwirth's comments on the coincidence of the "archaic" and the "puerile" in fables in *Fable* (New Orleans, 1980). Fables" primacy within pedagogical practice is as old as Plato, who allowed them to remain part of children's education. Seventeenth- and eighteenth-century writers, both English and French, were particularly conscious of the connection, which they felt Plato had authorized. "Platon [...] souhaite que les enfants sucent ces fables avec le lait," La Fontaine remarked in the preface to the 1668 volume of his *Fables choisies mises en vers* ((1668–1692) Paris, 1966), 29. The English fabulist Edmund Arwaker, also following Plato, advised "Mothers and Nurses to teach their Children Fables; and to use a Care and Diligence to inform their Minds by such Instructions, than

to shape and rectifie their Bodies by continual Stroaking." See Arwaker, *Truth in Fiction: or Morality in Masquerade* (London, 1708), sig. A4r. Fables were a staple of children's literature throughout the nineteenth century. Aesop of course today survives in the children's section of bookstores.

38 Addison, *Spectator* 183, 249.

39 Richard Blackmore, Preface to *Prince Arthur*, n.p. For contemporary commentary on the fable as a manifestation of "human delight in lying," see Samuel Butler's *Characteristics*; or John Toland's grim portrait of a time when "the whole World was overrun the Lyes and Fictions of the Practitioners" of fables," in *Two Essays Sent in a Letter* . . . (London, 1695), 32. Notions of fables as substitutes for historical truth and destined to be replaced by it can be seen at least as early as Francis Bacon's *Wisdom of the Ancients* (1607), which declares that "Fables . . . were formerly substitutes and supplements of examples, but now that the times abound with history, the aim is more true and active when the mark is alive" (p. 467). In 1709, John Trenchard's *Natural History of Supernaturalism* described the fable as a figural structure rooted in "something innate in our Constitution [that] made us easily susceptible of wrong impressions." See Trenchard, repr. in *The Rise of Modern Mythologies*, ed. Burton Feldman and Robert D. Richardson (Bloomington and London, 1972), 32.

40 Edmund Arwaker, Preface to *Truth in Fiction*, vi.

41 English acquaintance with this Sanskrit fable collection begins with Thomas North's *The Morall Philosophie of Doni* (1570) and the Brahmin philosopher remained visible throughout the seventeenth and eighteenth centuries. Variously known as Bidpai and Pilpay, his character was never as stable as Aesop's and his fables were typically more complex and obviously anthropocentric. Unlike the slave Aesop he was supposed to have been a governor of "Indostan" who told his apologues to "the most potent Monarch Dabschelim." His fables "lay before all Kings and Princes the best Methods of governing their Subjects, couched under the Disguise of histories of Things, which happened among Birds and Beasts, as well as those of his own Species." Bidpai's fables are full of images of mystery and secrecy: his "Counsels" are supposed, "like Tapers, to give life into the most hidden secrets" and, far more than Aesop's fables, they exemplify discursive structures that emerged under the tyrannical political structures associated with the east, for "the Eastern monarchies being for the most part absolute, their Subjects were always restrained from Freedom of Speech." Images of secrecy like caves, boxes, and holes abound throughout Bidpai; fables are often set within fables. See especially *The Instructive and Entertaining Fables of Pilpay, an Ancient Indian Philosopher* (London, 1757), iii and ix.

42 "Persian Tales" appealed to contemporary fascination with the exotic and lacked Aesop's important anti-classical within the classical characteristics. Periodicals like the *Tatler*, the *Spectator*, and the *Guardian* are full of short tales set in the Near East and, like Bidpai's fables, usually told to tyrants: see especially *Spectator* 512 (October 17, 1712). This tradition obviously leads up to works like Samuel Johnson's *Rasselas* (1759) and Frances Sheridan's *History of Nourjahad* (1767). Meanwhile, the first English translation of the *Arabian Nights* appeared as *The Arabian Nights Entertainment* (1705–1707), translated out of the French of Antoine

Galland. In this version, all of the tales are told by the remarkably bookish
Scheherazade, who, we learn, "had read in abundance" (p. 19) and is encouraged
on her wedding night, by her sister Dinarzade, to "tell one of the stories of which
she has read so many" (p. 31). Scheherazade complies and thus manages to keep
herself alive; like other Oriental tales, hers explicitly link power relations and
storytelling, with the latter tending to balance asymmetrical instances of the
former. On such narratives see Martha Conant, *The Oriental Tale in the Eighteenth
Century* (New York, 1966).

43 Addison, *Spectator* 183, II: 220.

44 Arwaker, Preface to *Truth in Fiction*, vi.

45 Gotthold Lessing's *Fabeln und Erzahlungen in Reimen* (1753) and *Die Erziehung des
Menschengeschlects* (1780), and Johan Gottfried Herder's essays "Aesop and
Lessing" (1767–1768) and "On Image, Poetry and Fable" (1787) are classic
German discussions of the form. Noel (*Theories of the Fable*, 85–101 and 122–139)
helpfully summarizes German pre-romantic and romantic fable theory.

46 For commentary on medieval uses of fables, see Blackham, *Fable as Literature*,
33–62. The Renard the Fox cycle current throughout medieval Europe is also
obviously related to the circulation of animal fables; Caxton even printed the
adventures of the wily Renard and Aesop's fables at virtually the same time, in
1486.

47 John Milton, "Of Reformation," in *Works of John Milton*, 18 vols. (New York,
1951), III: 47. To figure the "vitious and harden'd" – and dispensable – character
of monarchy, Milton develops a lurid anti-monarchical and anti-iconographic
Aesopian fable about a "huge and monstrous Wen" that, as it usurps the head's
power over what is clearly the body politic, is maligned by a "wise and learned
Philosopher" who threatens to "cut thee off, and ope[n] thee" (pp. 48–49). For
Renaissance uses of fables, see Patterson, *Fables of Power*, 45–80; Blackham, *Fable
as Literature*, 63–84; and William Meredith Carroll, *Animal Conventions in English
Renaissance Non-Religious Prose* (New York, 1954), 15–89.

48 See Patterson, *Fables of Power*, 81–86.

49 Dodsley's "Essay on Fable" is a useful compendium of earlier attitudes toward
fables, but it lacks the self-consciousness, the immediacy, and the materialist
preoccupations of earlier Aesopians. The preface's concerns are classificatory and
schematic, oriented toward literary models and metaphors very different from
those even of the predecessors whom it quotes. For example, Dodsley divides
fables between "the sublimer and the more complex kind, as the epick and
dramatick" and "the lower and more simple, as what has been called the
Esopean." In his generic obsession he concludes rather condescendingly that the
Aesopian "apologue has a right to some share of our esteem, from the relation it
bears to the poems before mentioned: as it is honorable to spring from a noble
stem, although in ever so remote a branch." See Dodsley, "An Essay on Fable,"
preface to *Select Fables of Esop and Other Fabulists in Three Books* (Birmingham, 1764),
lvii–lviii.

50 See Edward Moore, *Fables for the Female Sex* (London, 1744) and *New Fables Invented
for the Amusement of Young Ladies* (London, 1754); Christopher Smart, *Poetical
Translation of the Fables of Phaedrus* (London, 1761); and William Godwin, *Fables,*

Ancient and Modern (London, 1811), a most intriguing Jacobite work that bears little resemblance to Dryden's compendium of the same title.

51 Fables designed to improve women morally, and to instruct them how to behave, became increasingly common throughout the eighteenth century and into the nineteenth, reflecting a growing anxiety to modulate female propriety. See Moore, *Fables for the Female Sex* (1744), *The Economy of Beauty addressed to the Ladies* (1777), *Fables and Flowers for the Fair Sex* (1773), and *The Fables of Flora* (1804). A typical frontispiece, like that to Edward Moore's *Fables for the Female Sex*, shows a satyr holding a mirror up to a woman, who is visible only in the reflection. The caption promises that "Truth under Fiction I impart / To weed out Folly from the Heart," and the ensuing poems explore the fictive contours of women's lives, identifying their desirability with their powers of concealment ("The maid, who modestly conceals / Her beauties, while she hides, reveals') and, while assuming their susceptibility to fiction and romance, defining women primarily as imitative creatures. Real women themselves, however, were writing fables to protest against these constructions: see Anne Finch's many fables, discussed in Chapter 5 below, Mary Leapor's "The Cock and the Hen," and Elizabeth Griffith's fable of the lion and the man in *Letters between Henry and Frances*.

52 Maria Edgeworth included fables among the children's stories in her *Moral Tales* and *Popular Tales* (1801 and 1804); Anna Barbauld's *Evenings at Home* (1792) often inculcates domestic values through animal fables. Extracted from a box, the fables describe rebellious, selfish, overly ambitious small animals who are often punished with death or, in the case of one flying fish, with awkward or inadequate bodies. Barbauld's fables are complex, however, and often expose English ambitions to empire or hint that, as one little mouse discovers quite literally, domestic space is really a trap. For fables' place in the history of children's literature, see Geoffrey Summerfield, *Fantasy and Reason: Children's Literature in the Eighteenth Century* (Athens, Ga., 1985).

1 The English fable collection and its authors, 1651–1740

1 John Ogilby, "Prospectus for Lottery" (1665). Reproduced in Marian Eames, "John Ogilby and his Æsop." *Bulletin of the New York Public Library* 65 (1961), 82.

2 Edward Phillips, *Theatrum Poetarum, or a Compleat Collection of the Poets, especially the Most Eminent of all Ages* (London, 1674), 114. William Winstanley's *Lives of the Poets* (1687), sardonically quoted in Pope's *Dunciad*, likewise deemed Ogilby "the *Prodigy* of his time."

3 Ogilby, "Prospectus," 82.

4 Ogilby, "Proposal" (May 10, 1669). Oxford, Bodleian Library, Wood, 658, fol. 792.

5 John Aubrey, *Brief Lives and Other Selected Writings*, ed. Anthony Powell (London, 1949), 106.

6 Ogilby, "Prospectus," 82. Ogilby called himself an 'AUTHOR" though most of his work was paraphrase, translation, or, in the case of the Bible, merely textual reproduction. His lavishly embellished folio description of Charles II's coronation (1662) came closest to what we would consider an original composition.

7   Samuel Pepys, *Diary of Samuel Pepys*, ed. H.B. Whaley. 3 vols. (London, 1924), III:
    131. Pepys also won a copy of Ogilby's 1662 *Entertainment of his Most Excellent
    Majestie Charles II.*
8   Pepys, *Diary*, V: 213 (June 27, 1666).
9   "To convince them he published a 2d volume, which he calles his *Æsopiques*,"
    wrote John Aubrey (p. 106).
10 Phillips, *Theatrum Poetarum*, 114.
11 Alexander Pope, *The Dunciad* (1728), I: 121, and note.
12 James Shirley, "To My Worthy Friend Mr. John Ogilby," in Ogilby, *Fables of
    Æsop, Paraphras'd in Verse and Adorn'd with Sculptures* (London, 1651 and 1668), n.p.
13 Good discussions of Ogilby's *Fables* in its successive incarnations, and of his varied
    career generally include Katherine S. Van Eerde, *John Ogilby and the Taste of his
    Times* (London, 1976); Earl Miner's Introduction to Ogilby's *Fables* (Los Angeles,
    1965), i–xii; and Eames, "Ogilby and his Aesop," 73–88. On the lotteries, see
    Sarah L.C. Clapp, "The Subscription Enterprises of John Ogilby and Richard
    Blome," *Modern Philology* 30 (1933), 365–379; and C. L'Estrange Ewen, *Lotteries
    and Sweepstakes* (London, 1932).
14 Helpful discussions of Caxton's Aesop may be found in R.T. Lenaghan, *Caxton's
    Aesop* (Cambridge, Mass., 1967); and Jacobs, *Fables of Aesop*, 187–192.
15 These were William Barret's *Aesop's Fables with his Whole Life* (1651) and the
    anonymous *The Fabulist Metamorphosed and Mythologized* (1634).
16 Ogilby's topicality, including his use of political slang and his references to recent
    political events like the Root and Branch Bill, is treated in detail in Mary
    Pritchard's groundbreaking "Fables Moral and Political." Pritchard interprets
    Ogilby's fable collection as "an unhappy Royalist's response to the excesses and
    hypocrisies of his fellow countrymen of all persuasions during and immediately
    following the Civil War" (p. 6). Annabel Patterson's *Fables of Power* offers an
    incisive interpretation of some of Ogilby's fables as critiques of contemporary
    politics (pp. 85–94).
17 John Locke, Preface to *Æsop's Fables* (London, 1701), sigs. A2r–A3v.
18 Wallace, "'Examples are Best Precepts'," 278. For a more recent treatment of
    sixteenth-century ideas about the example, see Timothy Hampton, *Writing from
    History: The Rhetoric of Exemplarity in Renaissance Literature* (Ithaca, 1990).
19 Arwaker, Preface to *Truth in Fiction*, ii.
20 See for example Richard Steele's *Spectator* essay of March 13, 1711, where as
    "Arietta" Steele writes: "Your Quotations [from *The Ephesian Matron*, a fiction of
    female inconstancy] put me in Mind of the Fable of the Lion and the Man. The
    Man walking with that noble Animal, showed him, in the Ostentation of human
    Superiority, a *Sign* of a Man killing a Lion. Upon which the Lion said, justly, We
    Lions are none of us Painters, else we could show a hundred Men killed by Lions,
    for one Lion killed by a Man. You Men are Writers, and can represent us
    Women as Unbecoming as you please in your Works, while we are unable to
    return the Injury." *The Spectator*, ed. Donald F. Bond. 6 vols. (Oxford, 1965),
    I: 48–49.
21 Roger L'Estrange, "A Lyon and a Man," in *Fables of Æsop*, 209. The inversion is
    literal in L'Estrange's lion's fantasy of "*Twenty Men* under the Paw of a *Lyon*."

22 John Ogilby, "Of the Lion and the Forester," in *Fables*, 123.

23 Gerard Reedy gives an excellent summary of this crisis in "Mystical Politics," in *Studies in Revolution and Change*, ed. Korshin, 20–46. Not overlooking Ogilby's own role in crafting the iconography of Charles II's Restoration, Reedy points out that the "symbolic texture of the day" (p. 20), thanks to the "demythologiz[ing]" mania of the Interregnum, was characterized by a deep skepticism about the "mystical nature of noumenal essence" and by a conviction that kingly authority was little more than "a concept to be manipulated" (p. 45) as a "political tool" (p. 21). We can generalize this insight to suggest that all previously unchallengeable correspondences between "phenomenal" signifiers and "noumenal" signifieds found themselves under fire by 1660.

24 In *Stability and Strife*, W.A. Speck offers an overview of the conflictual structure of eighteenth-century English politics. Compelling essays on various conflicts of the period may be found in *Culture, Politics, and Society in Britain, 1660–1800*, ed. Jeremy Black and Jeremy Gregory (Manchester, 1991). Jean-Christophe Agnew's *Worlds Apart: The Market and the Theater in Anglo-American Thought, 1550–1750* (New York, 1985) traces and theorizes the way an emerging market shaped symbolic forms in early modern England.

25 This is how Roger L'Estrange described his own prodigious fable collection's metamorphosis from the diminutive to the mammoth, so that it might better "answe[r] all the *Parts* and *Pretences* of the *Undertaking*, as well *Publique* as *Private*." L'Estrange, Address to the Reader, in *Fables and Storyes Moralized, Being a Second Part of the Fables of Æsop* (London, 1692 and 1699), sig. A3v. Future references to this preface will be designated "Address."

26 L'Estrange, "A Fox and a Goat," in *Eminent Mythologists*, 80.

27 *Ibid.*; Samuel Richardson, "A Cock and a Fox" in *Æsop's Fables, with Instructive Morals and Reflections* (London, 1739), 20.

28 Arwaker, Preface to *Truth in Fiction*, vi.

29 Thomas Hobbes, "The Introduction" to *Leviathan*, ed. C.B. Macpherson ((1651) Harmondsworth, 1968), 81. For Hobbes's elaboration of the "generall use of Speech," "*Markes*, or *Notes*," and "*Signes*," see *Leviathan*, I.iv, "Of Speech." Hobbes's discussion of language's culturally constructive uses actually begins with a discussion of writing – "a profitable Invention for continuing the memory of time past" (p. 100), and his discussion of words very often seems to assume that at their most efficacious they would be graphic. On Hobbes's use of the exemplary potential of the page, and on its centrality to his notion of obedience to certain forms of cultural authority, see Richard Kroll, "*Mise-en-page*: Biblical Criticism and Inference during the Restoration," in *Studies in Eighteenth-Century Culture*, ed. O.M. Brack, Jr. (Madison, 1986), 3–40.

30 William Davenant, "To My Friend Mr. Ogilby, Upon the Fables of Æsop Paraphras'd in Verse," in Ogilby, *Fables* (1651), n.p.

31 Ogilby, "Of the Fox and the Lion," in *Fables*, 194–195. Patterson analyzes several of Ogilby's fables as instances of his having "appropriated fabulist tradition," rendering individual fables "vehicle[s] of protest and solidarity for the Royalist nobility and gentry" and thereby eventually "alter[ing] the *status* of the fable" (*Fables of Power*, 86–87). Her close readings of several of Ogilby's most tendentious

fables enhances Pritchard's interpretation of *Fables* as a sustained plea for cultural integration reflected in the "narrative unity" of the collection itself (p. 17).

32 Bernard Mandeville, "Remark P," in *The Fable of the Bees* (1705–1729), ed. F.B. Kaye. 2 vols. (Oxford, 1924), II: 178.

33 John Ogilby, "Of the Dog and Shadow," in *Fables of Æsop.* 4.

34 On Barlow's contributions to Aesopian representation in England, see Edward Hodnett, *Francis Barlow: First Master of English Book Illustrations* (London, 1978). Philip Hofer analyzes Barlow's fable collection as a "private venture" that was "in direct competition" with Ogilby's Aesop, even though Barlow apparently supplied illustrations for one of Ogilby's collections. Hofer sees Barlow as wishing to "produce a finer book" than Ogilby (pp. 281–282). See Hofer, "Francis Barlow's Aesop." *Harvard Library Bulletin* 2 (1948), 279–295.

35 Francis Barlow, Dedication to *Aesop's Fables with his Life, in English, French and Latin* (London, 1687), n.p. Future references to Barlow's Dedication and to Behn's fables will be to this edition (in Bibliography see *s.v.* Behn).

36 L'Estrange, "Address," sig. A3v.

37 Contemporary lampoons depicted L'Estrange as a dog with "a thousand dog tricks, viz. to catch for the Papists, carry for the Protestants, whine to the King … and cring [*sic*] to the Crucifix," none of which could compare with his "damn'd old trick of slipping the halter." See the anonymous "Hue and Cry" appended to "Strange's Case Strangely Altered" (London, 1680), n.p.

38 L'Estrange's biographer, George Kitchin, points out that, though L'Estrange was knighted much earlier, he only became "the celebrated L'Estrange" after he turned to polite letters. *Sir Roger L'Estrange: A Contribution to the History of the Press in the Seventeenth Century* (London, 1913), 390–407.

39 Patterson, *Fables of Power* (139–143), treats L'Estrange's *Fables* as political satire responding to England's return to constitutional government after 1688.

40 Roger L'Estrange, Preface to *Eminent Mythologists* (London, 1692), sig. A2v. L'Estrange berates the "Morose and Untractable Spirits in the World, that look upon Precepts in Emblem" as trivial, the strict province of "Women and Children" and uses the terms "Figure" and "Fable" interchangeably. Future references to this preface will be to this edition and will appear in the text.

41 L'Estrange, "Address," sig. A3v.

42 L'Estrange's choice of words here is not original. In the preface to *The Midwives Book* (London, 1671), Jane Sharpe remarks on her own choice to communicate anatomical, gynecological, and obstetrical precepts in lay words: "It is not hard words that perform the work, as if more understood the Art that cannot understand Greek. Words are but the Shell, that we ofttimes break our Teeth with them to come at the Kernel. I mean our Brains to know what is the Meaning of them" (pp. 3–4).

43 Mr. Spectator was voluble on the rampant "Humour of Shortning our Language" that, exemplified by L'Estrange, threatened to "have confounded all our Etymologies, and have quite destroy'd our Tongue." Joseph Addison, *Spectator* 135 (August 4, 1711), in *The Spectator*, ed. Bond, II: 35. For the most minute of many contemporary engagements with L'Estrange's fables, see *Some Observations on the Fables of Æsop, as Commented upon by Roger L'Estrange* (Edinburgh, 1700). The

"Divine of the Church of Scotland" responsible for the *Observations* added morals
to L'Estrange's fables, examined their sometimes contradictory relations to each
other, and furnished details that he felt L'Estrange might have mentioned. The
depth and detail of the *Observations* show how deeply L'Estrange's fable collection
engrossed contemporary readers and writers.

44 Samuel Croxall, Preface to *Fables of Æsop and Others* (London, 1722), sig. B5v.
    Future references to Croxall's preface are to this edition and will appear
    parenthetically in the text.

45 Croxall, "The Forrester and the Lion," in *Fables of Æsop and Others*, 96.

46 Richardson, Preface to *Æsop's Fables*, iv. Future references will appear parenthe-
    tically in the text.

47 As would his choice of names like "Charles" and "Charlotte" for protagonists in
    his last novel *Sir Charles Grandison* (1753–1754). For Richardson's uncommonly
    sympathetic response to L'Estrange, see Margaret Anne Doody, *A Natural Passion:
    A Study in the Novels of Samuel Richardson* (Oxford, 1974), 25–28. And on
    Richardson's possible Jacobitism, Doody's "Richardson's Politics," *Eighteenth-
    Century Fiction* 2 (1990), 113–126.

48 Samuel Richardson, *Pamela; or, Virtue Rewarded* ((1740) Harmondsworth, 1980),
    108. Future references to *Pamela* will be to this edition and will appear
    parenthetically in the text.

49 Terry Castle, *Clarissa's Ciphers: Meaning and Disruption in Richardson's "Clarissa'*
    (Ithaca, N.Y., 1982).

50 Richardson's footnotes to his novels notoriously multiplied over successive editions
    as he sought to protect the authority he had conceded by writing in the epistolary
    form. As they simultaneously assert and surrender the authority to control
    interpretation, we are thus encouraged to read the novels as we would fables.

51 For example, Lovelace cites a fable in which Mercury, disguised, asks a statuary
    "what price that same statue of *Mercury* bore," only to be told it is worth nothing.
    Lovelace applies this fable to his correspondent Belford, who like Mercury
    "prizes" Clarissa's "good Opinion" and whom Lovelace rewards with the
    bruising information that "she dislikes thee." Samuel Richardson, *Clarissa; or The
    History of a Young Lady* ((1747–1748) Harmondsworth, 1985), 355. Future
    references to *Clarissa* will be to this edition and will appear in the text.

52 Arwaker, Preface to *Truth in Fiction*, vi.

53 Antoine Houdart de la Motte, *One Hundred New Court Fables*, trans. Robert Samber
    (London, 1721), 331. La Motte, whose *Fables nouvelles* appeared in an ornate and
    theoretically eloquent edition in Paris in 1719, was extremely important for
    English fabulists (particularly Whiggish ones); Samber ventured that this was
    because he "seem[ed] to have the utmost Allusion to Arbitrary Government, and
    dares say so; Through all his Fables may be discovered a spirit of liberty" (ix). (Of
    course, La Motte's fables were also dedicated to the king.) All fables being
    translations at some level, English fabulists habitually made few, if any, qualitative
    distinctions between an original fable and a translation. I thus treat Samber's
    important collection as a full participant in English Aesopian conventions.

54 Philip Ayres, "Epistle Dedicatory to Lewis Maydwell, in *Mythologia Ethica, or Three
    Centuries of Æsopean Fables in English Prose* (London, 1689), sigs. A3r–A4v; John

Jackson, Preface to *A New Translation of Æsop's Fables, Adorn'd with Cutts* (London, 1708), lxvii.

55 Richardson, *Æsop's Fables*, x. Like Richardson, Croxall likewise wanted his book to "suit [...] the Hands of the Generality of Children." See Croxall, *Fables of Æsop*, B8v.

56 La Motte (trans. Samber), "The Sheep and the Bush, in *Court Fables*, 248. *Æsop Naturaliz'd: In a Collection of Fables and Stories from Æsop, Lockman, Pilpay and Others* (3rd ed., London, 1711), sigs. A3v–A4r.

57 Susan Stewart's *On Longing: Narratives of the Miniature, the Gigantic, the Souvenir, and the Collection* (Baltimore, 1984) touches on some of the ideological underpinnings of the culture of miniaturism in which Aesop's fables so openly participated. James H. Bunn gives a brilliant and persuasive account of how mercantilism informed eighteenth-century linguistic activity in "The Aesthetics of British Mercantilism," *New Literary History* 11 (1980), 303–321.

58 William Davenant, "To My Dear Friend Mr. Ogilby," in Ogilby, *Fables of Æsop* (1651), n.p.

59 La Motte (trans. Samber), *Court Fables*, 31.

60 *Free-Thinker* 47 (September 17, 1718), in *The Free-Thinker* I (London, 1722), 34; La Motte (trans. Samber), *Court Fables*, 61.

61 John Dennis, *The Stage Defended* (1726), in *Critical Works of John Dennis*, ed. Hooker, II: 308.

62 Jackson, "Preface," xvii–xviii.

63 Joan Hildreth Owen, "The Choice of Hercules and the English Fable," 57.

64 Ayres, *Mythologia Ethica*, 74.

65 Toland, "Of the Eagle and the Fox," in *Fables*, 427.

66 L'Estrange, "A Crow and a Pitcher," in *Eminent Mythologists*, 208.

67 Anon., *Fables, Moral & Political* (London, 1703), sig. A11r.

68 *Æsop's Fables with their Morals in Prose and Verse* (1651); facing page: British Library copy.

69 *Fables Moral and Political*, sigs. A4v–A4r.

70 On the "oppositional seam" that structures standard discursive formations of the period, such as the maxim, see Roland Barthes, "Reflections on the Maxims of La Rochefoucauld," *New Critical Essays*, trans. Richard Howard (New York, 1980), 3–19.

71 Shaftesbury document, reproduced in James Winn, *John Dryden and his World* (New Haven and London, 1987), 523.

72 "Westminster-School," in *The Gentleman's Magazine* 6 (October, 1736), 611.

73 Hoole, *Æsop's Fables*.

74 Hoole, "Of the Fox and the Stork," in *Æsop's Fables*, 22.

75 *Æsop Return'd from Tunbridge* (London, 1698), sigs. A2r–A3v; *Æsop at Epsom* (London, 1689), sig. A2v.

76 "To the Reader," *Æsop at Tunbridge* (London, 1698), 1.

77 "Sharpers and Cullies," in *Æsop Return'd from Tunbridge* , 13.

78 Locke's conception of language is set forth in Book III of *An Essay concerning Human Understanding* (1690); of particular relevance there is his commentary on "the Signification of Words," which requires that words be "external sensible Signs" that necessarily evolve historically through "a voluntary Imposition, whereby

such a word is made arbitrarily the Mark of such an Idea." Even in their private uses, words are thus publicly derived and, as "Mark[s]," they are implicitly visible and discrete. See Locke, *Essay*, ed. Peter H. Nidditch (Oxford, 1975), 405.

79 John Locke, *Some Thoughts concerning Education*, in *Educational Writings of John Locke*, ed. James Axtell ((1693) London, 1968), 259.

80 Charles Hoole's translation of the *Orbis* makes its resemblance to the fable collection obvious, for it uses "a Symbolical Alphabet set before it, to Wit, the Characters of the several Letters, with the Image of that Creature, whose Voyce that Letter goeth about to imitate, picured by it." Johan Amos Comenius, "Author's Preface to the Reader," in *Visible World, or the Pictures and Nomenclatures of All the Chief Things that are in the World*, trans. Hoole (London, 1675), n.p. On the naturalistic spatial arrangement of pages in Comenius's *Orbis Pictus*, especially in relation to his planned "Encyclopedia of Sensuals," see James Turner, "The Visual Realism of Comenius," *History of Education* I (1972), 113–138.

81 See Kroll, "*Mise-en-Page*," 6–7, and on Lockean empiricism as a rhetorical structure supported by certain duplicitous figural devices, Geoff Bennington, "The Perfect Cheat: Locke and Empiricism's Rhetoric," in *The Figural and Literal: Problems of Language in the History of Science and Philosophy*, ed. Andrew E. Benjamin, Geoffrey N. Cantor, and John R.R. Christie (Manchester, 1987), 103–123.

82 "Of the Countrey Man and the Snake," in *Æsop Improv'd*, ed. Thomas Singleton and Thomas Houghton (London, 1673); *Æsop's Fables with his Life*, ed. Robert Burton (pseud. of Nathaniel Crouch) (11th ed., 1754), 11.

83 L'Estrange, "A Wolf and a Lamb," in *Eminent Mythologists*, 3. L'Estrange's prefatory metaphor of the nutshell of Aesopic language is itself another instance of this effect.

84 Jonathan Swift, *A Tale of a Tub*, in *Writings of Jonathan Swift*, ed. Greenberg and Piper, 274. Future references to the *Tale*, and to *Gulliver's Travels*, will be to this edition and will appear parenthetically in the text.

85 Terry Castle, "Why the Houyhnhms Don't Write: Swift, Satire, and the Fear of the Text," *Essays in Literature* 7 (1980), 26–38.

86 Swift wrote to Gay: "There is no writing I esteem more than Fables, nor any thing so difficult to succeed in, which, however, you have done excellently well, and I have often admired your happiness in such a kind of performance, which I have frequently endeavoured at in vain. I remember I acted as you seem to hint; I found a moral first, and then studied for a fable, but could do nothing that pleased me, and so left off that scheme for ever." *Correspondence of Jonathan Swift*, ed. F. Elrington Bell. 6 vols. (London, 1913), IV: 34. For Swift's own use of fables, see Albert Ball, "Swift and the Animal Myth," in *Transactions of the Wisconsin Academy of Science, Arts and Letters* 48 (1959), 239–248; and Colin J. Horne, " 'From a Fable Form a Truth': A Consideration of the Fable in Swift's Poetry," in *Studies in the Eighteenth Century* I, ed. R.F. Brissenden (Canberra, 1968), 193–205.

2   Augustan fable theory and the birth of the book

1 Croxall, "Preface." sig. B2v; Addison, *Spectator* 183, Bond, II: 247. Future references to Addison's essay will be to this edition and will be indicated parenthetically in the text.

2 George Farquhar, "A Discourse upon Comedy in Reference to the English Stage," in *Love and Business* (London, 1702), 137. Future references to Farquhar's "Discourse" will be to this edition and will appear parenthetically in the text.

3 William Davenant, "To My Dear Friend, Mr. Ogilby," in *Fables of Æsop*, n.p.

4 Arwaker, "Preface" to *Truth in Fiction*, iii.

5 Singleton and Houghton, Preface to *Æsop Improv'd*, n.p.; John Toland, *Essay concerning the Rise, Progress and Destruction of Fables and Romances* (London, 1704), 30.

6 Ayres, "Preface" to *Mythologia Ethica*, sig. A8r.

7 Both the structure and the incipient contradictions and ambivalences of this best known of cultural projects are analyzed in Weinbrot's *Augustus Caesar in "Augustan" England*.

8 Richard Blackmore's preface to *Prince Arthur* held that "an Epick Poem [is] a feign'd or devis'd Discourse, that is, a *Fable*. ... The Word Fable at first signified indifferently a true or false story, therefore Cicero for distinction used *Fictas fabulas* in his book *De finibus*. But afterward Custom obtain'd to use the word always for a feign'd Discourse. And in the First Ages ... great use was made by Learned and Wise men of these feign'd Discourses, Fables or Apologues. ... So Thales, Orpheus, Solon, Homer, and the rest of the great Men have done, and the famous philosopher Socrates is by some affirm'd to be the Author of many of the Fables that pass under Æsop's name" (n.p.).

9 John Dennis, *The Stage Defended from Scripture, Reason, Experience, and the Common Sense of Man* (1726), in *Critical Works of John Dennis*, ed. Hooker, II: 302. Dennis's own fables – some translations of La Fontaine and some original – appeared in his *Miscellany Poems* of 1696.

10 René Le Bossu, *Mssr Bossu's Treatise of the Epick Poem*, trans. W.J. (1695), 2 vols. (London, 1719), I: 24. Future references to Le Bossu are to this translation and will appear parenthetically in the text.

11 In *Probability and Literary Form*, Douglas Lane Patey discusses Augustan literary theory's devotion to "hierarch[ies] of probable signs," with individual signifiers deemed meaningful through their probable coherence with larger clusters of signs. For neoclassical critics, the fable was the keystone in this literary hierarchy (pp. 110–116). For a general survey of neoclassical fable theory, see Thomas Noel, *Theories of the Fable*.

12 Dennis, "To Sir Richard Blackmore on the Moral and Conclusion of an Epick Poem" (1719), in *Works*, II: 110.

13 Swift's *The Battel of the Books* (1704), discussed at length below, encapsulates the conflict. For a sensible modern reassessment of the ancient–modern controversy, see Joseph M. Levine, *The Battle of the Books: History and Literature in the Augustan Age* (Ithaca, N.Y., 1991).

14 Two important exceptions are Richard Kroll's *Material Word*, which shows how epicurean poetics assimilated atomistic evidences to the neoclassical imperative; and Helen Deutsch, *Resemblance and Disgrace* (Cambridge, Mass., 1996), which examines the way the image of Alexander Pope, at once classicized and deformed, shaped and menaced that very opposition.

15 Mikhail M. Bakhtin's *Rabelais and his World*, trans. Helene Iswolsky (Bloomington, Ind., 1984), inaugurates the classical/grotesque distinction, whose historical and

political relevance has been explored by Peter Stallybrass and Allon White in *The Politics and Poetics of Transgression* (Ithaca, N.Y., 1986).

16 *Royal Magazine* 93 (September, 1760), 118.

17 John Toland, *Second Essay concerning the Rise, Progress, and Destruction of Fables and Romances* (London, 1704), 29.

18 William Temple, "An Essay upon the Ancient and Modern Learning," in *Five Miscellaneous Essays*, ed. Samuel Holt Monk ((1690) Ann Arbor, 1963), 64.

19 *The Craftsman* 75 (December, 1727), 325.

20 The actual overlapping of oral and literate modes in antiquity, with particular reference to Plato, is a central concern in Eric A. Havelock's *A Preface to Plato* (London, 1963), especially pp. 141–145.

21 *The Adventurer* 18 (January 6, 1753). In *The British Essayists*, ed. Lionel Thomas Berguer, 45 vols. (1823), XXII: 114.

22 William Warburton, *The Divine Legation of Moses, Demonstrated*, 4 vols. (London, 1728), IV: 36.

23 Temple, *Essays*, 50.

24 Edward Stillingfleet, *Origines Sacrae*, 2 vols. (London, 1662), II: 133.

25 Jacques Derrida's model of "*différance*" is most explicitly set forth in *Writing and Difference*, trans. Alan Bass (Chicago, 1978), 196–231.

26 For a preliminary discussion of the ancients–moderns controversy, see Gilbert Highet's *The Classical Tradition: Greek and Roman Influences on Western Literature* (Oxford, 1949). Richard Foster Jones's influential *Ancients and Moderns* (Saint Louis, 1961) reads the battle of the books as a function of and within the scientific academy. Jones's argument has been revised and sophisticated in recent years by Joseph M. Levine, who interprets the battle as a complicated debate "about history, about the meaning and use of the past and about the method of apprehending it." See Levine, "Ancients and Moderns Reconsidered," *Eighteenth-Century Studies* 15 (1981–1982), 84. For more extensive analyses of the quarrel, see Levine's earlier essays, "Ancients, Moderns and History: The Continuity of English Historical Writing in the Later Seventeenth Century," in *Studies in Change and Revolution*, ed. Korshin, 43–75; and "The Battle of the Books and the Shield of Achilles," *Eighteenth-Century Life* 9 (1984), 33–61. Continental versions of the *querelle* are outlined in Ira O. Wade, *The Intellectual Origins of the French Enlightenment* (Princeton, 1971).

27 William Wotton, *Reflections on the Ancient and Modern Learning* (London, 1692), 376.

28 Temple, *Essays*, 49.

29 Robert Adams Day, "Richard Bentley and John Dunton: Brothers under the Skin." *Studies in Eighteenth-Century Culture* 16 (1984), 127. For the relevant historical background, see Eisenstein, *The Printing Press*; Marshall McLuhan, *The Gutenberg Galaxy* (Toronto, 1962); and Walter J. Ong, *Orality and Literacy* (London and New York, 1982).

30 Levine, "Ancients and Moderns Reconsidered," 86.

31 In the war of words that ensued, Phalaris's bull became an emblem of rhetorical manipulation, and a figure for misquotation and other textual machinations. Combatants accused rival writers of absorbing quotations into their own texts and twisting their implications just as the bull distorted the voices of its prisoners.

See for example Bentley on Boyle: "In the End of his Book, he has got me into Phalaris's Bull; and he has the pleasure of fancying that he hears me 'begin to bellow.'" *Dissertation concerning the Epistles of Phalaris* (London, 1697), xxii.

32 Jonathan Swift, *The Battel of the Books*, in *A Tale of a Tub, with Other Early Works*, ed. Herbert Davis (Oxford, 1957), 149. Future references to the Battel will be to this edition and will appear parenthetically in the text. The Bookseller's ironic declaration that the "Discourse . . . seems to have been written about . . . the Year 1697, when the famous Dispute was on Foot about *Ancient and Modern Learning*" (p. 141) lets us assume that the *Battel* is exactly contemporary with Bentley's dissertation on Phalaris and the accompanying essay on Aesop.

33 On the ambiguity of Swift's fidelity to the ancient cause, see Philip Pinkus, who cleverly challenges the terms of the ancients–moderns controversy and Swift's relationship to it in "Swift and the Ancients–Moderns Controversy," *University of Toronto Quarterly* 29 (1959), 46–58. Deborah Baker, in *Jonathan Swift and the Vested Word* (Chapel Hill, N.C., 1988), 61. Wyrick also points out that "both insects are ambivalent images."

34 Swift's poetry often experiments with the fable form, while Bentley annotated an edition of fables penned by Aesop's Latin successor Phaedrus.

35 Terry Castle, "Why the Houyhnhnms Don't Write," 32.

36 Surprisingly few critics have devoted real attention to the role the animal fable plays in Swift's *oeuvre*. See Albert Ball, "Swift and the Animal Myth." *Transactions of the Wisconsin Academy of Sciences, Arts and Letters* 48 (1959); and Colin J. Horne, "'From a Fable Form a Truth': A Consideration of the Fable in Swift's Poetry," in *Studies in the Eighteenth Century*, ed. R. F. Brissenden, 4 vols. (Canberra, 1968), I: 193–205. Special considerations of *The Battel of the Books* may be found in Robert F. Sarfatt Borkat, "The Spider and the Bee: Jonathan Swift's Reversal of Tradition in *The Battel of the Books*," in *Eighteenth-Century Life* 3 (1976), 444–445; and in Richard N. Ramsey's interesting "Swift's Strategy in *The Battel of the Books*" in *Papers on Language and Literature* 20 (1994), 382–389.

37 The complexity of seventeenth-century negotiations with the figural and the literal is apparent in *The Figural and Literal*, ed. Benjamin, Canton, and Christie (Manchester, 1987). Of particular interest is Geoff Bennington, "The Perfect Cheat: Locke and Empiricism's Rhetoric," 103–123.

38 Bentley, "Of Æsop's Fables." In *A Dissertation*, 19. Future references to the essay are to this edition and will appear parenthetically in the text.

39 One recent classical scholar points out that Herodotus too was positioned between the opposing symbolic practices dictated by the eye and the ear. See François Hartog, *The Mirror of Herodotus*, trans. Janet Lloyd (Berkeley and Los Angeles, 1988).

40 Bentley refers to a fable where an ass hides under a lion skin and makes a short but happy career of impressing his fellow asses. His long ears ultimately expose him and the ass is dragged into the open, an emblem of the folly of pretense. Roger L'Estrange's *Eminent Mythologists* (1692) proposes both oral and visual betrayals: "He had the Hap in the Conclusion, partly by his *Voice*, and partly by his *Ears*, to be Discover'd, and consequently Uncas'd" (p. 196).

41 Francis Atterbury, *A Short Review of the Controversy between Mr. Boyle and Mr. Bentley* (London, 1701), 5.

42 John Ogilby, Dedication to Heneage Finch, *Fables of Aesop*, sig. A1r.
43 John Ogilby, Preface to *Africa* (London, 1670), sigs. C2v–C2r.
44 Ayres, "Preface," sig. A2v.
45 John Jackson, Preface to *A New Translation*, vi.
46 Richardson, "Preface," x.
47 For commentary on these commentaries, see George Kitchin, *Sir Roger L'Estrange: A Contribution to the History of the Press in the Seventeenth Century* (London, 1713), 401–404. And on the jest books and cheap "little books" to which the fable collections are here compared, Margaret Spufford, *Small Books and Pleasant Histories* (London, 1981).
48 *Spectator* 185 (May 4, 1711).
49 Robert Dodsley, "An Essay on Fable," in *Select Fables of Esop*, lxxvii.
50 Arwaker, Preface to *Truth in Fiction*, x.
51 The *Spectator* papers" relationship to their readership, and the social strategy that drives them, are brilliantly delineated in Michael Ketcham's *Transparent Designs: Reading, Performance and Form in the Spectator Papers* (Athens, Ga., 1986).
52 Livy, *Ab urbe condita*, II.xxiii, trans. B.O. Foster. 3 vols. (Cambridge, Mass., 1902), I: 373–375.
53 Addison, *Spectator* 512 (October 17, 1713), in *The Spectator*, ed. Bond, IV: 318.
54 Croxall, Preface, sig. B7r.

3   Common and uncommon characters: the lives of Aesop

1 In *A Narrative of the Life of Mrs. Charlotte Charke* ((1755) London, 1930) the author (whose father Colley Cibber had played Aesop in John Vanbrugh's *Æsop, A Comedy* (1696)) describes her adventures selling sausages on the streets of London with her daughter: "Our Loads were like *Æsop's* when he chose to carry the Bread, which was the weightiest Burden, to the Astonishment of his Fellow-Travellers" (p. 114). During the reign of Anne, one Eton cobbler evidently earned the appellation of Aesop, and lived the role to the hilt: "Deformed, similar to his fabled namesake of activity," and finding that "the Whig and Tory politicians so liberally bespattered one another, [this] Æsop was determined not to remain neuter, and, inspired by the classic air of Eton, he started in the treble pursuits of politics, poetry, and cobbling, and employed his pen and awl alternately to patch the state and old shoes and boots." Meanwhile, "the copious draughts of Sir John Barleycorn's delightful beverage enabled him to exercise his muse in many a drunken rhyme." See James Caulfield, *Portraits, Memoirs, and Characters of Remarkable Persons, from the Revolution in 1688 to the End of the Reign of George II*, 4 vols. (London, 1819), I: 73–74.
2 Bentley, "Of Æsop's Fables," 148.
3 Roger L'Estrange, "Preface," sig. B1r.
4 Saunders and Hunter certify the birth of modern fictions of authorial identity out of their actual dependence on various contingencies in "Lessons from the 'Literary': How to Historicise Authorship," *Critical Inquiry* 17 (1991), 479–509. A nearly canonical authority on the subject is Mark Rose's "The Author as Proprietor: Donaldson vs. Becket and the Genealogy of Modern Authorship."

Representations 23 (1988), 51–85; and of older vintage is Michel Foucault, "What is an Author?" in *Textual Strategies*, ed. Josué Harari (Ithaca, N.Y., 1979), 141–160. Helen Deutsch discusses the model of "monstrous contingency" in relation to Alexander Pope's famous efforts to create himself as an author in "The 'Truest Copies' and the 'Mean Original': Pope, Deformity, and the Poetics of Self-Exposure," *Eighteenth-Century Studies* 27 (1993), 1–26.

5 Patterson, *Fables of Power*, 18. For earlier discussions of Aesop's life, see Howard Baker, "A Portrait of Aesop," *Sewanee Review* 77 (1969), 557–590; and M. Ellwood Smith, "Aesop: A Decayed Celebrity," *Publications of the Modern Language Association*, 46 (1931), 225–236.

6 Jackson, "Life of Æsop," xii–xiii.

7 John Vanbrugh, *Æsop. A Comedy*. In *Sir John Vanbrugh*, ed. W.C. Ward (London, 1893), 168, 170.

8 "Preface" to *Æsop Naturaliz'd and Expos'd to the Publick View in his Own Shape and Dress* (Cambridge, 1697).

9 John Toland, Letter to Anthony Collins, in *The Fables of Æsop with the Moral Reflections of Mssr. Baudoin* (London, 1704), sig. A3v.

10 Robert Henryson, "The Taill of the Lyoun and the Mous," in *Morall Fabillis of Esope*, ed. George D. Gopin (Notre Dame, 1987), 111. Patterson speculates that Henryson himself was ignorant of the Planudes narrative.

11 On the genesis of Caxton's collection, and especially on its use of Steinhowel, see Lenaghan, ed., *Caxton's Aesop*. Edward Hodnett traces the influence of Steinhowel's motifs as they were reproduced in seventeenth-century collections in *Aesop in England: The Transmission of Motifs in Seventeenth-Century Illustrations of Aesop's Fables* (Charlottesville, 1979), as does John J. McKendy in *Aesop: Five Centuries of Illustrated Fables* (New York, 1964).

12 Croxall, "Preface," sig. B1v.

13 "To the Reader," *Æsop at Richmond* (London, 1798), n.p.

14 A short but lively discussion of Aesop as trickster figure in the classical period may be found in Winkler, *Auctor and Actor*, 280–291.

15 On Aesop as owner and author of his fables, see especially Charles Boyle, *Dr. Bentley's Dissertation on the Epistles of Phalaris and the Fables of Æsop Examined*. 2nd. ed. (London, 1699), 236.

16 Gregory Nagy explores Aesop's scapegoating, and his role as an "*aîton*" in a classical context in *Best of the Achaeans*, 281–286.

17 Patterson, *Fables of Power*, in *Politics of Discourse*, ed. Steven N. Zwicker and Kevin Sharpe (Berkeley and Los Angeles, 1988), 281.

18 Oliver Goldsmith, *Life of Æsop*. In Bewick, *Select Fables* ((1784) New York, 1932), iii.

19 "A Brief Prospect of the Life of Aesop," in *Æsop's Fables, with his Life*, 2.

20 George Dalgarno, *Didascalocaphus; or, The Deaf and Dumb Man's Tutor* (London, 1680). In *The Works of George Dalgarno*, ed. Henry Cochran and Thomas Maitland (Edinburgh, 1921), 129–130. Dalgarno's treatise aims to develop a sign language for the deaf and also a universal language that, for him, must be rooted in a material medium. The story in which Aesop appears is meant to demonstrate the merits of such a language – one through which, eventually, the blind Homer and

the deaf Aesop are able to patch up the often bloody differences related in the first part of the narrative and live as "good friends, passing the time in telling old stories, sometimes on their fingers'' ends and sometimes with hand in hand, traversing the alphabetical Ilias" (p. 130).

21 *Æsop's Fables with their Morals in Prose and Verse* (London, 1651), 267.

22 Patterson discusses some of these literalizing and corporeal elements in *Fables of Power*, pp. 22–30.

23 Barlow, "Prospect," 3.

24 "Life of Aesop," *Aesop's Fables with their Morals* (1651), 271.

25 Philip Ayres, Preface to *Mythologia Ethica*, sig. A8r.

26 *Æsop's Fables, with their Morals* (llth ed., 1751), 265.

27 *Ibid.*, 287.

28 Jonathan Culler discusses this aspect of the pun in "The Call of the Phoneme," in *On Puns: The Foundation of Letters,* ed. Culler (Oxford, 1988), 1–16.

29 L'Estrange, "Life," sig. A1r.

30 Ayres, Preface to *Mythologia Ethica*, A6v.

31 "An Essay of the Learned Martinus Scriblerus, concerning the Origin of Sciences," in *Life and Works of John Arbuthnot*, ed. George A. Aitken (Oxford, 1892), 363. The essay was first published in 1727, in Pope's *Miscellanies in Prose and Verse.*

32 Barlow, "Prospect," 2.

33 Jackson, "Life of Æsop," xx; Barlow, "Prospect," 2; "Preface" to the Anon. *Æsop's Fables with Instructive Morals and Reflections* (London, 1734), vii.

34 Barlow, "Prospect," 1. English writers were actually reviving classical approval of Aesop's willingness to demystify authoritative "Signatures." Philostratus for example had considered Aesop the most authentic of poets precisely because "he cares more for veracity than the poets do: where they strain to make their stories sound credible, he frankly gives you to expect a fictitious story; and so every one knows that Aesop tells the truth when he announces that he is not going to tell you a true story … The author who gives you a fiction and then adds a moral, as Aesop does, shows how he has made use of fiction for the purpose of instruction." See Philostratus, *Philostratus in Honour of Appolonius of Tyana*, trans. J.S. Phillimore, 2 vols. (Oxford, 1912), II: 57.

35 Barlow, "Prospect," 1.

36 Contemporary conceptions of alphabetical characters are one object of inquiry in Cohen's, *Sensible Words*. But one especially vivid contemporary history of writing that emphasizes the evolution of institutionalized characters and also explores forms of representation that exploit "the voice of the sign" is Warburton's *The Divine Legation of Moses Demonstrated*, IV: 34.

37 Barlow, "Prospect," 1.

38 William Bullokar, *Aesopź Fablź in tru Ortography with Grammar Notź* (1585), in *The Works of William Bullokar*, ed. J.R. Turner, 4 vols. (Leeds, 1969), IV: sig. A4v.

39 Arwaker, Preface to *Truth in Fiction*, ii.

40 Singleton and Houghton, "Preface" to *Æsop Improv'd*, sig. A2v.

41 Ayres, "Preface," A8r.

42 *Æsop at the Bell-Tavern* (London, 1711), sig. A2r.

43 Barlow, titlepage *Æsop's Fables.*

44 Jackson, *A New Translation*, lxiv. The Delphians are subsequently "scourged, if not converted, into a true Sense of so heinous a Guilt'; then, "to appease offended Heaven, they erec[t] a Pyramid to [Aesop's] Memory, as some Part of an Atonement" (lxv).

45 On the text history of the anonymous *Life of Aesop*, see Perry, *Studies in the Text History*, especially pp. 2–4.

46 Boyle, *Dr. Bentley's Dissertation*, 280.

47 L'Estrange, "Preface," sig. A1r.

48 Samuel Richardson, "The Life of Æsop," In *Æsop's Fables*, xv–xvi.

49 Croxall, "Preface," sigs. A1r–A2v.

50 Henryson, *Morall Fabillis*, 111.

51 John Toland, *The Fables of Æsop*.

52 *Idem.*

53 L'Estrange, "Life," sig. A1r.

54 Madeleine de Scudéry, *Artamène, ou le grand Cyrus* (Paris, 1656), IV: 72. For a good discussion of these and other French uses of Aesop, see Terence Allott's preface to *Les Fables d'Esope, Comédie* (Exeter, 1988), v–xxvii.

55 Jean de la Fontaine, "La vie d'Esope le Phrygien." In *Fables choisies*, 33.

56 Boursault, *Fables d'Esope*, 15.

57 John Vanbrugh, Preface to *Æsop. A Comedy*, 220.

58 Toland, Letter to Collins, sig. A3v.

59 On Meziriac's biography of Aesop, see Patterson, *Fables of Power*, 33–36.

60 Bentley, "Of Æsop's Fables," in *A Dissertation*, 149. Future references to Bentley's essay will appear parenthetically in the text.

61 Boyle, *Dr. Bentley's Dissertations [...] Examined*, 233. Future references will appear parenthetically in the text.

62 Quoted in Maynard Mack, *Alexander Pope. A Life* (New Haven, 1985), 148.

63 Charles Draper, "Preface" to *Fables Translated from Æsop and Other Authors* (London, 1760), iii.

4   Aesop's fables and Dryden's later poetry

1 Charles Montague and Matthew Prior, *The Hind and the Panther Transvers'd to the Story of the Country Mouse and the City-Mouse* (1687), in *The Literary Works of Matthew Prior*, ed. H. Bunker Wright and Monroe K. Spears. 2 vols. (Oxford, 1959), II: 35.

2 The doctrinal points like infallibility and transubstantiation that Dryden was supposed to have confused were enumerated by contemporaries like Nathan Clifford, whose "Reflections on the Hind and Panther. In a Letter to a Friend" (London, 1687) concluded that Dryden defended these points so feebly "that his new Church will find it necessary in a little time to spue him out" (p. 25).

3 Thomas Heyrick, *The New Atlantis, with Some Reflections upon the Hind and the Panther* (1687), A1r.

4 Heyrick, *ibid. A Poem in Defence of the Church of England, in Opposition to the Hind and Panther* (London, 1687) also casts the poem as "dull Pennance" for the time when Dryden's Muse "unbaptiz'd, disdain'd the Christian yoke" (pp. 2–3).

5 Samuel Johnson, "Life of Dryden," in *Lives of the English Poets*, ed. George Birkbeck Hill, 2 vols. (Oxford, 1903), II: 446.

6 George Saintsbury, *Dryden* (New York, 1921), 92.

7 Sanford Budick, *Dryden and the Abyss of Light* (New York and London, 1970), 237.

8 James Kinsley, "Dryden's Bestiary," *Review of English Studies* 4 (1953), 531.

9 James Winn, *John Dryden and his World*, 423. Winn's reading of *The Hind and the Panther* is in many ways generous, insightful, and sympathetic: for example, he also classifies *In Memoriam, Four Quartets*, and *Leaves of Grass* as "fascinating, risk-taking failure[s]."

10 Winn (*ibid.*, pp. 414–416) helpfully summarizes Dryden's possible motives for conversion, but Walter Scott's discussion of this "remarkable incident" is subtle and psychologically compelling, concluding that the "conversion was not of that sordid kind which is the consequence of a strong temporal interest," see Scott, *The Life of John Dryden*, in *Works of Dryden*, ed. Scott and George Saintsbury, 10 vols. (London, 1808), I: 264. By contrast, a typical contemporary speculation may be found in Clifford's "Reflections': "Our Poet is not only contented to leave our Church, but all of a sudden he appears at the head of the Contrary Party; which … in him was so *Mercenary*, that none would have descended to act his *Part*, but one who could not get a Livelihood from a Playhouse" (p. 37).

11 For details of these and related grisly events, see John Kenyon, *The Popish Plot* (London, 1922), 181.

12 Scott, *Life of Dryden*, I: 276.

13 Clifford, "Reflections," 21.

14 A useful and succinct account of the Protestant position with respect to contemporary "political and epistemological anxieties" may be found in Richard Kroll's introduction to Abraham Woodhead's *The Protestants Plea for a Socinian* ((1686) repr. Los Angeles, 1987), iii–x.

15 Patterson, *Fables of Power*, 209; Zwicker, *Politics and Language*, 31; Winn, *Dryden and his World*, 422.

16 "A Miracle," Brown's Crites submits, "does the same Mischief, as the *Saxons* did in the case of the poor *Britains*. It ruins the very cause it was sent for to support. If you believe a Miracle is, as I told you, an appeal to the Sences, 'tis as impossible to justifie Transubstantiation by one, as if you can admit a Dispensing Power, as to suppose there can be … an inviolable Magna Charta for Liberty of Conscience." *The Reasons of Mr. Bayes Changing his Religion* (London, 1690), 29–30. Anglican theologians, on the other hand, often marked their own position as anti-fabulous. For example, the titlepage of Edward Stillingfleet's *Origines Sacrae* (1662) promised "a Rational Account of the Grounds of Christian Faith" and fetched its epigraph from II Peter 1.16: "For we have not followed cunningly devised fables, when we made known to you the power and cunning of our Lord Jesus Christ."

17 *Ibid.*, 23.

18 Sloman, *Dryden: The Poetics of Translation*, 18.

19 John Dryden, *The Hind and the Panther*: "Address to the Reader." in *The Works of John Dryden*, gen. eds. Edward Niles Hooker and H.T. Swedenberg, 20 vols. (Berkeley and Los Angeles, 1956–1992), III, ed. Earl Miner (1969), 122. All

references to the poem and to the address will be to this edition, and will appear in the text.

20 Sloman, *Dryden*, 18.

21 Clifford, "Reflections," 35.

22 *The Revenger. A Trage-Comedy Acted between the Hind and Panther and Religio Laici* (London, 1687), 9.

23 Gilbert Burnet, *A Reply to Mr. Varillas* (London, 1688), 139.

24 Clifford, "Reflections," 38 and 22.

25 Dryden, "Epilogue" to *Albion and Albanius*, in California *Works* XV, ed. Earl Miner, XV, 54.

26 Jacques Bossuet, *An Exposition of the Doctrines of the Catholic Church* (Paris, 1672), 34.

27 Dominique Bouhours, *The Life of Saint Francis Xavier*, trans. Dryden. In *Works*, ed. Miner, XIX, 5. Dryden's 1686 pamphlet war with Edward Stillingfleet over Anne Hyde's conversion to Roman Catholicism rehearsed similar issues, hinging as it did on the question of whether to interpret the language of Hyde's account as literal and performative or as ambiguous and untrustworthy.

28 Matthew Prior, "The Occasion of Writing the Country Mouse," in *Dialogues of the Dead and Other Works*, ed. A.R. Wallace (Cambridge, 1907), 130.

29 Alan Roper, *Dryden's Poetic Kingdoms* (London, 1968), 3.

30 John Ogilby, "The Forester, the Skinner and a Bear," in *Fables of Æsop*, 130.

31 Patterson's reading of this image is instructive. She connects it to the frontispiece of Barlow's *Æsop's Fables with his Life*, where Aesop seems to be a "mild and plebeian Adam surrounded by the animals, a spokesman for a peaceable kingdom" (p. 98) and explores at length the political implications of this model of authority – for, "in Dryden's argument, the survival of Catholicism in England is tied to the survival of a monarchy without constitutional limitations" (p. 98). I am suggesting that Dryden acknowledges authority's constituted (thus inherently discordant) nature without sacrificing its prerogative to compel belief.

32 Albert Cacicedo, "The Beast Fable in Dryden's *The Hind and the Panther*," *Restoration* 9 (1985), 76.

33 Montagu and Prior, *The Hind and the Panther Transvers'd*, 35–36.

34 Tom Brown, *The Reasons. . .*, 30.

35 Ogilby, "Of the Sun and Wind," in *Fables*, 166.

36 On other aspects of the dream of a "common language" in *The Hind and the Panther*, see Sloman, *Dryden*, 19.

37 Matthew Prior, "The Occasion of Writing the Country Mouse," 355–356.

38 Anon., *A Poem in Defence of the Church of England; in Opposition to the Hind and Panther* (London, 1678), 2.

39 Montagu and Prior, *The Hind and the Panther Transvers'd*, 35.

40 The most frequently cited influences are Edward Topsell's *History of Foure-Footed Beasts and Serpents* (London, 1658) and Wolfgang Franzius, *The History of Brutes, or a Description of Living Creatures*, trans. T.N. (London, 1670). Miner shows how Dryden revises assumed correspondences between natural and divine histories in order to accommodate a modern conception of history in *Dryden's Poetry*, 158–164.

41 Topsell, *History of Foure-Footed Beasts and Serpents*, 575.

42 Montagu and Prior, *The Hind and the Panther Transvers'd*, 36.

43 Sloman's creative and important reading of *The Hind and the Panther* notes that Dryden here "wittily uses the image of pointing, or punctuating time ... as if to say that memorable events break upon the seamless flow of history, just as commas, which are necessary only on the page, break up the flow of vocal sound. Points are also the marks denoting vowel sounds in written Hebrew which were often omitted from older texts, thus causing problems and ambiguities in interpretation" (p. 18).

44 Ogilby, "Of the Fly and the Ant," in *Fables*, 80.

45 Patterson applies this analogy to the Hind and the Panther, suggesting that "the Hind, as a nonpredatory representative of a faith now claimed as the only true one, has been chosen by Dryden to stand in for the innocent and yet highly intelligent lamb of *The Wolf and the Lamb*" (p. 96).

46 Montagu and Prior, *The Hind and the Panther Transvers'd*, 53.

47 In interpreting the fables of the Swallows and the Pigeons as images of the failure of accommodation that become legible only within shared assumptions about representation, I hope to reconcile two of the most cogent recent discussions of them – Sloman's, which finds the fables part of the dream of a common language (p. 18), and Bywaters's, which through an analysis of the parallels between the two tales show how the larger poem launches a "consistently thorough attack on the Anglicans" (p. 20).

48 Many Catholics, including Dryden, feared that the gains made by the Catholics were too many, and that James's enthusiasm would, as it did, eventually force him to abdicate the throne; thus, the Panther here speaks partly for the Catholic Dryden. On the complexity of this correspondence and for a survey of scholarly interpretations of it, see Miner's notes to the *The Hind and the Panther*, in his ed., *The Works*, 420.

49 Miner, Notes to *The Hind and the Panther*, 436.

50 Margaret Anne Doody shows how the ending of the Hind's fable complements that of Dryden's in *The Daring Muse: Augustan Poetry Reconsidered* (Cambridge, 1985), 79.

51 "The Cock and the Fox" is derived from Chaucer's *Nun's Priest's Tale*, but the story had been recounted more recently, and in a more Aesopian context, in Ogilby's *Fables of Æsop*.

52 Dryden, "Of the Pythagorean Philosophy," line 394. In *Fables, Ancient and Modern*, in *The Poems of John Dryden*, ed. James Kinsley, 4 vols. (Oxford, 1958), IV: 1728. All references to the fables in *Fables, Ancient and Modern* will be to this edition and will be indicated parenthetically in the text according to Kinsley's line numbers.

53 The term is Sloman's, set forth in her *Dryden: The Poetics of Translation*, which deals with *Fables, Ancient and Modern* at length. Cedric D. Reverand II's more recent *Dryden's Final Poetic Mode: The "Fables'* (Philadelphia, 1988) is the only long study of Dryden's *Fables*, and captures the metamorphic – indeed polymorphic and perpetually decentered – structure of the *Fables*.

54 Dryden, "Preface" to *Fables, Ancient and Modern*, 1458.

55 Sloman, "An Interpretation of Dryden's *Fables*," *Eighteenth-Century Studies* 4 (1970) 199.

56 *Fables, Ancient and Modern* (London, 1712). British Library copy, third blank page.

57 Dryden seems to have imagined *Fables* in terms of very concrete exchange, writing to his friend Elizabeth Steward, that "I may come to you with a volume in my hand, like a dog out of the water, with a duck in his mouth." See Charles E. Ward, *The Life of John Dryden* (Chapel Hill, 1961), 109.

58 Richardson, Preface to *Æsop's Fables*, vii.

59 Reverand (*Dryden's Final Poetic Mode*, 62–64; 130–135) points out the encoded references to William in *Fables*.

60 On Chanticleer as key to a political rewriting of Chaucer, see Patterson, *Fables of Power*, 106.

61 As Scott observed, "the fox in the fable of old Chaucer is translated into a Puritan" (*Life of Dryden*, I: 360).

62 See Reverand, *Dryden's Final Poetic Mode*, 164; Reverand suggests that we identify Chanticleer's father, rather than Chanticleer himself, with Dryden (p. 161).

5 Obstructions of poetic justice in Anne Finch's fables

1 Anne Finch, "The Goute and Spider," in *Poems of Anne, Countess of Winchilsea*, ed. Myra Reynolds (Chicago, 1903), p. 31, line 50. Though it contains some inaccuracies, Reynolds's edition of Finch's work remains the most comprehensive and definitive one to date; future references to Finch's poems will be indicated according to Reynolds's line numbers and incorporated into the text.

2 Jean de la Fontaine, "La goutte et l'araignée," in *Fables choisis*, ed. Adam, p. 105, III.viii. Future references to La Fontaine's fables will be indicated by book, fable, and line number, according to the numeration of this edition, and will, except when the title is not apparent, appear in the text in parentheses.

3 Here and throughout this chapter, my discussion of the ways in which a woman's text might mark its differences owes much to Nancy K. Miller's elegant and important "Emphasis Added: Plots and Plausibilities in Women's Fiction," *Publications of the Modern Language Association* 96 (1981), 36–48.

4 William Wordsworth, Letter to Alexander Dyce (*c.* April 19, 1830), in *Letters of William and Dorothy Wordsworth*, ed. Alan G. Hill, 5 vols. 2nd ed. (Oxford, 1979), V: 239.

5 Finch's life almost paradigmatically spans a political shift that incorporated a transition from one kind of literary culture – and one set of possibilities for literary women – to another. Before 1688, Finch belonged to the circle of writing women, including Anne Killigrew, that surrounded and was patronized by Mary of Modena, and that circulated manuscripts in an intimate and elite community. After 1688, that community perforce disbanded, and the private sphere began its famous drift away from the public and increasingly commercialized domain of letters.

6 Finch, "The Apology," lines 1–2; "The Introduction," lines 19, 53–54.

7 Finch, "Fragment," lines 1–2.

8 For a convincing study of early eighteenth-century gender identity in which women's estrangement from many domains of value and meaning is shown to be bound up with their metaphorical involvement in these very domains, see Ellen Pollak, *The Poetics of Sexual Myth* (Chicago, 1985). Although Pollak is concerned

with representations of women, chiefly in Swift and Pope, rather than with women writers, her argument is often applicable to them.

9 Reynolds's introduction to *Poems*, pp. cviii–cxi, and Katharine M. Rogers's to *Select Poems of Anne Finch, Countess of Winchilsea* (New York, 1979), pp. ix–xvii, both touch on the fables as they survey the body of Finch's work generally. Jean Mallinson acknowledges the "unusual" character of Finch's fables (p. 58) and, comparing her to John Gay, notes that she "had something no less serious but somewhat less elevated in mind" (p. 56). See Mallinson, "Anne Finch: A Woman Poet and the Tradition," in *Gender at Work: Four Women Poets of the Eighteenth Century*, ed. Ann Messenger (Detroit, 1990), 34–76. Messenger's chapter on Finch in *His and Hers* (Lexington, Ky., 1986), and Ruth Salvaggio's in *Enlightened Absences: Neoclassical Configurations of the Feminine* (Urbana and Chicago, 1988), pp. 105–126, concentrate on the lyric poetry. Only Charles H. Hinnant's *The Poetry of Anne Finch* (Newark, Del., 1994) comes close to appreciating fables" significance to the body of Finch's poetry. Hinnant suggests that the fable itself is "more complex and challenging than is commonly supposed" (p. 167) and shows how Finch engineered oblique political satires through her Aesopian pieces.

10 William Wordsworth, "Essay Supplementary to the Preface" to *Lyrical Ballads* (1820). In *Prose Works of William Wordsworth*, ed. W.J.B. Owen and Jane Worthington Smyser, 3 vols. (Oxford, 1974), III: 73. Wordsworth had a "female friend" transcribe extracts from some of Finch's work into a gift volume for his friend Lady Mary Lowther, and in 1825 another friend, Alexander Dyce, included some of Finch's nature poetry in his *Specimens of British Poetesses*.

11 See Reuben Brower, "Lady Winchilsea and the Poetic Tradition of the Seventeenth Century," *Studies in Philology* 42 (1945), 61–80. For representative feminist summaries of Finch's literary career, see Sandra Gilbert and Susan Gubar, *Norton Anthology of Literature by Women* (New York, 1985), 98–100; and Moira Ferguson, *First Feminists: British Women Writers, 1578–1799* (Bloomington, Ind., 1985), 247–248.

12 Salvaggio, *Enlightened Absences*, 107. See also N.K. Miller, "Arachnologies; The Woman, the Text and the Critic," in *The Poetics of Gender*, ed. Miller and Michael Riffaterre (New York, 1986), pp. 270–297. Miller discusses Finch's interesting "Description of One of the Pieces of Tapestry at Long-leat" in terms of women's arts of weaving and their registration in the text.

13 Wordsworth to Dyce, *Letters*, V: 237.

14 Virginia Woolf, *A Room of One's Own* ((1957) London, 1967), 62.

15 Finch, "The Spleen," lines 85–86. Also quoted in Woolf, *Room of One's Own*, 64.

16 It is also to imply that women were indiscriminately barred from Augustan literary culture. On the contrary, popular writers like Jane Barker, Delarivière Manley and Eliza Haywood flourished after 1688; as recent scholars have shown, the age of Anne (1702–1714) offered women writers a crucial, if also ambiguous, source of cultural authority in the figure of the monarch herself. Therefore, Finch's "noble" class and her political alterity must have shaped her poetry at least as much as considerations of gender did. Queen Anne's role as an empowering figure for women writers is taken up in Carol Barash, *English Women's Poetry, 1649–1714*, (Oxford, 1996) and in Toni Bowers, *The Politics of*

Motherhood (Cambridge, 1996). On women's full participation in Augustan print culture see Kathryn Shevelow, *Women in Print Culture* (London, 1988), and for Finch's biography, Barbara McGovern, *Anne Finch and her Poetry* (Athens, Ga., 1992). Reynolds's introduction to *Poems of Anne, Countess of Winchilsea*, pp. xvii–cxxxiv; and Katharine M. Rogers's introduction to *Selected Poems*, pp. ix–xxiv.

17 Finch, "The Introduction," lines 51–52.

18 See especially "The Petition for an Absolute Retreat," "The Bird and the Arras," and "To Sleep."

19 Finch, "Preface" to folio manuscript of 1689, in Reynolds, *Poems of Anne*, 7. Future references will be to this edition and will appear parenthetically in the text.

20 Miller, "Arachnologies," 272.

21 Finch, "Some Pieces out of the First Act of the Aminta of Tasso" ("THIRSIS persuades AMINTOR not to despair'), lines 41–50.

22 Finch's concentration on Athalia herself is significant: Racine saw the tragedy to be about Athalie's grandson, Joash, rather than about Athalie herself: "The subject of the work is the recognition of Joash and his restoration to the throne. According to these rules, I should have called the play *Joash*. But, as most people have only heard of it by the name of *Athaliah*, I felt that it was undesirable to present it under a different title." See Racine, Preface to *Athalie*, trans. John Cairncross (Harmondsworth, 1963), 234.

23 Poems that make translation their theme, like Finch's remarkable "Poem Occasion'd by the Sight of the 4th. Epist. Lib Epist. I of Horace," further dramatize the cross purposes that connect women's bodies to male homosocial communities of literary exchange which exclude them or, at best, experience them as dangerous seductions.

24 John Lockman, "Address to Fontenelle," in *The Loves of Cupid and Psyche, from the French of La Fontaine* (London, 1744), 2. See also La Motte's *Fables nouvelles* (1719), translated into English by Robert Samber as *One Hundred New Court Fables* (1726), 9; and the introduction to *The Looking-Glass*, a 1784 translation of some of La Fontaine's fables which classifies him as "an Author *sui generis*" (p. iii).

25 Lockman, "The Life of M. de la Fontaine with Characters of his Genius and Manner of Writing, and an Account of his Words," in *Loves of Cupid and Psyche*, 8. Roseann Runte's very interesting "La Fontaine: Precursor of the Eighteenth-Century Libertine," in *Eighteenth-Century Life* 3 (1976), 47–51, relates such aversions to restraint to libertine traditions in eighteenth-century French writing.

26 Lockman, "Life," 14.

27 La Fontaine, "La vie d'Esope le Phrygien," in *Fables choisies*, 34.

28 La Fontaine, "Testament éxplique par Esope" (II.xx), lines 3–4.

29 La Fontaine, "La Depositaire infidèle" (IX.i), lines 5–6; "Epilogue" to Book XI, lines 7–8.

30 English perception of La Fontaine's work is reflected in the title of Bernard Mandeville's *Fables after the Easie and Familiar Manner of Monsieur de la Fontaine* (1703).

31 Marianne Moore's *Fables* appeared in 1952. Ross Chambers discusses the way that La Fontaine himself played with "female speech" in some of his fables in

"*Histoire d'oeuf:* Secrets and Secrecy in La Fontaine's Fable." *Sub-stance* 32 (1981), 68–74.

32 *The Looking-Glass*, xix.

33 "Les deux rats ...", line 168.

34 "Le Statuaire et la Statue de Jupiter" (ix.vi), lines 33–36.

35 La Fontaine, "Epilogue," to Book xi, lines 12–14.

36 Recent criticism has focused on the ways in which his fables replace "l'origines du récit" with a recitation about formal origins that undercuts their authority, as in Louis Marin's "Le récit originaire, l'origine du récit, le récit de l'origine," in *Papers in French Seventeenth-Century Literature* 11 (1975), 13–38.

37 Antoine Houdart de la Motte, Antoine Furetière, Henri Richer, the Jesuits Jean Commire and Pierre Bouhours, and Francois Fénélon, among others, all produced copious volumes of fables throughout the early 1700s; none of these could be called Fontainean.

38 Joseph Addison, *Spectator* 183 (October 29, 1711), ed. Bond, II: 220. Lockman remarked that La Fontaine was "one of the few Writers of [France] who speak very Handsomely of *Englishmen* and *England*" ("Address," 4).

39 Lockman, "Address," 85.

40 Mandeville's "Preface to the Reader," in *Æsop Dress'd, or a Collection of Fables writ in Familiar Verse* (London, 1704) remarks that "Two of the [following] Fables are of my own Invention; but I am so far from loving 'em the better, that I think they are the worst in the Pack. And therefore in good Manners to my self I conceal their Names. Find 'em out, and welcom" (sig. B1r). Despite his flippancy, Mandeville's obsessive revisions of *The Fable of the Bees* suggest that La Fontaine was far more important to him than he wanted to admit in the beginning.

41 "The Atheist and the Acorn" was one of the few fables in Dyce's *Specimens of British Poetesses* (1825).

42 Chambers offers a clever and provocative reading of La Fontaine's ambivalent relationship to an existing "power-structure" in "Narrative in Opposition: Reflections on a La Fontaine Fable." *French Forum* 8 (1983), 216–231.

43 See "The Call of the Phoneme," Jonathan Culler's introduction to *On Puns* (Oxford, 1988), 1–16.

44 Hinnant, *Poetry of Anne Finch*, p. 20. Hinnant cites Finch's opening fable, "Mercury and the Elephant" (discussed below) as Finch's acknowledgment of the printer's interest in an author's works.

45 Ann Messenger also argues that Finch's most controversial work appears in her unpublished manuscripts. See Messenger, "Publishing without Perishing: Lady Winchilsea's *Miscellany Poems*," *Restoration* 5 (1981), 27–37.

46 L'Estrange, "The Doctor and his Patient," in *Fables of Æsop*, 351.

6 John Gay's *Fables* and the matter of reading

1 John Gay, "The Elephant and the Bookseller," in *John Gay, Poetry and Prose*, ed. Vinton Dearing, 2 vols. (Oxford, 1974), II: 314, line 6. Future line references will be to this definitive edition.

2 William Thackeray, *The English Humourists of the Eighteenth Century* ((1853) Chicago, 1893), 145.

3 "The Old Hen and the Cock," lines 37–38.

4 "The Elephant and the Bookseller," lines 29–30.

5 James Beattie, "On Fables and Romances," in *Dissertations Moral and Critical* (London, 1783), 507.

6 Patricia Meyer Spacks, *John Gay* (New York, 1965), 196.

7 Samuel Johnson, "The Life of Gay," in *Lives of the English Poets*, ed. George Birkbeck Hill, 2 vols. (Oxford, 1905), II: 283.

8 George Sampson, *Cambridge History of British Literature*, 166. Early nineteenth-century readers also objected to the "defective morality" of Gay's *Fables*. See John Lettice's letters on the *Fables* in *European Magazine* 68 (1815) and 69 (1816).

9 Like the rest of Gay's poetry, the *Fables* have been overshadowed by *The Beggar's Opera*, and relatively few later twentieth-century interpretations of them exist to begin with. The five book-length studies that deal with the *Fables* at any length are Sven M. Armens, *John Gay: Social Critic* (New York, 1954); Edwin Albert Graham, "John Gay's *Fables*'; Adina Forsgren, *John Gay: Poet "of a Lower Order'* (Stockholm, 1971); William Irving, *John Gay: Favorite of the Wits* (Durham, 1940); and Spacks, *John Gay*. Armens and Forsgren in particular treat the *Fables* primarily as satires, and thus delve helpfully into their contemporary political and philosophical contexts: both, for example, identify the 1738 *Fables* with Bolingbroke's *On the Idea of a Patriot King* (1738).

10 *The Craftsman* 41 (April 28, 1727), 155.

11 "The Painter who pleased No body and Every body," lines 1–2.

12 "The Monkey who had seen the World," lines 60–61.

13 *Gentleman's Magazine* 24 (February, 1754), 90.

14 Thackeray, *English Humourists*, 148.

15 Jane Austen, *Northanger Abbey* ((1818) Harmondsworth, 1972), 38.

16 "The Hare and many Friends," lines 7–12.

17 Gay's readers evidently empathized: at least one child "scarce was able/To finish the concluding Fable." See Mary Barber, "A TALE, Written by a Lady, (Mrs. Barber) on Reading MR. GAY's Fables." This poem was published prefatory to the 1747 *Fables by the Late Mr. Gay* and in *Poems by Eminent Ladies* (1755), n.p. French readers also expressed great sympathy with the hare's predicament: "La fin de cet apologue laisse le lecteur dans une grande peine a l'egard du malheureux Levre," M. Jauffret observed in his *Lettres sur les fabulists*. 3 vols. (Paris, 1827), III: 29.

18 Charles Cowden Clarke, *Poetical Works of Joseph Addison and Gay's Fables* (1875), 12.

19 Austin Dobson, "John Gay," in *Miscellanies* (Cambridge, 1898), 274.

20 James Sutherland, "John Gay," in *Eighteenth-Century English Literature: Modern Essays in Criticism*, ed. James L. Clifford (New York, 1959), 131.

21 Christopher Smart, Introduction to *Poetical Translation of the Fables of Phaedrus* (London, 1761), iv. The *Fables*" first epitomizer, Daniel Bellamy (1740), also produced an edition of *Phaedri Selectae*.

22 Letter to Pope, October, 1727. In *Letters of John Gay*, ed. C.F. Burgess (Oxford, 1966), 66.

23 Letter to Swift, in *Letters*, ed. Burgess, 133.
24 It is fitting that Gay was Lottery Commissioner while he was writing the 1727 *Fables*, not only because Ogilby had sold his fables by lottery but also because in Gay's own day the English lottery ran according to the *classis* system that assigned winning and losing values arbitrarily to different classes of ticket. Conscious that value and significance are produced through the aleatory but influential distribution of interpretive authority, the *Fables* play to this disheartening cultural arrangement.
25 On the illustrations of the *Fables*, see Vinton Dearing, introduction to *Fables* (repr. Los Angeles, 1967), iv–v.
26 Barber, "ʌ TALE," n.p.
27 See Madame de Kéralio, *Fables de M. Gay, suives du poem de l'éventail, le tout traduit de l'anglois* (Paris, 1759).
28 "The Turkey and the Ant," lines 29–30.
29 See Addison's famous dictum: "Upon the reading a Fable, we are made to believe we advise our Selves" (*Spectator* 512 (October 17, 1713), ed. Bond, IV: 318).
30. "The Lyon, the Tyger, and the Traveller," lines 81–82.
31 "The Poet and the Rose," line 38.
32 "Introduction to the *Fables*. The Shepherd and the Philosopher," lines 9–10.
33 A "lay" is not only a song but also a wager and a lair. All three descriptions apply to the fable, which is at once a poem, a gamble in its bid for patronage and, like the lion's "regal den," a discursive trap.
34 "Pythagoras and the Countryman," lines 8–9.
35 "The Two Owls and a Sparrow," lines 17–18.
36 For a vigorous and relevant discussion of conflict between metonymy and metaphor in *The Beggar's Opera*, see William Bowman Piper, "Similitude as Satire in *The Beggar's Opera*." *Eighteenth-Century Studies* 21 (1988), 334–351.
37 John Gay, *The Beggar's Opera*, (1728), III.ii.
38 See Ian Donaldson, " 'A Double Capacity': *The Beggar's Opera*," in *Modern Essays on Eighteenth-Century Literature*, 141–158.
39 "The Old Woman and Her Cats," lines 9–10.
40 "The Fox at the Point of Death," lines 45–46.
41 "The Wild Boar and the Ram," lines 1–2.
42 The elephant's many admirable accomplishments are taken up in Pliny's *Naturalis historia* (Book VIII), where this impressive creature "understands the language of its country," climbs ropes, deceives itself, feels shame, and falls in love. One even "learnt the shapes of the Greek letters and used to write out in words [...]: 'I myself wrote this.'" See Pliny, *Naturalis historia*, trans. H. Rackham, 10 vols. (Cambridge, Mass., 1957), III: 3–5.
43 "*Tim* and the *Fables*," in *The Poems of Jonathan Swift*, ed. Harold Williams, 3 vols. (Oxford: Clarendon Press, 1937), III: 782–783. Swift's assumption that his own reader knows the plot of "The Monkey who had Seen the World" gives us a hint as to how familiar Gay's *Fables* had become.
44 "The Raven, the Sexton, and the Earth-worm," lines 17–22.
45 On the 1738 *Fables* as political satires whose tag words, like "spies," "pension," and "treasurer" presumably link them with the opposition publication *The*

Craftsman, see Edwin Graham, "John Gay's Second Series: *The Craftsman* in *Fables*," in *Papers on Literature and Language* 5 (1969), 17–26.

46 Joseph Warton, *Essay on the Genius and Writing of Pope*, 2 vols. ((1956) London, 1806), II: 245.

47 Thackeray, *English Humourists*, 146.

48 *Ibid.*

49 Gay to Swift (May 16, 1732), in *Letters*, ed. Burgess, 122.

50 In *John Gay: Favorite of the Wits* (New York, 1968), for example, William Irving praises the 1738 *Fables* as follows: they "have a power lacking in the first lot, a higher imagination and emotional reach which are reflected in matters like diction and figures" (p. 144).

51 "Advertisement," to *Fables* (1738), sig. A1r.

52 See especially the fable of the town mouse and the country mouse in Horace's Satire, II. 6 (*Horace: Satires, Epistles and Ars Poetica*, ed. R. Rushton Fairclough (Cambridge, 1957), 224–235).

53 "The Degenerate Bees," line 36.

54 "The Dog and the Fox," lines 1–2.

55 *Ibid.*, line 27.

56 "The Vulture, the Sparrow, and other Birds," lines 1–4.

57 Rachel Trickett, *The Honest Muse: A Study in Augustan Verse* (Oxford, 1967), 16.

58 "The Countryman and Jupiter," lines 95–96.

59 "The Man, the Cat, the Dog and the Fly," lines 1–2.

60 "The Ant in Office," lines 81–82; "The Jackall, the Leopard, and other Beasts," line 72; "The Bear in a Boat," line 69.

61 Machiavelli himself offered an Aesopian figure as the ideal device for educating the successful prince: "*Achilles* and several other Princes were committed to the education of *Chiron* the Centaur, who was to keep them under his Discipline, chusing them a Master, half Man and Half Beast, for no other reason but to show how necessary it is for a Prince to be acquainted with both, for that one without the other will be of little Duration. Seeing, therefore, it is of such Important to a Prince to take upon him the Nature and Disposition of a Beast of all the whole Flock, he ought to imitate the Lyon and the Fox: For the Lyon is in Danger of Toils, and Snares, and a Lyon to Fright away the Wolves, but they who keep wholly to the Lion, have no true notion of themselves." See Niccolo Machiavelli, *The Prince*, trans. Henry Neville ((532) London, 1695), 223. In *Mythologia Ethica*, Philip Ayres recognized the Machiavelli connection: "*Achilles*, and many other Princes were committed to *Chiron* the Centaur, to be brought up under his admirable Discipline; who being half a Man and half a Beast, and having a perfect understanding of both these Natures, might instruct them by Wise Precepts. [...] This Centaurs [*sic*] Methods of Instruction, were probably by Fables and Hieroglyfics [*sic*]" (sigs. A1v–A2r). The Machiavellian example had been a favorite with English fabulists of the later seventeenth century: L'Estrange's "Matchiavel Condemn'd" shows "*Matchiavel's* putting *Dogs Teeth* by Night into the Mouths of the *Sheep*" in order to incite rebellion in the peaceful flock; the moral captures precisely the political implications of such a gesture. "The Secrets of Government ought not to be Touch'd with Unwash'd Hands, and Expos'd to

the Multitude; for upon Granting the People a Privilege of Debating the Prerogatives of Sovereign Power, they will Infer naturally enough aright, and a Title to the Controlling and over-ruling it." See L'Estrange, "Matchiavel Condemn'd," in *Fables of Æsop*, 469.

62 See Dianne Dugaw, "Folklore and John Gay's Satire." *Studies in English Literature* 31 (1991), 521–528.

7 The moral

1 See *Works of William Hazlitt*, ed. P.P. Howe, 24 vols. (New York, 1967) IV: 332; XVI: 48; and Warton, *Essay*, II: 12.
2 See Cohen, *Sensible Words*, XXV.
3 Barbara Maria Stafford, *Body Criticism: Imaging the Unseen in Enlightenment Art and Medicine* (Cambridge, Mass., 1991), 2–5.
4 Charlotte Lennox, *The Female Quixote*, ed. Margaret Dalziel ((1752) Oxford, 1970), 377.
5 A good discussion of Bewick's technique may be found in *Fables*, ed. Anne Stevenson Hobbs (London, 1986), 86–87.
6 "The Cat, the Monkey and the Chesnuts," in *89 Fugitive Fables* (London, 1780), 1.
7 Robert Dodsley, "Essay on Fable," in *Select Fables of Esop*, lviii and lxxiii.
8 Jean Jacques Rousseau, *Emile, or On Education*, trans. Allan Bloom (New York, 1979), 112.
9 William Cowper, "Pairing-Time Anticipated. A Fable," in *Cowper, Poetry and Prose*, ed., Brian Spiller (London, 1968), 99.
10 Warton, *Essay*, I: 245.
11 James Beattie, "On Fables and Romances," in *Dissertations, Moral and Critical*, 507.

Select bibliography

PRIMARY WORKS

Addison, Joseph, and Richard Steele. *The Spectator*, ed. Donald F. Bond. 5 vols. Oxford, 1965.

Anon. *Æsop at Amsterdam*. London, 1698.

Æsop at Bathe; or, A Few Select Fables in Verse. London, 1698.

Æsop at the Bell-Tavern. London, 1711.

Æsop at Oxford. London, 1709.

Æsop at Paris, his Letters and Fables. London, 1701.

Æsop at Tunbridge; or, A Few Select Fables in Verse. London, 1698.

Æsop Return'd from Tunbridge; or, Æsop out of His Wits. London, 1698.

Æsop Naturaliz'd: In a Collection of Fables and Stories from Æsop, Lockman, Pilpay and Others. London, 1711.

Æsop Naturaliz'd and Expos'd to Publick View in His Own Shape and Dress. Cambridge, 1697.

Æsop Unveil'd, or the Beauties of Deformity. London, 1730.

Fables, Moral and Political. London, 1703.

The Fabulist Metamorphosed and Mythologized. London, 1634.

Some Observations on the Fables of Æsop, as Commented upon by Roger L'Estrange. Edinburgh, 1700.

A Poem in Defence of the Church of England, in Opposition to the Hind and Panther. London, 1687.

The Revenger. A Trage-Comedy Acted between the Hind and the Panther and Religio Laici. London, 1687.

"Westminster School." *Gentleman's Magazine* 6 (October 1736), 611.

Arbuthnot, John. "An Essay of the Learned Martinus Scriblerus, concerning the Origin of Sciences." *Life and Works of John Arbuthnot*, ed. George A. Aitken. Oxford, 1982.

Arwaker, Edmund. *Truth in Fiction; or, Morality in Masquerade*. London, 1708.

Atterbury, Francis. *A Short Review of the Controversy between Mr. Boyle and Mr. Bentley*. London, 1701.

Aubrey, John. *Brief Lives and Other Selected Writings*, ed. Anthony Powell. London, 1949.

Ayres, Philip. *Mythologia Ethica, or Three Centuries of Æsopean Fables in English Prose*. London, 1689.

Barret, William. *Æsop's Fables with his Whole Life*. London, 1651.

Beattie, James. *Dissertations Moral and Critical*. London, 1783.

Beck, Cave. *Universal Character*. London, 1657.

Behn, Aphra. *Æsop's Fables, with his Life*. London, 1687.

Bentley, Richard. *A Dissertation concerning the Epistles of Phalaris, with an Essay on the Fables of Æsop*. London, 1697.

Bewick, Thomas. *Select Fables*. London, 1799 (New York, 1932).

Blackmore, Richard. *Prince Arthur*. London, 1695.

Blackwell, Thomas. *Enquiry into the Life and Writings of Homer*. London, 1730.

Bossuet, Jacques. *An Exposition of the Doctrines of the Catholic Church*. London, 1672.

Boursault, Edmé. *Fables d'Esope, Comédie* [1690], ed. Terence Allott. Exeter, 1988.

Boyle, Charles. *Dr. Bentley's Dissertation on the Epistles of Phalaris and the Fables of Æsop Examined*. London, 1699.

Brown, Tom. *The Reasons of Mr. Bayes Changing His Religion*. London, 1690.

Bullokar, William. *Aesopź Fabelź in tru Ortography with Grammar Notź* (1585). In *Works of William Bullokar*, ed. J.R. Turner. 4 vols. Leeds, 1969.

Bulwer, John. *Chirologia and Chironomia*. London, 1644.

Burnet, Gilbert. *A Reply to Mr. Varillas*. London, 1688.

Caulfield, James. *Portraits, Memoirs and Characters of Remarkable Persons, from the Revolution of 1688 to the End of the Reign of George II*. 4 vols. London, 1819.

Caxton, William. *The Book of the Subtyll Historyes of Æsop*. London, 1486.

Charke, Charlotte. *A Narrative of the Life of Mrs. Charlotte Charke*. London, 1930.

Clifford, Nathan. "Reflections on the Hind and Panther. In a Letter to a Friend." London, 1687.

Comenius, Johan Amos. *Visible World, or the Pictures and Nomenclature of all the Chief things that are in the World*, trans. Charles Hoole. London, 1675.

Creech, Thomas. *The Epicurean Philosopher*. London 1682.

Croxall, Samuel. *Fables of Æsop and Others*. London, 1722.

Dalgarno, George. *Didascalocaphus; or The Deaf and Dumb Man's Tutor* (London, 1680). *The Works of George Dalgarno*, ed. Henry Cochran and Thomas Maitland. Edinburgh, 1921.

D'Anvers, Caleb, ed. *The Craftsman*. 14 vols. London, 1731–1737.

Dennis, John. *Critical Works of John Dennis*, ed. Edward Niles Hooker. 2 vols. Baltimore, 1939–1943.

    Miscellany Poems. London, 1697.

Dodsley, Robert. *Select Fables of Esop and Other Fabulists in Three Books* (1761). Birmingham, 1764.

Draper, Charles. *Fables Translated from Æsop and Other Authors*. London, 1760.

Dryden, John. *Poems of John Dryden*, ed. James Kinsley. 4 vols. Oxford, 1958.

    Works of John Dryden, ed. Edward Niles Hooker and H.T. Swedenberg. 20 vols. Berkeley and California, 1956–1992.

Farquhar, George. *Love and Business*. London, 1702.

Felton, Henry. *A Dissertation on Reading the Classics*. London, 1709.

Finch, Anne. *Miscellany Poems on Several Occasions: Written by a Lady*. London, 1713.

    Poems of Anne, Countess of Winchilsea, ed. Myra Reynolds. Chicago, 1993.

Franzius, Wolfgang. *The History of Brutes, or a Description of Living Creatures*, trans. T.N. London, 1670.

Godwin, William. *Fables, Ancient and Modern*. London, 1811.

Gay, John. *Fables*. London, 1727.

   Fables of the Late Mr. John Gay. London, 1738.

   John Gay, Poetry and Prose, ed. Vinton Dearing. 2 vols. (Oxford, 1974).

   Letters of John Gay, ed. C.F. Burgess. Oxford, 1966.

Henryson, Robert. *Morall Fabillis of Esope*, ed. George D. Gopin. Notre Dame, 1987.

Heyrick, Thomas. *The New Atlantis, with Some Reflections upon the Hind and the Panther*. London, 1687.

Hildrop, James. *Free Thoughts upon the Brute Creation*. London, 1742.

Hobbes, Thomas. *Leviathan* (1651), ed. C.B. Macpherson. Harmondsworth, 1968.

Hoole, Charles. *Æsop's Fables, English and Latin*. 1687, 2nd ed. London, 1700.

Holder, William. *The Elements of Speech*. London, 1667.

Jackson, John. *A New Translation of Æsop's Fables, Adorn'd with Cutts*. London, 1708.

Johnson, Samuel. *Lives of the English Poets*, ed. George Birkbeck Hill. 2 vols. Oxford, 1903.

La Chambre, Marin Cureau de. *Traité de la connoisance des animaux*. Paris, 1645.

La Fontaine, Jean de. *Fables choisies, mises en vers* (1668–1692), ed. Antoine Adam. Paris, 1966.

La Motte, Antoine Houdart de. *One Hundred New Court Fables*, trans. Robert Samber. London, 1721.

Le Bossu, René. *Traité du poème épique*. Paris, 1675.

   Mssr Bossu's Treatise of the Epick Poem, trans. W.J. (1695). 2 vols. London, 1719.

L'Estrange, Roger. *Fables of Æsop and Other Eminent Mythologists*. London, 1692 and 1699.

   Fables and Storyes Moralized, Being a Second Part of the Fables of Æsop. London, 1699.

Livy, *Ab urbe condita*, trans. B.O. Foster. 2 vols. Cambridge, Mass., 1902.

Locke, John. *Æsop's Fables*. London, 1703.

   Some Thoughts Concerning Education. In *Educational Writings of John Locke* (1693), ed. James Axtell. London, 1968.

Lockman, William, trans. *The Loves of Cupid and Psyche, from the French of La Fontaine*. London, 1744.

Mandeville, Bernard. *Æsop Dress'd, or a Collection of Fables writ in Familiar Verse*. London, 1704.

   The Fable of the Bees (1705–1729), ed. F.B. Kaye. Oxford, 1924.

   Fables after the Easie and Familiar Manner of Monsieur de la Fontaine. London, 1703.

Montagu, Charles and Matthew Prior. *The Hind and the Panther Transvers'd to the Story of the Country-Mouse and the City-Mouse* (1687), in *Literary Works of Matthew Prior*, ed. H. Bunker Wright and Monroe K. Spears. 2 vols. Oxford, 1959.

Moore, Edward. *Fables for the Female Sex*. London, 1744.

   New Fables Invented for the Amusement of Young Ladies. London, 1754.

North, Thomas. *The Morall Philosophie of Doni* (1570).

Ogilby, John. *Æsopicks, or A Second Collection of Fables, Paraphras'd in Verse*. London, 1675.

   Fables of Æsop, Paraphras'd in Verse, and Adorn'd with Sculptures. London, 1651 and 1668.

Pepys, Samuel. *Diary of Samuel Pepys*, ed. H.B. Whaley. 3 vols London, 1924.

Phaedrus. *The Aesopic Fables of Phaedrus*, ed. Ben Edwin Perry. Cambridge, Mass., 1945.

Phillips, Edward. *Theatrum Poetarum, or a Compleat Collection of the Poets, especially the Most Eminent of all Ages*. London, 1674.

Philostratus. *Philostratus in Honour of Appolonius of Tyana*, trans. J.S. Phillimore. 2 vols. Oxford, 1912.

Prior, Matthew. *Dialogues of the Dead and Other Works*, ed. A.R. Wallace. Cambridge, 1907.

Richardson, Samuel. *Æsop's Fables, with Instructive Morals and Reflections*. London, 1739.
Clarissa; or the History of a Young Lady. (1747–1748). Harmondsworth, 1985.
Pamela; or, Virtue Rewarded. (1740). Harmondsworth, 1980.

Scott, Walter. *The Life of John Dryden*. In *Works of Dryden*, ed. Scott and George Saintsbury. 10 vols. London, 1808.

Singleton, Thomas and Thomas Houghton. *Æsop Improv'd*. London, 1673.

Smart, Christopher. *Poetical Translation of the Fables of Phaedrus*. London, 1761.

Sprat, Thomas. *History of the Royal Society*. London, 1667.

Stillingfleet, Edward. *Origines Sacrae; or, A Rational Account of the Christian Faith*. 2 vols. London, 1662.

Swift, Jonathan. *Correspondence of Jonathan Swift*, ed. F. Elrington Bell. 6 vols. London, 1913.
Writings of Jonathan Swift, ed. Robert A. Greenberg and William Bowman Piper. New York and London, 1973.

Temple, William. *Five Miscellaneous Essays* (1690), ed. Samuel Holt Monk. Ann Arbor, 1963.

Thackeray, William. *The English Humourists of the Eighteenth Century* (1853). London, 1983.

Toland, John. *Essay concerning the Rise, Progress and Destruction of Fables and Romances*. London, 1704.
The Fables of Æsop with the Moral Reflections of Mssr. Baudoin. London, 1704.

Topsell, Edward. *History of Foure-Footed Beasts and Serpents*. London, 1658.

Trenchard, John. *Natural History of Supernaturalism*. In *The Rise of Modern Mythologies*, ed. Burton Feldman and Robert D. Richardson. Bloomington, Ind., 1972.

Vanbrugh, John. *Esop. A Comedy*. London, 1728.

Wallis, John. *Grammatica Linguae Anglicanae*. London, 1653.

Warburton, William. *The Divine Legation of Moses, Demonstrated*. 4 vols. London, 1728.

Wilkins, John. *Essay towards a Real Character and a Philosophical Language*. London, 1668.
Mercury: Or the Secret and Swift Messenger. London, 1661.

Willan, Leonard. *The Phrygian Fabulist*. London, 1650.

Wotton, William. *Reflections on the Ancient and Modern Learning*. London, 1692.

SECONDARY WORKS

Agnew, Jean Christophe. *Worlds Apart: The Market and the Theater in Anglo-American Thought, 1550–1750*. New York, 1985.

Armens, Sven M. *John Gay: Social Critic*. New York, 1954.

Baker, Howard. "A Portrait of Aesop." *Sewanee Review* 77 (1969), 557–590.

Bakhtin, Mikhail. *Rabelais and His World*, trans. Helene Iswolsky. Bloomington, Ind., 1984.

Barthes, Roland. "Myth Today." *Mythologies*, trans. Annette Lavers. New York, 1972, 109–159.

Benjamin, Andrew E., Geoffrey N. Cantor and John R.R. Christie, eds. *The Figural and the Literal: Problems of Language in the History of Science and Philosophy*. Manchester, 1987.

Blackham, H.P. *The Fable as Literature*. London and Dover, N.H., 1985.

Boas, George. *The Happy Beast in French Thought of the Seventeenth Century*. Baltimore, 1983.

Bunn, James H. "The Aesthetics of British Mercantilism." *New Literary History* 11 (1980), 303–321.

Cacicedo, Albert. "The Beast Fable in Dryden's *The Hind and the Panther*." Restoration 9 (1985), 75–82.

Carroll, William Meredith. *Animal Conventions in English Renaissance Non-Religious Prose*. New York, 1954.

Castle, Terry. "Why the Houyhnhms Don't Write: Swift, Satire and the Fear of the Text." *Essays in Literature* 7 (1980), 26–38.

Clifford, Gay. *The Transformations of Allegory*. London, 1974.

Cohen, Murray. *Sensible Words: Linguistic Practice in England, 1660–1720*. Baltimore, 1977.

Culler, Jonathan, ed. *On Puns: The Foundation of Letters*. Oxford, 1988.

Daniel, Stephen. "Political and Philosophical Uses of Fables in Eighteenth-Century England." *The Eighteenth Century: Theory and Interpretation* 23 (1982), 151–171.

Day, Robert Adams. "Richard Bentley and John Dunton: Brothers Under the Skin." *Studies in Eighteenth-Century Culture* 16 (1984), 125–128.

Doody, Margaret Anne. *The Daring Muse: Augustan Poetry Reconsidered*. Cambridge, 1985.

  A Natural Passion: A Study in the Novels of Samuel Richardson. Oxford, 1974.

  "Richardson's Politics." *Eighteenth-Century Fiction* 2 (1990), 113–126.

Eames, Marian. "John Ogilby and his Aesop." *Bulletin of the New York Public Library* 65 (1961), 78–86.

Eisenstein, Elizabeth. *The Printing Press as an Agent of Change*. New York, 1979.

Forsgren, Adina. *John Gay: Poet "of a Lower Order."* Stockholm, 1971.

Graham, Albert Edwin. "John Gay's *Fables* Edited, with an Introduction to the Fable as an Eighteenth-Century Genre." Ph.D. dissertation, Princeton University, 1960.

Gutwirth, Marcel. *Fable*. New Orleans, 1980.

Hinnant, Charles H. *The Poetry of Anne Finch*. Newark, Del., 1994.

Hodnett, Edward. *Aesop in England: The Transmission of Motifs in Seventeenth-Century Illustrations of Aesop's Fables*. Charlottesville, 1979.

  Francis Barlow: First Master of English Book Illustration. London, 1978.

Hofer, Philip. "Francis Barlow's Aesop." *Harvard Library Bulletin* 2 (1948), 279–295.

Jacobs, Joseph. *The Fables of Aesop*. 3 vols. New York, 1889. Repr. New York, 1970.

Jones, Richard Foster. *Ancients and Moderns*. Saint Louis, 1961.

Ketcham, Michael. *Transparent Designs: Reading, Performance and Form in the Spectator Papers*. Athens, Ga., 1986.

Kitchin, George. *Sir Roger L'Estrange: A Contribution to the History of the Press in the Seventeenth Century*. London, 1913.

Kroll, Richard. *The Material Word: Literate Culture in the Restoration and Early Eighteenth Century*. Baltimore, 1991.

Lenaghan, R.T., ed. *Caxton's Aesop*. Cambridge, Mass., 1967.

Levine, Joseph M. *The Battle of the Books: History and Literature in the Augustan Age*. Ithaca, N.Y., 1991.

Marin, Louis. "Le récit originaire, l'origine du récit, le récit de l'origine." *Papers in French Seventeenth-Century Literature* 11 (1978), 13–38.

McKendy, John J. *Aesop: Five Centuries of Illustrated Fables*. New York, 1964.

Messenger, Ann. "Publishing without Perishing: Lady Winchilsea's *Miscellany Poems*." *Restoration* 5 (1981), 27–37.

Miller, Nancy K. "Arachnologies: The Woman, the Text and the Critic." *The Poetics of Gender*, ed. Nancy K. Miller and Michael Riffaterre. New York, 1986.

   "Emphasis Added: Plots and Plausibilities in Women's Fiction." *Publications of the Modern Language Association* 96 (1981), 36–48.

Miner, Earl. *Dryden's Poetry*. Bloomington, Ind., 1967.

Nagy, Gregory. *The Best of the Achaeans: The Hero in Archaic Greek Poetry*. Baltimore, 1979.

Noel, Thomas. *Theories of the Fable in the Eighteenth Century*. New York and London, 1975.

Owen, Joan Hildreth. "The Choice of Hercules and the Eighteenth-Century Fabulist." Ph.D. dissertation, New York University, 1974.

Patey, Douglas Lane. *Probability and Literary Form: Philosophic Theory and Literary Practice in the Augustan Age*. Cambridge, 1989.

Patterson, Annabel. *Censorship and Interpretation*. Madison, Wisc., 1974.

   Fables of Power: Aesopian Writing and Political History. Durham, 1991.

Perry, Ben Edwin. *Aesopica*. 2 vols. Urbana, Ill., 1932.

   Studies in the Text History of the Life and Fables of Aesop. Philological Monographs 7. Haverford, Penn., 1936.

Pritchard, Mary. "Fables Moral and Political." Ph.D. dissertation, University of Western Ontario, 1974.

Quilligan, Maureen. *The Language of Allegory*. Ithaca, N.Y., 1979.

Reedy, Gerard. "Mystical Politics: The Imagery of Charles II's Coronation." *Studies in Revolution and Change*, ed. Paul J. Korshin. Merston, Yorkshire, 1972, 19–35.

Reverand, Cedric D. *Dryden's Final Poetic Mode: The "Fables"*. Philadelphia, 1988.

Roper, Alan. *Dryden's Poetic Kingdoms*. London, 1968.

Rose, Mark. "The Author as Proprietor: Donaldson vs. Beckett and the Genealogy of Modern Authorship." *Representations* 23 (1988), 51–85.

Saunders, David and Ian Hunter. "Lessons from the 'Literary': How to Historicise Authorship." *Critical Inquiry* 17 (1991), 479–509.

Serres, Michel. *The Parasite*, trans. Lawrence W. Schehr. Baltimore, 1982.

   Literature, Science and Philosophy, ed. Josue Harari and David F. Bell. Baltimore, 1982.

Smith, M. Ellwood. "Aesop: A Decayed Celebrity." *Publications of the Modern Language Association* 46 (1931), 225–236.

Sloman, Judith. *Dryden: The Poetics of Translation*. Toronto, 1985.

Spacks, Patricia Meyer. *John Gay*. New York, 1965.

Speck. W.A. *Stability and Strife: England, 1714–1760*. Cambridge, Mass., 1977.

Stafford, Barbara Maria. *Body Criticism: Imaging the Unseen in Enlightenment Art and Medicine.* Cambridge, Mass., 1991.

Stewart, Susan. *On Longing: Narratives of the Miniature, the Gigantic, the Souvenir, and the Collection.* Baltimore, 1984.

Summerfield, Geoffrey. *Fantasy and Reason: Children's Literature in the Eighteenth Century.* Athens, Ga., 1985.

Trickett, Rachel. *The Honest Muse: A Study in Augustan Verse.* Oxford, 1967.

Van Eerde, Katherine S. *John Ogilby and the Taste of His Times.* London, 1976.

Wallace, John. "Dryden and History: A Problem in Allegorical Reading." ELH 36 (1969), 265–290.

   " 'Examples are Best Precepts': Readers and Meaning in Seventeenth-Century Poetry." *Critical Inquiry* 1 (1975), 273–290.

Weinbrot, Howard, *Augustus Caesar in "Augustan" England: The Decline of a Classical Norm.* Princeton, 1978.

Winkler, Jack. *Auctor and Actor.* Berkeley and Los Angeles, 1985.

Winn, James. *John Dryden and His World.* New Haven and London, 1987.

Wray, William. "The English Fable," 1650–1800. Ph.D. dissertation: Yale University, 1950.

Zwicker, Stephen. *Politics and Language in Dryden's Poetry: The Arts of Disguise.* Princeton, 1984.

Index

Addison, Joseph, 33, 137, 220 n. 29, 190 n. 2;
  The Spectator, 1, 10, 18, 48, 51–52, 54, 66–69,
  201 n. 43
Aesop, 10–11, 12, 17, 64, 71–98, 132, 136
Æsop at Amsterdam (1698), 38
Æsop at Bathe (1698), 38
Æsop at Epsom (1698), 38, 39
Æsop at Tunbridge (1698), 38
Æsop at Westminster (1698), 38
Æsop at Whitehall (1698), 38
Æsop Naturaliz'd (1697), 33
Æsop from Islington (1698), 38
Æsop Return'd from Tunbridge (1692), 38, 39
Allen, Don Cameron, 192 n. 20
Allott, Terence, 211 n. 54
Anglican Church, 99, 101, 110, 114
Ancients and Moderns, 57–60
"The Ape and the Fox," 23
Arbuthnot, John, 210 n. 31
Aristophanes, 92
Aristotle, 53, 54
Armens, Sven M., 219 n. 9
Arwaker, Edmund, 66; *Truth in Fiction; or,
  Morality in Masquerade* (1708), 32, 65, 194
  n. 26, 195–196 n. 37
Atterbury, Francis, 51
Aubrey, John, 198 n. 5
Austen, Jane, 160
authors and authorship, 14–15, 71–72, 77, 85–
  88, 124
Avianus, 86
Ayres, Philip, 10, 80, 82–83, 86; *Mythologia Ethica*
  (1689), 32, 65, 194 n. 26, 221 n. 61

Babrius, 86
Baker, Howard, 209 n. 5
Bakhtin, Mikhail, 205 n. 15
Ball, Albert, 204 n. 86, 207 n. 36
Barash, Carol, 216 n. 16
Barbauld, Anna, 12, 198 n. 52
Barber, Mary, 160, 219 n. 11
Barlow, Francis, 20–24, 73, 79; *Æsop's Fables with
  his Life* (1666, 1687), 4, 17, 22–24, 102, 109
Barthes, Roland, 9, 195 n. 35, 203 n. 70
battle of the books, 57–63, 95, 125

Baudoin, Jean, 11, 92
Bayle, Pierre, 92
Beattie, James, 188
Behn, Aphra, 23, 86–87, 102, 130
Beck, Cave, 192 n. 19
Bennington, Geoff, 204 n. 81, 207 n. 37
Bentley, Richard, 6, 11, 50, 56, 57–58, 89, 95–97,
  106; "Of Æsop's Fables," 56, 60–63, 71
Bewick, Thomas, 11–12, 162, 185, 186
Black, Jeremy, 191 n. 13
Blackham, H.P., 9, 191 n. 5
Blackmore, Richard, 192 n. 16, 196 n. 39, 205
  n. 8
Blackwell, Thomas, 7
Blake, William, 162
Boas, George, 192 n. 21
Boccaccio, Giovanni, 122
Boissat, Pierre, 11, 137
Borkat, Robert F.S., 207 n. 36
Bossuet, Jacques, 105
Bouhours, Dominique, 105–6
Boursault, Edmé, 92, 190 n. 1
Bowers, Toni, 216 n. 16
Boyle, Charles, 51, 57, 63, 96–97, 209 n. 15
Brower, Reuben, 216 n. 11
Brown, Tom, 102, 212 n. 16
Budick, Sanford, 212 n. 7
Bullokar, William, 17, 84–85
Bulwer, John, 192 n. 20
Bunn, James H., 203 n. 57
Bunyan, John, 108
Burnet, Gilbert, 104
Bywaters, David, 102, 214 n. 47

Cacicedo, Albert, 108
Caroline, Queen, 163
Carroll, William Meredith, 197 n. 47
Castle, Terry, 29, 46, 59
Caxton, William, 11, 17, 77, 78
Chambers, Ross, 140–141, 217 nn. 15, 31, 218
  n. 42
Charke, Charlotte, 71, 208 n. 1
Chaucer, Geoffrey, 11, 122, 124–126
Cibber, Colley, 190 n. 1
Cicero, 49

Clarke, Charles Cowden, 219 n. 18
Cleyn, Francis, 16, 21
Clifford, Gay, 193 n. 26
Clifford, Nathan, 102, 211 n. 2
"The Cock and the Fox," 125–126
"The Cock and the Gem," 20
Cohen, Murray, 6, 186, 192 n. 19, 193 n. 22, 216 n. 36
Comenius, Johan Amos, 41, 204 n. 80
Conant, Martha, 197 n. 42
"The Countryman and the Serpent," 44
Cowley, Abraham, 5, 7, 192 n. 17
Cowper, William, 187
Coxe, William, 163, 187–188
The Craftsman, 53, 159
Creech, Thomas, 193 n. 24
Croxall, Samuel, 73, 89, 90–91, 94, 185; *Fables of Æsop and Others* (1722), 73, 89, 90–91, 94
Culler, Jonathan, 210 n. 28

Dalgarno, George, 79, 192 n. 20, 209–210 n. 20
Daniel, Stephen H., 190 n. 4
Davenant, William, 21, 48
Dearing, Vinton, 220 n. 25
Dennis, John, 34, 49, 51, 56, 138, 190 n. 3
Derrida, Jacques, 206 n. 25
Deutsch, Helen, 205 n. 14, 209 n. 4
Dobson, Austin, 161
Dodsley, Robert, 11, 65, 185, 186, 192 n. 49
"The Dog and the Shadow," 22, 108, 114
Donaldson, Ian, 167–168
Doody, Margaret Anne, 28, 202 n. 47, 214 n. 50
Draper, Charles, 98
Dryden, John, 2, 4, 5, 6, 12, 13, 15, 99–127, 132, 155, 164, 176; *Absalom and Achitophel*, 101; *Æneis*, 123; *Albion and Albanius*, 104; *Fables Ancient and Modern* (1700), 122–126, 130; *The Hind and the Panther* (1687), 12, 99–101, 103, 106–122, 129, 130, 146, 154, 178; *Religio Laici*, 101–102; *Sylvae*, 123
Dugaw, Dianne, 222 n. 62
Dyce, Alexander, 216 n. 10

"The Eagle and the Fox," 23
Edgeworth, Maria, 12, 198 n. 52
Eisenstein, Elizabeth, 191 n. 13, 206 n. 29
Evelyn, John, 193 n. 24
English Civil Wars, 1, 4, 5, 7, 17, 19, 186

fable, classical uses, 9, 11, 40, 49; collections, 14–45; definition and theory, 10, 48–56, 66–70; illustration, 17, 23–24, 28, 169; morals, 9, 20, 36, 44, 119–120; political uses, 20, 21, 38–39, 174
Fables, Moral and Political (1703), 36, 43–44, 195 n. 36
Farquhar, George, 48, 50, 53
Felton, Henry, 6
Fénelon, François, 11

Ferguson, Moira, 215 n. 11
Finch, Anne, Countess of Winchilsea, 4, 5, 12, 13, 100, 128–155; *Athalia*, 134–135; "The Atheist and the Acorn, 139–140; "The Battle of the Rats and Weazels," 141–142; "The Bird and the Arras," 154–155; "The Brass Pot and the Stone Jugg," 142–143; "The Critick and the Fable-Writer," 147–148; "Five Pieces out of Tasso's Aminta," 133–134; "For the Better," 150; "The Goute and Spider," 128–129, 131, 135, 155; "The Jester and the Little Fishes," 143–144; "Jupiter and the Farmer," 151–153; "The King and the Serpent," 149; "Mercury and the Elephant," 144–147; *Miscellany Poems* (1713), 131, 144–154; "The Owl Describing her Young Ones," 153–154; "The Poor Man's Lamb," 148; "There's No To-Morrow," 151
"The Fly and the Ants," 115–116
Forden, Thomas, 66
Forsgren, Adina, 219 n. 9
"The Fox and the Crow," 8, 185
"The Fox and the Goat," 20
"The Fox and the Grapes," 44
"The Fox and the Stork," 37–38
Freeman, Rosemary, 194 n. 26
France, 3, 11, 49, 92–94, 135–138
Franzius, Wolfgang, 213 n. 40
"The Frog and the Ox," 20

Gay, John, 4, 5, 12, 13, 47, 100, 156–184, 185; *The Beggar's Opera*, 159, 167–8; "The Cookmaid, the Turnspit, and the Ox," 180; "The Degenerate Bees," 180–182; "The Dog and the Fox," 177–178; "The Elephant and the Bookseller," 157–158, 171–172, 187–188; *Fables* (1727), 159–161, 164–173, 182; *Fables of the Late Mr. Gay* (1738), 173–184; "The Fox at the Point of Death," 168; "The Hare and Many Friends," 160–161; "The Lyon, the Tyger and the Traveller," 165–166; "Jupiter and the Countryman," 179; "The Old Woman and her Cats," 168; "The Ravens, the Sexton, and the Earth-Worm," 173, 182–184; "The Shepherd and the Philosopher," 164–165; "The Turkey and the Ant," 163–179; "The Wild Boar and the Ram," 169
Gentleman's Magazine, 37, 159–160
George II, 156
Gilbert, Sandra M., 216 n. 11
Gildon, Charles, 144
Goldsmith, Oliver, 79
Godwin, William, 12, 185
Gordon, Thomas, 65
"The Gourd and the Pine," 109
Graham, Edwin Albert, 190 n. 4, 219 n. 9, 221 n. 45

"The Grasshopper and the Ant," 30
Gravelot, Hubert, 174
Griffith, Elizabeth, 18
Grub Street, 38–39, 45, 50, 86
Gubar, Susan, 216 n. 11
Gutwirth, Marcel, 195 n. 37

Hartog, François, 207 n. 39
Harwood, Dix, 192 n. 21
Havelock, Eric, 206 n. 26
Hazlitt, William, 185
Hegel, Georg, 9, 194 n. 35
Henryson, Robert, 11, 89
Herder, Johan Gottfried, 11, 197 n. 45
Heyrick, Thomas, 99, 100
Highet, Gilbert, 206 n. 76
Hildrop, John, 192 n. 21
Hinnant, Charles H., 144, 216 n. 9, 218 n. 44
Hobbes, Thomas, *Leviathan* (1651), 21, 22, 200
    n. 29
Hodnett, Edward, 201 n. 34, 209 n. 11
Holder, William, 192 n. 20
Holland, Peter, 193–194 n. 26
Hollar, Wenceslaus, 16
Homer, 11, 49, 79, 122
Hoole, Charles, 37–38, 41
Horace, 49, 176, 193 n. 24, 221 n. 52
Horne, Colin J., 204 n. 86, 207 n. 36
Hunter, Ian, 72
Hunter, J. Paul, 194 n. 29
"The Husband-Man and the Wood," 109
Hutchinson, Lucy, 193 n. 24
Hyde, Anne, 213 n. 27

Irving, William, 221 n. 50

Jackson, John, 32, 35, 65, 211 n. 44
Jacobitism, 25–26, 28, 41, 90
Jacobs, Joseph, 194 n. 34
James II, 101, 117, 121
Johnson, Samuel, 100, 124, 158, 166
"The Jay in Peacock Feathers," 20, 31, 101

Kenyon, John, 212 n. 11
Kernan, Alvin, 191 n. 13
Kinsley, James, 217 n. 8
Kitchin, George, 201 n. 38
Korshin, Paul J., 191 n. 12, 193 n. 26
Kroll, Richard, 6, 191–192 n. 13, 192 n. 20, 193
    n. 24, 204 n. 81, 205 n. 14, 212 n. 4

La Chambre, Marin Cureau de, 192 n. 21
La Fontaine, Jean de, 3, 10, 13, 33, 86, 128–
    129, 133, 135–144, 149–150, 151–153, 161,
    187; "Le berger et le roi," 149; "Le combat
    des rats et des belettes," 140–142; *Fables
    choisies* (1668–1694), 135–138; "Le Gland et la
    citrouille," 139; "La goutte et l'araignée,"
    128–129; "Jupiter et le métayer," 151–153;

"Le pot de terre et le pot de feu," 142; "Le
    rieur et les possons," 143–144
La Motte, Antoine Houdart de la, 3, 32, 33, 34,
    137
Leapor, Mary, 198 n. 51
Le Bossu, Rene, 49, 93
Lenaghan, R.T., 199 n. 14; 209 n. 11
Lennox, Charlotte, 186
Lenoble, Eustache, 92
L'Estrange, Roger, 5, 10, 88, 90, 102, 130, 138,
    145, 150–151, 164, 221 n. 61; *Fables of Æsop
    and Other Eminent Mythologists* (1692; 1699), 2,
    14, 24–26, 27, 28, 29, 33, 36, 44–45, 61,
    65–66, 69, 73
Lessing, Gotthold, 197 n. 45
Levine, Joseph M., 206 n. 26
Life of Aesop, 71–98
"The Lion and the Man," 14, 18–19, 27–28
Livy, 54–55, 67, 68
Locke, John, 20, 130, 203 n. 78; *Æsop's Fables*
    (1703), 17, 41–43, 69; *Some Thoughts concerning
    Education* (1693), 40
Lockman, William, 135–136, 137, 218 n. 38
lottery, 14, 15, 162, 220 n. 24
Louis XIV, 92
Lucian, 91
Lucretius, 6, 193 n. 24

Machiavelli, Niccolo, 221 n. 61
Mallinson, Jean, 216 n. 9
Mandeville, Bernard, 2, 22, 138, 191 n. 11, 218
    n. 40
Manley, Delarivière, 144
Marin, Louis, 195 n. 36, 218 n. 36
McGovern, Barbara, 217 n. 16
McKendry, John J., 209 n. 11
Messenger, Ann, 216 n. 9, 218 n. 45
Méziriac, Claude de, 89, 92, 93–94
"Martinus Scriblerus," 83
Mary of Modena, 130
Miller, Nancy, K., 134, 215 n. 3, 216 n. 12
Milton, John, 11
Miner, Earl, 107, 109, 117, 123, 190 n. 5, 213
    n. 40
Montagu, Charles, 5, 109; *The Hind and the
    Panther Transvers'd* (1687), 105, 108, 116–117,
    192 n. 14
Montaigne, Michel de, 133
Moore, Edward, 12, 185, 197 n. 49
Moore, Marianne, 136, 217 n. 31
"The Mouse and the Lion," 23

Noel, Thomas, 190 n. 5
North, Thomas, 196 n. 41
Nagy, Gregory, 194 n. 34, 209 n. 16

Ogilby, John, 3, 14, 50, 72, 73, 109, 115,
    126, 129, 130, 164, 176; *Aesopicks* (1675),
    15–18; *Africa*, 64; *Fables of Æsop, Paraphras'd*

in Verse (1651), 2, 14, 15, 19, 20–22, 64, 73, 117
Old Æsop at Whitehall (1698), 38
Oldham, John, 179
Ong, Walter J. 206 n. 29
Ovid, 122
Owen, Joan Hildreth, 35, 190 n. 4

Patey, Douglas Lane, 193 n. 25, 205 n. 11
Patterson, Annabel, 2, 3, 9, 21, 72, 78, 79, 82, 85, 102, 191 n. 7, 195 n. 36, 200 n. 31, 209 n. 17, 210 n. 22, 214 n. 45, 213 n. 31
pedagogy, 3, 6, 10, 20, 25, 36–37, 40–41
Phaedrus, 10–11
Pepys, Samuel, 15, 17
Perry, Ben Edwin, 194 n. 34
Peters, Julie Stone, 194 n. 29
Petrarch, 133
Phaedrus, 49, 60–61, 86, 161, 206 n. 31
Philipott, Thomas, 23
Phillips, Edward, 15
Philostratus, 210 n. 34
Pilpay, 10, 34, 196 n. 41
Pinkus, Philip, 207 n. 32
Planudes, Maximus, 77, 78, 84, 88, 91, 94, 96
Plato, 54–55, 62, 92
Pliny, 171, 220 n. 42
Plumb, J.H., 2, 191 n. 10
Plutarch, 91, 92
A Poem in Defence of the Church of England (1687), 110, 211 n. 4
Pope, Alexander, 6, 98, 156, 174, 176; *The Dunciad* (1728, 1742), 15, 50, 55
Pollak, Ellen, 215 n. 8
Porta, Giovanni, Baptista, 177
Popish Plot, 101
Praz, Mario, 194 n. 26
print culture, 4, 12, 17, 33, 39–40, 50, 55–56, 57, 65, 77, 85
Prior, Matthew, 10, 105, 106, 108, 109, 110, 112
Pritchard, Mary, 3, 21, 190 n. 4
Prodicus, 54, 68

Queensbury, Duke and Duchess of, 162, 174, 176
Quarles, Francis, 108
Quilligan, Maureen, 193 n. 26

Racine, Jean, 134–135, 217 n. 22
Reedy, Gerard, 5, 191 n. 12, 200 n. 23
The Revenger (1687), 104
Reverand, Cedric D., 125, 214 n. 53
Revolution of 1688, 24, 34, 101, 128, 130, 194 n. 33
Reynolds, Myra, 216 n. 9
Richardson, Samuel, 73; *Æsop's Fables* ([1739] 1740), 2, 17, 28–29, 33, 65, 88–89, 124; *Clarissa* (1747–8), 29, 30–31; *Pamela* (1740), 21, 29, 30

Rogers, Katharine M., 216 n. 9, 217 n. 16
Roman Catholicism, 13, 24, 57, 90, 99, 100–102, 105–106, 114, 117, 125
Roper, Alan, 106–107
Rousseau, Jean Jacques, 187
Rowe, Nicholas, 131
Runte, Roseann, 217 n. 25

Saintsbury, George, 212 n. 6
Salvaggio, Ruth, 216 nn. 9, 12
Samber, Robert, 202 n. 53
Saunders, David, 72
Scheherazade, 196–197 n. 42
Scotin, Gerard, 174
Scott, Sir Walter, 15, 101
Scudéry, Madeleine de, 92–93
Seneca, 24
Serres, 195 n. 35
Sharpe, Jane, 201 n. 42
Sheridan, Frances, 196 n. 42
Sheridan, Thomas, 190 n. 1
Shevelow, Kathryn, 217 n. 16
Shirley, James, 21, 199 n. 12
Sidney, Philip, 23
Sloman, Judith, 102, 103, 123, 190 n. 5, 214 nn. 43, 47, 53
Smart, Christopher, 10–11, 12, 161, 185
Smith, M. Ellwood, 190 n. 4, 209 n. 5
Socrates, 54, 62, 67
Some Observations of the Fables of Æsop (1700), 201–202 n. 43
Speck, W.A., 2, 191 n. 10, 200 n. 24
Sprat, Thomas, 192 n. 17
Spenser, Edmund, 11, 18, 108, 124
Spufford, Margaret, 208 n. 47
Stafford, Barbara, 222 n. 3
Stallybrass, Peter, 206 n. 15
Steele, Richard, 199 n. 20
Steinhowel, Wilhelm, 77
Stewart, Susan, 203 n. 7
Summerfield, Geoffrey, 198 n. 52
Stillingfleet, Edward, 56, 212 n. 16
Stockdale, William, 159
Stoope, Robert, 16
"The Sun and the Wind," 109
Swift, Jonathan, 6, 50, 65, 131, 156, 172–173, 174, 177, 204 n. 86; *The Battel of the Books* (1704), 57, 58–60, 71; *Gulliver's Travels* (1726), 46–47, 58–59, 156, 157, 193 n. 23; *Tale of a Tub* (1704), 45–46

Turner, James, 204 n. 80
Tacitus, 24
Tasso, Torquato, 133–134
Temple, Sir William, 51, 52, 57, 63
Terence, 24
Test Act, 101
Thackeray, William, 156, 160, 174
theriophilism, 6

Toland, John, 35–36, 52, 59, 93–95, 196 n. 39
Topsell, Edward, 112, 213 n. 40
Trenchard, John, 196 n. 39
translation, 123–126, 128–129, 133–144
Trickett, Rachell, 128

Vanbrugh, John, 171, 190 n. 1
Van Eerde, Katherine S., 199 n. 13

Wallace, John, 18, 193 n. 26
Wallis, John, 192 n. 19
Walpole, Horace, 185
Walpole, Robert, 162, 173
Warburton, William, 55, 210 n. 36
Ward, Charles E., 215 n. 57
Warton, Joseph, 155, 156, 174, 187–188
Weinbrot, Howard D., 191 n. 8, 201 n. 7
Westminster School, 36
White, Allon, 206 n. 15
Wilkins, John, 192 nn. 19, 20

William and Mary, 24, 101, 130
William of Cumberland, 156, 160, 165, 173, 177
William of Orange, 24, 101, 125, 130
Winkler, Jack, 9, 194 n. 34, 209 n. 14
Winn, James, 102, 212 nn. 9, 10
Winstanley, William, 198 n. 2
"The Wolf and the Lamb," 20, 115–116
"The Wolf and the Stork," 37–38, 39
Woolf, Virginia, 128, 131–132
Wooten, John, 169
Wordsworth, William, 128, 129, 131–132, 216 n. 10
Wotton, William, 57
Wray, William, 190 n. 4
Wyrick, Deborah Baker, 207 n. 33

Xanthus, 78, 80, 82

Zwicker, Steven N., 102, 190 n. 6, 195 n. 35

CAMBRIDGE STUDIES IN EIGHTEENTH-CENTURY ENGLISH LITERATURE AND THOUGHT

General Editors

Professor HOWARD ERSKINE-HILL, LITT.D., FBA, *Pembroke College, Cambridge*
Professor JOHN RICHETTI, *University of Pennsylvania*

1 *The Transformation of* The Decline and Fall of the Roman Empire
by David Womersley

2 *Women's Place in Pope's World*
by Valerie Rumbold

3 *Sterne's Fiction and the Double Principle*
by Jonathan Lamb

4 *Warrior Women and Popular Balladry, 1650–1850*
by Dianne Dugaw

5 *The Body in Swift and Defoe*
by Carol Flynn

6 *The Rhetoric of Berkeley's Philosophy*
by Peter Walmsley

7 *Space and the Eighteenth-Century English Novel*
by Simon Varey

8 *Reason, Grace, and Sentiment*
A Study of the Language of Religion and Ethics in England, 1660–1780
by Isabel Rivers

9 *Defoe's Politics: Parliament, Power, Kingship, and* Robinson Crusoe
by Manuel Schonhorn

10 *Sentimental Comedy: Theory & Practice*
by Frank Ellis

11 *Arguments of Augustan Wit*
by John Sitter

12 *Robert South (1634–1716): An Introduction to his Life and Sermons*
by Gerard Reedy, SJ

13 *Richardson's* Clarissa *and the Eighteenth-Century Reader*
by Tom Keymer

14 *Eighteenth-Century Sensibility and the Novel*
The Senses in Social Context
by Ann Jessie Van Sant

15 *Family and the Law in Eighteenth-Century Fiction*
The Public Conscience in the Private Sphere
by John P. Zomchick

16 *Crime and Defoe: A New Kind of Writing*
by Lincoln B. Faller

17 *Literary Transmission and Authority: Dryden and Other Writers*
edited by Earl Minor and Jennifer Brady

18 *Plots and Counterplots*
Sexual Politics and the Body Politic in English Literature, 1660–1730
by Richard Braverman

19 *The Eighteenth-Century Hymn in England*
by Donald Davie

20 *Swift's Politics: A Study in Disaffection*
by Ian Higgins

21 *Writing and the Rise of Finance: Capital Satires of the Early Eighteenth Century*
by Colin Nicholson

22 *Locke, Literary Criticism, and Philosophy*
by William Walker

23 *Poetry and Jacobite Politics in Eighteenth-Century Britain and Ireland*
by Murray G. H. Pittock

24 *The Story of the Voyage in Eighteenth-Century England*
by Philip Edwards

25 *Edmond Malone: A Literary Biography*
by Peter Martin

26 *Swift's Parody*
by Robert Phiddian

27 *Rural Life in Eighteenth-Century English Poetry*
by John Goodridge

28 *The English Fable: Aesop and Literary Culture, 1651–1740*
by Jayne Elizabeth Lewis

Printed in the United Kingdom
by Lightning Source UK Ltd.
109921UKS00001B/263